THE LAST
INNOCENT WHITE MAN
IN AMERICA

THE
LAST INNOCENT
WHITE MAN
IN
AMERICA

and other writings

JOHN LEONARD

THE NEW PRESS
NEW YORK
1993

PUBLISHED IN THE UNITED STATES BY THE NEW PRESS, NEW YORK
DISTRIBUTED BY W.W. NORTON AND COMPANY INC.
500 FIFTH AVENUE, NEW YORK, NY 10110

LIBRARY OF CONGRESS CATALOGING-IN-PUBLICATION DATA
Leonard, John.
The last innocent white man in America and other writings / by
John Leonard. — 1st ed.
p.   cm.
ISBN 1-56584-072-0
1. Title.
PS3562.E56L36   1993
814'.54—dc20   92-50838
                                                                 CIP

First Edition

ESTABLISHED IN 1990 AS A MAJOR ALTERNATIVE TO THE LARGE, COMMERCIAL PUBLISHING
HOUSES, THE NEW PRESS IS INTENDED TO BE THE FIRST FULL-SCALE NONPROFIT AMERICAN
BOOK PUBLISHER OUTSIDE OF THE UNIVERSITY PRESSES. THE PRESS IS OPERATED EDITORIALLY
IN THE PUBLIC INTEREST, RATHER THAN FOR PRIVATE GAIN; IT IS COMMITTED TO PUBLISHING
IN INNOVATIVE WAYS WORKS OF EDUCATIONAL, CULTURAL, AND COMMUNITY VALUE, WHICH,
DESPITE THEIR INTELLECTUAL MERITS, MIGHT NOT NORMALLY BE "COMMERCIALLY VIABLE."
THE NEW PRESS'S EDITORIAL OFFICES ARE LOCATED AT THE CITY UNIVERSITY OF NEW YORK.

★

THIS IS FOR SUE, WITHOUT WHOM
THERE WOULDN'T HAVE BEEN A BOOK,
NOR AN AUTHOR

CONTENTS

INTRODUCTION:
AN EXPLANATION OF
WHAT FOLLOWS   ix

PART I:
THE WORLD, THE FLESH
& THE DEVIL

The Day of the Locust:
The Burning of Los Angeles   1

*The Blame Game: We Might
As Well Be Haitians*   6

The Curse of the "Resting" Classes   10

Betsy Ross Meets Staggerlee   13

Rip Van Winkle Meets Caliban   15

Who Will Tell the Children?   19

Invasion of the Cyberpunks   22

The Imperial City:
Rewriting New York   27

The Way We Are   27

Vanities   29

*The "Delirious Professions"…
Fear…(and)…Shoes*   30

*There Are More Than
Three Worlds*   33

Making Fifth Avenue Safe for
Our Only Mayor   38

Crazy Eddie Sweeps the Streets   38

Rooting for the Titanic   39

The Iguana That Ate Chrysler   42

Heidegger in New York   44

Censorship:
The Angels and the Ax   45

*Where We Go to Talk
About Censorship*   45

What I Told Them, Being Pious   47

*What I Didn't Tell Them,
Being Ambivalent*   54

Recovering from the Sixties:
Heroes, Criminals
& Iconic Clowns   58

*Chicago '68:
Tales of the Hoffmans*   58

Tricky Dick and Elvis   63

*Dr. King, Who Made
Connections and Waves*   68

Kissinger Laughs   70

*Allen Ginsberg,
Angel-Headed Hipster*   72

*Kissinger Again,
That China Card*   75

Is Abbie Hoffman Really Dead?   77

Studs Terkel, a Wired Diogenes   79

Abbie Again, the Long Good-Bye   82

The Golden Age of Izzy Stone   84

★

Hunter S. Thompson, *Duke of Despair*	85
Captain Kangaroo in Court	87
Nancy Reagan, Ugly Duckling	90
Country-and-Western Ghostwriters	91
Election '88: Let's Not Talk About It	93
Do We Gotta Have Hart?	93
The "L" Word	95
Gary Redux	98
Jackson for President— The Kiss of Death	99
Despairing of Duke	102
The Turkey Shoot	104
Gulf War (1): Send Quayle	104
Gulf War (2): Bloody Farce	106
Gulf War (3): Glitterdome	108
Gulf War (4): Whatever Happened to Civilization?	110
Gulf War (5): How to Love an Arab	112
Gulf War (6): The Software in the System	114
Taking Back the Night	116
Buchanan Knows What He Doesn't Like	118
Patterns and Ghosts	121
Graham Greene Forgives Kim Philby, But I Hold a Grudge	123
1992: Fear and Loathing on the Campaign Trail	125
If Mario Doesn't Run, the Rest of Us May Have To	125
The Women Are Restless	128
Madison Square Garden: The Pillsbury Doughboys Go to a Sun Dance	130
The Republicans in Houston, with Kali and Gilgamesh	140

PART II: BOOK WORLD

At War and Peace on the Home Front	149
Toni Morrison: She Can Give You Dreams	149
Kurt Vonnegut: The Last Innocent White Man in America	165
Don DeLillo: Who Killed John F. Kennedy? (The CIA)	173
Maxine Hong Kingston: Buddha in Berkeley	179
Norman Mailer: The Trouble with Harry	185
E.L. Doctorow: Boy Gangster	198
Thomas Pynchon: Down Among the Thanatoids	205
Robert Stone: Jonah in the Whale	213
Mary McCarthy, R.I.P.	225
Hemingway's Women	227
Other Voices, Other Rooms	233
Gabriel García Márquez versus Simon Bolívar	233
Salman Rushdie: Two Brown Men, Falling Hard	249
The Hit Men	257
Günter Grass: Bad Boys and Fairy Tales	260
Milan Kundera Wants to Be Immortal	274
Jean-Paul Sartre: Problematic Pillhead	283
Wole Soyinka: A Garden of Too Many Cultures	289
Doris Lessing Returns from Outer Space	292
Sad Sam Beckett	295

★

INTRODUCTION:
AN EXPLANATION OF
WHAT FOLLOWS

In 1947, a young American and a middle-aged Japanese climbed a tower in Toyko to look at the bombed temple and the burnt-out plain of the Asakusa. The twenty-three-year-old American, in a PX jacket, was the critic Donald Richie. The forty-eight-year-old Japanese, wearing a kimono and a fedora, was the novelist Yusunari Kawabata. Kawabata spoke no English, Richie no Japanese, and their interpreter stayed home, sick in bed with a cold. So they talked in writers. Richie said: "Andre Gide!" Kawabata thought about it, and then replied: "Thomas Mann!" They both grinned. They'd go on grinning all afternoon, trading names like Flaubert, Edgar Allan Poe and Stefan Zweig.

It's a lovely story, isn't it? Two men on a tower, after a war, waving the names of writers as if they were signal flags or semaphores...

For a living, I chase the ambulances of the culture. I review television every Monday for *New York* magazine; and books every Tuesday for National Public Radio; and politics and other cultures every Thursday for *New York Newsday*; and media of several sorts every Sunday morning on CBS; and I will be found otherwise, four or five times a year, in *The Nation*, where I am encouraged to rhapdsodize about new novels at whatever length I think I need—with the understanding that I will be underpaid. What I look for and care about in these various bunkers is the slice of the strange, the surprise of the Other, the witness not yet heard from, the archaeologies forgotten or ignored or despised. What I think about almost anything, from Henry Kissinger to Deng Xiaoping, from the doctrine of transubstantiation to the theory of surplus value to a tax on capital gains, from *Murphy Brown* to *Thelma and Louise* to *Jelly's Last Jam*, is a mess of juxtapositions, miscegenations, transplants and hybrids; atavisms and avatars, landlords and tenants, ghosts and gods; grace-notes and cognitive dissonance— Chaos Theory, with lots of fractals.

And, almost always, you will see me waving the name of some writer. Instead of the usual suspects at the State Department, the Heritage Foundation, the Hoover Institution and the Rand Corporation, the dopesters, pollsters, think-tank rent-an-academics, ministers of mystification and doctors of spin in the megagovernment, ready at the drop of a message unit to leak all over you, to supply-side a convenient sound-bite on every global crisis from Czechoslovakian "lustration" to campus speech codes, I call up writers—for witness and scruples and laughs. Books are my Rolodex. From them I've learned to read everything else. The library is where I've always gone—for transcendence, of course, a zap to the synaptic cleft, the radioactive glow of genius in the dark; but also to get more complicated; for advice on how to be decent and brave; for narrative instead of scenarios, discrepancies instead of euphemism. In the library, that secretariat of dissidents, they don't lie to me.

In other words, besides transcendence, I'm looking for help. I'm the least disinterested of critics. How literature is taught, according to which theory from a French lab or the Frankfurt School or Dover Beach or Vanderbilt, absorbs me less than how we use it to civilize ourselves. I *like* the Canon; I just wish there were more of it; pluralism is my middle name. After the Great Debate on Great Books at Stanford, they added one women and one wog. This seems stingy. Meanwhile, at least once a week, another novel is published telling us something we need to know on matters never dreamed of by Dr. Gallup or the *New York Times*/CBS News Poll.

My politics began in high school, in southern California in the fifties, with a saturation in Dos Passos, after which there was Allen Ginsberg. It's no surprise that the sixties started with novels like *The Tin Drum*, *The Golden Notebook* and *Catch-22*; *One Flew Over the Cuckoo's Nest* and *V*. I reviewed all of them, for Pacifica radio in Berkeley, in the middle of the Cuban missile crisis, on the eve of the Free Speech

Movement, along with James Baldwin, Norman Mailer and Betty Friedan. Since then, in the *New York Times* during the Vietnam War and Watergate, or at *The Nation* and on National Public Radio during the Reagan gerontocracy (that theology of greed) and the Gulf War (that turkey shoot), if I've spent too much time abroad, among the Latin Americans and the Eastern Europeans, García Márquez and Milan Kundera, it's because they seemed to have a more interesting politics to construe, landscapes in sharper relief, nightmares and heresies worth fighting about and dying for. While at home, in search of my minimum daily requirement of magic tricks, radiance, blood-threads of the mother-tongue and passionate conviction, I have been partial to the fiction of writers who happen to be women with double identities, like Toni Morrison, Maxine Hong Kingston, Mary Gordon and Cynthia Ozick—as if, by the abrasions of sex on race on class on culture, they will rub up something combustible; as if by these plate tectonics, I'll get the continental drift I need.

To me, the most interesting thing so far about Bill Clinton, besides Hillary, is his professed admiration for García Márquez's *One Hundred Years of Solitude*. That the Republicans failed to make an issue out of this suspicious enthusiasm for a left-wing Spanish-speaking Castro-symp suggests that Republicans just aren't educated or serious about people who talk funny. If more of us had read Václav Havel before 1989, the collapse of the nonprofit police states might not have seemed so astounding. A David Grossman, in Hebrew, and a Jacobo Timerman, in Spanish, prophesy every bit as much as they report, and so has Nadine Gordimer, in novel after novel, for South Africa. Likewise, there were Filipino novelists and playwrights presaging that fairy tale, the Princess Bride in yellow taking charge when the Wicked Frog left town with his Dragon Lady, in an American whirlybird. A close reader of the Chinese "Misties" could have predicted Tiananmen. Nor would I would be shocked if Milorad Pavic, in his *Dictionary of the Khazars*, proves more reliable than anybody at the United Nations on what's wrong with Yugoslavia.

Those of us who read for a living already know there's an international multiculture. This isn't a multiculture of blue jeans, gangster movies and rock music; of bank loans, arms credits and microchips; of Kentucky Fried Chicken and the CIA and the spider-speak in green decimals of international currency speculation. It's a multiculture of distinctions and connections and the exchange, in translation, of our

deepest meanings and darkest chords and coded identities. It's a Philip
Roth discovering a Jiri Weil. It's a García Márquez reading Faulkner
and Flaubert (and Kafka in a Borges translation). It's Kobo Abe reading García Márquez in Japanese, and Salman Rushdie reading him
(and Bulgakov) in English, and Maxine Hong Kingston rewriting
Journey to the West to include Abbie Hoffman as the Monkey King. It's
Wole Soyinka, Octavio Paz, Naguib Mahfouz and Ismail Kadare. It's a
parliament of hungry dreamers.

I'm not saying that in such a parliament our writers are wizards and
their books totemic. It's a little foolish to worship literature, as if we
were one part Hegel and one part Tinkerbell, as Sacred Text and Pure
Thought (what Mallarmé called "absolute contour" and Wallace
Stevens a "counter-geography" and Keats "the egotistical sublime"),
when most of those dead trees in the chain stores have titles like *How I
Lost Weight, Found God, Sold Junk Bonds, Shot Sandinistas and Changed My
Sexual Preference in the Bermuda Triangle*. I *am* saying that good writers are
better citizens than most of the rest of us because they have found or
invented the language to think out loud about what's surprised them
on the edge, at the margin, inside a labyrinth or the whale.

In thirty years, I've looked at books through binoculars, periscopes
and kaleidoscopes. Like a New Critic, I've worn Christ as a campaign
button to every symposium on Moral Fatigue and the Seven Ambiguities. Fugitive! Agrarian! Like a New York intellectual, a Modernist
flack, I've been promiscuous with my problematics, transparencies,
synoptic recitations, and gratuitous actings-out. Partisan Reviewer!
Like a Freudian, I've always looked under the bed for oedipal cycles,
reaction formations, repetition compulsions and masochistic cy-
clothymia. Projection! Like a Marxist, I could explain absolutely anything, including television, as a function of class relations determining the deepest communal fantasies of the culture. Vomit-eating cryp-
to-fascist hyena! Trotskyite nose-picker! I even let a hundred Harolds
Bloom, after which I had to be deconstructed in order to speak *Klang
und nicht Sprache*—"the mocking sound-trace of some primal cleavage:
fall, babel, parricide, castration," because otherwise I'd turn into
what Roland Barthes calls an "obtuse meaning," incapable of hacking
away at my base predicates with a semantic axis, incapable of distinguishing a paratax from a syntagm; and the usurpation of poesis by
mimesis would be *my* fault. Anyway, according to the busy French, "a
text is not a line of words releasing a single 'theological' meaning (the

'message' of the Author-God) but a multidimensional space in which a variety of writings, none of them original, blend and clash."

Actually, all these mirrors are fun to stare through and sometimes even useful. The more we know, the more we see; the more we see, the greater our pleasure. It does occur to me, however, that critics could learn something about style from Author-Gods. Thorstein Veblen was, as usual, right on the money when he said that "except where it is adopted as a necessary means of secret communication, the use of a special slang in any employment is probably to be accepted as evidence that the occupation in question is substantially make-believe."

How does it work? Late this summer, while watching on C-SPAN the Republican festival of hatred for (and denial of) anybody who was different, I was also, as one of the fiction judges for the 1992 National Book Awards, reading some two hundred new American novels. The democracy of these fictions doesn't look at all like Houston's. It is a star-spangled bazaar of styles, subjects, genders, complexions and epistemologies, from which everybody levitates.

From a John Updike and a Joyce Carol Oates, we more or less expect a book a year, and here they are, on James Buchanan and on Teddy Disappointment. Among the not-quite-so-prolific: a new William Kennedy with a lot more Albany; a new Reynolds Price, and the same old Larry McMurtry and Harry Crews. It's been too long, but we can stop waiting for the new Robert Stone, the new Maureen Howard and the new Cormac McCarthy. We seem to have waited almost forever for a new Ken Kesey and a new Terry Southern. Surprise! And who could have imagined a Susan Sontag from whose pages the dead rise up, in Naples, to curse British imperialism?

Just look, in this small sample on my office floor, at those distant territories heard from, old contours and new textures. If I had had an extra month or two, I'd have written this year, at unconscionable length in *The Nation*, about Maureen Howard, who has done for Bridgeport what Kennedy does for Albany, Faulkner for Yoknapatawpha, and Joyce for Dublin, with Walt Kelly, Walter Benjamin and P. T. Barnum looking on; and about Robert Antoni, whose *Divina Trace* is also Joycean, a sort of Caribbean *Finnegans Wake*, with as much magic as Macondo, more puns than *Pale Fire*, and four and a half religions (if you count Santeria and obeah)—a frog-child and a Black Madonna and Hanuman, the Monkey King, in a West Indian rewrite of the *Ramayana* by Valmiki...But there are also new novels about poor whites in the rural Carolinas, and persecuted homeless in New York City, and orange groves and barrios in Pomona, California; about homeboy gangs in Oakland, Tlingit Indians in Alaska, French Jesuits and the Iroquois in sixteenth-century Canada, and Montana feminists; about Columbus in Vermont and the Dominican Republic, motherhood in Miami and Havana, fathers and sons and identity crises in Boston and Guatemala, Irish Catholics in Bridgeport, in Brooklyn and on Long Island; Americans abroad and adrift in Crete, Morocco and Nigeria; Vietnamese displaced to New Orleans, and Japanese to Chicago.

Talk about your gorgeous mosaic. And I haven't even mentioned Fiction of Color in 1992, when the wealth and resonance of this fiction is what's so dazzling about the year. Imagine Toni Morrison *and* Alice Walker *and* Gloria Naylor, plus Terry McMillan and Thulani Davis. Imagine Albert Murray *and* John Edgar Wideman *and* Walter Mosley, plus a remarkable first novel by Darryl Pinckney and a breathtaking handful of stories from Edward P. Jones.

From these riches, we pick one for a National Book Award. I'm not even happy about our nominations. I know enough about awards committees to wish writers wouldn't care as much as they do about prizes. But writers of fiction especially care, because the writing of fiction is so peculiar, almost unique in its disregard for the claims of sociability and respectable behavior. Like a monk, a hermit, a yogi or a shaman, you disappear for years at a time behind closed doors to talk to the ghosts in your machine. It is a brave solitude, but also crazed with doubt. Your book takes longer than any baby to gestate and is then delivered naked into the care of strangers. From these strangers you need approval and the assurance that your inwardness isn't diseased, that you aren't as sick as Narcissus, that you brought back something precious (mystical, revolutionary) from your dreamy desert. But this writer's solitude is experienced by the reader in a competing solitude. It is not communal. It's intimacy to intimacy, one on one, down there with the demons. Similar solitudes also write book reviews, variously wet from their own emotional weathers. The reviewers sit in separate splendid singularities on prize-giving panels, groping for a group-mind. More often than not, the ultimate winner is everybody's second-best, agreed upon in order to sacrifice the least of each panelist's embattled self-esteem.

This, too, is very much like democracy, except with more parties,

and livelier primaries, and a love of language. From such a democracy, I seek counsel and courage. Why not? Listen to a young Jean-Paul
Sartre, in his grandfather's library, drawing near "to observe those
boxes which slit open like oysters, and I would see the nudity of their
inner organs, pale, fusty leaves, slightly bloated, covered with black
veinlets, which drank ink and smelled of mushrooms."

Or Marshall McLuhan, quoting the African Prince Modupe: "I came
gradually to understand that the marks on the page were trapped
words. Anyone could decipher the symbols and turn words back
again into speech. The ink of the print trapped the thoughts; they
could no more get out than a *doomboo* could get out of a pit."

William Gass has explained: "The purpose of a literary work is the
capture of consciousness, and the consequent creation, in you, of an
imagined sensibility, so that while you read you are that patient pool
or cataract of concepts which the author has constructed; and though
at first it may seem as if the richness of life had been replaced by
something less so—senseless noises, abstract meanings, mere shadows of worldly employment—yet the new self with which fine fiction and good poetry should provide you is as wide as the mind is,
and musicked deep with feeling. While listening to such symbols
sounding, the blind perceive; thought seems to grow a body; and the
will is at rest amid that moving like a gull asleep on the sea."

Bernard Malamud spoke for the German-Jewish refugees of World
War II: "Articulate as they were, the great loss was the loss of language—that they could not say what was in them to say. You have
some subtle thought and it comes out like a piece of broken bottle."

A box, then, Pandora's, of trapped words, and oysters, mushrooms,
histories and dreams; broken glass and surplus value; trapdoors and
rainbows; a levitation and a cure for stupidity. Maybe an axe. "A
book," said Kafka, "must be an axe for the frozen sea in us." Or even
a tree. Octavio Paz asks us to consider "the pain of roots and broken
limbs, the fierce stubbornness of plants, no less powerful than that of
animals and men....They do not have blood or nerve, only sap, and
instead of rage or fear, a silent tenacity possesses them."

And it often seems to me, much as I hate to sound like a UNICEF
greeting card, that we are all trying to tell each other pretty much the
same story. This happens at twelve-step meetings. It happens at political rallies. It happens whenever I answer the latest fire alarms of the

culture, sometimes only to pour more gasoline on them. And it happens when I open, so much at random—one last example—a book like Eva Hoffman's *Lost in Translation*.

As childhood memoir, *Lost in Translation* has the colors and nuance of Vladimir Nabokov's *Speak, Memory!* As an account of a young mind wandering into great books, it recalls Sartre's *Words*. As a ghost story of the emigrant experience, a counterpoint of discarded and invented selves, it belongs with Lore Segal's *Other People's Houses* and Kingston's *The Woman Warrior*. As an anthropology of Eastern European émigré life, American academe and the Upper West Side of Manhattan, it's every bit as deep and wicked as anything by Ozick (or Mary McCarthy).

I don't look like any of these writers. Nor was I, like Hoffman, born female and Jewish in Poland in 1945. I didn't grow up in Cracow, a gifted pianist. I wasn't obliged by anti-Semitism to emigrate, at age thirteen, to Canada and "a whole new geography of emotions." I didn't miss, in high school in Vancouver and in college in Houston, the "plenitude" of Cracow, the "frame" of Polish culture, the "weight" of European history. I hadn't in graduate school to slough off "excess darkness," or "deconstruct" my self-conscious "rage" or "triangulate" my fragments on each passing moment before deciding to become that most difficult of beings, a New York intellectual with her own psychiatrist. Why then should it seem to me that *Lost in Translation* is my story, too?

I don't mean mindlessly to universalize; I *do* mean to identify. Many of us (especially bookies) have felt, like Hoffman, at times a "mosaic," and at times a "hybrid," and even at times an "oxymoron." We would like to be as "spontaneous" as everyone else but we're wary of "the space sickness of transcendence," the unbearable lightness of American being. Groping our way into our politics, our marriages and our work, we've been strangers, too, and like her wondered how to "stop reading the exterior signs of a foreign tribe and step into the inwardness." She built a second language "from the roof down," and wrote her way to brand-new meanings. When at last she came to trust "the specific gravity" of English enough to let it speak her childhood being—"the molten force" she felt herself made of, in Cracow, under a chestnut tree, when time like a river pulsed through her blood—her translation was complete: into this polyphonic book that is itself an act of faith, a Bach fugue, a kind of heroism.

There are other languages just as mysterious, other Polands, other

Europes, whole alphabets of antarctic Americas; of class and race and sex; of disappointment and disease; of faith and love and cowardice; of dreamscapes, I Chings, Books of the Tibetan and Egyptian Dead; selves we find in the solitude of our reading as thrilling as Goethe's Faust, Hegel's history-devouring sage, Holderlin's Empedokles, Lautreamont's Maldoror, Nietzsche's Zarathustra; into whom, like Eva in her Tales of Hoffman, we are translated, overnight and forever, citizens of the international multiculture and a Republic of Dreams. Beyond translation, this is metamorphosis.

Although everything in this book has been to one degree or another revised and rearranged, most of the literary essays appeared originally in The Nation *and most of the political commentaries in* New York Newsday, *with interpolations here and there from National Public Radio,* New York *magazine,* CBS Sunday Morning, Ms., The Village Voice *and* Vanity Fair. *I have been more than lucky in my editors; I've been blessed. I am grateful to Elizabeth Pochoda, Art Winslow and Victor Navasky, at* The Nation; *Phyllis Singer, John Van Doorn, Mort Persky and John Anderson, at* New York Newsday; *Naomi Person, at* Fresh Air *on NPR; Ed Kosner, Chris Smith, Rhoda Koenig, and, especially, Celia McGee at* New York; *and Linda Mason, Bud Lamoreaux and Charles Kuralt at CBS. My agent for almost thirty years, Marilyn Marlow at Curtis-Brown, is also a heroine.*

PART I:
THE WORLD, THE FLESH
& THE DEVIL

THE DAY OF THE LOCUST:
THE BURNING OF LOS ANGELES

When the bird grew silent, he made an effort to put Faye out of his mind and began to think about the series of cartoons he was making for his canvas of Los Angeles on fire. He was going to show the city burning at high noon, so that the flames would have to compete with the desert sun and thereby appear less fearful, more like bright flags flying from roofs and windows than a terrible holocaust. He wanted the city to have quite a gala air as it burned, to appear almost gay. And the people who set it on fire would be a holiday crowd.

—Nathanael West

"Back in Los Angeles," wrote Randall Jarrell, "we missed Los Angeles." I grew up there. A friend telephones during the insurrection to tell me that, from the Greek Theatre where all of us went from high school to see Harry Belafonte, after which we'd eat at the only French restaurant known to our pubescent social set, the Taix, with its red-checkered tablecloths and bread sticks, you could see the flames, like tracer-fire, like Nathanael West. Another friend, my oldest, is a political scientist at UCLA, and lives in Venice, but he isn't answering the phone, so what good is he? I wanted to know if this friend knew that they had burned down the Pathfinder Bookstore at Pico and Berendo, which is where the two of us first met Leon Trotsky, with the axe in his head, back in 1955, which is why the FBI has files on both of us.

On the other hand, in South Central, they also burned down two public libraries; and the oldest bookstore in the country owned by African-Americans, the Aquarian; and the district offices of two of L.A.'s better politicians, Representative Maxine Waters and Councilman Mark Ridley-Thomas; not to mention the headquarters of the Watts Labor-Community Action Council. On a third hand, unlike the Watts riots of '65, there seems not to have been much anti-Semitism. A Wilshire District mini-mart was reduced to cinders, but a synagogue a block away remained untouched. Koreans, this time, were the target. The rapper Ice Cube is on record as hating Koreans. He is to be distinguished from the rapper Ice-T, who hates cops. Neither of them is Sister Souljah, the rapper who dismayed Bill Clinton, the candidate who plays the saxophone.

There'd been, of course, another California fire, just last October in Oakland, during which the novelist Maxine Hong Kingston lost the only copy of the manuscript of a new book, and what she said to a reporter was this: "Did you know that when paper burns, it is very beautiful? It's just amazing to look at a burned book. It looks like feathers, the thin pages, and it's still book-shaped, and you touch it and it disintegrates. It makes you realize that it's just air. It's inspiration, and air, and it's just returned to that." Nobody blamed anyone for *that* fire, not even Gaia. And there would be another *riot*, almost immediately after Los Angeles, in Chicago, with a thousand arrests and very little publicity, because Chicago was just basketball.

Los Angeles was a lot more personal. As usual, most of those who died were people of color. And also as usual, many of the fires turned out to have been convenient slumlord arsons. And the number of those fires seems now to be in dispute; after having been exaggerated originally, for apocalyptic effect, to as many as 7,000, they are now being minimized, for public-relations purposes, to as few as 600, if we are counting city blocks instead of individual "structures."

Besides Koreans, Salvadorans also got it. I have been reading *L.A. Weekly*, the alternative newspaper. Its correspondents were everywhere, and reported in a hurry, so I know about the devastation done to Salvadorans, just one of so many warring tribes in a municipal multiculture that speaks ninety-three languages. Police Chief Darryl Gates, bonkers on some sort of bombazine, tried at first to blame the riots on illegal aliens. And the Immigration and Naturalization Service used them as an excuse to round up thousands of "undocumented" people. Meanwhile, nobody except *L.A. Weekly* mentions Goodyear, Ford and Max Factor, all of which moved out of town during the *last* recession—a different species of emigration. Nor Pia Zadora's husband, Meshulam Riklis, who bought all the Zody discount stores in South Central and then got rid of severance pay for 3,000 employees, closed the stores, sold the land, and reaped a $1-billion stock profit on which George Bush would rather he didn't pay a capital-gains tax.

How much of this do you want to hear? What I find demystifying may seem to other people merely more confusing. For instance: South Central used to be mostly black. Now it's at least half Latino. The violence and arson seem to have been mostly by African-Americans, whereas the looting was racially mixed—"an equal-opportunity riot," says *L.A. Weekly*. Those much-feared gangs never showed up; no one knows why. Conspiracy theorists on the Left are floating a hot-air balloon according to which the Crips and Bloods plotted together to waste Koreans, but this seems so much jailbird blowhard vainglory.

The median household net worth for Anglos in Los Angeles in 1991 was $31,904; for non-Anglos, the median household net worth was $1,353. Imagine that.

On the phone, I have been listening to my stepdaughter, Jen Nessel, through several rough drafts of the article she's writing, from the front on Ivar and Hollywood Boulevard, for *The Nation*. According to Jen, about whom, naturally, her parents were frantic:

Los Angeles has to be the most surreal place in the world a person could experience rioting. On Thursday afternoon, in the midst of the torchings, beatings and rampaging, our Mayor urged us—no, implored us all—to stay home and watch The Cosby Show. *Arsenio Hall was hangin' in the missions and Edward James Olmos was taking a broom to the streets. Over on a soundstage in Burbank, celebrities were lining up to film public service announcements to stop the violence: Debbie Allen; Wesley Snipes; Chris Rock from* Saturday Night Live; *Luke Perry, teen heartthrob from* Beverly Hills 90210 *(probably the ZIP code least affected during the whole insurrection); Anjelica Huston (Anjelica Huston?) and Sean Penn. The pugnacious Penn telling us that violence wasn't the way to deal with our anger wasn't even the height of absurdity during the crisis. I'm not sure what was.*

Maybe it was the Scientologists in their paramilitary uniforms forming a human barricade around the 12-story L. Ron Hubbard Life Exhibition building on Hollywood and Ivar Friday night. Or maybe it was the brainless woman interviewing Blair Underwood of L.A.Law who asked him to make a comparison with the Watts riots of '65 based on his having been in a movie about them (too many years of Reagan's movie war stories, I guess).

The most absurd moment I witnessed personally came during a break in the cleanup in South Central on Saturday afternoon. A young actress who once starred in a long-running sitcom and later in a babes-in-a-band-at-the-beach movie felt the need to make an inspiring speech to the assembled crowd. Shovel in hand, she began, "Guys, this is like a zit. We've popped the zit but now we have to get at the acne underneath." More facials and deep-pore cleansing for Los Angeles—now there's a rallying cry. I don't mention her name because she really did mean well, and hell, at least she was out there.

Jen approved of local TV coverage the first two days ("no commercial interruptions and no spin"), till the graphics took over, and then the politicians: "One local politician had criticized the stations for acting like 'the home looting network,' telling everyone where the newest target was and essentially inviting people to come on down. I can tell you the people who were looting were not dashing home to plug in their newly acquired TV sets to find out where to hit next." From Frederick's of Hollywood to the Compton mini-malls...from Baskin-Robbins ice cream to Payless shoes: "You wonder why Payless got hit so hard and not Ferragamo. It looks like people hit the places where they resent spending their money every day: grocery stores, liquor stores, discount clothing stores, gas stations, 7-Elevens. There are people here and around the country saying that after the first couple of hours it wasn't political. Sure, it wasn't exactly, 'This CD player is for Rodney King,' but a woman looting an armload of diapers that she couldn't afford to buy would suggest to me that the insurrection was entirely political. Since when are poverty, unemployment, pent-up rage, alienation and disenfranchisement not political?"

I've also been reading *Sex, Death and God in L.A.*, a new collection of essays on everything from Movieland to Little Tokyo to the barrio to the sweatshops to the subway boondoggle. Mike Davis tells us that downtown L.A. is "paradigmatic" because it embodies *the rise of new, globalized circuits of finance and luxury consumption amid the decline of much of the old mass-consumption and high-wage industrial economy. But there is no single, master logic of restructuring, rather the complex intersection of two separate macroprocesses: one based on the overaccumulation of bank and real-estate capital (most recently, from the recycling of the East Asian trade surplus to California); the other arising from the reflux of low-wage manufacturing and labor-intensive services in the wake of unprecedented mass immigration from Mexico and Central America.*

Left out in the battle between Bradley's pro-development (and ghetto-dispossessing) coalition of fatcats and absentee landlords, on the one hand, and, on the other, a populist homeowners' rebellion (Not in Our Neighborhood) on the white West Side, are, of course, the working poor. While a diagram of the players is as complicated as the *Tabula Smaragdina* of the Egyptian Thoth, they include MCA's Lew Wasserman, Lockheed's Roy Anderson, Tom Jones of Northrup, greedy "zaitech" Japanese and the Canadian overreachers Olympia and York, plus Henry Waxman, Zev Yaroslavsky, the Berman brothers, the *Los Angeles Times*, the University of Southern California and even the Kuomintang with Hong Kong funny money. Outside this charmed circle of Inner Clubbies, there is an important African-American player, Diane Watson in the State Senate, who, along with Maxine Waters, performed heroically during the riots. There are some Latino players—Esteban Torres in the Congress; Mike Hernandez on the City Council; Gloria Molina on the powerful L.A. County Board of Supervisors—but they were awfully quiet when everything was most combustible, maybe because their own East L.A. kept the lid on. And there's also an important Asian-American player, Michael Woo, who'd like to graduate from the City Council to Tom Bradley's larger digs. The problem for the outsiders wanting in is that so many Latinos are illegals and so many East Asians don't vote.

In the last decade, a million immigrants have crammed into older black and Chicano slum housing, without the ghost of a social policy to accommodate them; with federal housing assistance slashed 70 percent since 1981; *without a single new public housing unit since the 1950s.*

"Paradoxically," says Davis, "as high-productivity manufacturing in Los Angeles has collapsed, sweated and labor-intensive production has boomed. This is explained by the emergence of a Third World sector within the regional economy, based on the minimum-wage labor of immigrants without citizen rights." And even in L.A.'s low-wage market, blacks and Chicanos are discriminated against in hiring, because noncitizens and illegals will work cheaper. In black Los Angeles, unemployment has risen by nearly 50 percent since the early 1970s—*in a city that spends* nothing *on social programs for the poor*. While L.A. rhapsodists liken their metropolis to ancient Alexandria, every day it looks more like Cairo, Canton and Sao Paulo.

Homelessness, moreover, is a crime. At first, the forces of law and order—Gates, again—punished this crime only by destroying those makeshift sidewalk shelters that the homeless had fashioned to save themselves from hypothermia. "The camping aspect is what we are trying to get at," said the chairman of the Century City East business association, "the jumble of furniture on the street, the open fires. But no one is telling people they can't sleep on the streets." Such a nicety vanished in May 1987, when Gates, backed by the mayor, declared that the homeless had a week to get lost, after which they were carted away, just like garbage.

THE BLAME GAME:
WE MIGHT AS WELL BE HAITIANS

> *But not even the soft wash of dusk could help the houses. Only dynamite would be of any use against Mexican ranch houses, Samoan huts, Mediterranean villas, Egyptian and Japanese temples, Swiss chalets, Tudor cottages, and every possible combination of these styles that lined the slopes of the canyon.*
>
> —Nathanael West

It *couldn't* have been Simi Valley's fault. (Did you know Simi Valley is where they hid the Ronald Reagan Library?) Nor Daryl Gates's, nor yours, nor mine, nor, especially, the Bush Administration's. According to Marlin Fitzwater, the Mortimer Snerd who waffles for the biggest collection of empty suits since the Congress of Vienna, the riot was the fault of sixties liberal programs like Head Start, Medicare, the Job Corps, and food stamps. Tough love means always saying that you're not the least bit sorry. The answer for South Central L.A., as for the newly liberated nonprofit police states of Eastern Europe, is...Free Enterprise Zones.

The heart goes pitty-pat. Free Enterprise Zones! More tax breaks and zoning variances for a handful of fast-buck businessmen to build something ugly on cinder blocks, surround it with barbed wire, bring in a few managers from outside the neighborhood for the high-paying jobs, hire a couple of hundred locals at minimum wage (nonunion, of course; no health plan), and so compete, on a Third World level, with the sweatshops of Santo Domingo and Singapore.

Whereas according to Dan Quayle the fault resides in a deterioration of family values typified by the unwed motherhood of Murphy Brown on sitcom television. Dan Quayle vs. Murphy Brown isn't as funny as it ought to be, or as we've tried to make it. I'm as guilty as the rest. I suggested elsewhere, in a review of Sigourney Weaver's *Aliens 3* (talk about your Single Mothers!), that if only Quayle and Marlin Fitzwater had been invited to appear on *FYI*, like Walter Cronkite, Linda Ellerbee and Connie Chung, we'd have been spared this White House production of *Goof Balls from Outer Space*. Instead of which, we got…Murphy Envy: an infantile disorder.

But this is frivolous. Sure Quayle's a windup doll; twist the key in his head and he malaprops, while the dreaded Marilyn seethes. And our only president, as has been pointed out on the funny pages, is "a monogrammed wind-sock." And Clinton is a mushpuppie; he had a genuine campaign issue and instead, through his sax, he blew smoke. And Ross Perot, who got rich on government contracts to dun by computer the Medicared-for, is less the chivalric knight he imagines himself—with, for his ducal coat-of-arms, a bald eagle rampant on a rabble of rabid bunny rabbits—than Puff the Magic Dragon, proposing to govern by *Gong Show* plebescite.

But the whole country watches television *hoping* it's real. That's why the L.A. riots came as such a shock. There we were, imagining that we're one big prime-time family because Bill Cosby and Michael Jordan spend so many hours in our living rooms, and a city had to burn down before we realized there are African-Americans who aren't overpaid athletes and entertainers. Cities in general and ghettos in particular had been wholly missing from the hot-air primaries, without a propheteering Jesse to keep them honest: the Invisible Man all over again.

From my own mail, I know that before Quayle ever opened his mouth, there were lots of people who *hated* the whole idea of Murphy's fictitious pregnancy. Mr. "Potatoe" Head speaks for these peo-

>>>>>>   *

ple, who believe in the nuclear family despite the 50 percent divorce statistics and the ten million unwed mothers and almost as many runaway children who are fleeing abuse at home; who dream on, in the Hollywood movies and Tin Pan Alley music of their fictitious Reagan youth, of apple pies, aproned moms, and the melting pot as a machine for spinning cotton-candy, from which we'll all emerge uniformly pink and squeaky clean; who are opposed, simultaneously, to birth control, abortion, day-care, job training, national health insurance, and maybe even sex (if it involves proletarians); for whom the only poverty is one of "values."

"Family values": like the House of Atreus, the Brothers Karamazov, the Mafia and Charlie Manson. This is how the White House hopes to line up its right-wing ducks and distinguish itself from Ross Perot. Besides running against Loose Women—one of the "reality-based programs" of this campaign ought to be *Thelma and Louise vs. the Supreme Court*—Bush will run against the poor. And the defenseless environment. Not to mention Haitians.

Nothing new here. A decade ago, sociologist Herbert Gans pointed out that poverty is profitable. Poverty is good for the economy because it makes sure that there's a low-wage labor pool to do our dirty work and creates jobs for social workers and penologists. Poverty is good for society because poor people can be punished as deviants, guaranteeing the status and legitimacy of the rest of us—even the working class. Poverty is good for politics because poor people are a handy symbolic constituency to be fought over by the far right and the radical left. And poverty is good for culture; the poor gave us jazz, and slang, and blue jeans.

What a shame that when these poor want to speak for themselves, the only way they can be heard is by burning down a city in primetime. Couldn't they have FAXed? Inside the Beltway, the various "neos" appear to believe that if there are more young black men in prison than in college, it's only because we're too wimpy about capital punishment.

It's too bad Joan Didion went to press with *After Henry* before the L.A. riots. She's just the stylist for them—a seismograph registering every tremor on the culture's fault line, alert to every paranoid vibration, crouched there in the blank uneasiness like a gryphon, lion colored, eagle eyed, waiting for the Big One: a Manson or a quake or anything that scourges Malibu. But she does remind us in a review of Nancy Reagan's memoirs that the Ronnies never had to worry about a roof over *their* heads. It was the habit of Hollywood studios to provide housing for actors on location. When their studio days were over in the late fifties, Ronnie's TV sponsor, GE, picked up his tab in Pacific Palisades. Later on in Sacramento a group of wealthy businessmen bought the house the Reagans stayed in as well as an eleven-acre site on which Nancy ordained their brand-new Governor's Mansion. These same plutocrats forked over a million bucks for the renovation of the Reagan White House, and paid as well for the Bel Air house on St. Cloud Road to which the Reagans have retired, between memory lapses and junkets to Japan. We are told, too, that the street number of the house on St. Cloud Road was changed from 666 to 668 "to avoid association with the Beast in Revelations." In a country where the average family on welfare receives goods and services worth less than $4,600 a year, Nancy wore $46,000 worth of clothes to her husband's inauguration. From her memoirs we learn she was dismayed at having in the White House to pay for her own food and toothpaste. You will remember she also used to borrow clothes from famous designers and forget to return them, like Imelda Marcos. Isn't this special?

During the reign of King Babar and Queen Celeste, while the federal deficit more than tripled, not counting Social Security flimflam and other forms of double-entry bookkeeping, federal funds for the poor—for income maintenance, for Medicare and Medicaid, for food stamps and for Aid to Families with Dependent Children—were cut $57 billion. And, for hot-lunch programs in our public schools, ketchup became a vegetable. This is special, too.

About George, we already know that he was born "with a silver foot in his mouth" (Ann Richards) "on third base...and thinks he hit a triple" (Tom Harkin). Nor has Danny ever worked for a living. When Danny's done disserving the public, if his father doesn't provide for him, the Pentagon will. One of his favorite projects is a U.S. Department of Defense brain-bender called "Island Sun." Island Sun's a nuclear war contingency plan to deploy a convoy of lead-lined tractor trailers containing a cargo of the nation's top military officials. These miniature Pentagons will roam the nation's interstate highways weeks after everything and everybody else have been destroyed, and launch what's left of our nukes. In the 1991 budget, Bush upped the ante on Island Sun to $84.6 million, a 46 percent increase over 1990. This is more than the $33 million the Air Force spent to purchase 173 heavy-duty FAX machines from Litton Industries, plus $40 million more for support and spare parts, for a tidy $421,000 per machine, but it's peanuts compared to the billions still to be squandered on the Star Wars duel of laser light, Dungeons and Dragons—and we may be sure that a hard rain is never gonna fall on the Bushel and his Peck.

Maybe, after all, we *deserve* Ross Perot. Perot could have been the character in Nathanael West's novel who stands to speak in the Tabernacle of the Third Coming, from some colony in the desert where "he had been conning his soul on a diet of raw fruit and nuts," with the "countersunk eyes, like the heads of burnished spikes." This man was very angry: "The message he had brought to the city was one that an illiterate anchorite might have given decadent Rome. It was a crazy jumble of dietary rules, economics and Bibical threats. He claimed to have seen the Tiger of Wrath stalking the walls of the citadel and the Jackal of Lust skulking in the shrubbery."

Compared to such a messenger, George reminds me of West's Homer: "Yet there was something wrong. For all his size and shape, he looked neither strong nor fertile. He was like one of Picasso's great sterile athletes, who brood hopelessly on pink sand, staring at veined marble waves." It's mystifying. Why should you want so passionately, and stoop willingly to anything, to be elected and then reelected when you haven't an interest in, or a talent for, or a clue about, *governing*? What's in it for you? Class interest? *Let them eat broccoli!*

According to this White House, those of us who aren't good enough for a capital-gains tax cut probably watch public television, anyway, and we might as well be Haitians.

THE CURSE OF THE "RESTING" CLASSES

An American, I said, sighing, but understanding my love of my adopted country perhaps for the first time: an American looks like a wounded person whose wound is hidden from others, and sometimes from herself. An American looks like me.
—Alice Walker, *Possessing the Secret of Joy*

If there's a "working" class, there's also a "resting" class. If there's a black "underclass," there is also a white "overclass." "They did not sow," says Barbara Ehrenreich in *The Worst Years of Our Lives: Irreverent*

Notes from a Decade of Greed, "neither did they reap, but rather sat around pushing money through their modems in games known as 'corporate takeover' and 'international currency speculation.' Hence their rage at anyone who actually works—the 'unproductive' American worker, or the woman attempting to raise a family on welfare benefits set below the average yuppie's monthly health spa fee."

I'm about to lay on some numbers. In the first four years of Reagan's gerontocracy, with reduced taxes for the well-off and reduced social spending for the poor, the richest one-fifth of American families gained $25 billion in disposable income, while the poorest one-fifth lost $7 billion. During the go-go years, from 1977 through 1989, 70 percent of the increase in average family income went to the top 1 percent of our resident plutocracy. The richest 2 percent of American families now controls half of all the personal wealth in the economy. The top 1 percent owns more wealth than the bottom 90 percent. According to *Forbes,* the "Capitalist Tool," despite a recession and layoffs all over the country, more than 400 top corporate executives earned more than a million dollars each in 1990, with Heinz CEO Anthony F.J. O'Reilly pulling down a svelte $75 million. To quote Barbara Ehrenreich again, we've become "a society divided between the hungry and the overfed, the hopeless and the have-it-alls."

Meanwhile, not only will a Savings & Loan bailout cost taxpayers more than $500 billion—to which we should add the tab of such similar socialisms-for-the-rich as the bailouts of Chrysler, Boeing, Franklin National, Continental Illinois and Conrail—but the federal government holds billions of dollars more in properties foreclosed when the so-called *thrift* industry went belly-up along with its pet senators. There are vacant office buildings, apartment houses, private homes, shopping centers, restaurants, golf courses, marinas, even churches. The Resolution Trust Corporation, created to manage this bailout, can't sell any of these properties in any area of the nation designated as "distressed" (like overcrowded and decrepit South Central) *for less than 95 percent of their appraised value.* This is to protect the real-estate "market."

A similar $500 billion, by the way, is what the Rainbow Coalition, meeting in Las Vegas, proposed to use in pension funds, plus a new gasoline tax or an oil import fee, to attract private investors to projects for rebuilding the American economy. Suspicious as we should be of any plan devised by Felix Rohatyn, I'd like to have heard more details, but they were trampled under by reporters on their way to sound-bites from Bill Clinton and Sister Souljah.

Before we actually hate the needy, it is necessary to abstract and stigmatize them, which is what our entire discourse about poverty has been about from the beginning. In *The Undeserving Poor*, Michael Katz traces this discourse: from "lumpenproletariat" to "culture of poverty" to "femininization of poverty"; from "relative deprivation" to "family pathology" and "workfare" and "value stretch" and "benign neglect." Then he disabuses us of some of the cherished myths that have determined recent social policy. Only 0.8 percent of our Gross National Product is spent on welfare, mostly for Social Security. Since 1972, Aid to Families with Dependent Children has *declined* 20 percent. Most poor people, 69 percent, are white, although almost half of all black children live in families with incomes below the poverty line. Between 1970 and 1980, the birth rate of unmarried black women *dropped* 13 percent, while the birth rate of unmarried white women *increased* 27 percent.

How to measure the nation's homeless? Nobody knows. We talk about a million. As many as three million are homeless off and on. As many as seven million are at "extreme risk." One thing we do know is that, between January '83 and December '84 alone, the number of families seeking shelter in New York rose 67 percent; and that, by 1987, most American cities reported a 15 to 20 percent annual increase of homeless. Of these about a third are families with children; most are single men, many of them Vietnam vets, though single women are increasing; and perhaps a third suffer from some sort of psychiatric disorder, or alcoholism, or drug problems.

In a nation where a million are homeless, three million of us own more than one. Ehrenreich, the only known socialist left in America with a sense of humor, notes that the number of rich white men who have never married is almost exactly the same as the number of poor black single mothers: "In the absence of all the old-fashioned ways of redistributing wealth—progressive taxation, job programs, adequate welfare, social services, and other pernicious manifestations of pre-Reaganite 'big government'—the rich will just have to marry the poor."

BETSY ROSS MEETS STAGGERLEE

They did not believe doctors could heal—for them, none had ever done so. They did not believe death was accidental—life might be, but death was deliberate. They did not believe Nature was ever askew—only inconvenient. Plague and drought were as "natural" as springtime. If milk could curdle, God knows robins could fall. The purpose of evil was to survive it and they determined (without ever knowing they had made up their minds to do it) to survive floods, white people, tuberculosis, famine and ignorance. They knew anger well but not despair, and they didn't stone sinners for the same reason they didn't commit suicide—it was beneath them.
—Toni Morrison, *Sula*

Alas, such forbearance has been withdrawn, such communities are no more, and not just because of drugs, which are mostly passing through, anyway, on their way to pink junkies in paisley ties and red suspenders. The fact is that, since Watts in 1965, for poor people, everything has gotten *worse*—housing, schools, jobs, health. For all our think-tank hermeneutics, it would seem as if the purpose of evil were despair.

Between the time I took his course at Harvard in the fifties and the time he had to write a paper for the 1969 report of the National Commission on the Causes and Prevention of Violence, Louis Hartz revised himself. He had always celebrated America's lack of a feudal past (because it finessed class animosity) and our John Locke sort of liberal consensus (because it exempted us from ideological gang warfare). But the sixties changed his mind. Hartz developed a new theory for the commission, speculating that the "aborigine," whether Afro or Australo or Inca, threatens the consensus culture of the European "fragment." Either we accommodate that "aborigine," or we exterminate him. Hartz—and doesn't this make you nostalgic?—looked hopefully to the Supreme Court, because the Court embodied "the notion that there is enough moral agreement in the political world to permit the adjudication of even its largest questions."

A couple of years later, in a novel about black migrant workers in the apple orchards of New Hampshire, I wrenched poor bleeding Hartz out of his academic context, into the mouth of a Roxbury militant called Raja Born. According to "The Raj":

The European frag…You be getting away with it in the 19th century. None of that French shit here, no ma'am. Let all them little ide-ol-o-ets run around acrost the Atlantic cutting up each other. You got your boo-jew-wash liberpimples to keep you warm. Bunch of Anglo saxophones, offing the Indos, trashing wigwams, eeternal vigilantes, let the micks and wops rumble for their shithouse, the state is quo is us. Suspended sentence of the U.S. of Candy-Ass. But the Century Number Twenty come along. Your con-sen-sus is concussed. By the Aborginal—the Peru dude, Inca-dinca-doo! The bushman, we don't waltz no mother Matildas! The Afro, black trash-eater, voodoo to you do, groin and bare it! I am 1789, caught up with you at last!

I don't do dialect any more. Or novels. My favorite question on the TV talk shows after the burning of L.A. was the one they asked obsessively, about whether *you* as a honky feel more apprehensive on the street when you meet a group of young black men than when they're white folks. As a cerified honky, I can tell you that if you *aren't* worried about those young black men, you just haven't been paying attention. As well as being melanin deprived, you've a deficiency of imagination. What *I* imagine happening to me is more or less what I think we deserve. This is a projection: If I were a young black man I know how I'd feel about *me*. And it wouldn't do this me any good at all to whip out my glowing reviews of the novels of Toni Morrison, or my columns on Jesse Jackson, or my teaching credentials from a Boston ghetto during that War on Poverty.

Nor would it make much difference in my night-sweats whether these bloods included, say, a Michael Jordan, with his space-age sneakers and endorsements. Why does everybody want to hear from Michael Jordan? What makes us think he likes us any more than, say, Farrakhan? Hasn't Jordan enough to worry about in a country where black men wear out fast; where Jackie Robinson, after a pit stop for Rockefeller Republicanism, went angry to an early grave; where Muhammad Ali is a saintly vegetable; where Richard Pryor set himself on fire; where all Wilt Chamberlain will talk about is his wall-to-wall carpet of arctic wolves' noses and his 20,000 one-night stands? Having made it, one of the ways you make sure you keep it is by lying low.

There's a T-shirt, popular in Harlem, that says: BO KNOWS RACISM. Does anybody remember Paul Robeson? He just wouldn't shut up. Never mind that he did all right by himself for the grandson of a slave…went to Rutgers on a scholarship and made all-America in football...went to Broadway in some plays by Eugene O'Neill...went to Hollywood, where he sang "Old Man River" in *Show Boat*...went to England, where they let him do *Othello*...went to Russia and got uppity...couldn't go anywhere when we took away his passport...and so went crazy, from the sadness and electroshock. This Robeson, when he wasn't singing spirituals at benefits for his disenfranchised people, or for labor unions, or for Progressive party presidential candidates...when he wasn't going to bed with white women like Peggy Ashcroft before she became a Dame, or Uta Hagen while she was still married to Jose Ferrer...when he couldn't, because of his skin color, get a room in a hotel or a table at a restaurant or a concert hall to sing like an angel in, in cities like New York and Seattle and Los Angeles...this black Captain Marvel, who should have been grateful white Americans liked him more than they liked most other black folks, insisted instead on complaining about racism, colonialism, imperialism and Red-baiting. Roy Wilkins of the NAACP didn't like him any more than J. Edgar Hoover of the FBI liked him any more than either of them later on would like Martin Luther King, Jr., who was very different but just as uppity. So what our government couldn't do to Robeson, the doctors did. They cured his depression by "electroconvulsive therapy"; they seized his brain. He didn't die until 1976, but he'd been missing for at least a decade before that. He wouldn't have liked us, either.

When I said all this to Peter Freundlich at CBS, he agreed: "Yes," said Peter. "You seldom hear them say on the news that after all the looting and pillage, the broken windows and burning buildings and the helicopters and police dogs, eight white liberals were found left standing."

RIP VAN WINKLE MEETS CALIBAN

Might have been killed for the prize of her gum boots, mask and bubble suit in the raid. The unrecognizable children who run the streets taking over abandoned social service agencies and subways and concert halls and armories finally taking her over too. Offspring of the children who roamed in vacant lots and city dumps years before when old smoke detectors leached americum into the dirt, their clothes, their genes. Kids who dug up for fun the contaminated uniforms of workers hunted by the angry mob awakened too

*late and misdirected in their hatred. Those kids grown up twisted and wast-
ed giving birth to the ones shunned, turned out, driven off who found each
other and ran in packs and found her on the street, beat her down...*
—Toni Cade Bambara, *The Salt Eaters*

It could have happened here, in New York City. And would have, too,
if Ed Koch were still in charge, that demagogic Chicken Little Big
Foot. It helps a little that the races see each other in this city on a daily
basis. The whole point of the L.A. freeway system is to avoid places
like South Central, as if it were Soweto. At least in New York, on the
buses and the subways, we can pretend we're all going in the same direction. But I can remember a week in 1989, just across the bridge.
That Wednesday, in the mostly white Bensonhurst section of Brooklyn, a sixteen-year-old black was chased by a mob with baseball bats,
and shot to death. Yusef Hawkins was wrongly suspected of going to
a birthday party for Gina Feliciano, a white woman. That Saturday and
Sunday, demonstrators, mostly black, marched in Bensonhurst. They
were jeered by counterdemonstrators, entirely white, who taunted
them with watermelons, and signs that said, "We Got One!" and
many shouts of "nigger." We watched all this on the late-night local
news. That Monday the mayor, who was up for reelection, seemed
more upset by the marches in Bensonhurst than by the murder in
Bensonhurst, for which he was booed Tuesday, at a wake for Yusef
Hawkins in Bedford Stuyvesant, and Wednesday, at the funeral in
Brownsville, where we also heard from everybody's favorite black
anti-Semite, Farrakhan, and all this, too, was on the late-night news.
With dogs and hoses, it would have looked like Selma.

Now we all knew, back in 1989, that not everybody in Bensonhurst
killed Yusef Hawkins. That Bensonhurst was not much worse than
other neighborhoods we could name, including mine in Manhattan,
where the NYPNS ("Neat Young People in Neat Situations") don't
want a homeless shelter or an AIDS clinic or even a 7-Eleven to attract
riffraff. And that, to a degree, the demonstrations and counterdemon-
strations were made for television, almost choreographed, like student riots in Korea. And that Ed Koch, Al Sharpton, Morton Downey,
Jr., Louis Farrakhan and all those TV cameras conspired at a circus.
Maybe none of this would have seemed so disgraceful if we hadn't at
that minute been deciding whether, like Chicago or Los Angeles or
Detroit, to elect our first black mayor, or vote instead for Crazy Eddie

or Rudy (Robocop) Guiliani. In the event, we knew Bensonhurst
would end up as a TV movie or a miniseries, in the manner of other
New York neighborhood stories, like Howard Beach the previous fall
on NBC, or the preppie "rough sex" murder case the following fall on
ABC, after which we'd never have to think about it again.

But it was interesting, wasn't it, that Spike Lee also went to Bensonhurst that week, a visit arranged by the New York newspaper for
which I am a columnist. And they *loved* Spike Lee in Bensonhurst, as if
he were a basketball player or a rock star...as if he *weren't* Yusef
Hawkins...as Michael Jordan isn't Rodney King.

Anyway, we elected David Dinkins. He has so far given us some
breathing space, and pretty blue ribbons, and a night at the Cathedral
of St. John the Divine—like one of those Festivals of Life they used to
stage during the French Revolution, those carnivals in favor of the
Goddess of Pure Reason, pitching the "good" magic of a civic religion
(called the Gorgeous Mosaic) against the "bad" magic of armed and
bristling ethnic enclaves. Dinkins says he *wants* to give us more, but
there isn't any money, *certainly not from a federal government that takes away
$21 billion more in taxes from New Yorkers than it returns in services.* Still, he
plays the usual New York game of The Suddenly Discovered Surplus
So We Won't Have to Close the Zoo, After All; and you'd think that a
mayor who really cares about the homeless would not have permitted
Grand Central Station to reduce its public seating to six benches; nor
allowed the Port Authority Bus Terminal to refuse entry to anybody,
after 1:00 A.M., without a bus ticket; nor tolerated a transit-cop crack-
down on anyone trying to beg, sleep or sing in the subways.

In the parks, of course, we burn them alive.

During his brief tenure as minister of propaganda for the Dinkins
regime, Albert Scardino was quoted as saying, in *Vanity Fair* of all unlikely places: "Most white people in this city have had no experience
with blacks. They think black men are felons and black women are
maids."

One assumes he didn't mean the real world of mailmen, bank
tellers, cops, teachers, local TV anchorpeople, baseball or the theater.
He was probably talking about *social* experience. You know: in our
living rooms. If so, he had a point. I probably know more African-
Americans, socially, than most middle-class whites in this city, but
they're usually writers. The pool I swim in is a library, after which I
wear their panther skins. In my kitchen the novelist Toni Morrison

has actually felt sorry for the felon Mike Tyson. The playwright Wesley Brown has told me what it was like to be a conscientious objector
during Vietnam and what it is like to be a single black *father* today in
this city. Plus…well, let's see. On one occasion, my wife and I were
the only white folks at a gathering of the East Coast black intelli-
gentsia, up the Hudson, in a gazebo, for a New Year's party that Spike
Lee abandoned early because the others were insufficiently worship-
ful of his success; and while Lee hadn't yet begun his Malcolm X film,
everybody at this party had gone in 1982 to an off-Broadway production of a play about Malcolm, called *When the Chickens Come Home to
Roost*, that *I'd* never heard of, starring (surprise!) Denzel Washington;
and I felt like a country bumpkin. (Malcolm X…meet Andy Warhol.)

On another occasion not so long ago, I went to a dinner party to
celebrate John Edgar Wideman for his quasi-novel, *Philadelphia Fire*.
Commingling socially at this dinner party were the likes of Charlayne
Hunter-Gault and E.L. Doctorow, Quincy Troupe and Grace Paley.
Back in the sixties, I'd imagined this was the way most of the dinner
parties one went to would look like in the future. But they don't;
there's the despair. In my living room there's a brass birdman totem
from the Ivory Coast that I see a dozen times a day. I see John Edgar
Wideman once a decade.

And Wideman's career in its way is as instructive as Paul Robeson's.
I reviewed his novel *Hurry Home* in 1970, and he invited me to talk to
a class he taught at the University of Pennsylvania. I wouldn't see him
again till a lunch in 1981. He had given up trying to find a hardcover
publisher and brought out three new books, simultaneously, in Avon
paperback. In those paperbacks, Wideman tried to go home again—
from Penn, from his Rhodes scholarship, from years in Europe, from
James Joyce, to the Pittsburgh ghetto where he had grown up, and
which he felt himself in some obscure way to have betrayed. And
now…now he's Caliban.

In *Philadelphia Fire*—part fiction, part memoir, part deconstruction
of the text of black American manhood—Wideman's alter ego, Cudjoe, who ran away from marriage and America to an Aegean island,
tries to go home again to West Philly in 1985. What has happened to
his old neighborhood, instead of a gorgeous mosaic, is the murder,
on Osage Avenue, of the Move cult. A SWAT team shot up the house
where Move lived, a police helicopter dropped a bomb on it, six
adults and five children died, 53 houses were destroyed, and 262

people were left homeless. Do you see how once you start thinking about Los Angeles, everything fits and everything hurts?

Cudjoe, a graduate of Penn, hopes to write a book about Osage Avenue, and to find a child, "a naked boy, a forked stick," a creature of ash and wind who escaped the fire and vanished into the city to become a hero, Simba. Meanwhile, Wideman, the creator of Cudjoe, is worried about his son in prison. Together, Wideman and Cudjoe will write another sort of book, *Philadelphia Fire*, about politics and history and Indian ghosts with flame-colored bodies, about adults left out of Western culture and children lost to drugs and rage, about failed marriages, exile, basketball and *The Tempest*, a play by Earl the Pearl Shakespeare. It's a book of brilliant correspondences that can't find closure because the *culture* is schizophrenic. Simba is Wideman's lost son. If Osage Avenue burns, so will the library in the novelist's head. Besides that Greek island, there is also Shakespeare's, with Caliban, the "dark thing," the first slave and the first "dead Indian." Before he went away, Cudjoe wanted to mount an all-black children's production of *The Tempest* in a city park, with Caliban as hero—as if black intellectuals, having gone to Penn instead of Osage Avenue, could take Shakespeare away from the Canon, from T.S. Eliot and *The Wasteland*. But, of course, Prospero, the first imperialist, with his magic books, will always be the hero, and Caliban will never sleep with Miranda, and the black children of Philadelphia—those who haven't been shot, blown up, burnt, drowned or hanged from basketball rims—run wild, in war paint, on the city streets, not speaking sonnets. This is the fire next time.

WHO WILL TELL THE CHILDREN?

You go along for years knowing something is wrong, then suddenly you discover that you're as transparent as air. At first you tell yourself that it's all a dirty joke, or that it's due to the "political situation." But deep down you come to suspect that you're yourself to blame, and you stand naked and shivering before the millions of eyes who look through you unseeingly. That is the real soul-sickness, the spear in the side, the drag by the neck through the mob-angry town, the Grand Inquisition, the embrace of the Maiden, the rip in the belly with the guts spilling out, the trip to the chamber with the deadly gas that ends in the oven so hygienically clean—only it's worse because

you continue stupidly to live. But live you must, and you can either make pas-
sive love to your sickness or burn it out and go on to the next conflicting phase.
—Ralph Ellison, *Invisible Man*

Let's be a little less literary, more downhome. There was an article a
year ago in *New York Newsday* about teenagers and a police lineup.
Asked by cops at the Ninth Precinct station house in lower Manhattan
to supply some warm Hispanic bodies for a November lineup, the
dean at the School for Career Development obligingly forwarded ten
male teenagers to pose as perps. Now: the School for Career Development specializes in kids who are "emotionally disturbed or learning
disabled." The "volunteers" weren't told what they'd be doing, nor
were their parents asked for permission. One fifteen-year-old burst
into tears. *Then* they told him he wasn't a suspect.

As indecencies go, this one's routine. And like all routine indecencies, it also has a history. *Newsday* reported the previous May that several city high schools were in the habit of supplying students for police lineups. Schools Chancellor Joseph Fernandez promptly banned
the practice. The appropriate memo apparently never reached such
special education schools as Career Development. There was also a Police Departmental memorandum, issued in June, saying that before
detectives used teens under eighteen for their lineups, they needed
the written consent of parents or guardians. A police spokesman told
Newsday, "The problem was, many of the old-time detectives figured
that when they [students] are in school, the principal was the legal
guardian."

Well, no, that isn't the problem. The problem is depersonalization
and contempt. My wife, for instance, teaches history to teenagers at a
private school in Manhattan. It would never occur to cops to ask for
any of *her* students in their chorus line, nor would her school have tolerated such a request. But all male Hispanic teens look alike don't
they, sort of suspect, like black kids on subways? We've already
thrown them away. Why not this convenient recycling program?

Perhaps the child in you recalls cherished teachers in classes that
weren't overcrowded in buildings that weren't falling down in neighborhoods that didn't look like Beirut, when education was about distinctions and connections, about surprise, wonder, passion, regret
and citizenship, instead of drugs and guns and AIDS, back when the
public-school system was a trampoline, from which we bounced into

the future, instead of a detention camp for refugees. In this day and age, another child drops out of the public high school warehouse system *every eight seconds*. Of those who stick with it, 700,000 graduate each year unable to read their own diplomas.

I find that I don't have the words to describe how I feel about a school system that imagines its custodianship of our children so casually. Let me borrow some. From, say, Elizabeth Bowen: "Two things are terrible in childhood: helplessness (being in other people's power) and apprehension—the apprehension that something is being concealed from us because it was too bad to be told." And from Lillian Hellman: "God help all the children as they move into a time of life they do not understand and must struggle through with precepts they have picked up from the garbage can of other people, clinging with the passion of the lost to odds and ends that will mess them up for all time, or hating the trash so much they will waste their future on the hatred."

Mary McCarthy assured us that "people with bad consciences always fear the judgment of children." But do we really? I doubt it. We've come a long way in this society from Rousseau's idea of a child, or Wordsworth's, or even Freud's. Our war on children is personal: Millions are sexually abused each year not by Black Mass pedophiles who snatch them off the city streets, but at home, by family, relatives, friends. And this war is institutional: A third of the homeless in this city are families with children. Half of all our young people who are black or Hispanic are unemployed. During the narcoleptic reign of Ronald the Reposeful, the poor were shunned, and funds for them slashed, and we actually seemed to *want* to be a culture that measures everybody by his ability to produce wealth; a culture that morally condemns anyone who fails to prosper; a culture that babbles hysterically all day long about "family values" and goes to bed comfortably at night with apartheid. According to Charles Lamb, "I am determined that my children shall be brought up in their father's religion, if they can find out what it is."

HE WHO DIES WITH THE MOST TOYS WINS.

INVASION OF THE CYBERPUNKS

He was carried through the exit to the back street and lifted into a police car. The siren began to scream and at first he thought he was making the noise himself. He felt his lips with his hands. They were clamped tight. He knew then it was the siren. For some reason this made him laugh and he began to imitate the siren as loudly as he could.
—Nathanael West

A week after the L.A. riots, *TV Guide* sponsored a symposium on "The New Face of Television Violence," at the Center for Communication on Lexington Avenue, in New York City. Educators, psychologists and other social scientists felt bad, at length, into a tape recorder. I was included for comic relief, and not only because I'm a notorious First Amendment absolutist who believes that there's already too much censorship of television, particularly self-censorship, especially when it comes to politics. But I was also included because I actually watch this stuff. I did not then and I do not now believe the other members of this panel watched television like the rest of us, if they watched at all. Mondays, I watch *Murphy Brown* and *Northern Exposure* because I want to laugh, the way Fridays I want to eat Italian. There's this talking furniture in our living rooms, a twenty-four-hour machine for grinding out narrative and novelty and distraction, news and laughs, high culture and group therapy, a place to celebrate, a place to mourn, a circus, a wishing well and a cure for loneliness. Before midnight, anthropology. After midnight, archaeology. Commercials themselves are a crash course in economics: overproduction and forced consumption. We should worry less about what's *on* television, and more about what's *not*.

Certainly, such symposiasts never "surf." But, like a Marlin Fitzwater and a Dan Quayle, they are looking for somebody (else) to blame.

At our symposium, naturally, much was made of the repeated reruns of the cam-recorded videotape of Rodney King's Golgotha. As much was also made of the subequent coverage, "live," of the riots. Nothing got in the way of their many theories about how TV violence, somehow simultaneously, both "desensitizes" and "incites" a reciprocal violence on the part of audience. But it should have been obvious that no one anywhere in the country had the slightest difficulty grasping the difference in kind between what happened to Rod-

ney King and what *seems* to happen in TV movies and serials. After
decades of cartoonlike, aestheticized, even kinky mashings and mutilations, we are still capable of distinguishing between fact and fancy,
and what we saw appalled us, as it should have. Nor were we under
any illusion that what happened to Rodney King, or to Los Angeles,
was in any way aberrant, anomalous or ahistorical. There were causes,
connections and consequences. And to judge by the results of the subsequent California primary (most of the law-and-order heavy
breathers lost), and by the national polls (a surprising majority of
Americans seemed to agree that we've neglected our cities), we may
have learned something.

And this is a surprise. I had feared, and I was not alone, that during
the Gulf War our government and television perfected a kind of electronic grid to dazzle the eye and cloud the mind, a Social Control
video game. Pac-Man, said many of us, analogizing promiscuously;
and Nintendo. Call this video game "Showtime" or maybe "Spectacle": a mythological creature, part goat, part bull, with a fiery sign; a
supercommercial for the first consumer war. Barbara Ehrenreich has
said that when TV commercials want us to buy cars, they sell us *adventure*; and when they want us to buy beer, they'll sell us *friendship*. What
was the war commercial really trying to get us to buy? Let's nibble
some texts. According to the critic Eugene Goodheart:

> *The apocalypse may be the dominant media trope of our time; its endless re-
> play has inured us to the real suffering it might entail. We repeatedly wit-
> ness the assassination of Kennedy, the mushroom cloud over Hiroshima, the
> disintegration of the Challenger space shuttle in the sky. Repetition wears
> away the pain. It also perfects the image of our experience of it. By isolating
> the event and repeating it, its content, its horror, evaporates. What we have
> before us is its form and rhythm. The event becomes aesthetic and the effect
> upon us anesthetic. The phenomenon is called kitsch.*

Kitsch! Goodheart defines it as "a term of contempt for art of little
value or an art that is meretricious, a misleading, ingratiating semblance of the real thing....Ordinary kitsch covers over reality with the
appearance of art: It appeals to the desire for the pleasant and harmonious. But there is a kitsch of death: a juxtaposition of the kitsch aesthetic and of the themes of death; an aestheticizing of experience." In
The Unbearable Lightness of Being, Kundera was talking about the same

thing when he described kitsch as "a folding screen set up to curtain off death." Kitsch, he said, "always serves up 'the intelligible lie'... It is endowed with a tireless capacity to swallow up reality and churn it out as something plastic...It has a special appetite for death."

Well, yes, but: I know people, and so do you, who must leave the room whenever there's a rocket lift-off on television, because that *Challenger* launch with the teacher inside is burned on their mind's own retina. How often must we burst into tears at a snippet of film from the death camps, before media theorists admit that what's going on in our image-filled heads is something more or other than aesthetic? It's not the mushroom cloud that breaks the heart in this atomic age; it's home movies of the deformed children of Hiroshima and Nagasaki. When we've forgotten everything else about the Vietnam War, Americans will remember a single snapshot, of a little girl and her baby brother burning alive in napalm. And no matter how many times we saw the Rodney King videotape in reruns, we weren't "inured" to a real suffering; the horror never evaporated; it was neither aesthetic nor anesthetic; to no one did it ever become "plastic"—except to the Simi Valley jurors who acquitted the cops. And that tape was replayed endlessly for those jurors *in slow motion*, as if to stone them. *They weren't watching it in Real Time.* In the courtroom "theater," it became for them a *Bonnie and Clyde*, a kind of self-hypnosis after which they voted the way you'd expect a bedroom community of cops to vote.

In his new novel *Immortality*, Kundera moves on from kitsch to what he calls "imagology." Imagology's taken over from ideology. It's the agitprop of journalists dependent on advertising agencies. Imagology, says Kundera, is stronger than reality. Public-opinion polls enable imagology to live in absolute harmony with the people, because

> *they create a truth, the most democratic truth that ever existed...The wheels of imagology turn without having any effect on history. Ideologies fought with one another and each of them was capable of filling a whole epoch with its thinking. Imagology organizes peaceful alteration of its systems in lively seasonal rhythms. Imagologues create systems of ideals and anti-ideals, systems of short duration that are quickly replaced by other systems but that influence our behavior, our political opinions and aesthetic tastes, the color of carpets and the selection of books...*

Again, we assent, but there are these niggles. Just look, today, at the disarray of the spin doctors in the White House; at the mad scramble of the ad agency account executives to come up with anything as fraught, this time around, as Willie Horton was four years ago, after the flag no longer works and Panama is worse off than before we "rescued" it from Noriega; at approval ratings that flipflop as porpoiselike for the president as they did for Mike Dukakis, in spite of White House control of the media agenda and policies calculated to pander to the perceived whim of the people. With our magic "remotes," we skip commercials, and lie to pollsters, and consult in secret the compass of our own pain, and maybe even our own shame. As much as we seem to despise incumbent politicians, we seem even more to despise those media that imagine they can engineer our consent. In a recession of ideas, there is every sign that we just aren't buying.

Besides, between the time Kundera started writing *Immortality* and the time it appeared, all of Eastern Europe, watching itself on television, decided on a change of histories.

Don DeLillo's always written wonderfully about TV in his novels. Remember the academic in *White Noise* who wanted his students to look at TV

> *as children again....Root out content. Find the codes and messages. TV offers incredible amounts of psychic data. It opens ancient memories of world birth, it welcomes us into the grid, the network of little buzzing dots that make up the picture pattern. There is light, there is sound. I ask my students, "What more do you want?" Look at the wealth of data concealed in the grid, in the bright packaging, the jingles, the slice-of-life commercials, the products hurtling out of darkness, the coded messages and endless repetitions, like chants, like mantras. "Coke is it, Coke is it." The medium practically overflows with sacred formulas...*

But this most media-savvy of our novelists changes *his* mind too. DeLillo introduces us in *Mao II* to Karen, a former Moonie who watches so much TV news that she seems "lost in the dusty light, observing some survivor of a national news disaster, there's the lonely fuselage smoking in a field, and she was able to study the face and shade into it at the same time, even sneak a half second ahead, inferring the strange dazed grin or gesturing hand, which made her seem involved, not just in the coverage, but in the terror that came blowing through the fog."

TV news for Karen is neither aesthetic nor anesthetic: "She was thin-boundaried. She took it all in, she believed it all, pain, ecstasy, dog food, all the seraphic glitter, the baby bliss that falls from the air...She carried the virus of the future."

But is there anybody anymore who believes it all? We believe *something*, but maybe not what they want us to. Whatever they're selling, we seem to have purchased Dread. When that Death Commercial took over the networks during Desert Storm, and the public appeared to have bought it, overnight, I thought we had entered the "virtual reality" of cyberspace, that hacker's cosmos of computer simulations. But in the year or so since the Gulf War, somehow, the Grid...well, the Grid *leaked*. Maybe it was pictures of the Kurds. Or maybe it was Bush throwing up in Japan. Or maybe, as June Jordan suggested in the *New York Times*, in the middle of all the yellow-ribbon waving, when you couldn't hear anything over the noise of the marching bands, the high of war wears off like a hit of crack. And maybe something else goes on while we're watching even the cleverest television, and just takes awhile to find a way to articulate itself, like an alarm clock on a bomb.

If we had become, to whatever degree, agnostics about reality itself, something happened to us while we were memorizing Rodney King. And then we saw Los Angeles, live and unrehearsed. Who says violence never changes anything? Had anybody ever seen so many black faces all of a sudden on all the TV news shows? Where did they find these people, that they couldn't have found them before L.A. went up in flames? Why were we, suddenly, talking about all the issues we had so studiously ignored throughout the campaign? If you've read any cyberpunk fiction, you know that in the cyberspace of "virtual reality" there's always supposed to be a matrix, a datasphere, which the punks attack. While it's hard to think of *this* government as anything so grand as a matrix, it does seem as though the Master Narrators and the Imagologists have lost control of the story line, and what the Grid leaks is blood, and this means there's blood on our kitsch, and the next face we see through those computer simulations could be one of our homeless...and then a Haitian...and then maybe, even, a Palestinian. Out there, anyway, outside the glitter-dome and the dancing dots and the obscene light show, are all the dispossessed: Boat People, everywhere. What we'll do with them if we ever let them in, I can't say. "Writers don't give prescriptions," explained the Nigerian novelist Chinua Achebe; "they give headaches."

But this isn't very complicated. People who have homes and schools and jobs and respect don't riot in the streets. Besides the Sermon on the Mount, another, older religion has reliably informed us: Without work, there is no bread, and without bread, there is no *Torah*, and thus no love of learning.

THE IMPERIAL CITY: REWRITING NEW YORK

THE WAY WE ARE

We live in this imaginary city, a novel that needs a rewrite, where the only politicians not in jail probably ought to be (except for Ruth Messinger), and all of them are Democrats; where the unions don't care, and the schools don't work, and the cops deal drugs, and the mayor has his own foreign policy and I can't leave home without stepping over the body of a runaway or a derelict. We didn't elect Felix Rohatyn to anything, but the Municipal Assistance Corporation is more important than the City Council. Nor did we vote for Steinbrenner, Trump, Sharpton or the rest of the bullies and crybabies who bray on our battlements and wave the bloody pennants of their imperial omophagous selves. And yet Mort Zuckerman will have his Zuckermandias at Columbus Circle, his finger in the sun on the same Coliseum site from which Robert Moses before him dispossessed an entire neighborhood. And because none of these pop heroes ever takes the subway, there isn't a Bernie Goetz to shoot them. Maybe more than Tom Wolfe or a bunch of disappointed intellectuals, we need Jeremiah.

But Wolfe, in *The Bonfire of the Vanities*, and *Dissent* magazine, in a special anniversary issue called "In Search of New York," have written their New York novels anyway. Wolfe, the parajournalist, looks pretty much the same as always, still grinning at us out of the nimbus of his double-breasted signature white suit, a vanilla-colored Mau Mau. *Dissent*, on the other hand, has had a format face-lift and for the first time in thirty-three years you can read the socialist quarterly without an O.E.D. magnifying glass. In both their novels, the underclass is the stuff of dreams, the return of the repressed, a kind of history-making black magic. They disagree, of course, on whether this is a good thing.

Listen up to Wolfe:

You don't think the future knows how to cross a bridge*?...you Wasp char-
ity-ballers sitting on your mounds of inherited money up in your co-ops with
the 12-foot ceilings and the two wings, one for you and one for the help, do
you really think you're impregnable? And you German-Jewish financiers
who have finally made it into the same buildings, the better to insulate your-
selves from the* shtetl *hordes, do you really think you're insulated from the*
Third World*?*

Dissent wants this very same Third World—2.5 million "newcomers" since 1965—to be an energizing principle. In diversity, we've always found our jumping beans. From abrasions of culture on culture
we rub up a public philosophy, a civic space. Surely the new immigrants, this ethnic muscle, will rescue us from a mood grown "sullen,
as if in contempt of earlier feelings and visions" and "a peculiar kind
of social nastiness" (Irving Howe); a "trained incapacity to see the
city as a human environment or as anything more than a machine for
generating money" (Marshall Berman); "a way of life not much better than jungle warfare" (Ada Louise Huxtable); and "a world devised
in its entirety by Dostoevski's Smerdyakov" (Paula Fox).

It's odd that Wolfe is so much better than *Dissent* on the details of
class animus. He knows exactly where to look for them. Whereas *Dissent* can barely bring itself to mention cops, Wolfe goes underground
into the criminal-justice system, where the hatred is naked. If *Dissent*
is too polite these days to call anybody an out-and-out racist, Wolfe
has been to the fancier dinner parties and taken notes, like St. Simon,
and bites the hand that scratched his ears, like Truman Capote. It's
equally odd that Ed Koch, who certainly deserves it, is all over the
pages of *Dissent*, while Wolfe entirely ignores him. A New York novel
without Koch is like a French court without a Sun Kinky. Even Danny
Ortega took time out to rub Crazy Eddie's lucky hump.

But there are many oddities. Neither New York novel has much of
anything to say about drugs or organized crime. Both mention
Alexander Cockburn.

VANITIES

Sherman McCoy is a thirty-eight-year-old Yalie who decided to sell bonds on Wall Street instead of going into his father's good-bones law firm. He made almost a million dollars last year but when he sits himself down on his oxblood Moroccan leather swivel chair in front of the tambour door of his *faux*-Sheraton TV cabinet, he's still broke because of his $2.6-million tenth-floor Park Avenue duplex, the Southampton house on Old Drover's Mooring Lane, a wife who decorates her interiors with Thomas Hope chairs, plus three servants, a handyman, club dues, car insurance for the Mercedes and private-school tuition for cute little Campbell who, "supremely ladylike in her burgundy Taliaferro jumper and white blouse with a buttercup collar," bakes bunny rabbits in the kitchen and writes short stories about sad koala bears.

Sherman also has a bimbo. Wolfe's no better than Bill Buckley at heavy breathing, but he knows enough to borrow from his betters. Poor-white-southern-trashy Maria, faithless wife and merry widow, slinks right out of a 1940s detective novel, into Sherman's nerveless arms: "Her medium was men...the way a dolphin's medium is the sea." At night on an off-ramp in the darkest Bronx at the wheel of Sherman's Mercedes, Maria will hit, run down and run away from a young, black, fatherless, "honor student" belonging to the nearby bombed-out Projects, and Sherman will be blamed.

This malefaction will excite a black, Sharpton-like demagogue, the Reverend Reginald Bacon of Harlem; a white, Kunstler-like attorney, the radically chic Amos Vogel; an English reporter for a Murdoch-minded tabloid, the alcoholic Peter Fallow; a Jewish district attorney up for reelection in a Bronx that's 70 percent black and Hispanic, the publicity-hungry Abe Weiss; a Jewish assistant D.A. who 'd rather be an Irish cop, the poor and horny Lawrence Kramer; plus assorted Communists, "the lesbos and the gaybos," welfare bums and fluffy-headed nightly-newsies.

Poor Sherman. In his rent-controlled love nest, he's menaced by the landlord's hired Hasidic muscle. ("These...unbelievable people... could now walk into his life.") When the cops ("insolent...Low Rent...*animals*") come to take him to the Bronx for his arraignment, they're driving ("*brutes* from the outer boroughs") an Oldsmobile Cutlass! When he looks down from his tenth-floor co-op, a black mob is howling for his blue blood. (The *Other* is gaining on *him*!)

Only Tom Wolfe could descend into the sewers of our criminal-justice system and find, for his hero, a *white* victim in a city where Goetz gets six months, Ray Donovan and John Gotti walk, Robert Chambers blames the victim and Eleanor Bumpers and Michael Stewart are still dead. Only Wolfe could want to be our Balzac and yet not notice the real-estate hucksters and the homeless, nor send a single character to a concert, a movie, a play, a museum, a ball game, a Chinese restaurant or an all-night deli. So what if the women are Tinkertoys, the blacks corrupt cartoons, the homophobia flagrant, the politics a surly whelp of Evelyn Waugh and Joseph de Maistre and the author less amusing than he was when he trashed modern art. Nobody's perfect. Satire means never having to say you're sorry, no matter how much there is for which you ought to apologize.

But on several subjects, all but disdained by *Dissent*, Wolfe can really sweat our socks.

THE "DELIRIOUS PROFESSIONS"...FEAR...(AND)...SHOES

By the "delirious professions" Paul Valéry meant "all those trades whose main tool is one's opinion of one's self, and whose raw material is the opinion others have of you." In other words, Creative People, who in New York are not merely artists, writers, actors, dancers and singers, but journalists, editors, critics, TV and radio producers, anchorheads and talkshow hosts, noisy professors of uplift or anomie, experts on this week's Rapture of the Deep at the Ninety-second Street Y, even advertising account execs, swinging bankers and Yuppies in red suspenders on the stock and identity exchange. Each is asked every minute of the day to be original: *unique.* Only then will they be lifted up by the epaulets to Steinbrenner's box in the Stadium sky, there to consort with city presbyters the likes of the late Roy Cohen, where you can't tell the pearls from the swine.

Dissent isn't interested in these people, their white suits and their bonfires. When *Dissent* nods at the market, it's merely to observe that "a multi-billion dollar, cost-plus, militarized economy virtually guarantees spectacular profits to investors in the West and South" (Berman). When it mentions the media at all it's only to complain of their role in a "bipartisan incumbent-protection society," and their "'objective' contempt" for politics as anything other than "sport"

(Jim Chapin), or to make fun of *Manhattan, Inc.* and *Spy* (Brian Morton). Where, for heaven's sake, is an analysis of the *Times*? How come *Newsday* was the only daily to oppose the reelection of Al D'Amato (whom Irving Howe calls "Picklehead")? For *Dissent*, the "delirious professions" are lumped anonymously into a "service sector" as remote from the new Third World as Mars.

Yet these are the blimps and billboards who make images, taste and deals; write the city's Zeitgeist; call down the heat wave, cold fronts, snow jobs and acid rain of our emotional weather. Without their complicity, there will be no change. Change needs better p.r. Dazzle them into some kind of sentience. At least take seriously their many failures of intelligence and character.

Wolfe can't get enough of them in his zippy jetstream and jazz fugue of the latest language: "They were moving about in an agitated manner and sweating early in the morning and shouting, which created the roar. It was the sound of well-educated young white men baying for money on the bond market." Prestaggered cash flows! Convertible asset management! Capital-sensitive liquidity ratios! He's got their number: "He was wearing a covert-cloth Chesterfield topcoat with a golden brown velvet collar and carrying one of those burgundy leather attaché cases that came from Madler or T. Anthony on Park Avenue and have a buttery smoothness that announces: 'I cost $500.'" He also knows his way around the *Post*: the press are "fruit flies." And TV types are print-dependent bubblebrains, even though demonstrators only appear to protest the latest outrage when they're sure the camera's rolling. And "dancers, novelists and gigantic fairy opera singers [are] nothing but court jesters" to the bond-selling "Masters of the Universe."

Wolfe knows too that his delirious professionals—"frisky young animal[s]...of that breed whose natural destiny it was...to have what they wanted!"—are scared to death, especially on the subway: "Into the car came three boys, black, fifteen or sixteen years old, wearing big sneakers with enormous laces untied but looped precisely in parallel lines...They walked with the pumping gait known as the Pimp Roll...They drew closer, with the invariable cool blank look...Such stupid self-destructive macho egos."

It's the attitude. Compare Wolfe's hyperventilating to a lovely riff from Wesley Brown, in *Dissent*, who goes underground to see that "a display of bravado by a young, indigo-skinned black male moving

through a crowded subway car like a point guard bringing the ball up
court, sporting a haircut that makes the shape of his head resemble a
cone of ice cream, and wearing barge-sized sneakers with untied laces
thick as egg noodles, is immediately considered a dangerous presence
whether he is or not." By whom? By the delirious professionals. On
the subway, the First World and the Third coincide, at least until the
express stop at Columbus Circle.

They are afraid, too, that what they do is make-believe; that their
luck and charm will run out; that they'll look in the mirror one morning and see, if not the other side of the room, then maybe something
no longer new and unique...someone *found out,* like Sherman. They
will lose their co-op and our good opinion. As cops, press and mob
close in on Sherman, his megabucks Paris deal on Giscard bonds is
also falling apart, and his panic is palpable. (Nobody writing for *Dissent* seems to be afraid: angry, maybe, tired, sad, or contemptuous,
but not scared.) Wolfe makes us buzz. As bad as he is on sex, he's terrific on money and hangovers and...*shoes.*

There are no shoes in *Dissent.* (There are two references to "shoe-
makers," but that's just left-wing atavism.) Whereas shoes are
Wolfe's big story, from "the Boston Cracked Shoe look" to Maria's
"electric-blue lizard pumps with white calf caps on the toes" to Sherman's $650 bench-made half-brogued English New & Lingwoods,
with the close soles and beveled insteps. Shoes for Wolfe are character. Sherman's dandified defense attorney wears brown suede shoes.
Assistant D.A. Kramer wears Johnston & Murphy clodhoppers. A witness for the prosecution is partial to snow white Reeboks, but they
make him change to leather loafers for the grand jury. Ballet slippers
or "go-to-hell" sneakers with Velcro straps, Wolfe's gone that extra
mile and worn them.

What does this mean? More than you think. I have consulted Krafft-
Ebing's *Psychopathia Sexualis,* and Sacher-Masoch's *Venus in Furs,* and
Kurella's *Naturgeschichte des Verbrechers.* I know more than I ought to
about high-buttoned patent-leather boots and "Hungarian high-
heels," the legend of Aschenbrodeland, the toe-sucking (later beati-
fied) Marie Alacoque, foot-fetishists East (Junichiro Tanizaki) and
West (Restif de la Bretonne), not to mention vampirism, anthro-
pophagy and koprolagnia, and not even to think about "shoes of the
fisherman" Christian symbolism. On one level, the meaning of shoes

in Wolfe is upward mobility, but there is, naturally, a subtext. Not one, but two Primal Scenes in *Bonfire* make this obvious.

These young men baying for money on the bond market spend most of their time with their mouth on a telephone and their shoes in a stirrup: Felix, the middle-aged black shoeshine man,

> *was humped over…stropping Sherman's right shoe, a New & Lingwood half-brogue, with his high-shine rag.…Sherman enjoyed the pressure of the rag on his metatarsal bones. It was a tiny massage of the ego, when you got right down to it—this great strapping brown man, with the bald spot in his crown down there at his feet, stropping, oblivious of the levers with which Sherman could move another nation, another continent merely by bouncing words off a satellite.*

But these Masters of the Universe will be punished. Shoes in Wolfe's novel are like guns in Chekhov's plays; they have to go bang. Before Sherman is fingerprinted in the Bronx, he's made to stand outside in the rain and soak his New & Lingwoods. And before he's tossed in the holding pen, where surly men of color want to wrinkle his friskiness, he is made to remove his belt *and his shoelaces*. His pants fall down and his shoes fall off and he has to…*shuffle*: "The shoes made a squishing sound because they were so wet." At the end of *Bonfire* he changes into hiking boots, and we know why. Shoes are sex organs and status symbols. We are what we feet.

THERE ARE MORE THAN THREE WORLDS

From Wolfe you wouldn't know that we've got one big problem with real-estate developers, and another with the homeless. For *Dissent* these are strophe and antistrophe, as in an old Greek choral ode, with everybody moving right to left and back again. To be sure, Deborah Meier—the heroine of District 4—has important things to say about "teaching for testing" and alternative schools; and Maxine Phillips would like to pay for the care of 60,000 children who are abused or neglected each year, by taxing cooperative apartments like Sherman's; and Theresa Funicello is furious about "workfare," wondering why "a black woman hired as a nanny for an upper-class white family is a 'worker,' while a mother struggling under adverse conditions to raise her own children on welfare…is a parasite on society"; and Anthony Borden points out that 55 percent of all our AIDS victims are black or Latino, and so are 90 percent of our AIDS children, who never had a chance to say no to anything; and Gus Tyler looks at what happened to labor-intensive light manufacturing in this city (it went to Korea and Taiwan); and Michael Oreskes follows the garment industry to nonunion sweatshops in Chinatown or Queens; and Jewel Bellush explains the "room at the top" for black women in organizing hospital, school and clerical workers; and John Mollenkopf can't find a "good government" reform movement anywhere.

Moreover, *Dissent*'s a lot more cultured than Wolfe. This novel has a chapter by Paul Berman on the sexual confusion and political ambivalence of those "prisoners of culture" who live below Fourteenth Street, and therefore have to read Kathy Acker, look at David Salle, listen to Peter Gordon and go to plays by Albert Inauratto; and a chapter by Juan Flores on the convergence of black and Puerto Rican cultures in "hip-hop," by way of Bo Diddley, Joe Cuba, Frankie Lymon, doo-wop, *capoeira*, break dancing and rap; and a chapter by Ellen Levy on group theater versus performance art. And then it's Memory Lane: Michael Harrington, who has less to be ashamed of than any other man of the Left I know, admires Ruth Messinger and tries hard to remember when Crazy Eddie was…a liberal. Morris Dickstein and Robert Lekachman feel bad and write agreeably about the Upper West Side and our favorite slumlord, Columbia. Rosalyn Drexler and Leonard Kriegel go back to the Bronx (all that Art Deco on the Grand Concourse); Kriegel finds a whole new *Irish* community Wolfe must have missed while soaking Sherman's shoes. Alfred Kazin has fun spanking such avatars of agitprop as N. Podhoretz, A. Cockburn, H. Kramer and G. Vidal, and then he gets serious: "When the great Reagan counterrevolution is over, what I shall remember most is the way accommodating intellectuals tried to bring to an end whatever was left among Jewish intellectuals of their old bond with the oppressed, the proscribed, the everlasting victims piled up now in every street."

Which brings us back to the grubby and the brutish. Marshall Berman itemizes everything Tom Wolfe never noticed:

> *spectacular giveaways to real estate operators; the attacks on the poor, depriving them of industrial work, low-income housing, public hospitals;… the casual brutality that has come to permeate our public life, as in the recent*

wave of mass arrests to drive homeless people out of the railway terminals that the city's own development policies have driven them into; the triumphal march of the city's rejuvenated political machines, whose movers have made the 1980s one long carnival of white-collar crime; the rescue of the city from the clutches of a hostile federal government by selling it (or giving it away) to rapacious real estate empires that will tear down anything or throw up anything, if it pays; the long-term transformation of New York into a place where capital from anywhere in the world is instantly at home, while everybody without capital is increasingly out of place.

In this corner: the Cross-Bronx Expressway, the Coliseum, Lincoln Center, Westway, Zuckermandias, Trump Television City, Times Square as Alphaville and Disney World. In the other corner: the homeless—the usual ghosts on the brownstone stoop with little green bottles, the bag lady who reads *Vogue*, the portly sociopath with the green beret and the eight-inch pigsticker, as well as the ambassador of this month's zombie mushroom, nodding off on his way to where the action isn't. But they were our "regulars," and they've been overwhelmed by a deindustrialized proletariat, a ragged army of the dispossessed, a supply-side migratory tide of angry beggars, runaway refugee children and almost catatonic nomads. Have you seen the cold-water crime-ridden disease-spreading shelters in which we "warehouse" these dropouts and castaways? They're safer on the streets, except for Crazy Eddie and his net. In the parks, they're barbecued.

There are an estimated *100,000* homeless in the imperial city today. In the last twenty years, the years of the 2.5 million "newcomers," housing production has *decreased* from 60,000 new units in 1966 to 7,000 in 1985 (Huxtable). Twenty-five percent of us live below the poverty line. After World War II there were a million jobs in New York light industries; it's down today to 400,000. White unemployment is 7.2 percent; blacks, 11.5; Hispanics, 13.4; among the white young, 22.5; among black young, *47.9* (Tyler)—all of them Wolfe's Pimp Rollers?

Meanwhile why do you suppose that the developers, brokerage houses and their law firms forked out over $4 million in 1985 campaign contributions to Koch and seven other members of the Board of Estimate? Maybe because Koch and the Board have given these people $1.3 *billion* in property tax breaks and zoning variances since 1978 (Jim Sleeper). Since 1981 we have as much *new* commercial space—

45 million square feet—as the total commercial space in Boston and San Francisco *combined* (Sleeper); yet there's still no room for the homeless. There isn't even any room for a simple idea like San Francisco's, where you can't put up new commercial space downtown unless you pay for day-care for the children of the people who will work there (Messinger). Of course, the Reagan Administration won't invest in permanent housing for New York's poor; *that* would be socialism, the dreaded "S" word. But Crazy Eddie doesn't want unions or churches or foundations or grass-roots community groups or anybody else except his favorite developers in the business of rehabilitating the 100,000 condemned properties the city already *owns*. Nor are a big developer's tax breaks available to these groups. Why not? Maybe because this kind of low-cost community initiative is bad for the Profit Motive and the Power Base. Certainly permanent housing for the poor—the ever-unpopular "free ride"—is bad for the Work Ethic, like aid to dependent children.

It's not just the money. It's a social philosophy that is at the same time greedy and punitive. We might scrounge the money. Messinger reminds us of that mysterious $500 million in unspent revenues, mostly from "Big MAC," World Trade Center and Battery Park City surpluses that the city "rolls over" every fiscal year until it disappears whenever anyone wants to spend it on basic decencies. Dan McCarthy can find another half billion in a capital-gains tax on real estate. If we tax cooperative apartments for mortgage-recording and real-property transfer, as Phillips suggests, that's another $60 million. Suppose we killed off "gratuitous tax abatements to Smith-Barney or AT&T" and decided instead to use the city's zoning clout to insist on social services, to help low-income communities "establish themselves in properties that the marketplace has abandoned" (Sleeper). We aren't talking here about anything so radically Scandinavian as income restribution. We *are* talking about more than anybody now in power has the inclination or the guts to attempt. What we need is a change of philosophy and philosophers.

For this change, *Dissent* looks to those 2.5 million "newcomers," with mixed feelings. We have been a "minority-majority" city since the middle of this decade: blacks and Puerto Ricans joined by Dominicans, Cubans, Caribbeans and other Latin Americans, plus Africans and 350,000 Asians. (The indefatigable Sleeper tells us that by 1995, "with revolution in Korea and the defenestration of Hong Kong," our

Asian population will have tripled.) To this "Third World" of Wolfe's swamp-fever dreams—Koreans in the fruit and vegetable trade, Indians in the newsstand business, Arabs in neighborhood groceries and head shops, and Senegalese street vendors—add some 200,000 Russian Jews, Israelis, Poles, Italians, Greeks and the Irish in Kriegel's Bronx. That's a lot of clout waiting to be mobilized.

But Sleeper, Chapin and Philip Kasinitz are also cautionary tale-tellers. Blacks and Hispanics haven't got their act together, except in "hip-hop," even in Brooklyn. Many newcomers can't speak English, aren't citizens, aren't registered, or aren't old enough to vote. Why should Korean shop owners in Washington Heights or Cuban doctors in Jackson Heights join a coalition that cares about the interests of welfare mothers in Bedford-Stuyvesant? It isn't Popular Front-romantic when blacks resent Koreans, Russians are "rednecks," Chinese won't join unions, and the unions are mostly right-wing, anyway. Chapin is cold eyed: "Immigrant insurgencies are generally pluralist rather than radical in nature; some are even regressive." He asks the Left (census figures on this minority have been unavailable since the Molotov-Ribbentrop pact) to "stop mistaking ethnicity for politics; while ethnicity may be more important than class to voting, economics is more important to governing policy than ethnicity."

This doesn't exactly sing, but we had better learn to hum it. To be sure, even the broadest coalition—of immigrants and intellectuals, teachers and preachers, ethnics who've yet to get their taste, limousine liberals, Republican "goo-goo" types, low-income community organizers and "delirious professionals"—can't save the city all by itself. Even the federal government (another bunch of once-and-future jailbirds) can't control oil prices or the dollar or the deficit or international drug traffic. No government in the world, says Berman, knows how to regulate "the vastly accelerated mobility of capital, propelled by breakthroughs in information technology," that "is fast bringing about the deindustrialization of America." But if we begin by being ashamed of ourselves, and then start working the streets, we might find enough conscience and will to make over again the city Randolph Bourne once called "a federation of cultures."

On the other hand, tourism is up, from 3.3 million in 1975 to 17.5 in 1987. Just like Venice: a theme park. See the pretty Winter Palace.

MAKING FIFTH AVENUE SAFE
FOR OUR ONLY MAYOR

CRAZY EDDIE SWEEPS THE STREETS

Our only mayor congratulates himself. During the holiday season, he saved Fifth Avenue from illegal vending. To decontextualize Donald Barthelme, "Dusky warriors padded with their forest tread into the mouth of the mayor," and he spat them out. A task force of hundreds of cops and undercover detectives, on foot beat, horseback and motorized patrol, for merely $300,000 in overtime, issued 14,378 summonses, made 221 arrests, seized three vehicles, and confiscated 14,735 cubic feet of merchandise. That's one cubic foot per summons—and a lot of gloves, umbrellas, coloring books, beaded earrings, Maxell tapes, incense and falafel.

Like St. Sebastian, that favorite pincushion of so many Renaissance painters, the mayor has lately been arrow prone. What with Donny Manes and Stanley Friedman and Bess Myerson and so on, it's been too long between occasions for self-hug. Who would begrudge him this one? After all, $300,000 can't be much less than Leona Helmsley spends on jewels before dinner—without, of course, bothering to pay a sales tax.

But the heart does not leap up. It's not just that the latest body count of the homeless would suggest other priorities. Nor even that crack dealers are clicking like castanets on the corner of Third and Eighty-seventh every afternoon when the movies and schools let out. In this city, we are used to the downbeat. "We have rots, blights and rusts capable of attacking the enemy's alphabet," says Barthelme, not to mention "real-time online computer-controlled wish evaporations." But the heart does not leap up because the mayor's declared himself in favor of Fifth Avenue, against the rest of us, those of us who resort to illegal vendors because we can't afford to go inside the Ice Palace and lick the Gucci boots of the merchant prince. We'll never be important enough to make an interesting campaign contribution or wheedle a tax write-off. And we've never been welcome on Fifth Avenue anyway—certainly not on shopping days—because we look, talk and eat funny.

ROOTING FOR THE *TITANIC*

I ask you: What does Fifth Avenue mean? If the Heartland and the Sunbelt bespeak; if Yankee Ingenuity and Southern Hospitality connote; if Wall Street, Bourbon Street, Main Street, Main Line, Beacon Hill, Tobacco Road, Cannery Row and Hollywood & Vine *signify*—and they do—then what does Fifth Avenue advertise, connecting as if by accident two of our more sinister and exotic symbolizations, Harlem and Greenwich Village?

You won't get much help from serious literature. Henry James was, as usual, ambivalent, liking the old Waldorf in 1905 but confronting, four years later in a Fifth Avenue mansion, the ghost that embodied his "American fate," "evil, odious, blatant, vulgar." Edith Wharton in 1906 wrote a play about the Fifth Avenue marriage of Carrie Astor and Orme Wilson, computing the probable value of the wedding gifts at a million pretax dollars. Whitman liked the Avenue, but Whitman liked everything. O'Henry liked Madison Square. Scott Fitzgerald liked the food at the Plaza; Zelda, the fountain. Hemingway kept silent about the time he did secretly at the Sherry-Netherland. Amy Lowell liked holing up at the Belmont and the St. Regis with Ada Russell; they reserved vacant rooms on either side of their suite, stopped the clocks and drew the shades.

Before the Civil War, Washington Square was a potter's field, with a gallows. During the Civil War, draft rioters—a mob of people, your basic lumpen, who couldn't afford to buy a substitute to carry their swords into battle at Gettysburg—burned down the Colored Orphan Society at Forty-third and Fifth. After the Civil War, with the help of the American Jockey Club, Old Money followed its trotters uptown brownstone by brownstone. By the turn of the century, New Money—the "dinosaurs" of unsainted memory, über-lumpen, fattened on terrapin and canvasback, champagne-tipsy, swapping railroads, dance halls and banana republics—had gobbled up the Old, and built mansions they thought looked like châteaux in the Loire Valley; toilets resembling throne rooms; "clubs" that wanted to be temples.

It was as if Veblen had written a racy novel, called *Conspicuous Consumptives*. "Two miles of millionaires," said Paul Bourget in *Outre-Mer*. The men—stock swindlers, price fixers, slumlords, politician-bribers, Indian killers, union busters, copper kings and anti-Semites—specialized in horses and chorus girls and had to be taught to eat with a fork.

The women dressed up like Mrs. Astor as the Empress Theodosia in the Ravenna mosaics, and were partial to onyx, ormolus, bear claws, porcelain goose girls and dead birds in bell jars. The children went mad, or sank on the *Titanic*…while my potato-famine Irish grandfather was rooting for the iceberg.

Had Veblen written a sequel, much less thrilling, it might have been called *The Loopholes*. Contemplate the guilt money and the tax breaks it took to endow all those galleries, foundations, libraries, hospitals, small colleges, large skating rinks and muddy racetracks. A university like Vanderbilt would not have been possible without the foul-mouthed commodore who committed his wife to the Bloomingdale Asylum because she nagged him. Before there could be a subway stop at Astor Place, John Jacob had to chop down most of the sandalwood trees—and slaughter most of the otters—in Hawaii. Museums like the Guggenheim exist only because the Founding Family made a deal with Porifiro Diaz to strip Mexican silver and exploit Mexican workers, and helped out King Leopold II of Belgium, who was having a little trouble with his Congo. Carnegie Hall is brought to you by the Homestead Strike.

A new biography of August Belmont, *The King of Fifth Avenue*, runs 804 pages. This is 799 pages more than David Hume devoted to his memoirs. Belmont introduced French wines to New York City; Hume introduced Jean-Jacques Rousseau to London.

And why Fifth Avenue? A sensible city would have used its waterfront to aggrandize the filthy rich. Think of the Tiber and the Seine, of Thames and Neva, of Tigris and Euphrates. If you don't have a river, use a hill: look *down* on everybody. With no hills to speak of, New York went right up the middle of itself as if to cleave, to disembowel. The manifest destiny of the dinosaurs would seem to have been to squat where they could neither see nor swim.

But the dinosaurs were reptiles. Too big for their brains, too far from water, they were doomed in the avenue's evolutionary scheme. Money grows up to need sponge-handed managers who are so busy moving it around in the night—*information*; magic markers—from memory bank to memory bank in computerized spider-speak, that they'd rather not show up in novels or S.E.C. regulations. They live on the margin. They want anonymity. Even their schools are private. Have you ever *seen* a line of credit?

Along the avenue, banks needed room, and luxury hotels, and cor-

porations, and diplomatic missions, and merchandising marts. Not to
mention airlines, later on, selling one-way tickets to Brazil. The dinosaurs sold out to plant their bad seed in Newport and Palm Beach.
The managers moved in, as if on escalator clauses, now that the
neighborhood was safe for business. What sort of business? Listen:

In 1913, a very good year, a commission was appointed to advise
the Board of Estimate on how to regulate "the height, size, and
arrangements of buildings in the City of New York," and to decide if
the city should be divided into zones. Behind the commission was the
Fifth Avenue Association. It was, as Seymour Toll makes clear in *Zoned
American*, a historic moment. If the dinosaurs had borrowed their notion of culture from the French, the merchants, bankers and their
silent partners at Tammany Hall borrowed their idea of what consti-
tuted urban planning from the Germans. If zoning worked in Ham-
burg, why not Manhattan? Never mind that Germany was oversup-
plied with public administrators, and that Germans were accustomed
to taking orders from their city-states on every little this and that, and
that German city-states already owned upwards of 40 percent of the
local fatherland. What happened was that almost from the start of
American urban planning, the special interests that needed regulation,
like the realtors, sat on the commissions that did the regulating.

Realtors dominated the 1913 commission, which is just as the Fifth
Avenue Association would have wished. What did they want, the Elli-
mans and Brentanos? Besides restrictions on the size of buildings, they
wanted, and got, restrictions on the nature of the business conducted
in those buildings. Why? On the high rhetorical road, counsel for the
association told the commissioners:

> *Fifth Avenue is not only the common property, but the common pride, of all
> citizens, rich and poor alike, their chief promenading avenue, and their prin-
> cipal shopping thoroughfare. Thus all alike are interested in maintaining the
> unique place that the avenue holds not only in the traditions of this city and
> in the imagination of its citizens, but in the minds of countless hundreds of
> thousands from other cities and countries...*

Another spokesman took a lower road:

> *The high-class retail business for which Fifth Avenue is so well-known is
> the most sensitive and delicate organism imaginable, depending, first, on the*

*exclusiveness of the neighborhood; second, on its nearness to the homes of the
rich and the large hotels; and third, on its lack of congestion, especially on
the sidewalks, so that customers may not be crowded or jammed in a hurly-
burly crowd...*

This spokesman spelled it out:

*The loft buildings have already invaded the side streets with their hordes of
factory employees. If an adequate move were made restricting the occupancy
of the buildings so that no manufacturing could be done on Fifth Avenue, or
from Madison over to Sixth, the matter would be solved. The employees
from these loft buildings cannot be controlled. They spend their time—lunch
hour and before business—on the avenue, congregating in crowds that are
doing more than any other thing to destroy the exclusiveness of Fifth Avenue.
If the exclusiveness and desirability are destroyed, the value of real estate on
Fifth Avenue will depreciate immediately.*

In the lofts, of course, they spoke Russian, Italian, Greek, Yiddish
and my very own Ogham and brogue. We are talking about your
basic immigrant hordes—garment workers, short on pennies and
long on body language, clogging up the circulatory system of dispos-
able income for which Bonwit Teller, Bergdorf Goodman, F.A.O.
Schwarz, Elizabeth Arden, Saks, Tiffany's, Cartier's and Lord and Taylor are the liver and the bladder. As Barthelme has put it:

*The aristocrats heard Jacques talking. They all raised their canes in the air,
in rage. A hundred canes shattered in the sun, like a load of antihistamines
falling out of an airplane. More laughing aristocrats arrived in phaetons
and tumbrels....Laughing aristocrats who invented the cost-plus contract...Laughing aristocrats who invented the real estate broker...Charles
poured himself another brilliant green Heineken.—To the struggle!*

THE IGUANA THAT ATE CHRYSLER

Flash-forward from 1913 to 1978. On October 4, 1978, members of
this very same Fifth Avenue Association, a sort of Opus Dei and KGB
for hierophants of greed, had every reason to feel smug about themselves. It was a "A Salute to Fifth Avenue Day" and began early. More

than 400 VIPs including your Lindsays and your Plimptons showed up for lunch at the Plaza. After lunch, there would be cocktails in the Terrace Room. After cocktails, models of the female persuasion, wearing "Fifth Avenue Look" fashions from Saks, were introduced to the VIPs by a stud in Calvin Kleins. That night everybody special went to fireworks in Central Park, as if to admire the fall of Saigon. This was not a telethon for anorexia. It was, instead, the unveiling of a new style on four wheels—the Chrysler "Fifth Avenue" automobile, at $12,000 per internal combustion. Chrysler, thanks to socialism for the rich, picked up everybody's tab. The new car came in only one color: "blonde." I am serious: *Blonde* was the color of Fifth Avenue.

Three and a half weeks later, on Halloween, 1978, the iguana appeared. Marx would have explained this dialectically; Freud would have chatted up hysteria and the return of the repressed; Newton would have leaned on his Third Law of Motion. Dryden might have reminded us that, after too much license, poetry can be just; couplets, heroic. Anyway, Fifth Avenue deserved it. It was a huge lizard on the roof of the Lone Star Cafe at Fifth Avenue and Thirteenth. Basilisk eyed, warrior tailed, and muscled together with wire and mesh, it was forty feet long, weighed 3,000 pounds, and wasn't blond. Was it, however, art? Inspectors for the Fifth Avenue Association didn't think so. What do you do with an iguana in a restricted neighborhood? What if it ate a Plimpton? It certainly looked omophagous. According to Barthelme:

> *The bad zombies place sheep ticks in the Bishop's ear. If a bad zombie gets you, he will scarify your hide with chisels and rakes. If a bad zombie gets you, he will make you walk past a beautiful breast without even noticing.*

I went downtown on election day to check out the omophagous lizard. Talk about your Nemesis. Think Eumenidesiacal: Alecto, Megaera, Tisiphone! If a frog is Kermit or Conrad, this was Hotspur, Rhadamanthus and Set. Like a Druid, it looked uptown, *older* than Ogham, prerunic, unimpressed. Before the Plaza, there had been a sacred grove. Before the Fifth Avenue Association, there had been ashes and ice, a pair of ragged claws, wing-shadow, jigsaws of cosmic radiation, some final energizing bolt that wrinkled the waters of the primordial earth-borscht and formed the first self-replicating greed. This lizard knew from Genesis. St. Patrick would have loved him. They were both in the snake business. And it was as if I no longer needed to march in the St. Patrick's Day parade, with my pipes and my harp, my Moynihan and my stomping boots, just to depreciate the real-estate values. *Geas*, said the iguana on top of the Lone Star Cafe, speaking the ancient death-taboo of the blue-faced Celts before the first imperialism. GEAS!

But as I type, mysteriously, the iguana, like journalists in Argentina, like street vendors from Senegal, has been wish-evaporated. For a zoning violation. He probably talked funny, too.

HEIDEGGER IN NEW YORK

Fifth Avenue has never wanted us, the unlicensed and unwashed. It resents cleaning up the democratic litter after our prideful parades, so many ethnics and peaceniks, veterans and Easter Bunnies, blacks and gays. Once upon a time our only mayor had been one of us and knew it in his street-genes. But that mayor, like the iguana, has been disappeared. This mayor, if we ever get him out of office, should be sentenced to read Heidegger on *Schuld* (guilt) and *Geschick* (destiny) and *Sein zum Tode* (being-for-death). And one day, maybe, we'll live in Barthelme's New York: "There are flowers all over the city because the mayor doesn't know where his mother is buried..." Not yet, not with Crazy Eddie and his Pinkertons. On the streets, however, a few of us will go on selling ideas as well as falafel. And many years from now, after there's cable television in Queens, a child will ask: "Daddy, before the Revolution, why were you in jail?" And her father will reply: "I was an illegal vendor." Barthelme has promised:

> *High in the air, working on a setback faced with alternating bands of gray and rose stone capped with grids of gray glass, we moistened our brows with the tails of our shirts, which had been dipped into a pleasing brine, lit new cigars, and saw the new city spread out beneath us, in the shape of the word FASTIGIUM. Not the name of the city, they told us, simply a set of letters selected for the elegance of the script. The little girl dead behind the rosebushes came back to life, and the passionate construction continued.*

CENSORSHIP:
THE ANGELS AND THE AX

WHERE WE GO TO TALK ABOUT CENSORSHIP

Please picture two hotels.

The first is the Westin Bonaventure in Los Angeles. From the sky, it looks like the revolving cylinder on a Colt .45 with one of its chambers missing. From the freeway, it's a huddle of monoliths, like a basketball team before the jump. Inside its skin of smoky glass libido seethes: spire, sphere and spume. Escalators from a checkpoint in the maximum-security garage rise to lap at a lobby that wants to be a labyrinth: no bell hops. Elevator bubbles fall, like time capsules for nasal congestion, through figure eights of shopping mall to a free-form fish pond in which frogmen wade to no apparent purpose: Dragging for ideas? The vegetation is abstract, the towers color-coded, the rooms trapezoidal and once, trying to find a committee meeting at which I was supposed to save the world, I missed my exit ramp because the elevator wouldn't stop on even-numbered floors, and managed to get myself locked outside, precipitous, on a yard-wide concrete lower lip that proved to be for jogging—jogging!—five stories up from a drizzled Figueroa Street and at least two hours by Porsche from the nearest quart of milk.

Think of Godard's *Alphaville*, De Gaulle's airport, Disney on acid, a world-devouring video game and a huge bowl of Froot Loops. That's the Bonaventure.

The second hotel is the Rossya in Moscow: instant drab, Stalinoid tacky, spy-flecked, with a watchful troll on every floor. You are being visited by an emissary from two Soviet dissidents. How he achieved your room at all is a mystery; the elevators seldom work and the troll never sleeps. You assume the room is bugged, and so you communicate on a child's Magic Slate. Questions are asked by scribble and answered in scrawl and promptly "disappeared," like journalists in Chile. Talk about writing on the wind...

Think of Kafka's Castle, Potemkin's village, Lenin's tomb. That's the Rossya.

At the Bonaventure I was asked by the Modern Language Association to deplore censorship at ten in the morning. At the Rossya I was asked by a perfect stranger—he drank my vodka, he smelled of salami—to smuggle a statement out of Mother Russia into a New York art gallery. The Rossya is the foot of censorship, in our face, on our neck. The Bonaventure's more problematic, like a bowl of brain, a spaghetti of synapses. I knew what I was doing in Moscow. In Los Angeles, I had my doubts.

These days the angels of light who gather in classrooms, boardrooms, courtrooms and committee rooms to deplore censorship have more to deplore than ever before: heavy breathing on the telephone, alarm clocks in the mail. Are the censors busier or the century more obscene or everybody quicker to take offense or the news just running away from us so fast, in circles, that when we go after it we have to look over our shoulder because scissors might be gaining on us?

Networks and publishing houses and school boards and theaters and museums and courts have censored artists, teachers, moviemakers, mathematicians, newspaper reporters, assistant librarians, conscientious objectors and novel-writing ex-spies. Not every instance may seem equally urgent. Among those censored, there are some who are boring or untalented, several bullies, lots of creeps. (Andrew Dice Clay comes to mind.) Even an angel of light is entitled to mixed feelings. For every professor from Belgium or Zimbabwe who isn't permitted to profess in these United States because he's actually read Marx and favors the Class Struggle, there is a pornographic color photograph of, for instance, a razor and a woman's breast. If books by Maya Angelou and Margaret Atwood are banned from high schools in Seabeck, Wash., and Rohnert Park, Calif., in the greater Boston area there are dirty old men who say out loud that sodomizing little boys is perfectly normal and very Greek. Our pink and squeaky children (born of course under cauliflowers) aren't allowed to listen to a foulmouthed Richard Pryor or George Carlin on FM radio, but they can watch bestiality on cable television as if it were just another hockey game. Do American fascists have civil rights? Leather bars, the CIA, filthy music, Moral Majorities, rape fantasies, prior restraint, antiSemitism and the best-selling blacklist...every physicist knows that light is not invariably coherent. Thomas Jefferson, call home.

But the angels respond, anyway, weary, stretched thin, elastic, generous, predictable and good. Having sat on the committee to watch Helsinki and its accords, having funded free expression from Gdansk to Kinhasa, they feel obliged to defend even the nasty-kinky down the block, in the candy store. On being advised of a Hefner or a Guccione, they wish it were the heroic Polish union leader Walesa or the Chinese feminist jailbird Ding Ling, but gulp, sigh, lie down with a pneumatic theory or a bromide, rise up full of qualms, swallow, call a meeting, speechify, resolve: It's not what you *say*, it's what you *do*; the First Amendment and I refuse to edit *anyone*.

Nat Hentoff can be counted on to be at every meeting of the angels, and Kurt Vonnegut. Toni Morrison, Floyd Abrams, Sophie Silberberg, Anthony Lewis and Aryeh Neier are among many other heroes and heroines of the U.S. Constitution who have stolen time from jobs and families to insist, without a reservation, that our young Republic really meant it when it said that Congress shall make *no* law prohibiting or abridging what We the People publish. Such angels (citizens) have written a social contract (another petition) I'm proud to sign.

Yet the angels need an occasional dose of the Bonaventure, where dope's sold in the shopping malls and someone got mugged (a dissident jogger?) between a bubble and a trapezoid, before we deplored. In this glitterdome, brains storm. Anything imaginable might as well happen. Saying is halfway to doing. Ideas blow up in the unwrapping: in science, in religion, in politics, in bed.

WHAT I TOLD THEM, BEING PIOUS

We deplored, nevertheless.

The scholar, an Iranian-born American novelist who teaches comparative literature in San Diego, described the wretched situation of intellectuals in his country before and after the Shiite takeover. Names like Said Soltanpur, Homa Nategh, Qolam-Hosein Sa'edi and Sadegh Chubak ring no bells in American ears. The scholar also confessed to a critical dilemma. Such writers must be read, as it were, through prison bars: "I know that I do not read Solzhenitsyn the way I read Flaubert." And he despaired at the destruction of entire libraries, the Magic Slating of whole categories of difficult thought—not merely censorship but "deculturization."

The editor, guilty of books himself about the Hollywood Ten and some Kennedys, spoke of the management of news: by monopoly, with copyright as a truncheon; by leak, to sabotage a policy or a career; by suppression. Editors, said this editor, censor themselves and their reporters, paralyzed in advance by the contemplation of libel suits, advertising dollars, Post Office tax exemptions, reader prejudice, and the good opinion of well-connected buddies in the agreeable spas of the power structure.

The futurist, a "long-range planning consultant," so handsome he must eat miracle chips while watching his VDTs, made the same speech about censorship that he probably makes about dioxin, or angst, or acne: all this will have disappeared by the year 2000. In a global village, unlike a Potemkin, everybody "telecommunicates." Having "accessed," we will "impact."

The journalist said the sort of things I usually say when, as a part-time angel, I show up at committee meetings to thicken the light.

We can't talk about censorship without talking about sex, though we keep trying to. We'd like to leave the sex out of discussions of censorship because pornography bothers us more than, say, treason. But the weather of censorship consists equally of sex and politics. They are variable. Put them together, and it isn't surprising to get religion or violence.

The last time I spent three hours saving the world in Southern California, we discussed sex and television. We had been organized into T-groups, with an emphasis on heavy petting. My T-group included two talented writers of TV sitcoms and a network vice president for broadcast standards. A network vice president for broadcast standards is a censor. Let's call the two sitcoms Jim and Ed, because those are their real names. Let's call the veep George, just because.

Jim had heard that anytime a writer submits a script to George's network and that script touches in any way on the subject of homosexuality, the script is sent by George for approval to a gay dentist in New Jersey. Was it true, Jim wanted to know, that one man, a gay dentist, is deciding what's copacetic to say on national television about bent people in straight America?

Untrue, said the veep. This particular gay dentist in New Jersey is not only sincere; he is also a part-time psychotherapist.

We looked for a while at the clouds in our coffee, until the second sitcom, Ed, waggled his hand. "You mean," he said to George, "you mean...there really is a Tooth Fairy?"

Have I offended anyone? I hope so. If Andy Rooney told this story, he'd catch so much flak that CBS would probably suspend him for another month until the *60 Minutes* ratings faltered. I don't know, nor do I care, whether Ed or Jim is into bicycle seats or Twinkies. Any

number of sitcom insults to ethnicity and "life-style" are permitted by
the First Amendment: lazy blacks, impotent Wasps, Irish drunks,
dumb Swedes, Jewish slumlords and Puerto Rican janitors. (It's only
on college campuses today that you can't offend anybody; the colleges have "codes" of verbal behavior to protect the feelings of the
cauliflower children.) And a gay dentist in New Jersey has every right
to feel that his life has been lied about on television; if he can get some
money from television, television doubtless owes him. Thomas Jefferson would have allowed Ed's joke and forgiven the dentist. He
would have been offended by networks that have dentists.

But Jefferson wasn't around long enough to understand television's
special relationship with industrial democracy. There is, in this industrial democracy, official speech, about which more later. And there's
semiofficial speech, like newspapers of record and television networks. The TV we see is a form of sympathetic magic—a sort of symbolic dramaturgy. It sits there, very centered, authenticating and legit-
imizing and sedating. According to Ed Sullivan, Elvis and the Beatles
were peachy-keen. According to Johnny Carson, Nixon overnight became a dirty bird. According to Mary Tyler Moore, it was okay for
young women to go to work and go to bed without permission or
guilt. According to Rather, Brokaw and Jennings, that's not only the
way it was, but the way it ought to be, because that's all we're going
to tell you. What you see is news; what you don't, wasn't...Who
needs Head Start, or decent public schools, when we've got *Sesame
Street*? Who needs psychotherapy, when we've got Phil and Oprah?
What a Magic Slate! No wonder, in the sixties, the Malcolms and Yip-
pies petitioned the tube for redress of grievance.

Legitimizers like Carson and the Anchorheads are dentists. Religions and governments are networks. The planet's paved with dentists
and networks and always has been. Syracuse deported Plato. Christ on
the Cross was a free-speech issue. Dante died before Florence forgave
him. The Vatican has a long memory, and used to have an even longer
Index. The bulls Luther gored were papal. The stage has bothered the
State since the Middle Ages: Moliere was hassled because of *Tartuffe*;
England's Lord Chancellor is an official dentist. After 1744, Montesquieu, Voltaire and Rousseau had to publish in Switzerland. Czar
Nicholas I—in case you thought that censorship in Russia was invented after 1917—took it upon himself to edit Pushkin, and they almost
shot Dostoyevsky for reading aloud to friends a letter from the critic

Belinsky to that dead soul, Gogol. By the 1920s the bourgeoisie had been so often alarmed by avant-garde irreverence that *Time* magazine had to be invented as an early-warning system.

Then came Hitler and Stalin, Dachau and the Gulag. The penal colonies and the psychiatric wards of South Africa and South Korea are full of difficult poets. Until the "decolonization" of Eastern Europe in 1989, its best writers had to publish in the West—Kadare, Konrad and Kundera among them. Latin Americans as illustrious as Gabriel García Márquez and Ariel Dorfman and Isabel Allende and Eduardo Galeano didn't quite dare go home again. (The dentist Peron turned the poet Borges from a librarian into an inspector of chickens, by Magic Slate.) It was a lousy idea to be an intellectual during Mao's Cultural Revolution; it is not such a good idea to be one today in Castro's Cuba. The Ayatollah Khomeini can't be said to have been an improvement, especially for women, on the Shah of Iran; both believed the best place for a Reza Baraheni was the torture chamber. (Not even the shah, of course, put out a global all-points hit-contract on the Salman Rushdies of the world.) The Sandinistas in Nicaragua closed *La Prensa*. There was a man in the Philippines before the revolution of the yellow flowers—I met him; he followed me around Manila, as sleek as an eel in his short-sleeved, baby blue jumpsuit—whose job it was to measure column inches of "negative news" versus "positive news" in the daily papers, and to report his tally to the dragon lady, Imelda Marcos. The French filmmaker Marcel Ophuls made *The Sorrow and the Pity* for television in 1970; it was shown everywhere *except* on French TV, until the election of François Mitterand. And France thinks of itself as a free country.

And so do we think of ourselves as a free country, right here in the kindergarten of the Enlightenment, as if the Alien and Sedition Acts, the Smith Act and the raging hormones of Tailgunner Joe McCarthy had never happened; as if Nixon had never edited his tapes, Ollie North had never used his shredder, Richard Helms had never lied to Congress and Bill Casey's brain hadn't gone dead with Iranscam secrets left untold; as if congressional investigators weren't, even as we speak, turning up desks and ransacking file cabinets at the National Endowment for the Arts, looking for lesbians. Quick now: Exactly *why* did Dalton Trumbo and Ring Lardner, Jr., go to jail?

If we read Ronald Reagan right—was there another direction in which to read him?—the whole point of his Howdy Doody era was to regulate speech while deregulating greed. One Cabinet bureaucracy, HEW, would cut off funds for family-planning clinics that mentioned abortion as an option. Another, the Treasury, wanted us to go to jail if we drank Nicaraguan coffee. Selective Service was sicced on students who failed to register for a draft we were no longer conducting. (These students would be refused federal loans for their college educations. They'd also be tracked down through Social Security.) The Department of Justice, under that gerbil Meese—when it wasn't trying to prevent the publication of articles about making hydrogen bombs in *The Progressive*, when it wasn't saying we couldn't buy *Playboy* at 8,000 newsstands—had nothing better to do with its Young Republican legal beef than ask them to watch out for propaganda in Canadian movies about acid rain. And the FBI was sent to lean on libraries. (Libraries, said FBI director William Webster, "are places where hostile foreign intelligence persons seek both to gather information and to recruit people who will be their agents in this country.")

Lyndon Johnson's Justice Department would have approved. His Justice Department put Dr. Spock on trial. Richard Nixon would have approved, too. *His* Justice Department sought to convict the Chicago 8 for having conspired, in 1968, to cross state lines in an unlawful frame of mind; and in 1971 the case to bury the Pentagon Papers went all the way to the Supreme Court. (In the Nixon years, only the Plumbers could be said to have been pro–Freedom of Information; they thought Dan Ellsberg's psychiatrist hadn't the right to keep any secrets, so they burgled his office, as if they were gay-rights activists "outing" a Malcolm Forbes.) Nixon, of course, bugged himself, as if the White House were the Rossya. He was also his own dentist.

Let's see how many Nobel Prize–winning Latin American novelists we can keep out of New England and New Mexico with our Immigration and Nationality Act. Let's circumvent, before we abolish, the Freedom of Information Act. Let's make sure Mapplethorpe doesn't get any taxpayer money for taking dirty pictures. If you ever worked for the CIA, and now you want to write a book, that piece of paper they made you sign is more binding, according to the Nixonburger Supreme Court, than the Constitution of the United States. If you work for the FBI, you might find yourself infiltrating a Trotskyist sect, a cell of black nationalists, the pubescent Left or the Ku Klux Klan, as often as not a provocateur, inciting to riot—by *your* free speech—a cadre of hyperventilating hopheads. And when the nation goes to

Holy War against dastardly Panama or Hitlerite Iraq, the only free speech allowed on the front belongs to the Pentagon briefers and the network rent-a-generals speaking technoblab.

If, however, we blame all censorship in this country on the State, we're lying to ourselves. In what way, on television in the 1950s, was Larry Adler's harmonica subversive? How does the hit list of the Moral Majority, which includes Marlo Thomas's *Free to Be You and Me*, differ in spirit from the hit list of *Red Channels*, which included Leonard Bernstein, Lena Horne, Zero Mostel, Edward G. Robinson and Orson Welles? When CBS was young, it canceled one loudmouth, John Henry Faulk; now that CBS is all grown up, it only suspends another, Andy Rooney of the sermonettes. Terry Rakolta and the Reverend Donald Wildmon are out there, agitating against deviant sex on television, not to mention any program that mentions abortion without condemning it. Mainstream newspapers and network TV news organizations refuse to follow up on Pete Brewton's articles in the *Houston Post* connecting the CIA to the S&L scandal. Vanessa Redgrave is suddenly unemployed because of her opinions on the Middle East. Some blacks, having entirely missed the moral point of Mark Twain, would keep *Huckleberry Finn* out of our schools. Some gays, as if in imitation of Anita Bryant, disrupt the filming and obstruct the screening of movies they don't like whether they've seen them or not. And you should hear the wrangling in my own kitchen between gay men who think *The Silence of the Lambs* is homophobic, and lesbian women who consider Jodie Foster a feminist role model. Some feminists campaign against pornography as if such toads in the erotic garden as Larry Flynt weren't *nice* enough to deserve our Bill of Rights. Some exurbanites in Island Trees, Long Island, would spare their children Bernard Malamud, Desmond Morris and Langston Hughes. Some farmers in Drake, N. D., burn in a furnace the words of that radical enthusiast of Robert's Rules of Order and the Sermon on the Mount, Kurt Vonnegut. Harper & Row, the publisher of presidents, sues Victor Navasky, editor of *The Nation*, for having treated Gerald Ford's memoirs as if they were newsworthy; and Susan Sontag sues the *SoHo News* as if she were as newsworthy as Gerry Ford; and Simon & Schuster, the book subsidiary of the conglomerate that produces and distributes *Friday the 13th* splatterflicks, refuses to honor its contract to publish *American Psycho*; and the L.A. chapter of the National Organization of Women calls for a boycott of the company that *does* publish *American Psycho*.

I have seen the Tooth Fairy, and he is everywhere: right, left, centered, ubiquitous. If I weren't a part-time angel of light, I'd like to be a dentist, too. I think TV commercials are often obscene, and Muzak, and American medical semicare, and such covert "intelligence" activities as the assassination of incovenient heads of foreign states. I think a government that hides its mistakes behind "national security" and "executive privilege"—when it can't find a pet journalist on whom to leak—is also obscene. Obscene, as well, is our official speech: euphemisms like "destabilize" and "eliminate with extreme prejudice," graffiti like "heuristic" and "incursion," spray-paint like "pacification" and "free-fire zone" and "generating refugees," disinformation like "prophylactic random terror bombing" and "peace with honor." The Gulf War, that smarty-pants bombfest, gave us "collateral damage" (which used to be "civilian dead") as well as "human remains pouches" (which used to be "body-bags"). This is Newspeak on its Orwellian way toward that linguistic netherworld that talks about "Aryan science" or "the Democratic People's Republic of Kampuchea." It also seems to me that racism and homelessness are pornographic.

But I'm not your dentist. There's been censorship as long as there's been society, because society, any society, gets along just fine, thank you, in efficient silence, or with a happy hum, no whistle blowing, whereas free speech of its essence is discordant and heretical. Call it smut or sedition: This discord, this black magic, nevertheless articulates an underground refusal of established morals and manners, a critique of contemporary social and economic arrangements, an execration of the dominant culture and the prevailing pieties, a secession from clout. It is weepy, feral, parodic, blasphemous, stammering, paranoid; it says no, *other*, or *instead*. Most of it's swill, because most of everything is swill. But what isn't swill persists, returning again and again like the repressed in a scary dream, a denied symbol of the forbidden, a strangled self.

There is, I agree, no reason to suppose that a laissez-faire economy of ideas will work any better than a laissez-faire economy of moral conduct, or a laissez-faire economy of primitive accumulation. But who knows? Nobody's ever tried it before. Would Thomas Jefferson really want us to be just like all the other guys, the Tooth Fairies in Moscow and Johannesburg and San Salvador? Wouldn't he feel ashamed of us? Shouldn't we feel ashamed of ourselves?

WHAT I DIDN'T TELL THEM, BEING AMBIVALENT

What am I saying? This is the faith of the angels of light. Ideas don't kill; people do.

That would be nice. But we raise our children on the understanding that there's some sort of causal relationship between thinking and saying, between saying and doing. And people show up at all those committee meetings to start something, or to stop it, with their words. And I am writing this article to discourage dentists, to change their ways. And if speech didn't lead to action, we wouldn't have censors. For that matter, we wouldn't have culture. Let's regroup.

You'll have gathered from my description that the light in Los Angeles was mottled. There were shadows in the Bonaventure. It is one thing to speechify in the morning about wisdom and justice. It is another, at night, in a color-coded tower in a trapezoidal room, to confront your own discrepancies. On your way to the bottom of your discrepancies you are not seraphic.

Most speech isn't free. Somebody owns it, officially or semiofficially: the president, the chairman of the board, the media mogul. Most of our publishing houses are owned by giant corporations in business to print money as well as books: witness what happened to poor Pantheon when beancounting bottomliners took over Random House and turned an editorial umbrella into a boot. What's left of our academic freedom, after rules and regulations against offensive speech, is brought to us by federal, state and local sponsors: the land-grant university, the government contract. (For that matter, most of our pornography is owned by what used to be called the Mafia, before we passed a resolution against hurting anybody's ethnic feelings.)

This is obviously a social problem, but the Bill of Rights can't do anything about it. I wish I had a printing press and you had a cable-television program, but the fact that we don't is not the First Amendment's fault.

On the other hand, Jefferson isn't around to look at color photography, 16-mm movies, and video cassettes. A technologizing of the imagination indubitably magnifies its power to suggest, persuade and disgust. Gutenberg can't compete with Polaroid—much less *Gidget Goes to a Gang Bang* at the local drive-in or couch-potato rental. We flounder as if in a sea of very expensive commercials for fishy sex and affectless violence.

Sex, of course, antedates Edison, and the state still owns most of the violence, and technology also gave us such agreeable wondertoys as the long-playing record, the Picasso print, the pacemaker and my mackintosh. But nobody can pretend that *Caligula* was what Jefferson had in mind, or *Deep Throat* either. How do I know? Because I've seen both. Do you want to hear something? They didn't grow hair on my palms. Would I want my children to see them? No, I want my children to believe in the cauliflower and the stork, but aren't there other ways to protect our children that don't involve telling anybody what movies he can't make? And ask yourself this: Are those societies in which such images are banned—for instance, Saudi Arabia—healthier, wealthier and wiser than ours? (There is more pornography, and less violence against women, in Amsterdam than in any other city in the Western world.) Besides, you can't have the politics without the sex, not unless you rewrite the entire organism and get rid of some basic engrams.

Ah, well, what about advertising, those billions of dollars spent to make us want what we don't need? Is that free speech, too? Yes, it is. You can't say that everybody has a right to his own opinion and then tell him he's not allowed to spend his own money spreading that opinion around. Obviously this means that the richer he is, the more his opinion is going to be foisted on us. I wish this weren't so, and I wish that I'd been born with a ninety-mile-an-hour fastball, and I wish that Mozart hadn't died, or Thomas Jefferson.

The most depressing thing about advertising is that it works. It would never have occurred to any of us to want to smell like prunes or sawdust, but someone talked us into it. Advertising is expensive proof that speech leads to action, that thinking out loud modifies behavior, that talk *isn't* cheap. Of course we know ideas have consequences. But we'd like to believe that no particular consequence is inevitable, that each idea is only one idea in a world of ideas, happening to us by accident. We shop around, striking attitudes like matches; we will have many ideas before selecting a behavior; for our behavior, not for our ideas, we are properly accountable. The idea, in any event, is as blameless as a ghost.

Dream on.

At night, in the Bonaventure, this seems impossibly innocent. In such a dark, attitudes *are* matches: incendiary. Ideas combust, derange; scribblers are arsonists; radical speech means to cut our throats; obscene speech means to screw us. Physicists play with symbolic equations and Hiroshima burns. We remember: somebody *dreamed up* snuff movies, kiddie porn, Jonestown, Auschwitz. We have only to consult ourselves, like Dostoyevsky, to know the worst. "The earth is trembling," were De Maistre's last words to the Russian liberals, "yet you want to build." De Maistre hated the Enlightenment; having spent too many nights alone with himself, he was afraid of his own thinking. And he had a point, like Dostoyevsky's Grand Inquisitor: Freedom is terrible. The earth trembled; a world was about to end; ideas came out of the sewers like rats; the streets were bloody theater, in Paris first and then in Petersburg; the leading actor was an axe.

Why am I telling you any of this? To remind you that when a world ends, the politics are radical, left and right, and so is the sex, up and down, and religions veer to violence and mysticism, and the emotional weather is invariably iffy. The philosophers of new orders always think they know what they're doing, their categories lined up, neat like bureau drawers. (A surprising number of them have been journalists: Saint-Just, Marx, Lenin, Trotsky, Maurras, Mussolini and Mao.) But extreme situations hatch extremes of personality—as if the culture itself were throwing up. Just before a revolution, almost anybody who doesn't belong to some subversive cell is likely to join some secret society, with its mixture of the bloody and the erotic.

Imagine France before its Revolution: while they wrote the Rights of Man, they were also, like Mirabeau, Marechal, de Sade, Laclos and Restif de La Bretonne, writing pornographic novels, and dabbling in Pythagorean numerology. Imagine Russia before the Finland Station: While Herzen was in London being civilized, and Turgenev was in Paris being superfluous, at home in the Motherland the Rosicrucians, the self-castrating *skoptsy*, the nihilists and the Nechayevs had a bloody field day. If, in nineteenth-century prerevolutionary Russia, you wanted to be a member in good standing of Aleksandr Ilyich Ulyanov's Terrorist Faction of the People's Will, you would be asked to plant a bomb in a gift-wrapped dictionary.

"Sasha" Ulyanov, by the way, was Lenin's older brother.

So in France, Russia, Germany and China, somebody had a revolutionary idea, after which other ideas—Terror, Gulag, Final Solution, the Red Guards—took over. These ideas wore uniforms, and before long it was necessary for people like Albert Einstein and *their* ideas to leave home, where no one was permitted anymore to listen to the atonal music of Anton Webern.

Does this mean that our censors are right to worry; that the earth trembles under the Reeboks of the American Imperium because of flag-burning, chocolate-covered Karen Finleys and American Psychos, *Married…with Children* and *The Last Temptation of Christ*, 2 Live Crew and Frederick's of Hollywood and telephone-sex (dial a wet dream); that our ball game will be called off on account of decadence?

Certainly not. For one thing, no censor can stop a dangerous idea whose time is come. Shut every mouth and the body finds another way to speak, like the flagellants of Origen or the *tricoteuses* of Robespierre. Yogis don't say much, shamans mumble, monks and hermits don't have to talk at all and there's the anti-speech of autism and catatonia, the anonymous bomb in a crowded cafe or a busful of burning children, sniper fire and madness. Just listen to the martial music and the dirge. We can always find another way to communicate that hurts more than speech.

For another thing, some of the worst ideas are the ones that turn into the religions and governments that hire the censors:

Why should freedom of speech and freedom of the press be allowed? Why should a government which is doing what it believes to be right allow itself to be criticized? It would not allow opposition by lethal weapons. Ideas are much more fatal things than guns. Why should any man be allowed to buy a printing press and disseminate pernicious opinions calculated to embarrass the government?

The date was 1920. The place was Moscow. The speaker was Sasha Ulyanov's kid brother, Vladimir Ilyich, who would buy himself a famous tomb.

What all this means is that, while angels of light are mostly innocent, ideas seldom are. If recorded history has anything interesting to say on the subject, it's that there are more bad ideas than good ones, and that the bad ones, systematized, tend in the short run to prevail. In the long run, Confucius had the last laugh on the Ch'in dynasty; and Galileo was right and the Inquisition was wrong; and a hundred years from now, when we read Solzhenitsyn and Pasternak, who will care about the Soviet Writers' Union?

Why then the First Amendment, *my* First Principle? For the occasional Galileo; and maybe because we need to know what the next Lenin has to say, so that he won't kill us by surprise; and also because nobody's ever tried it before, not another civilization that we've heard about, so why not give this Sacred Text a chance? Our social business is far from finished. Out there, after long dumbfounded silence, there may be saving speech: songs, truth, grace.

RECOVERING FROM
THE SIXTIES: HEROES, CRIMINALS
& ICONIC CLOWNS

CHICAGO '68: TALES OF THE HOFFMANS

In 1968, all over the tom-tom world, the natives were restless, and student braves rose on their campus reservations to shake some feathers and rattle some gourds, and after the music there were tanks and helicopters and commissars and Nixon, and civilization was safe again for greed and red suspenders. It was nasty, but also cute.

David Caute, an English historian-journalist whose specialty in books like *The Great Fear* and *The Fellow-Travellers* has been the romance of the twentieth-century intellectual with revolution on the Left, taught in the middle of this student turmoil at the Free School in New York and the Anti-University in London, and also went to Prague as a reporter. In *The Year of the Barricades: A Journey Through 1968*, he wants to tell the big story. David Farber was an eleven-year-old Chicago schoolboy at the time of the '68 Democratic Convention. In *Chicago '68*, he wants to recover for tidy scholarship an incoherent past. Between them, they tell us everything we need to know in order to feel bad all over again.

The Year of the Barricades is lots of Zeitgeists looking for a Weltanschauung. For instance, and almost at random: In Paris that revolutionary springtime, student "Situationists" of the Atelier Populaire met each morning at the Ecole des Beaux Arts to discuss "urgent themes" and decide which ones needed illustration. Designers sketched, communards criticized, and the silk-screen process permitted the immediate printing of thousands of cheap posters (skulls in police helmets; a cartoon of the French press as a bottle of poison: "Do Not Swallow"). Overnight, these posters became collectors' items, with surplus value. And the Atelier Populaire was indignant:

> *The posters…are weapons in the service of the struggle and are an insepa-*
> *rable part of it.…To use them for decorative purposes, to display them in*
> *bourgeois places of culture, or to consider them as objects of aesthetic interest*
> *is to impair both their function and their effect. Even to keep them as histor-*
> *ical evidence of a certain stage in the struggle is a betrayal.*

Put this together with Ed Sanders and the Yippie program, quoted by Farber in *Chiacgo '68*: "Poetry readings, mass meditation, demagogic Yippie arousal speeches…the Chicago offices of the National Biscuit Company will be hijacked on principle to provide bread and cookies…Demand respect from the stodgy porcupines that control the blob culture…" What you get is that distinctive sixties confusion of styles, of politics and art, technology and passion, parody and self-righteousness, anarchy and cooptation, a fetishism of commodities and the perfidy of the marketplace, ad hoc class analysis and gee-whiz Götterdämmerung. All that's missing is the music in the air and the blood on the streets, the Tinkertoy sex and red-dwarf drugs. And Caute will tell us at length about them, too.

First he must tell us why in Chicago, Paris, Rome and Madrid, in Tokyo, Berlin and Mexico City, in Warsaw, Prague and the London School of Economics and as far away as Red Guard China, the natives were so restless. Obviously, there was something oedipal about the multiplicity of insurrections: kill the father, abolish the past. But just as obviously, the students weren't *all* revolting because they wanted to sleep with their mothers, or because of Vietnam or marijuana, or because they felt alienated in technocratic societies and "postscarcity" economies, or because their parents, with one eye on Freud and the other on Spock, pampered them too permissively, or at the behest of the Comintern or the CIA, or because Chairman Mao wanted to get his jollies.

In the United States, the issues in addition to Vietnam were racism and the draft. In Poland they were censorship and anti-Semitism. In France, they were coed dorms, sociology as a capitalist fraud and Claude Levi-Strauss. In Germany they were Third World poverty, consumerism, the ideology of science, Axel Springer and the Shah of Iran. In Spain, Franco and American military bases; in Czechoslovakia, basic democracy; in Britain, nuclear bombs; in Italy, university reform; in Mexico, every misery imaginable. Japanese medical students wanted to practice before they received their degrees, Belgians hated the Greek colonels, and Yugoslavs needed a job.

But why were fathers so various all called simultaneously into question, and how come the children always lost? Caute can't really explain it. He nods briefly at "the 'epidemic' factor," by which he seems to mean that everybody saw everybody else doing the same thing, at the same time, on TV, and it was contagious. We have to think again, alas, about McLuhan's global village, the electronic media as a central nervous system. Maybe what that picture-system telecast was a Third World iconography altogether inappropriate to a postindustrial Fat City status quo.

Farber is clearer on this than Caute. His tripartite *Chicago '68* gets claustrophobic, trapping us inside hermetically sealed chambers of Yippie freakview, cop paranoia and the Castroite delusional system of SDS and Mobe. But he has a livelier sense of the odds: in the city, 12,000 cops on 12-hour shifts; as backup, 6,000 National Guardsmen and 1,000 agents of the FBI; standing by in the 'burbs, another 6,000 Army troops, including units of the crack 101st Airborne, with flamethrowers and bazookas. Against this law and order, at best, 4,000 dissidents, 1 in 6 an undercover fed, and Allen Ginsberg. Still, the blood lust was up in a Tom Hayden and a Jerry Rubin, who saw in the streets their manly chance to stop being white and middle-class.

Caute and Farber remind us that Rubin was a poisoned Twinkie long before his first pair of red suspenders. Caute quotes him on Charles Manson after a prison visit: "One of the most poetic and intense people we ever met...his words and courage inspire us." Farber quotes him on the death of Robert Kennedy: "Sirhan Sirhan is a Yippie!" We meet all of them again: gurus, shock troops, media brats: Herbert Marcuse, Timothy Leary, R.D. Laing, Abbie Hoffman, Rudi Dutschke, Eldridge Cleaver, Danny (the Red) Cohn-Bendit and many, many avatars of "Che" Guevara.

Have you noticed an absence of women on this list? Caute did, and he's particularly ferocious on the subject of New Left male chauvinist pigginess, in spite of which (or perhaps because of which) feminism is its most enduring legacy. This leads him to wonder whether the revolution, at least in this country, fell apart because the blacks and women went their separate ways. (Farber is brief on blacks, and doesn't mention women at all.) Maybe.

But maybe the numbers just weren't there. (Only one out of every

twenty-eight American students was politically active in 1967–68.)
Maybe the shock troops—ten-to-one male on the streets of Chicago—
could have learned something about patience from what Dutschke
later called "the long march through the institutions" by nonviolent
black preachers and pacifist Quakers, SANE and Women Strike for
Peace, Michael Harrington's "conscience constituency" and all those
kids with no place to go when Kennedy died and McCarthy blew
them off. Maybe, in spite of so many SDS position papers, Yippie
freak-outs, Mobilization crisis meetings, TV guerrilla warfare and
endless discussions on, say, the correct attitude toward the Red
Guards, after which everything tasted like tar, just maybe the New
Left analysis of the situation was bananas.

And maybe I'm prejudiced. Chicago '68 was my first and only presidential nomination convention as a working reporter. I was there by
accident. Czechoslovakia had been my ticket. For the English weekly
The New Statesman, Andy Kopkind was supposed to file from inside the
International Amphitheatre, and my old friend Nora Sayre from the
streets. But when those Russian tanks rolled on Czechoslovakia, Kopkind was on the next plane to Prague. Sayre talked the Brits into letting
me substitute, and I was available because any number of magazines
had turned down my idea of eavesdropping on the California delegation where I had an inside source: my mother.

I'd sleep each night either with friends in Hyde Park, where a marriage was dying and its partners were afraid to get in their own VW
bug without a shillelagh for the muggers; or at the La Salle Hotel with
a traumatized California delegation pledged to a dead Kennedy, disdained by a Eugene McCarthy who had expected somehow to be appointed (or anointed) president, and about to opt for George McGovern. I'd awake each dawn to a phone call from a frantic editor who
was positive (in London!) that Teddy Camelot was about to be drafted
without my knowing it. I'd proceed each afternoon by chartered bus,
behind a squad-car escort, past checkpoints to the barbed-wire ring
around the slaughterhouse, where I surrendered my briefcase for inspection against bombs and guns, after which I was permitted into a
press gallery already preempted by municipal serfs from Mayor
Richard J. Daley's Department of Sanitation and Counterterrorism.

On the slaughterhouse floor, Hubert's whips trashed the peace
plank, Mike Wallace and Dan Rather got jostled, and John Chancellor
got arrested. Far away from these deliberations, in the parks and on

the streets, everybody I'd ever known in the antiwar movement, including many I wish I hadn't, got the crap kicked out of them. To get to the scene of this action, I had to leave the slaughterhouse without my charter bus, on foot in the middle of a transportation strike, on Chicago's very black South Side, where it turns out I was safer than I'd be in front of the Hilton.

From the bowels of the Hilton, which smelled of rotten eggs, I Telexed my copy to *The New Statesman*, reporting what I'd seen as if it were Marat/Sade: *The Persecution and Assassination of the Democratic Party by the Inmates of the Asylum in Chicago.* Then I went outside to stand around in my press credentials, where the nightsticks found me. Two months later, *Esquire* magazine would ask me to stop reviewing books long enough to write a politics column every month that Dwight Macdonald forgot to turn his in, and so I pedaled away on my career as if it were a tricycle. I had seen the system, and it turned my stomach.

But we all think we own the sixties, even Allan Bloom, whose feelings were hurt. The descent, or regression, of a wonderful idea like "participatory democracy" into little-league Leninism and then the tantrum of the cadres—Weatherpeople, Baader-Meinhof—injures us in the decency, and skews the historical sense. Those of us who did hard time on this incoherent Left tend to blame ourselves and our friends for its failures, forgetting that the short-hairs won on brute force. *They* had most of the violence, and all the cynicism. We were children who wanted our country to be a better place. We also wanted a meaning for our lives beyond class privilege and the profit motive; and, of course, we wanted this meaning immediately, and when we didn't get it, some of us went berserk and the rest went into hiding.

And what have we done in this hiding? "The spirit of the Movement," according to a hopeful Caute, "shows itself in local action, tenants associations, ecology groups, squatters' communes. There are more 'people's lawyers' today, more 'people's architects' and not a few business people keen to place their entrepreneurial skills at the service of poor communities. Journalists and media people who grew to maturity in the sixties are less respectful of state power and state secrecy." According to Farber, who's prone to the stentorian as well as a bit patronizing for someone who missed the rumble, "The successes of the movement are legion. They range from the deauthorization of the government and most other American institutional bases of power and authority among a sizable number of Americans to the creation of a whole range of new political forces and approaches, to the legit-imization of leftist and other alternative critiques in the universities, to the ongoing declaration to the warmakers that they will not be able to wage a war without facing a skeptical and even resistant force of American people."

To which, when I'm feeling optimistic, I'd add the securing of women's reproductive rights; a richer literature and popular culture; a livelier, more embracing sense of politics as the way we connect to one another in communities and living rooms. Patience in exile, and cunning: If, as Michael Walzer has suggested, the state won't wither away, we'll just have to hollow it out.

But almost as often, what I feel instead of optimism is a kind of postmodern blues. André Malraux in *Antimemoirs* tells us some ancient history. A Roman general and his legionnaires, after a bad time at the gates of Sheba, were misdirected to an inland sea. According to Malraux, this general "decided that, having failed to take the city, he'd take the sea. Crazed by the sun god

> *he dreamt of returning to the Capitol with his army laden with the shells in which he saw the spirit of this sea no Roman had ever beheld. He drew his troops in order of battle facing the waves. The beetles of Rome entered the tepid water at the command of the war trumpets; each soldier stooped, cuirass flashing in the sun, filled his helmet with shells, and went back without breaking ranks, holding a helmetful of echoing conches, to meet death by sunstroke. For two centuries, Arab travelers reported seeing an army of skeletons up to their breastplates in the sand, each with its skinny fingers holding up toward the sun a helmetful of shells.*

Like that.

TRICKY DICK AND ELVIS

They finally opened the Nixon papers, at least the first 1.5 million non-Watergate pages of them, and I'm all shook up. There is Elvis Presley: The King. Elvis Presley wrote to Richard Nixon in 1970, say-ing, according to an Egil Krogh memo, that "the Beatles had been a real force for anti-American spirit." Besides which, "those who use drugs are also those in the vanguard of anti-American protests." In return for this information, Nixon privately "deputized" Elvis as a federal drug enforcement agent, and gave him an "unofficial" badge.

Never mind that Elvis, of course, got his subscription canceled on account of chemicals. Who knew that Nixon had even heard of Elvis? The news that they were in bed together would have punched out the counterculture. I mean, Sammy Davis, Jr., is one thing—but Elvis? The whole point of Elvis was a working-class white boy's crossover dreams. He opened the locked doors to the attic and the basement and the bedroom of the Eisenhower culture. After such a long sedation, all that sexual energy was just waiting to explode. It was one thing to blame "dirty dancing" on black people, who had nothing better to do with their bodies when they were out of menial work. It was quite another when duck-tailed poor-white southern trash insinuated some rockabilly/hubcap-outlaw variant of this same R & B into the ears and hearts and glands of the Wonderbread children of the suburban middle class, bored and skeptical and horny. What Elvis meant, along with Ginsberg, Kerouac and the rest of the motormouth Beats, was that the sixties were coming. Some chairs were going to be broken, and some categories, and some hearts.

And *that* music was about, well, you'll recall, some sort of Dionysiac revolution. Children who'd grown up on Ed Sullivan and *Gilligan's Island* were now watching different tapes on differrent television sets in different rooms as if they lived on different planets with separate gravities and alternative moons, like Selma and Saigon. Flower-smoking media apaches took over the campuses and the parks, the Stock Exchange and the Evening News. Rock was political, and hair, and sex, even whales. Culture was politics and politics was culture and this confusion of realms perceived itself to be in opposition to a tone-deaf, anal-retentive, body-bag Establishment.

That's why the heavyweights on the Left, like Richard Poirier, wrote long articles for *Partisan Review* explaining why the Beatles should be taken seriously, while heavyweights on the Right like Irving Kristol filled up page after page of *Commentary* lamenting the West's decline in Electric Kool Aid and acid rock. (This was before a bat bit Norman Podhoretz, and he rushed by night to Cambridge, Massachusetts, to kick over the tombstones in Mt. Auburn cemetery in search of un-American Brahmins like Henry Adams, but that's another farce.) According to William F. Buckley, Jr., the Beatles "are so unbelievably horrible, so appallingly unmusical, so dogmatically insensitive to the

magic of the art, that they qualify as crowned heads of antimusic."
And this was before Disco and Salsa, before Heavy Metal and the
Punks, before Rap and Hip-Hop, before, and wouldn't you know it,
Harvard University Press published a book on the Sex Pistols!

They had the guns, and we had the guitars.

All right, about Elvis maybe we shouldn't be surprised. Jack Kerouac, after all, also ended up a right-wing pro-McCarthyite crackpot.
But did Garry Wills know this about Nixon?

Until now, I thought the craziest reimagining of Tricky Dick belonged to Robert Coover—not in *The Public Burning*, but in *Whatever
Happened to Gloomy Gus of the Chicago Bears?* In this short and wicked
novel, Gus was a star halfback for the Bears in the 1930s. He came
from Whittier, California, where he was known in college as "the
Fighting Quaker." He could've been president of the debating team,
and then run for Congress instead of daylight, but because he was so
badly coordinated and had endlessly to practice everything he did,
and because there's only so much practice time in life, he had to
choose at Whittier between debate and student politics, on the one
hand, or football and girls on the other. He chose to score, and so pro-
grammed himself (beep, beep) till his circuits went haywire and he
was shot to death running a picket line during the big 1937 strike
against Republic Steel. History pulled his plug.

We see this Gus through the eyes of Meyer, your typical, Chicago-
style, left-wing Russian-Jewish intellectual, who, when he isn't feeling bad about the Spanish Civil War, is hard at work on a scrap-metal
mask of Maxim Gorky. Meyer has lots of funny things to say about art,
socialism and sexual dialectics, but Gus obsesses him: "an absolute
materialist," "a naked superego," who lives entirely in the present
tense, without metaphor and without imagination. Meyer even *identifies* with this Gloomy Gus, whose real name, of course, turns out to be
Dick: "Both of us were fulfilling myths about ourselves, his the rags-
to-riches drama of the industrious American boy, mine the curse of
the Wandering Jew. And we were both—captives of alienating systems—divided within ourselves."

But there I go, already confusing the cultures. There might very
well have been another American president who watched football on
television instead of the antiwar rallies on the streets outside his White
House. The one we're reading about in the Nixon papers didn't want
to be a halfback; he wanted to be a hound dog.

Personally, I'm injured in my psychobabble and my semiotics. As recently as Thanksgiving, I was accused of having "stuffed the sixties down the throats" of my children just because those children know all the words to "Alice's Restaurant." And for months I've been working on an essay for *The New York Review of Books* comparing Baudelaire to Randy Newman.

According to Baudelaire, in "Jewels":

My darling was naked, or nearly, for knowing my heart
she had left her jewels on, the bangles and chains
whose jangling music gave her the conquering air
of a Moorish slave on days her Master is pleased.

Whereas, according to Randy Newman:

Baby take off your coat...(real slow)
Baby take off your shoes...(here I'll take your shoes)
Baby take off your dress
Yes. Yes. Yes.
You can leave your hat on
You can leave your hat on
You can leave your hat on

Talk about a confusion of cultures! Since another French poet, Rimbaud, is known to have abandoned his muse to run guns to Africa, maybe Ollie North has his own secret rock dreams—a duet, with the Sultan of Brunei, doing "Money Honey"?—and was in bed all along with those French commandos who blew up the Greenpeace ship in its New Zealand harbor. (If Ollie, as we're told, called himself "Steelhammer," whereas Hakim and Secord called him, behind his back, "Bellybutton," can you imagine the pet-rock code name the French would have come up with?) Why not try the same thing in the Strait of Hormuz or the Lago de Ometepe while we're at it, since our foreign policy, anyway, seems to have been written by S. J. Perlman, Harpo Marx and a roomful of Frank Zappa's "coke-tweezed rug-munchers"? This appeals to the paranoid in me. At heart, I'm a Wobbly: one big union and one big conspiracy, most of which is undisclosed because they took out Bill Casey's brain.

But this isn't getting us anywhere. Nixon's followed me around my whole life. I'm not old enough properly to remember Jerry Voorhees, but the red-baiting of Helen Gahagan Douglas happened next door when I was ten. His Checkers speech, when I was twelve, started off the crybaby style of the fifties, the Jack Paars, Charles Van Dorens and Dave Garroways. His reviling of Adlai Stevenson, who'd dared to suggest a moratorium on nuclear testing, was a highlight of my puberty. I reviewed *Six Crises* for KPFA Radio, and was there with a Pacifica microphone, in 1962, for what was supposed to be his last press conference. The only way I could vote for Hubert Humphrey in 1968 was to close my eyes and think of the Supreme Court. The Plumbers were no surprise to me nor the anti-Semitism on the White House tapes. Look what Daddy brought home from the Oval Office, *a secret bombing of Cambodia!* I bought the Garry Wills thesis, that Nixon embodied the self-made man who was diminished by his Making It, "the least 'authentic' man alive....He lacks the stamp of place or personality because the Market is death to style, and he is the Market's servant." I've also always seen him as my Doppelgänger or my Dorian Gray. We invented ourselves together in our southern California childhoods, out of tickytack, in the debating societies, and the essay contests, and the locker rooms...*for* the American marketplace, the Identity Exchange. What's been creepy is that, somehow, I seem to dream *through* him, and experience, in those scattered seeds, those electromagnetic dashes and dots, the terror of being out of phase, out of synch with myself. I've felt at times impossibly *approximate* to some receding essence of a personality, some longed-for definition, intelligence trapped in the inauthentic: the boy at bay. I've wanted to scream: It's not *my* fault!

Not only that, but he looks like a foot.

Clearly, I underestimated him. I imagined him in his last days alone at night in a darkened wing of the White House, listening to himself on tape—as if Watergate were a play by Samuel Beckett. He was apparently listening instead, with his hat and his jewels on, to "Heartbreak Hotel" and "Blue Suede Shoes." This, my friends, is scarier than a rerun of *Bedtime for Bonzo* meets *The Icelandic Sagas*. He went away by whirlybird; he returns as the Repressed.

CULTURE HEROES (1):
DR. KING, WHO MADE CONNECTIONS AND WAVES

Nothing unbecomes the Reagan White House more than his leaving of it with a snide crack about civil-rights leaders. There he was, this rutabaga, in the last spasm of his gerontocracy, on *60 Minutes* the Sunday night of Martin Luther King's birthday, bad-mouthing black folks who just won't hush up about the state of American race relations.

I wasn't going to write another King column, but the president made me. Had he lived to this birthday, Dr. King would still be causing trouble. That's why they murdered him in Memphis. What he did was make connections between, say, poverty and racism, and then make waves. His Poor People's "I Have a Dream" speech of 1963 was dandy with white America; let black people go on dreaming. But in 1966 he moved into our northern neighborhoods. And in 1967 he connected what the inner city looked like to the bombs we were dropping on Vietnam. Well, an editorial in the *New York Times* accused him of doing a disservice to his race. Hush up, boy.

Switching off Howdy Doody, what I see instead is a home movie of a Second American Revolution. What did such a revolution want? A place on the bus, a seat at a lunch counter, a desk in the classroom, a minute in a polling booth, nothing more complicated than the Fourteenth Amendment. How could such a revolution fail, with those anthems and that imagery, those marches, sit-ins, freedom rides; black preachers, black teachers and their children, against Klansmen, bombs and dogs? It was the shape of moral passion made coherent, a curve in time and space. Then the film speeds up, from "Freedom Now" to "Black Power"; from backwoods and bayou to urban wasteland and concrete jungle; from black suits and blue jeans and flowered dresses to dashikis, berets and guns; from gospel to rock. And it all fell apart. Economic injustice in the North was harder to beat than Jim Crow in the South. Simultaneous movements—against apartheid at home and war abroad—confused, divided and exhausted everybody. The Social Gospel couldn't compete with a theology of greed. And they kept killing our best people.

Read Taylor Branch's brilliant account of the King years, *Parting the Waters*. Although it stops in 1963, there's more than enough to wash out our mouths of the aspirin taste of Reagan, and of movies like *Mississippi Burning* in which the FBI was an ardent defender of civil rights.

I read Garrow and Oates and Mary King and saw *Eyes on the Prize* and served awhile myself as a foot soldier in King's movement of nonviolent civil disobedience. But Branch has something new on nearly every page—about the nightly tactical improvisations of voter registration, lunch counter sit-ins and Trailways freedom rides; about the almost mystical courage and loneliness of Bob Moses in Mississippi in the seasons of blood; about Bobby Kennedy and J. Edgar Hoover, Reinhold Niebuhr and Mahatma Gandhi; about witness and sacrifice.

Did you know that blacks voted 60 percent to 40 percent for Eisenhower over Stevenson in 1956, and 70 percent to 30 percent for Jack over Dick in 1960 after the Kennedy brothers intervened to get King out of a Georgia jail? Remember how close the 1960 election was? Branch also explains just how Hoover with his dirt on White House playgirls like Judith Exner blackmailed the Kennedys into tapping King, then tried to blackmail King with his own sex life. King never seemed to get the hush-up. At five feet seven inches, he was the biggest man I ever met, till we cut him down to a coffin.

Summer of 1967 was the only time I met him. We'd come from an antiwar umbrella group in Boston—Quakers, SCLC, Mobe, SANE, Women Strike for Peace—to seek his approval for a full-page ad we hoped to place in the *Times* "Week in Review." We'd stitched together snippets from his speeches to support our cause. Then as now the "Week in Review" section of the *Times* was a sort of Democracy Wall, by which secessionists from the prevailing pieties sought to communicate with those opinion makers whose influence and moral scruple we overestimated.

We were very white and nervous. He was very black and sad. We were nervous because the Black Power militants had kicked us out of their neighborhoods. I don't know why Dr. King was sad. Maybe he was depressed by the personal attacks, the mosquito bites, of bubblehead separatists like H. Rap Brown and Yippie pimples like Jerry Rubin. Maybe he knew he'd be dead in a year. More probably, he hadn't asked to be a hero. I sometimes think he didn't believe he *was* a hero, except when his own people, in a church or at a demonstration, gave him their energy and faith—their magical assent. And we were there, as pink as Easter bunnies, to steal some heat from his afflatus, the aura about him that he seemed himself to suspect. He was more complicated than our desires, although he let us put his name on them.

I've since met a president. A president arrives like the elephants in

Aïda. He's videotaped through coats of shellac and yards of yashmak. There is supposed to be a buzz on; I didn't feel it. With Dr. King, for all his sadness, I got that light, a scimitar; and heard those chords, a surge; and felt as well a sense of trespass, as if upon the music in a poem by Rilke:

> *when the innermost point in us stands*
> *outside, as amazing space, as the other*
> *side of air:*
> *pure,*
> *immmense,*
> *not for us to live in now.*

Later, in "Sonnets to Orpheus," Rilke met an angel, a tough audience: "You can't impress *him* with a glorious emotion; in the universe where he feels more powerfully, you are a novice."

As well as a maker of connections and waves, Dr. King was an integrationist. It's a measure of how far we haven't come, President-emeritus Babar to the contrary notwithstanding, that we seem as a nation more polarized today than we were when he died. I've fewer black friends; maybe it was easier to have them in Third World capitals like Berkeley or Cambridge. I live now in journalism and literature. You'd think that in those worlds too there'd be spectrum and striation and nuance; rainbows like croquet hoops. But not so. As much as conscience, we lack luster.

CULTURE CRIMINALS (1) :
KISSINGER LAUGHS

He's back, like Dracula. Of course, he never really went away, but I didn't have to think about him so long as he confined himself to board meetings of the many corporations for which he is a paid consultant, or to those gossip columnists in business to bootlick the guest list at the charity racket's latest black sabbath. (Alex Solzhenitsyn, Leona Helmsley and the late Roy Cohn Invite You to Feel Bad About the Boat People at the Museum of the American Indian.) But all at once I feel him closing in again, ubiquitous, and I wonder if garlic still works.

I'm talking about Henry Kissinger, who has been following me around since Harvard in the late 1950s. Simon & Schuster informed us earlier this month that Kissinger is writing a new book. According to his editor, Michael Korda, "It will do for diplomacy what Carl Sagan did for astronomy." It's Korda's job to say things like this from his command post at a power table in the Grill Room of the Four Seasons, but the rest of us must be less thrilled. When Carl Sagan got done with astronomy, astronomy was just the same. I mean, astronomy goes on doing whatever it does—red dwarfs and black holes and stuff— whether Sagan's around or not. We can't really say the same about diplomacy and Kissinger, can we?

A week later, Dr. K himself was interviewed by the *London Sunday Telegraph*. If he were asked to serve yet again as Secretary of State, would he say yes? "Anyone who says no would be ridiculous." (*Anyone*? Joseph Brodsky? Martha Graham? Chuck Norris?) Besides, "If offered, you have a duty to accept it." (No wonder we have a drug problem in this country.) Did he "regret" being barred from the presidency because of his foreign birth? A long pause; then: "Probably, yes. It would have stirred great passion." And Kissinger, according to the *Sunday Telegraph*, "gave a hearty laugh." You could hear it all the way to Cambodia.

It's even funnier when we remember Kissinger's excuse for dumping Allende in 1970: He had been elected president "through a fluke of the Chilean political system"; like six American presidents including Nixon in 1968, Allende won a plurality, instead of a majority, of the votes. Not so funny is an article in this week's *Nation*, telling us that Dr. K may have encouraged Argentina's generals, back in June 1976, to kidnap and murder 9,000 people before Jimmy Carter and his human rights fetishists could take over Washington. Dr. K liked to go to soccer games with Argentina's generals.

But Argentina will bounce off of him too, like Chile and the secret bombing of Cambodia and everything else except that extraordinary Nobel Prize. Amazing. Back in 1979, it fell to me to review the first volume of his memoirs. This worried my *Times* editors. I'd liked *Sideshow* too much, the William Shawcross book that savaged Kissinger for Cambodia. Nor would I leave the room if somebody said "war criminal" and "Kissinger" in the same sentence. But *White House Years* was more interesting and better written than the memoirs I'd reviewed recently by Gerald Ford and George McGovern. It did bother me that, in all his years of imperial service, he'd spent only a single sleepless night, on the eve of his first China visit, but after a couple of paragraphs of huff-and-puff about Allende and Sihanouk, I played far too fair.

And I would regret it. Almost immediately, the phone rang inviting me to a black-tie dinner for him. First, I'd been left off Nixon's Enemies List, and now this. My mother wouldn't let me go home again until 1983, when William Golding won the Nobel Prize for literature, and the MacNeil/Lehrer show on Channel 13 asked me to comment, and I said that Golding seemed to me to have done far less damage to literature than Kissinger had done to peace. Later on that same year, Seymour Hersh published his book on Kissinger and I asked him on TV whether he thought Henry should have had a few more sleepless nights. Hersh, a well-known softie, said: "I think generally when the rest of us go to bed at night we do, you know, Bambi or lambs or whatever we dream about. I really do think Henry Kissinger has to spend his evenings counting maimed and burned Vietnamese, Laotian, Thai, Bangladesh and Chilean babies."

I thought about this not long ago at a party William Buckley gave. Kissinger was there, and so was Walter Cronkite. They stood a few feet apart, in the separate solitudes of all they'd seen and done, case-hardened and secure in their celebrity; and they had a glow, these silent radiant beings, a kind of nimbus. Being equal, neither spoke; they needed, if not a court, at least a toady. I thought to introduce them—a joke, of course—but they stared right through me as though I were Cambodian. They were already communicating, nimbus to nimbus, with a hum heard only in the higher spheres. Then Buckley joined them—and all three laughs were hearty. I remembered an old English proverb: "They agree like bells; they want nothing but hanging."

CULTURE HEROES (2):
ALLEN GINSBERG, ANGEL-HEADED HIPSTER

In the same week that the Supreme Court decided that a high-school principal in Missouri had every right to tell his students what they could and couldn't say about teenage pregnancy and divorce in the campus newspaper—in other words, permission to go to the bathroom and permission to think: the First Amendment as a hall pass—

WBAI in New York dared not broadcast a reading of Allen Ginsberg's notorious *Howl* in a week-long radio series on censorship, for fear of the smutty-minded Federal Communications Commission.

Of course, predictably, I'm outraged. But why don't we pretend that I've already spent two or three paragraphs stamping my foot and get on with the real business of this column, which is to be nice to Allen Ginsberg?

Howl is 32 years old, Ginsberg is 61 and the Constitution's 200. That's three consenting adults we're still afraid of, and I'm secretly pleased at their continuing power to subvert. (*I have the secret, I carry/ subversive salami in/ my ragged briefcase/ Garlic, Poverty, a will to Heaven.*) *Howl* subverted a twerpy me in San Francisco in 1956, that North Beach summer before I went off to be inappropriate at Harvard.

It wasn't Ginsberg's sexuality that subverted me. (Technically speaking, I didn't even understand it till James Baldwin explained how in *Another Country*.) Nor his druggy evangelism. (I got high on paperback books.) Nor later on would it be what Morris Dickstein calls his "spiritual push-ups." ("Om Om Om Sa Ra Wa Du Da Da Ki Ni Yea," and so on unto stupefaction.) It was his Other America, an alternative nation of Tom Mooney, Sacco and Vanzetti, the Scottsboro boys, the Wobblies and his Communist Jewish mother: "Get married Allen don't take drugs."

I'd never met any of these people. They'd been left out of the textbooks in my southern California youth to make room for Richfield Oil and Father Serra. But Ginsberg included everyone, all of the children who had ever disappeared into Moloch. A closet history! When the alarm bell rang to end the fifties snooze, for many it sounded like Elvis. For me, it was Ginsberg and his elegy for the beautiful losers. At Harvard, I would write, inappropriately, about the Beats (and Fats Domino and Chuck Berry) for a student newspaper that was basically a prep school for the Luce magazines, but what I was really saying was that I didn't belong and would rather not: *When can I go into the supermarket and buy what I need with my good looks?*

Thirty-two years later, he seems to be following me around, except he's always been there first. Once at lunch in 1959 I met Whittaker Chambers, which was sort of like meeting the Brothers Karamazov. Although his favorite poet was Rilke ("every angel is terrible"), Chambers thought Ginsberg was the only Beat with genuine talent. I shouldn't have been surprised. Chambers and Ginsberg had Lionel

Trilling in common; Trilling had been bewildered by both of them.

In Barry Miles's biography of Ginsberg, we meet the gentle poet-father, Louis, and the crazy Communist mother, Naomi. We grow up in New Jersey with a kid whose favorite writer was Poe, whose favorite book was *Dr. Doolittle*. We accompany this kid to Columbia, where he met and bedded Kerouac, William Burroughs and Neal Cassady; where he confounded Trilling. We smoke his pot when he writes a paper on Cézanne for Meyer Schapiro, and when God talks back to him, through William Blake. We ship out with the Merchant Marine. We're there on North Beach for *Howl*; in Tangier for Burroughs, morphine and the machete; in Machu Picchu when God talks to him again after the death of his mother and tells him to love women; in Castro's Cuba where they kicked him out for talking too much about dope and homosexuality; in London, Moscow, Budapest, Jerusalem and Chicago '68—hobnobbing with the Stones, the Beatles and R.D. Laing, writing lyrics for Bob Dylan and the Clash, turning Robert Lowell on to LSD, phoning Henry Kissinger, telling Ezra Pound "but I'm a Buddhist Jew," composing *Kaddish*, loving Peter, hating cocaine, becoming, with a Pulitzer, *respectable...*

What we don't get from Miles is any sense of the civil-libertarian/anarchistic politics, of what's emblematic about him. For a while I thought he'd gone away forever in the early sixties, "washed up desolate on the Ganges bank, vegetarian & silent hardly writing," but in 1965, at Charles University in Prague, dissident students crowned him "King of the May." Novotny was no more amused by Ginsberg as king than Trilling had been by Ginsberg as student; the poet was expelled from Czechoslovakia, as he had been from Columbia and Cuba. If everywhere an exile, he was also everywhere a king of all our Maydays, at the levitation of the Pentagon, in the parks for the Chicago convention, in Judge Hoffman's kangaroo court, on Bill Buckley's *Firing Line*: Ban the bomb; hands off Nicaragua; Om. *America I'm putting my queer shoulder to the wheel.*

This "lonely old courage-teacher" looks somehow younger every time I see him, as though "the grey sign of time in my beard" had been painted on to disguise an untamed boy-subversive. What makes him so special? Well, like Rob Roy, Dick Turpin, Pancho Villa, Jesse James, Cartouche and the Opportune Rain Sung Chiang, he is of course a social bandit. But he's a *nonviolent* social bandit, an incorruptible pacifist even when it hurts, like Dr. King and Joan Baez. Maybe because he contained in himself all countercultures, he was the bridge in the sixties between the Yippie media brats and the New Left Little-League Leninists, but his ultimate role, at every engagement in this second Civil War, seemed to be that of a nurse, like his friend Walt Whitman.

Sending up his Oms, his toy balloons, against the technostructured Superstate, Ginsberg is all these—bandit, subversive, nurse—but also magical, like a shaman, in the sense that all magic is a sleight-of-mind, a symbolism of spontaneity elaborated to preserve and defend the self from a devouring society. "The only poetic tradition," he has said, "is the voice out of the burning bush." But there's another tradition, equally "metrical, mystical, manly," and no less honorable in a time of lesions. There is the Medicine Man.

CULTURE CRIMINALS (2):
KISSINGER AGAIN, THAT CHINA CARD

Writing for a living, I wear several hats—tricorn, straw, deerstalker, dunce—and sometimes it rains on this Easter parade. What am I saying, to whom, and why? There is an ethic, even on Grub Street. When you suspect yourself of a hidden agenda, fess up, or shut up, or bite the hand that feeds you.

For instance, if I were to tell readers of *Newsday* that Julie Baumgold's report on the Malcolm Forbes brouhaha, in the October 2 *New York* magazine, is the best article ever written on the subject (which it is), you're entitled to know that *New York* magazine has paid me to review television for almost seven years.

And if I were to tell readers of *New York* magazine that all the new programs on CBS this fall are wonderful (which they aren't), those readers are entitled to know that I'm paid by CBS to have opinions on the media every Sunday.

And if I were to tell the audience of *Sunday Morning* on CBS that *Newsday*, the only paper in New York to oppose the reelections of Al D'Amato and Ed Koch, has the best columnists in the whole country (which is arguable), that audience is entitled to know that I hunker down with Mona Charen to chew the same chicken bones.

Now suppose you are an ex-Harvard professor and ex-Secretary of State, with a syndicated newspaper column as well as a first-dibs retainer from a major television network. Suppose that network, ABC, asks you to comment on what American policy ought to be toward China, after the massacre in Tiananmen Square. Suppose you tell Peter Jennings of ABC that "I wouldn't do any sanctions." And suppose that then you go on to write a newspaper column, full of praise for Deng Xiaoping's economic reforms, reminding us that "no government in the world would have tolerated having the main square of its capital occupied for eight weeks."

Do you suppose you ought also to have told your readers and your TV audience that you have a vested interest in Deng's regime? That you just happen to run a couple of consulting companies that advise American firms on how to do business with China, and a third, called China Ventures, in a $75-million limited-partnership deal with one of Deng's ministries that stands to earn you, personally, hundreds of thousands of dollars—so long as there aren't any sanctions?

I know I promised never to write another Henry Kissinger column, but I lied.

I didn't hear about Kissinger Associates—or its subsidiary, Kent Associates; or their fancy clients, like American Express; or the lucrative China Ventures limited partnership—from any of the Doctor's many enemies. Seymour Hersh didn't tell me, and *The Nation* is preoccupied with the less compelling question of whether or not Alexander Cockburn is a Stalinist. I read all about it instead on the front page of the *Wall Street Journal* on Friday, September 15, after which the story sank without a trace.

This, ah, mystifies. You'd think the world might be interested in what Peter Jennings had to say when *Journal* reporter John Fialka called him to talk about Kissinger's various hats and many-fingered money-pies. Jennings told Fialka: "If I knew then what I know now, I would not have wanted him on that broadcast, plain and simple. And I think my management would have understood that perfectly." Of course, by the time Fialka called Jennings, Kissinger had already left ABC for CBS.

Maybe you knew all this—somehow—and it doesn't bother you. Maybe Kissinger would admire Deng Xiaoping no matter how many workers and students he killed, and whether or not it was bad news for the CEO of China Ventures. *Realpolitik*—the original game show from which *You Bet Your Life* derives. And maybe I'm just picking on Kissinger because I'm jealous of anybody who wears more hats than I do, and makes a better living at it.

But these people are amazing. Dr. K complains to the *Journal*: "What other former Secretary of State has been submitted to this scrutiny?" And did you see that his former boss, the Fighting Quaker, after failing to copyright his name, has switched his telephone service from AT&T to MCI to protest AT&T's sponsorship of the forthcoming TV movie version of *The Final Days*? According to *The Final Days*, Bob Woodward and Carl Bernstein's account of the decline and fall of the Nixon presidency, Nixon and Kissinger, at Nixon's insistence, fell to their knees in the White House bunker to pray for guidance through the long night of Watergate, and Nixon actually cried. Now think about that. Who do you suppose leaked the fact that Nixon cried to the dynamic duo from the *Washington Post*? Not Julie, nor Deng. *They* weren't there.

On the fifteenth anniversary of *Saturday Night Live*, Robin Williams wondered, what exactly do you *say* to a Kissinger if you meet him at a party: "Hi there, I *loved* all your wars"?

ICONIC CLOWNS (1):
IS ABBIE HOFFMAN REALLY DEAD?

I'm not sure I want to know why Abbie really died, especially if he did it to himself. This country doesn't need any help knocking off our Bobby Kennedys, Martin Luther Kings and Allard Lowensteins. Why volunteer? Shakespeare was easier on his clowns. And my Abbie stories—Dennis the Menace in Chicago; the levitation of the Pentagon; notes from the underground—are no better than anybody else's. He played the straight press like an ocarina, pumped and squeezed us like the bladder of a goat. He told the Walker Commission he favored the overthrow of the government "by any means necessary": "I'd prefer to see it be done with bubble gum, but I'm having some doubts." Compare this to the always quotable Jerry Rubin: "Sirhan Sirhan is a Yippie!"

Media apache! From this file, now closed, one paragraph: In Washington, D.C., a couple of years ago some of us sat on a panel of the National Endowment for the Arts to which Abbie had applied for money for *Radio Free America* on WBAI. You should have seen the grins on our faces as we listened to his tapes. After so many years, he was still at it. We voted to fund him, knowing the National Council would never approve. We were voting, really, for a memory-trace of our braver, more whimsical selves, before we'd emigrated to the Comfort Zone.

Captain Happen! In the sixties, I resented Abbie's badmouthing of King and the Quakers, of Allen Ginsberg and Movement women. Now I'm tired of sorting out the pacifisms, feminisms, absurdisms and Castroite delusional systems of those years. Against our bubble gum, the guys in the baby blue riot helmets had flamethrowers and bazookas, and the New Left went Baader-Meinof or bananas, and maybe I missed the point, but I never imagined that Abbie wouldn't be around to argue it. "As in tragedy, every comedy needs a scapegoat, someone who will be punished and expelled from the social order represented mimetically in the spectacle," wrote Susan Sontag: "In the happening, this scapegoat is the audience."

A weird and maybe preposterous analogy comes to mind—just because I'm reading Simon Schama's *Citizens*. Schama hates the French Revolution, and everybody who was anybody in it. But he's such a lively writer, and so much in love with the prurient details of social and cultural history, that he's dragged me kicking and screaming all the way to 9 Thermidor, 1794. Before I got there, I had to hear a lot about Montgolfier and his balloons.

According to Schama, hot-air ballooning in the 1780s "was much more than a fashionable amusement. Its public was enormous, elated and unconstrained, and spoke not with the accents of polite society but with the emotional vocabulary of Rousseau's sublimity." What fell apart in skies above Paris, Lyon and Versailles was the king's "ceremonial control of spectacle through which the mystique of absolutism was preserved and managed." These balloonists established "a direct and unmediated relationship of comradeship with enormous multitudes of people." Instead of state-licensed "official forms of art" and "processions [expressing] the corporate and hierarchical world" of the monarchy, a balloon belonged to the People: "In the air, it became democratic." As a consequence of this "charismatic physics," Louis XVI "was no longer the cynosure of all eyes. He had been displaced by a more potent magus: the inventor."

Or, to get even fancier: Listen to Octavio Paz, in *Sor Juana*, talking about "spectacles." If "the Renaissance introduced the triumphal arches and other elements that evoked the Roman past and at the same time announced the new absolutist state," the Baroque "theatricalized politics into popular pantomime and allegory. Thus began the reign of illusion...The festival left the city plaza and took refuge in the hamlet and the baroque palace. It would not be until the French Revolution that the public celebration would be revived. A bloody resurrection."

If we think of media reporting of our Vietnam era as "theatricalized politics" and "official forms of art" and the "pantomime and allegory" by which the State, at war, "preserved and managed" its mystique, then what Abbie did was to send himself up like a hot-air balloon. From his basket-cage, he lobbed cherry bombs into all that decorum and sedation, that death-denying etiquette. He was a magus. He democratized. If this wasn't politics—politics is what's left over, after television (and after the Supreme Court, too), on the streets, to which he returned at the end to organize—it was nonetheless an astonishment and a liberation, "charismatic physics." Already, I miss him and the point.

CULTURE HEROES (3): STUDS TERKEL, A WIRED DIOGENES

Studs Terkel was eighty years old Monday night. So what Studs did was publish another book, *Race: How Whites & Blacks Think & Feel About the American Obsession.* And what some of the rest of us did was go to a party for him, which he wasn't permitted to tape-record. He had to sit there, being admired, which is one of the few things he isn't good at. If you stay put, you might miss the action. While we were admiring Studs, for instance, they abolished democracy in Peru.

About the party, I won't tell you everybody there; they already know who they are. Many of them have been fighting losing causes since the Spanish Civil War. But mention must be made of two celebrants I've never seen before in almost a quarter-century of New York literary cocktail parties. One was Pete Seeger, in the kitchen, without his guitar. The other was Kenneth Clark, who started testifying to the pathologies of American apartheid as far back as 1952, in Clarendon, South Carolina, when the NAACP began its legal suit to desegregate our public schools.

(Time flies away. Back in 1953, it was Ike, not Ronald Reagan, who had this to say about the American South to his new chief justice, Earl Warren: "These aren't bad people. All they're concerned about is to see that their sweet little girls are not required to sit in school alongside some big overgrown Negroes.")

Clark, who must have had another party to go to, wore black tie.

Seeger, of course, did not. Studs was his usual vision of red checkerboard, looking, as always, like the sportswriter he had impersonated in *Eight Men Out*, the John Sayles/Chicago Black Sox movie—a hard-boiled leprechaun. The rest of us lacked such dash.

The last time Studs went Out There and Reported Back, in *The Great Divide*, his subject was what had happened in the Age of Reagan to the American dream of social justice. He is, of course, the opposite of a public-opinion poll. He goes anywhere, but when he gets there he stays put long enough to let people explain themselves. In *The Great Divide*, he talked to farmers, dentists, Teamsters, stockbrokers, disk jockeys and juice-bar cashiers; cement masons and gay activists; Gray Panthers and neo-Nazis; a congressman, a novelist and a cop; Yuppies and religious fundamentalists, social parasites and burnt-out cases, couch potatoes and NYPNS ("Neat Young People In Neat Situations"). What he heard were states of mind—like greed and doubt and anger and despair. What he found was an absence of memory, as if the whole nation had forgotten the Depression, never heard of the Civil War, never read the Bill of Rights. *The Great Divide* was the past we've lost, back when we were a caring country.

But because he's Studs he kept on looking till he also found pockets of resistance and renewal: organizers of union locals and community action groups, teachers who wouldn't quit, doctors committed to low-cost health-care clinics, police chiefs who knew something about the social pathology of crime, and a Sanctuary movement for refugees from Latin American death squads. These voices massed in *The Great Divide* to a choral movement of energy and dissent—decency on the march. For instance, Jean Gump, a grandmother who went to prison for eight years for having physically opposed the deployment of nuclear missiles. About life in jail, Gump told Studs: "As inmates, we're property. We belong to Mr. Meese, we belong to the Bureau of Prisons. A month ago, a young woman had come here from another federal institution. She'd been locked up for fourteen months without seeing the light of day. On arriving here, she was so happy to be out in the sunlight, she lay down and got herself a sunburn. They wrote a shot—that's an incident report. The shot read: Destruction of government property." *The property was her skin, which she had burned.* Think about it. According to Studs, it was time that we worked on our tans.

Now imagine him in action for this new book, on the streets of Chicago, on foot because he can't drive, in a raincoat and battered hat, with a hearing aid and a tape recorder, bluffing his way into the Ida B. Wells housing project on the black South Side and sitting down in somebody's kitchen to talk about race. Our premier oral historian is also one of the last of the integrationists—a throwback to Martin Luther King; and before Dr. King, to the left wing of the CIO; and before that, to Jewish socialism and the French Revolution. He's kept the faith by continuing to test it. He will talk to anybody, and he listens twice, first right there in the kitchen, and then again when he edits the tapes for his books, where intelligence is made somehow musical, where conversations become cantatas. I'm tempted then to call him an oratorio historian. This is what Walt Whitman must have meant when he said he heard America singing.

Not all the songs in *Race* are cheerful. Everybody—white, black, brown and yellow—seems to agree that relations between the races are worse than they've ever been, worse than they were in the sixties riots. Most blame the go-go greedhead Reagan years and the drug epidemic. Farrakhan gets mentioned more often than I'd have thought imaginable (or desirable). As if in counterpoint to Farrakhan, there's also a lot of country blues singer Big Bill Broonzy.

But nobody Studs talks to has given up. (Certainly not Emmett Till's mother, Mamie Mobley, who became a teacher after her son was murdered.) They have all got jobs to find, children to raise, neighborhoods to save and a nation to recover from its waste of scruple, its conscience gone up in smoke like garbage or the blues.

Where does he find these people? Mostly, but not always, in Chicago. Some, but not most, he's talked to before. Male or female, without exception, it's their *working* lives that give them their perspective. They are paramedics, firefighters and flight attendants; carpenters and computer-software salesmen; steelworkers, musicians, hairdressers, medical students, hospital aides and chauffeurs; union reps, evangelists, black separatists and Ku Klux Klanners; ex-Communists, ex-priests, retired domestics and many, many teachers, most of them despairing.

Each new Terkel book I make a big deal about this amazing democracy of occupations. Why? Because the brain, too, is a muscle and it's nice—it's more than nice, it's thrilling—to see it exercised by people who have never shown up on *Face the Nation* or Ted Koppel, where all we hear from are the male and pale with their credentialed feedback Vid-Blab of "underclass" and "trickle-down"; the mellowspeak salesmen in their Beltway blisterpacks, pushing a capital-gains tax cut as

the pep pill/miracle cure for moral fatigue, social paralysis and economic catastrophe.

Disappointed, hesitant or driven as they may be, there's no doubt at
all that America would be a better place if *everybody* listened to these
working people, not just radical-humanist Studs Terkel, that passionate old man with the brave songs and the magic hearing aid.

ICONIC CLOWNS (2):
ABBIE AGAIN, THE LONG GOOD-BYE

We would have felt worse at the "No Regrets" memorial for Abbie
Hoffman at the Palladium on Saturday afternoon if we'd known I. F.
Stone would die on Sunday, while the Mets were trading Lenny Dykstra. I do not mix my media; the culture does it for me, a crazy salad of
brave hearts.

"No Regrets" started late and only got to intermission fifteen minutes after it was supposed to be over. Sixties excess! But it was an excess
without the corollary paranoia. In Maxine Hong Kingston's very sixties
novel, *Tripmaster Monkey*, Wittman Ah Sing wonders, "What if Chubby
Checker does not mean us well? What if Chubby Checker is up to no
good?" It was impossible at the Palladium to believe that Peter Yarrow,
David Amram and Buster Poindexter were up to anything but good, although I'm not so sure about the Fugs. Under four giant video
screens—two of them reticulated—and a Mao-sized portrait of the
grinning Hoffman, small children wandered innocent as balloons.

Before this excess, in a weirdly aquatic green room, the usual suspects had been rounded up. A softshoe Norman Mailer, looking like
Ed Asner, had opinions on typewriters versus word processors and
what they do to your style. Mailer, of course, has a secretary, which
permits him to compose illuminated manuscripts.

Victor Navasky explained that *The Nation* had made a tender offer for
Time, Inc. How could *The Nation* afford to compete with Warner and
Paramount? The same as everybody else in the takeover racket: *The Nation* would borrow from the banks against the assets of the property it
sought to purchase. Navasky also promised to emancipate Time, Inc.'s
various divisions. *Sports Illustrated*, free at last…Power to the *People*!

Paul Krassner of *The Realist* needed to be disabused of the notion
that I'd tried to suppress a book of his, under orders of the CIA, back

in 1971. In fact, I seem to have been alone among my peer group in never having been recruited by the CIA. This has bothered me for years. What did they know and when did they know it, down at Langley, that theocracy of secrets?

Sydney Schanberg of *Newsday* told a nifty story about his cousin Abbie and Bill Walton, the red-haired vegetarian professional basketball player (a left-wing center). Schanberg would tell this story again onstage, and my wife would miss it again, the second time, because the zonkers at the balcony table next to us wanted her to smoke an illegal substance while she wanted them to listen instead to Schanberg.

I didn't want to talk to Allen Ginsberg because I happened to be in the middle of reading a biography of him; and in this biography Ginsberg was in the middle of discovering, under the influence of ayuhuasca, in the jungles of Peru, that God was an octopus; and I was embarrassed to know more about Ginsberg than he knew about me.

Onstage: Bob Fass, Marshall Efron, Jacques Levy, Ed Sanders, Abbie's kids, Anita and etc. "Abbie's not here," said Anita, "but we are. Let's take the nineties!" On the giant video screens: home movies of Brandeis, Berkeley, Mississippi, the Lower East Side, the Stock Exchange caper, the Grand Central Yip-In. Amram, singing "Pull My Daisy," reminded us of Kerouac. (Do you remember that Kerouac loved Joe McCarthy? That William Burroughs hated socialists and women?) By intermission, we were on the verge of Chicago '68, having crossed state lines in an illegal frame of mind. (Sunday the *Times* reported that Bobby Seale was "one of the Chicago 7." But, of course, the whole symbolic point of Bobby Seale was that, bound and gagged, he was the Eighth Man Out.) I left after Poindexter, missing Mailer and Ginsberg.

I left not just because I'd promised to be elsewhere at five o'clock. And not just because I didn't want to hear about Abbie's coke bust, nor whatever William Styron had to say on manic-depression, nor any well-wrought homilies on suicide—an imponderable, an impoverishment, that awful solitude, a theft of heart. I left because "No Regrets" was so busy, too filling, a made-for-television overproduction. There wasn't time and space at the Palladium for us to contemplate our own failures of character, nor any silence in which to seek some courage.

Late on Sunday afternoon I went out to the Second Avenue street fair to buy a new wallet. I do this every summer. About New York, I like street fairs and buses that kneel, that sigh as they lean down to ac-

cept the aged and infirm, like Ferdinand the Bull. I thought it odd how
Abbie's memory tapes had displaced my own. About Berkeley and
Chicago I remember *him*; I've forgotten me. When I got back to the
house, they told me that I. F. Stone had died, and Dykstra had been
traded. I have a brand-new leather wallet, and I'm broke.

CULTURE HEROES (4): THE GOLDEN AGE OF IZZY STONE

I.F. Stone, maverick journalist, late-blooming Greek scholar, one-man
Amnesty International, died last week at eighty-one. A radical who
hated Stalin, a lifelong Zionist who worried about Palestinians, a Jef-
fersonian democrat who read the small print in the Social Contract,
Izzy was also our conscience. In the media biz, too many of us get our
stories by press release or leak. We play footsie with the powerful, decide for ourselves what the public would be better off not knowing,
and never let a newspaper strike get in the way of our tuition payments
to the private schools where we groom our children for the Ivy
League. In our $800 suits and our shrewd career moves, we aspire in
Washington to fancy dinner parties, Oval Office group-gropes and the
fast lane on the Beltway. We aspire, in New York, to Liz Smith and
Vanity Fair, to Oscar de La Renta and La Côte Basque, *Spy* and Nell's.
Izzy, working in his garage, was a different breed of journalist.

During all those Cold War years when they wouldn't let him into
the National Press Club, Izzy published his scoops in his own Washington newsletter, *I. F. Stone's Weekly*. By burrowing into government
documents nobody else had read, by legwork in the archives and the
boondocks, and by never trusting the official cover story, he was
ahead of everybody else on human rights atrocities, on Vietnam and
on Watergate. A typical Izzy scoop went like this: In 1957, we were
thinking about a treaty with the Soviet Union, with inspection sites to
guarantee a moratorium on nuclear testing. And our own Atomic Energy Commission sought to sabotage the treaty. The AEC exploded a
bomb underground in Nevada, and then announced to the world that
it hadn't been detected, even 200 miles from the test site. Izzy collected obscure newspaper stories of turbulence recorded as far away as
Rome and Tokyo. Thus equipped, he went in person to unwary government seismologists, who told him they had picked up the test in

Fairbanks, Alaska, and twenty-five other monitoring stations. Every newspaper in the country bought the AEC line, except the *St. Louis Post-Dispatch*, where Izzy had a friend he tipped off before he broke the inside story.

Time and again, he followed a paper trail to the truth…until he went blind. And Izzy did go blind, like Homer and James Joyce and Jorge Luis Borges and Ray Charles and other great storytellers. His grand enterprise in his last years was his book on Socrates, another loner. Izzy didn't like Socrates, who had been contemptuous of democracy, a lousy husband and a snob. Izzy made the case for fourth-century Athens. I had my doubts, and said so in a review. Socrates was one of the first nay-sayers; he saw difficulties. He belongs to a long line of philosophers who gnawed their way to the end of what they knew, then questioned how and if they really knew it. Worried about essentials, they tended to lose touch. A surprising number of them quit us, if not mad like Nietzsche or suicides like Lucretius, then at least quite oddly—Vico, for instance, lowered by coffin from a window, because the stairs to Naples were too narrow; or Kierkegaard, hating women and dead broke. Many were reactionary, politically, like the modernists of our own culture, who likewise thought their way to the end of art and then turned to tear at that art with their teeth. We consult them not for practical advice but to hear some dark chords.

Izzy, however, had heard enough. Our century deafens with its contempt for the citizenry. Too many idealisms have been brutalized. By disposition a child of the Enlightenment, by habit a hard worker at the homely truths, by sympathies a commoner, by conviction faithful to popular sovereignty, by bitter experience suspicious of official wisdom and statist social engineering, a skeptic but not a cynic, he took a personal dislike to Socrates. We were supposed to have dinner to discuss it. Sadly, that won't happen now. He was himself an Athens, an agora.

ICONIC CLOWNS (3):
HUNTER S. THOMPSON, DUKE OF DESPAIR

These were our unlovely options on election night: (1) We could stay home, knowing the news would taste like Styrofoam. (2) We could go by subway, bus, cab, tank or camel to the Ritz in Alphabet City, where

Dr. Hunter S. Thompson was scheduled to fulminate. (3) We could walk eleven blocks uptown to Elaine's, where Robert Altman was throwing a private party for the cast and crew of *Tanner '88*, the pay-cable TV series, written by Garry Trudeau, in which Michael Murphy had run a better campaign for the presidency than Michael Dukakis. Or (4) we could emigrate to Madagascar, about which I've been browsing.

I am equally afraid of Hunter Thompson and Elaine. I haven't been to Elaine's in twenty years. Twenty years ago, she wouldn't let me in because I didn't fame enough, and she was right. A decade ago, I reviewed *The Great Shark Hunt*, a 600-page anthology of Thompson's gonzo journalism, and from Aspen, Colorado, he wrote to say he wouldn't shoot me, though he'd thought about it.

Even so, I identify with Thompson. You may remember that he was a straight reporter for Dow-Jones before he rode with the Hells Angels; before he invented gonzo in the pages of *Rolling Stone*; before he was caricatured in Trudeau's "Doonesbury" comic strip; before he discovered Fear and Loathing on the campaign trail, in Las Vegas, at the Super Bowl and inside his own head, where Nixon turned into a werewolf. In *The Great Shark Hunt*, he'd reported as well on so much damage to his own body, so many uppers, downers and moonshots, so many bottles of bourbon, cases of Coors, guns and auto wrecks, that the surprise a decade ago was that he wasn't dead. He ought at least to have glowed in the dark, like Chernobyl.

Amazingly, he surfaced again last June with *Generation of Swine*, a collection of columns from Hearst's *San Francisco Examiner*. He seems to have written most of these columns in the Rocky Mountains, consulting his satellite dish for every whisper in the global village, although we meet him sometimes in the desert, among mobsters; or on the telephone with Pat Buchanan, with whom he has a hallucinatory relationship; or lost inside the many mystifications of the mind of Gary Hart. Ed Meese especially obsesses him, and Bush, and Ferdinand Marcos, as well as hurricanes. We aren't talking about a sober-sided pundit on the order of Anthony Lewis, nor a gaudy parrot of great quotations like George Will. It's as if, on his mountaintop, Thompson is picking up, by ham radio in his limbic wastes, all those radio signals from red dwarfs and black holes; as if he amplifies and modulates all the madness and paranoia of the dying culture.

I think he's going crazy so I won't have to. This is a dangerous favor. It means I owe him. So we went on election night to Elaine's instead, where nobody will ever do me any favors. I'm too old for the East Village, anyway. I have been losing ever since the Spanish Civil War, and it wears a body out.

At Elaine's, we were looked down on by three different television sets and the proprietor. The networks had already conceded the election. We talked to an expansive Altman, who is going to work with Carol Burnett; and to candidate Murphy, about candidate Bush; and to Pamela Reed, Murphy's campaign manager on *Tanner*, about Dukakis and sound-bites. All of this was weird enough because, after all, these people were *actors*; Trudeau had written their lines. (To Trudeau, we chose not to talk about Thompson.) And then it happened: Fear and Loathing at Elaine's.

I should explain that a recent gig of mine is to show up Sunday mornings in front of a CBS camera, tethered like a goat to the TelePrompTer, where I eat my words. On the first of these Sundays, the words I ate had been all about *Tanner*, which is why I had been invited to Elaine's. Altman had a copy of this tape. Suddenly, instead of Rather or Brokaw, there *I* was, on three TV sets, looking like one of those Mikea Pygmies from Madagascar whose feet are pointed backwards so they can't be tracked by their many enemies. I bolted Elaine's, into the cities of the night.

Later friends would call to say that Thompson had shown up at the Ritz only two hours late, waving a rifle, wearing a rubber Richard Nixon mask, embarrassing himself, just like Mailer at his fiftieth. It occurs to me in hiding that America hates the sixties and one reason for this hatred is that so many of us who came of political age in that decade are tiresome performers. Like Madagascar, we've detached ourselves from the Mother Continent, grown our own flora and fauna. Like the bottle-trunked crassulescent baobab or the bygone elephant bird or the dog-faced, monkey-bodied, panda-coated indri lemur, ours is an exotic act. On the cusp of extinction, we have been showing off instead of hunkering down. In the American bush, wild borks are waiting for us.

CULTURE HEROES (5): CAPTAIN KANGAROO IN COURT

I'm assuming Captain Kangaroo showed up, on Tuesday, in Danbury. He was the scheduled commencement speaker at Western Connecti-

cut State University, but there'd been complaints in the student newspaper that the host of a children's television program would have
nothing to say of "insight or inspirational impetus for our seniors to
attain career pursuits." The little greedheads probably wanted a booster shot of testosterone from Carl Icahn or Bobby Knight.

They need the Captain more than they think. On Sixth Avenue,
where networks live, and on Madison Avenue, where the ad agencies
live, our children are called "mice." Toy manufacturers alone spend
more than $300 million a year on commercials to manipulate these
mice. As the Captain on CBS, Bob Keeshan wouldn't play the "kidvid"
game. He refused to do any commercials and was particularly opposed to selling war. He told our children instead that it was possible
to be a man without killing anything. This idea, which won Peabodys
and Emmys, went out of fashion when the fast-buck gang-bangers
from southern California seized power in our nation's capital. They
canceled the Captain, along with many social programs and most decency. You will have noticed that CBS has had ratings trouble on
weekday mornings ever since.

The mice in my house grew up, before *Sesame Street*, on episodes of
Captain Kangaroo and Mr. Greenjeans, Bunnyrabbit and Mr. Moose,
the grandfather clock and the Ping-Pong balls. Of course, like spiders
at the leak of dawn, they'd watch anything—from Air Force documentaries and religious shorts to farm reports and lessons in Por-
tuguese—but the Captain most appealed to them, and to me. His benign bafflement was a kind of umbrella against brutishness.

Like the Captain, I'd like to believe that for every Grimm fairy tale
there has to be a Ferdinand the Bull. But I'll also admit that the Captain's bafflement has another meaning for me, more evasive, perhaps
imponderable. More than twenty years ago I abandoned my children
to their TV set in Brighton, Massachusetts, to work that autumn in the
apple orchards of southern New Hampshire with a gang of black migrant pickers brought up by yellow school bus from Florida, Georgia,
Virginia and the Dixwell Avenue slum of New Haven, not that far
from Danbury, but in another universe. Never mind the apocalyptic
politics, the grandiosity, of this abandonment—nor the ridiculous
figure I cut, with my flayed face, my crayons and paper punch, in my
fatigue jacket on a forklift, as the apples came down like Ping-Pong
balls. These were the sixties. Between pedagogies in a Roxbury ghetto
and a stint as minister of propaganda for a popular front of antiwar

agitators, I was looking for my head: *authenticity*. I bore witness: *self-aggrandizement*. I dreamed, maybe, of year-round jobs for the underclass, in snowmobile New Hampshire; of improving New England's gene pool; of black ice-hockey players sticking it to French Canadians.

I got instead indentured servants: a sullen, press-ganged proletariat, doomed to piecework; running a tab on marked-up cigarettes and beer at an unfriendly company store; without wheels to get to the town where nobody'd cash what was left of their much-docked checks anyway, any more than any white New Englander would pick them up as hitchers, any more than the hospital wanted them when they fell off their ladders or met a snake or knifed themselves. When, that is, they weren't being knifed by a black gestapo of Alabama bullyboys who extorted a commission on every bushel picked, come frost, hail, scald, scab or radioactive fallout. To all of this the Scots-Irish farmer, indentured himself to an absentee landlord, averting his cold blue eyes, turning his red plaid back, would say, "Ayuuhp," and complain when the *apples* were bruised.

The black barracks was a stone house that sloped below-ground, where once upon New England time the ham was smoked and maple syrup batched. I'd wait outside with my paper punch as they rose from their bunks on the cold October mornings. I could see their turbanned heads, in the blue lavatory window. I listened to the TV set they watched for breakfast. Like my children, they were watching *Captain Kangaroo*. I distinctly heard the Captain say, "Do what your mommy asks you to, and try to make her happy." Everybody everywhere, simultaneously, sees the same thing in this country. We are one big children's program. But somehow, to some of us, it looks different when the Ping-Pong balls come down.

There was a novel in it for me. There was also a bafflement. In *Lazarus*, André Malraux tells his doctor: "Modern man has been fashioned on the basis of exemplary stereotypes: saint, chevalier, caballero, gentleman, bolshevik, and so on." He left out Captain Kangaroo. I've long since commenced—and Captain Kangaroo, *c'est moi*.

NANCY REAGAN, UGLY DUCKLING

Many years ago, when I reviewed Kitty Kelley's biography of Elizabeth Taylor for the *New York Times*, my editor there wanted to know why I was wasting their time. I was supposed to be a highbrow. Now Kelley's published another biography, of another MGM contract starlet, and it was all over the *front* page of the *New York Times* last Sunday morning. And Monday on the funny pages, Garry Trudeau began a series of daily "Doonesbury" comic strips based on *Nancy Reagan: The Unauthorized Biography*. And Tuesday Donald Trump, the playboy masterbuilder, said that all that stuff about Frank Sinatra couldn't possibly be true. And I didn't even get *my* copy of the book, by Pony Express from Simon & Schuster, till *Wednesday*. And so I put aside the essays of Isaiah Berlin, and new novels by Don DeLillo and Milan Kundera, in order to be gallant.

I'll not detain you with the hairbrush used to bash poor Patti's face, nor the teddy bear, the casting couch, the Mafia, the astrology, the bulletproof slip and the Sinatra. It's always seemed to me that we picked on Nancy to avoid thinking about her husband. Now we're doing it again. It amounts to a denial of politics, a publicity-thrill like a hit of crack. We bought into the notion of King Babar and Queen Celeste. Kitty Kelley suggests, instead, something like Rip van Winkle and a sort of Ugly Duckling, who really wanted to be a czarina, with her very own Rasputin.

So what if she changed her name, her age, her family history and the shape of her eyes, by cosmetic surgery? Starting over from scratch, inventing a brand-new self, is as American as lynching bees; it's what modernism in literature is all about; it's what California is *for*.

So what if she wanted to crash the Big Party, just like the rest of her southern California friends, those fast-buck self-made multimillionaires who had to be trained to eat with a fork, and their upwardly mobile Gucci-girl wives with their pet decorators, their pet hairdressers and their tough-love children stashed in boarding schools? The wonderful thing about this country is that peasants have money.

So what if she was a lousy parent? So are a lot of us. It gives our kids something to talk about to their designer therapists, their Ranks and Horneys. Those children seem not to have been such bargains, anyway. And Nancy didn't like to pay for anything, even motherhood.

So what if she was greedy and stingy? Wasn't the Reagan Revolution all about deregulating greed? And so what if both of them turn out to have been hypocrites on premarital and extramarital sex, marijuana, abortion, homosexuality, family values and religion? For office seekers, hypocrisy *is* a religion. As Kelley tells us, George and Barbara Bush switched their positions on abortion and the Equal Rights Amendment to get onto the ticket in 1980.

So we thought they were vegetables, and they turned out to be ketchup. So what? I could tell you that Nancy's right-wing stepfather, Dr. Loyal Davis, got his start as a surgeon performing prefrontal lobotomies at $150 a pop. That, after Jane Wyman, Ronnie might have married Ann Sothern or Viveca Lindfors or Doris Day or Piper Laurie. That Imelda Marcos...but this is all beside the point. What really bothers people is that Nancy had some White House clout, as if Betty Ford and Rosalynn Carter didn't, nor Eleanor Roosevelt, nor Abigail Adams! What weird fantasies about marriage we must have for this to come as news; what a poor opinion of women.

Nancy thought Watergate was "a stupid, stupid, immoral, illegal thing to do." She opposed aid to the Contras. She was against a pardon for Ollie North. She also pushed Babar into an arms treaty with the Russians, because she wanted him to win a Nobel Prize. On some things, at least, we ought to be *glad* that he listened to her more than he did to the fastbuck Thugees and the nuke-Managua globocops. Even astrology's better than whatever those wiseguys were smoking.

COUNTRY-AND-WESTERN GHOSTWRITERS

Everybody else will have to explain Mandela, Gotti, Rooney and the Trumps. I'm worried about Peggy Noonan. Her memoir, *What I Saw at the Revolution: A Political Life in the Reagan Era*, got a passing grade from Wilfrid Sheed in the *Times* and a thumbs-down from Garry Wills in *Newsday*, but neither reviewer addressed the crucial question: Going free-lance, has she made a shrewd career move?

I speak as someone who left the *Times* because people a lot like Donald Regan—"He did not know what he did not know"—were always messing with my copy. Not until years later, while watching *Sweet Dreams*, the movie about Patsy Kline, did I realize that I was a country-and-western sort of writer. Whether at the Grand Ole Opry or in some honky-tonk, I'd always sing the same songs, if they let me. When they wouldn't let me, I'd mosey on. I can identify with Noonan, who went from all-news CBS radio to disinformation in Washington, and stuck around long enough to be lip-synched by two different presidents. The White House was her Grand Ole Opry.

She's a dandy maker of phrases, often of sentences, sometimes whole paragraphs. Listen to her justify her job: "A great speech from a leader to the people eases our isolation, breaks down the walls, includes people: It takes them inside a spinning thing and makes them part of the gravity." Listen to her describe the people who got in the way of her doing that job: "What I mean is, when men in politics are together, testosterone poisoning makes them insane." And listen to her on her ideological buddies:

> *Some of the movement conservatives just weren't very…well, the hard-core movement people were so…well, you know how it is with intense people in an intense environment, and so many of these guys are fish who swam upstream and add to that the difficult natures that politics often draws and movements draw, and, and…and add all that up and, well…what you get is a bunch of creepy little men with creepy little beards who need something to seethe on (State Department cookie-pushers! George Bush! the Trilateral Commission!), some hate to live for.*

But for the purposes of her memoir (and her deliverance from ghosting into a more agreeable career) she's invented a literary persona, a sassy crosscircuit of Holden Caulfield and Fran Leibowitz but right-wing smarty-pants too, like *National Review*, with class animus for seasoning, a weakness for the sarcastic, a bratty Irish appetite for grudge, and too many exclamation marks. This persona often leaves her sounding dumber than she ought to, and I'm not talking about her opinions on gun control, abortion, the Sandinistas and the ACLU, at all of which she stamps her foot. I'm talking more about a reflexive yahooism of the kind that rushes to assure us that, even though she owns a copy of Ezra Pound, she doesn't understand a single "Canto."

Likewise, she would like us to think she really believes that all liberals are guilty-rich nitwits who went to Harvard and Yale instead of Fairleigh Dickinson; that all activists on behalf of the homeless are cruel manipulators of the insane; that only Republicans can talk to janitors; that Paul Johnson and Jean-François Revel are intellectual heavyweights; and that George Gilder isn't merely foolish when he blathers about "the humane nature of the free market." To meet Gorbachev, and to tell us only that he looks like "a retired hockey goalie," isn't just to miss the boat of history, but to jump off after it's set sail, thumbing your nose as you drown.

But to succeed in her career move, Noonan will need the Liberal Media Establishment, and so she compensates for her yahooism by doing some surprising damage to a president she says she loves. Thus, Reagan's White House is compared to "a beautiful clock that makes all the right sounds, but when you open it up, there is nothing inside." Of Reagan himself, she says that his intellect was only "slightly superior to average," he didn't hear much of what was said around him but "assumed it was good," and that the battle for his mind "was like the trench warfare of World War I: Never have so many fought so hard for such barren terrain." She even quotes a friend(!) of his: "Behind those warm eyes is a lack of curiosity that is, somehow, disorienting."

So is her memoir, somehow, disorienting. Her real gripe seems to be that *they* messed with her copy. That was my gripe, too, with the *Times.* If you've seen the movie *Reds* you know it was also John Reed's gripe with the Russian Revolution. It always happens to flacks, after which we write for ourselves or die. Peggy, read Patsy's lips: Sweet dreams, pointy-headed light.

ELECTION '88:
LET'S NOT TALK ABOUT IT

DO WE GOTTA HAVE HART?

I ought to be more interested in what Gary Hart thinks about our budget and trade deficits than I am in what he does on his weekends when his wife is out of town, but I'm not. For one thing, he hasn't told us what he thinks about the budget and trade deficits. For another, I'll admit to Mary McCarthy's "prurient avidity for the details of moral defloration." Why else do we read novels? At least since the nineteenth century, novels have been about sex and money, and so is character, which is how we behave when we think that nobody's looking, not even *The Miami Herald.*

Look: I didn't ask Gary Hart to run for president. He is a philanthropist who gives away himself. We are entitled to look a gift horse in its boxer shorts. And it's probably even chastening for journalists to stay up all night on a stakeout, instead of quoting the usual press releases, seizing the usual photo opportunities, or being leaked on by the usual self-serving tipsters and suspect sources, which is the usual dreary stuff of too much Beltway metafiction.

Besides, the details are novelistic, too. You will remember an earlier "new idea" of Hart's. Her name was Marilyn Youngbird. She was the daughter of an Indian medicine man. She said she was Gary's conscience. *He* said he didn't sleep with her, *either*, although gourd dancers, being very "pantheistic," whisked their two sweet bodies with a broom of eagle feathers.

Youngbird, as someone not to sleep with, sounded a lot more interesting than Donna Rice, a biology major who advertised a Miami bar by posing with one bare breast and a Confederate flag. Is this Hart's southern strategy for the regional primary? Just how "neo" can liberalism get?

We hear a great deal about JFK and "womanizing" on the New Frontier. We're also told that JFK's revolving door and musical beds in no way compromised his presidency. Well I've studied Judith Exner's autobiography. What a career in the dumps of macho rubbish—entertainers like Sinatra, mobsters like Sam Giancana, politicians like Jack. How did the Kennedy boys get together in the first place with the mobsters who tried to take out Castro for them? And if the president's idea of himself is that of a swashbuckler, how else does he expect the CIA to behave in Latin America and Southeast Asia? Looking back at the Green Berets, the napalm, the AWAKs and all those gang-bang counterinsurgency scenarios, it seems to me that the Kennedy presidency was a James Bond movie from the Fleming novels he loved so much—witty violence, insolent cool, dry Martinis, brand-name snobbery, killer gadgets, the technological fix, a contempt for women and for other cultures, too: style without substance; history as wet dream. Camelot!

Max Lerner is rumored to have had a fling with Liz Taylor. I once asked a young woman in a seedy dive whether *she* would sleep with Max Lerner. She thought about it for a minute, then replied: "Well, I'd rather fuck him than read him." Unfortunately, we not only have to read our presidents, but they are writing our novels.

Of course, there's a double standard. Nobody mentions Jennifer

Fitzgerald. And not all the money Carl Channell raised to provision the Contras made it to the gallant freedom fighters and their cocaine-running flyboys. The IRS thinks some of that money went to someone described at the very bottom of the jump in mainstream newspaper stories as Channell's "roommate."

Come on, now. When we go to the doctor and lie down on the couch because we can no longer cope, what is it that we talk about? (And never mind that American psychoanalysis has been well-described as "Calvinism in Bermuda shorts.") Gary got a lot of his Hart from the sixties, when everybody seemed to understand that sexuality was the ground of being, and vital sexuality an assurance of the moral life. As critics like Irving Howe have pointed out, this thinking leads to "a psychology of unobstructed need." Anything that gets in our way is cultural neurosis.

Howe then went on to wonder what happens when "the needs and impulses of human beings clash," when "the transfer of energies from sexuality to sociality" doesn't go smoothly. He found "a curious analogue to laissez-faire economics...by means of which innumerable units in conflict with one another achieve a resultant of cooperation. Is there however much reason to suppose that this will prove more satisfactory in the economy of moral conduct than it has in the morality of economic relations?...Against me, against my ideas, it is possible to argue, but how, according to this new dispensation, can anyone argue against my *need*?" Or, say, Rasputin's?

Gary Hart *needs* to be president.

THE "L" WORD

I am a liberal. Being a liberal means always having to say you're sorry. This is because we are insufficiently red in tooth and claw.

In a world of murderous abstractions, scruple inhibits us. We are the children of qualm. Believing as we do in our fuzzy-minded way that people are basically decent and social justice is a good idea and democratic instutitions can do something about the discrepancies between what *is* and *ought* to be, we never go far enough to the bloody end of things, where human sinew's cut to fit the pattern of the state, and our masters wear our skins to bay at the moon. The first thing a Stalin, a Hitler or a Mao does is kill us. On the twentieth-century grid, we are the ultimate waffle.

A liberal sometimes feels ashamed. We could have done more, should have, wanted to, but we were lazy, preoccupied, frightened or just too cozy in our privilege. This is different from self-hatred. I don't hate myself but I'd imagined somebody better. A liberal imagination is rich in possibility, which multiplies the opportunities for action and for disappointment. Even our cultural relativism, so much disdained, is a way of seeing through other pairs of eyes, of dreaming in space and time. The more we imagine, the more we also measure, and often come up short.

So be it. What really amazes me is shamelessness. I intend to vote against it, and all those for whom Original Sin is permission to steal. Bush-league attacks on my sort of liberalism don't bother me; I deserve them; I'm even proud of them. I *am*, in fact, a political enemy of the Vice President for Noriega/Iranscam. But Bush-league attacks on my patriotism I take personally. I know what he means when he says "them," and "card-carrying member of the ACLU," and "Jane Fonda workout book." I pledge no allegiance to the Bush, nor to the pips for whom he squeaks, and they have nothing to tell me about my country that would make me love it more.

Listen to a story. In 1959, when I married into an old New England family, they had their doubts about a bog-Irish would-be novelist and college dropout. I thought of myself, and so did they, as my father's son, the great-grandchild of a nineteenth-century potato famine, a poet-warrior full of Celtic mist and Mexican jumping beans. Never mind that what this amounted to was a grandfather who consorted mysteriously with banks and the law and then just as mysteriously died of sadness during the Depression, before I was born. And a father, who should have been another Dennis Day, on the radio, singing tenor, drinking rye and dying young. (The last I heard of that side of the family was when they wired me cross country for some money to pay for my father's funeral, which is the first I'd known that he was dead. He was always good at keeping a secret. And the rest of them have vanished from the Book of Kells.) Never mind that this Irishness was always bogus, self-induced, a literary persona—some Yeats to go with the fatigue jacket, Joyce in paperback, singing "Danny Boy" on St. Patrick's Day in every saloon on Third Avenue, with the green beer, the green horses and the green cops. A terrible beauty, and so on. Because I wanted to write, I chose to be Irish—translated from the original pre-runic, older than Ogham, a blue-faced Celt, Cuchulain, with the built-in gene for not crossing picket lines.

My more practical mother dragged the paterfamilias of this family away from his diseased elm and his books of hellfire sermons, to knock over half the tombstones in southern New Hampshire till she found the buried body of a relative of *hers*, Captain John Pratt, who'd died fighting on the winning side of the Revolutionary War.

This was embarrassing. Wanting, like most Americans, to invent myself, I'd borrowed the romance of a middle passage, the immigrant dream. Nobody had ever told me we'd been around from the start, bashing Indians; that one of my very own grandmothers had been a member, not of the American Civil Liberties Union, but of the Daughters of the American Revolution. It was a family secret because this grandmother had resigned from the DAR, just like Mrs. Roosevelt, when they wouldn't let Marian Anderson sing in Constitution Hall, in our nation's capital, where I was born, as Born in the USA as you can get. My grandmother never spoke of the DAR again.

I still don't like to talk about it. If they'd known the truth, they might have rushed me for one of the Final Clubs at Harvard and I'd have turned into a social parasite, my own class enemy. I found out about John Pratt too late for him to mean much to me, though it's always nice to have a revolutionary hanging from the family tree. But I found out about my grandmother in time for her to mean a lot. She was an American liberal, and so is my mother, and so are my children.

The children have something else going for them in their bones and gene pool. The New England family into which I married to make them possible had its fair share of closet abolitionists. The parcel of land they settled on, in 1740, would later be a stop on the underground railroad. When one of them died in 1858—I imagine five feet of stringy woman wrapped in Bengal cloth, shovel jawed, poor at curtseying—she left a sum of money to erect a monument over her grave. It is there in the woods to look at, a granite obelisk. On three respective sides are chiseled the names of her great-grandfather's children, her grandfather's children, and her father's children. On the fourth side is inscribed: THIS SIDE OF THE PILLAR IS DEDICATED TO THE SACRED CAUSE OF EMANCIPATION. MAY GOD BLESS IT, AND ALL THE PEOPLE SAY AMEN!

Shall I tell you what American liberalism is all about? It's about the

First Amendment to the Constitution, and Lincoln's Second Inaugural Address, and Thoreau's essay on civil disobedience, and Martin Luther King's "Letter from a Birmingham Jail"—and, of course, the Sermon on the Mount.

GARY REDUX

The other voices in the other room are those of men at cheerful work. They're building my pool table, from scratch. They arrived two hours ago with a do-it-yourself kit, like a gigantic can of Tinkertoys, and instruments of radical surgery, and have been ever since assembling the eight-foot Brunswick Buckingham, with the automatic gully return, from carriage bolts, hex nuts, pan head screws, tie plates, apron corners, machine studs and self-taps. We have been playing billiards in this country since 1565. I can wait another twenty minutes.

I'll explain this pool table, as well as the Victorian gingergread dollhouse, when I feel like it. Right now I'm thinking about the Iowa caucuses. I'm thinking about them because I didn't get a Christmas card from Cuomo. You've heard about this card, quoting Teilhard de Chardin: "All that really matters is devotion to something bigger than ourselves." Not having got one, I don't know whether to be injured in my self-importance or just plain relieved. Years ago, Nelson Algren explained that Mortimer Adler is the Lawrence Welk of the philosophy trade. If Teilhard de Chardin isn't the Lawrence Welk of the theology trade, he is at least its Carlos Castaneda.

For Christmas, instead of the usual odd books and strange music, my wife gave me a Brunswick Buckingham and I gave her a Victorian gingerbread dollhouse. I don't know why, except that we needed something else to think about besides the Iowa caucuses, and I'd always wanted a pool table, and she'd always wanted a dollhouse, and so we exchanged infantilisms. This was ideologically incorrect, according to our professional-feminist daughters. (I forget their names: Enver Hoxha? Kim Il Sung? They fold their little minds like fans.)

What's there to think about the Iowa caucuses, after you've observed the obvious—Jesse Jackson's black; Paul Simon is Mo Udall or Estes Kefauver, only short; Cuomo quotes Teilhard; and Pat Schroeder cries? (Aloise Buckley Heath once pointed out that men commit ten times as many violent crimes as women, kill each other seven times as often, kill themselves four times as often and drop dead of heart at-

tacks at a six-to-one ratio. Whereas, of course, women *cry*. Why do
women cry? Because women are more emotional, that's why.)

Except, of course, there's Gary Hart, who is assembling himself in
the next room with hex nuts and self-taps and apron corners and pan
head screws. Gary is his own Carlos Castaneda, Teilhard de Chardin,
Lawrence Welk and Santa Claus. He gave himself to us again at Christmas, and such New Ideas as a smaller aircraft carrier: some dollhouse.
I intended to ignore him, this time around, but there he was, Monday, all over *The Des Moines Register* and Associated Press, telling us, "I
won't be the first adulterer in the White House." And: "The people in
this country in the last three weeks have been tremendously warm
and accepting." And there was Lee breaking into tears on advising a
reporter that a couple had sent $100 to the Hart campaign that "they
might otherwise have spent on a crib for the baby they were expecting." And I thought of Nixon and Checkers, Charles Van Doren and
the quiz-show scandals, Jack Paar, Johnny Ray, "The Little White
Cloud That Cried," and the rest of the fifties. Really, aren't these people *wallowing* in it?

The professional feminists in my house think so. According to
Hoxha and Il Sung, the lonesome ranger has more holes in his head
than a Brunswick Buckingham. But children go away, and Hart won't.
James Reston, *Times* columnist emeritus, may have explained the sexual politics of Gary Hart better than any feminist: "He treats [the Democratic party] the way he treats his wife: as a personal convenience."

In psychoanalysis, "narcissism" is defined clinically as "erotic grat-
ification derived from admiration of one's own physical or mental at-
tributes." "I want!" cried Henderson the Rain King. So does everybody else except Mario. Midas wanted gold, Richard III wanted a
horse, Citizen Kane wanted a sled, Hitler wanted Poland, Garbo wanted to be left alone. I've always wanted a pool table, my wife a dollhouse, and Gary to be president. Your move, Iowa.

JACKSON FOR PRESIDENT—THE KISS OF DEATH

Jesse Jackson's campaign for the presidency suffered a major blow last
Thursday night, when I said that I would vote for him. This happened
in the living room on my forty-ninth birthday, and the cuckoo
clocked. My wife, my daughter and my mother just sat there, as Ezra

Pound once put it, "cloaked as with a gauze of ether." Spokesmen for the Jackson organization declined comment, though they were bitterly disappointed. I am known in political circles as a Typhoid Johnny. Candidacies start coughing up blood the minute I care about them.

My mother hasn't really been enthusiastic about any candidate for president since 1968, when she was a member of the California delegation to the Democratic convention in Chicago, pledged to a murdered man. My daughter, who majors at Barnard in Gnostic heresies, refuses on principle to vote for anybody Reverend in either party. My wife decided months ago to support Jackson, but she burns with such a gemlike flame that my sudden agreement has wounded her in the purity of her commitment to a losing cause. Even as we speak, she is wondering, like Maud Gonne in the Yeats poem, if there's another Troy for her to burn.

What about "Hymietown"? It's obligatory in every article on Jackson to mention "Hymietown" in the third paragraph, as it used to be obligatory in every article on Bella Abzug to mention "abrasive." I wish he hadn't said it; when people of prominence open their mouths and toads hop out, we *should* be alarmed; it says something about a man when the man says something. For instance, George Bush was quoted by *Time* magazine on February 29, 1988, as having said last fall on a visit to Auschwitz: "Boy, they were big on crematoriums, weren't they?"

But people also change, and sometimes for the better, like Bobby Kennedy. I'm reasonably satisfied with Jackson's prime-time apology at the '84 convention. You might also have noticed that he hasn't tried to capitalize on recent events in Israel. He doesn't have to, of course, because he's been on record as favoring a Palestinian homeland longer than the competition has been on record as thinking at all about the Middle East. Moreover, his calm on this question has managed to up the ambivalence quotient at *The New Republic* and the *Times*, surely a desideratum.

And Jesse would never ask, "Why should we subsidize intellectual curiosity?"—which is what our only president said last month to *Omni* magazine. Nor would he explain to Congress, as Elliott Abrams did the second time around on Contragate, "I never said I had no idea about most of the things you said I said I had no idea about."

Issues? If you don't know where Jesse stands on social programs and defense spending, on abortion and the Third World, on low-income housing, health insurance, day-care, farm foreclosures, tax loopholes, education and the minimum wage, Central America and the Middle East, you haven't been paying attention. Just the other day in Asheville, North Carolina, although the *New York Times* seems to have missed it, he pointed out that the poorest Americans are white *and female*. Jesse stands a little to the left of the rest of them, and feels a whole lot more.

Experience? I'm inclined to think that a leader of the civil rights revolution knows more about this country than any Congressman from Missouri who can't remember how he voted last week, if he did. Eisenhower, before he ran for president, had never even voted. Wendell Wilkie...but you know all this. Experience, often as not, means upward failure. Reagan, after all, was twice the governor of Oz before he became Babar.

Electability? That's never stopped me before. And those whites who voted Jackson into a strong second place in Maine and Minnesota are telling us something, especially those of us on the Left who are always moaning that race prevails over class in American political behavior.

Finally, as usual, there's symbolic politics. It says here in my living room that all politics are symbolic. Symbolic thinking distinguishes us from corn starch, Diet Pepsi, Pringles and Spam. Here's what tipped me:

(1) A friend, a usually cynical network news producer, reports from the primaries with astonishment that "You can *touch* Jesse. He's *real*. The rest of them are holograms."

(2) My wife's students complain that when you ask Jackson a question, "he answers with a *poem*!" Exactly. To object to Jesse Jackson's poetry is like objecting to Toni Morrison's ghosts.

(3) Another friend, an unrepentant atavistic Sixties activist still in business on the West Coast, writes about Brian Willson, the Vietnam vet who lost his legs in Concord, California, when the train sped up on the tracks where he sat trying to block weapons on their way to the Contras. When Willson got out of the hospital and back to the tracks on artificial legs, the only candidate for president who walked with him was Jesse, as Jesse was the only candidate in Washington for the April 1986 peace demonstration, and the only candidate at the October 1987 rally for gay rights, and the only one to go shake hands with AIDS patients. That's my kind of demagoguery.

Yes. Well, Jesse's the mariner, and I've had plenty of practice as an albatross.

DESPAIRING OF DUKE

Back in the nineteenth century, before there were TV commercials, political parties published comic books to cloud the minds of the semi-literate. This year Bush and Dukakis spent almost $40 million each on a comic book equivalent: electronic cartoons. These cartoons talked to one another. The great debate on defense, for instance, began with Dukakis in a tank. To this photo op, George Bush was soon to reply with a cartoon, making fun of Dukakis in a tank. And now, on the eve of the vote, about the same time that Mike Dukakis is rediscovering Harry S. Truman, he massively retaliates with a cartoon of his own, in which he turns off Bush and the television set. It is, of course, too late. Any chance Duke had against the Willie Hortons was squandered in what should have been his finest hour, when Bernard Shaw asked him how he'd feel about a death penalty if his wife were raped. This was the moment for Duke to show us he was something more than a Liberal Robocop, and he blew it, as he would blow a second opportunity with Ted Koppel on *Nightline*, a third with Tom Brokaw on NBC, and a fourth, with Shaw again, on CNN. He had two minutes. Imagine what a Winston Churchill, a Charles De Gaulle, or even a John F. Kennedy would have made of those minutes. Hell, you don't have to be that fancy. Imagine what you or I might do, at least the second time around:

> *It's a disgusting question, Mr. Shaw. It plays on nightmare. Sure, I'd want to kill, in rage and fear. Maybe I'd kill him, or he'd kill me. But I'm a man, not the law, not a government. I want my government to be better than I am, not Charles Bronson, not* Death Wish. *I'm against the death penalty not just because there's no evidence whatsoever that it deters violent crime. And not just because the ones we kill are usually those who can't afford expensive lawyers to get them off. I'm against the death penalty because it's self-corrupting, after all the months and years of psychiatrists, judges, juries, courts of appeal and tabloid gloating, to kill in cold blood, to send a stranger—the state executioner—to gas, fry, hang by the neck or stick a needle in the arm of another stranger, to kill in the name of all of us, beyond mercy and grace. We are pretending to know everything about the mystery of life and death, and I don't know everything and neither do you. I refuse to believe a mistake-proof state has perfect knowledge in final things. That's what we've got God for.*

That bite of sound, read aloud, takes a minute.

But Duke is lost, and so may be our scruples about capital punishment. Now that Tom Hayden out in California has decided *he's* in favor of the death penalty, just like our bloodthirsty Justice Department, I hardly have anyone left to talk to except that Thomist philosopher Mario Cuomo. But I am unmanly, anyway. This became clear the other night while I was watching TV, mainly to look at Greta Scacchi in *The Coca-Cola Kid*. I don't know why I love Greta Scacchi (you may have seen her with Olivier in *The Ebony Tower* or with Gabriel Byrne in *Defense of the Realm*) but I do, hopelessly, in the same way I loved, at age eleven, Cecile Aubrey in *The Black Rose*. They arrest my development and throw away the key.

Time out for art-crit: We are supposed to grow up from, say, Vermeer's *Head of a Young Girl* and Van der Weyden's *Portrait of a Lady* and David's *Mlle. Charlotte du Val d'Ognes* to, ah, Botticelli's Venus, Rembrandt's Bathsheba and Delacroix's Liberty, or perhaps the portraits by Renoir, Manet, Modigliani and Holbein the Younger of Jeanne Samary, Berthe Morisot, Jeane Hefuterne and Lady Elizabeth Parker. In our decadence we will admire Utamaro's *Poem of the pillow* and Kuniyoshi's *Flowers with abundant benefits*. Not me. Nor am I sorry.

Anyway, instead of Greta Scacchi I was looking at a commercial for the National Rifle Association. A bunch of red-breasted Bambi-blasters stood around the salt lick, swapping Elizabeth Taylor jokes. They *belonged*, and we could, too. By joining the NRA, we entitled ourselves to an I D card, a magazine subscription, a window decal, a shooter's cap and an "accidental death or dismemberment" insurance policy. Think of that.

It's not that I've never known the heat of the hunt and the thrill of the kill. I was the first little boy on my block with a Lone Ranger atomic bomb ring; you peeked in at a color photo of the mushroom. And only a year after I fell in love with Cecile Aubry, I was sent for the summer to a hunting and fishing lodge in Wisconsin. We bashed bats; we menaced the bats from their rafters with broomsticks and then, as they flapped from wall to wall, we bashed them with tennis rackets. Bat-sonar picked up only the holes in the rackets and missed the deadly catgut grid.

But bat-bashing was kids' stuff compared to the stalking of the porcupine. The lodge housed a pair of Labrador retrievers. They went into the woods to bother a porcupine. They came back with quills in their muzzles. Grim men in their checkerboard motley took up arms in the forest primeval. I found the fierce porcupine, hiding up a tree. I shot it twice with a .22. It fell at my feet, a sweet kill. I can't remember whether we ate it. No bird sang.

How does Robin Williams put it? "Kill a small animal, drink a lite beer."

I don't belong to this club, this freemasonry of Bambi-blasters. Examining their faces, I thought I saw James Earl Ray, but Mario wasn't there, nor Vermeer, nor, of course, any women. Once these manly bigshots have run out of Bambis, porcupines and Moby Ducks, after the Dr. Kings and the Bobby Kennedys, they'll hunt Greta Scacchi, Cecile Aubry and Mlle. Charlotte du Val d'Ognes. And next they'll be after Jane Fonda. They've always wanted to bag women instead of painting them. Hell, they'd really like to waste a unicorn or hippogriff.

"Man," wrote Joseph de Maistre, "demands everything at once: the entrails of the lamb to play on his harp, the bones of the whale to stiffen the virgin's corset, the most murderous tooth of the wolf to polish light works of art, the defenses of the elephant to fashion a child's toy: his tables are covered with corpses."

I will never belong. I am dismembered, the last American wimp. But you knew that.

THE TURKEY SHOOT

GULF WAR (1): SEND QUAYLE

Really, I'd rather be writing about the January 21 editorial in *The New Republic* denouncing Salman Rushdie for having tried, like Galileo, to save his own life. A decade ago, in *Midnight's Children*, Rushdie prophesied: "Washing will hide him—voices will guide him! Friends mutilate him—blood will betray him…jungle will claim him…tyrants will fry him…He will have sons without having sons! He will be old before he is old! *And he will die…before he is dead.*" Some of this should happen to some of the editors of *The New Republic*.

But I sit down to type on D-Day of a war already endorsed by *The New Republic*. In several hours we will leave for a vigil at the United Nations. We will have to wait awhile before we vote Bill Green out of our congressional district. This is somebody else's novel.

Saturday night at the Mexican restaurant, old friends, who could have been counted on ordinarily to talk about our children and our careers and the burning leaves and cellulose we stuck into our food-holes, talked instead about oil and Islam, surgical strikes and Vietnam, a volunteer army and the Cuban Missile Crisis, Wimp Factors and Losing Face. In my opinion, Losing Face is preferable to losing an arm, a leg, an eye, or your life, but I'm a retro peacenik.

We were joined later on that night by a Barnard senior and a Columbia senior. These two attractive people had found each other— let's hear it for Natural Selection!—and intended to go forth, after their May graduations, to teach poetry and history in a high school somewhere. They wanted to know if they were right to be scared. In my opinion, all of us ought to be scared when men in suits play nuclear chicken on the all-news cable network.

Sunday morning at CBS, Charles Kuralt wanted to know if I thought there'd really be war. Not, of course, if Charles Kuralt were in charge. But he isn't. If there is a war, next Sunday I will be talking about Pentagon restrictions on reporting from the desert instead of the new public TV series on the sixties. In my opinion, talking about the sixties would be peachy-keen.

Monday, the National Public Radio people for whom I make literary remarks called to ask that I stand by to be profound about the Middle East. Then Ed Diamond, at *New York* magazine, called to say the French were up to something. I turned on CNN; already the French proposal (Saddam withdraws; we talk about Palestine) had been turned down by the Fabulous Bush-and-Baker Boys. Then my wife came home to report that children at her school were terrified; they imagined terrorist bombs exploding in American movie theaters. Then I called *our* children, in Madison and Berkeley: just counting, to make sure they're all there, that they still add up.

Do you know why Saddam is worse than Hitler? Because, says our only president, "I was told that Hitler did not stake people out against potential military targets and that he did, indeed, respect—not much else, but he did, indeed respect the legitimacy of the embassies. So we've got some differences there."

How about those Saudis? Haven't they bought the very best army available for their petrodollars? And aren't you glad to be in bed with Hafez-el Assad, who brought us Pan Am 103?

Already, the "Wild Weasels" of our 35th Tactical Fighter Wing are in the cockpits of their F-4Gs, ready to take out Iraqi radar and surface-to-air artillery. Already, computer models at the Pentagon are churning out body-bag estimates that Les Aspin can live with. Already, the nine large-screen TV sets at Mickey Mantle's Sports Bar are warming up for midnight. "This is the first time in my life I've heard of an actual deadline for war," says John Levy, the co-owner of Micky Mantle's: "It's fascinating, like football or basketball."

Sanctions are boring. What's the point of a deadline, anyway, if nobody dies? Not me, of course. My son was born in Berkeley in 1962. I'd been reading Jean Larteguy's novels about Dienbienphu; my son calls himself the First Berkeley War Protest. Nobody I knew then went to Vietnam. None of the children of anybody I know now will go to the Middle East. Whether we are talking about a volunteer army or a rigged draft, it's pretty much the same proletariat of blood.

What I'd really like to see, by the light of tonight's new moon, is Dan Quayle and the editors of *The New Republic* on their way to Baghdad in a whirlybird brought to us by the same gung-ho can-do cost-plus industrial knowhow that perfected the Stealth bomber and the Navy A-12.

GULF WAR (2): BLOODY FARCE

To get our minds off the war, we thought about the Big Bang and we went to a farce. We also went to protest rallies, but they don't count. After each protest rally, the crazy generals on the networks explain that our qualms, which shouldn't have been launched in the first place because the New World Order has argument superiority, were shot down anyway, by anti-qualm Patriot absolutes. In my living room, I'm beginning to think I need a gas mask.

Still, we can't stay home every night in the cyberspace of War Chat, the "virtual reality" of computer simulations where nobody ever really dies, of presidential babytalk and military technoblab and network fanspeak and Baghdad babblecast. And so we left the Tigris and the Euphrates for The Brearley and the farce.

I'm the spouse of a Brearley teacher. I've gone to student productions of plays and musicals for fifteen years. I've never laughed harder than I did last Thursday night, which seems insane when you consider that we abandoned our seats during both intermissions to climb the stairs and stand outside on East Eighty-third Street huddled around transistor radios to listen in on missiles falling on Tel Aviv, after which we sat back down to laugh some more at the slapstick of Brearley and Collegiate juniors and seniors in Michael Frayn's *Noises Off*.

In *Noises Off*, actors purport to stage a play called *Nothing On*, while their private lives are falling apart. We see the first act three times, once on the backside of the set. By the third time through, the farce on stage and the farce behind the scenes are indistinguishable. Even the props turn on the players and bite their necks with double meanings. Dan Walker, director-in-residence at The Brearley, had warned me by mail that I'd enjoy myself. He'd no way of knowing that when I enjoy myself I'm compromised in my seriousness, damaged in the depths of my morbidity. What right had I to chuckle myself sick at Elizabeth Brown's delicious impersonation of Frederick Fellowes/Philip Brent, while Saddam foamed and Bush frothed? Was this Weimar?

Of course, Saturday at the United Nations, Mario Cuomo starred in his own farce. And Ruth Messinger was booed for insufficient bloodthirstiness. We've already seen the first act dozens of times, and it's going to be a very long night at the Mesopotamian theater.

Which brings up the Big Bang. When in doubt, I go intergalactic, like the novels of Doris Lessing. It was easy last week because the American Astronomical Society met in Philadelphia. The papers were full of reports from the front lines of particle-physics theory. Whatever the COBE probe (Cosmic Background Explorer) found in Deep Space, it hasn't proved anything at all about neutrinos in a void and quasars at the edge of time; about "cold dark matter" and "cosmic afterglow"; about "great walls" of galactic "clumps" or the "unseen mass" of a "great attractor."

What these Big Bang astronomers, astrophysicists and cosmologists want to know is: (1) Is the universe mostly WIMPs ("weakly interacting yet massive particles"); and (2) has this universe achieved Omega, at which point the average density equals critical density, or about six hydrogen atoms per cubic meter, meaning that the whole shebang is poised perfectly "between an endless expansion and an ultimate collapse"? You would think there'd be more doubts about a theory that posits the beginning of time and space some ten *or* twenty billion years ago.

I mean, which is it? Give or take *ten billion years*? Plasma physicist

Eric J. Lerner will argue in a new book in April that cosmologies come into fashion in phase with ideologies; that the Big Bang death-of-the-universe cosmology became popular at the same time as social ideas like "zero growth" and the End of Progress, whereas notions of an "inflationary universe" made their comeback in the go-go eighties, like junk bonds. I'd'like to believe him, but I'm often wrong. I thought, for instance, that sanctions might work in the Middle East, with some patience; that we had quarantined the bacillus, cut off his life-support of oil revenues; that the community of nations had found a way, maybe even a model, for punishing aggression without bombs or body bags.

But Martin Luther King is dead. Nonviolence has never been fashionable. The day after the elections we doubled our troops in Saudi Arabia and drew a line in the sand. We will Big-Bang Baghdad into WIMPs or cold dark matter. And in the bloody laser snowcrash afterglow, when the cloud cover finally clears and the actual—as opposed to the theoretical—dying begins, political debate will be seen to have been, as always, a farce.

GULF WAR (3): GLITTERDOME

Some background to suggest there's nothing new under the desert sun—not even military censorship. War correspondents were invented in the middle of the nineteenth century, just in time for the Charge of the Light Brigade. They were followed, immediately, by the invention in England of government counterpropaganda and official censorship. In our own Civil War, Lincoln's Cabinet fiddled with the casualty figures, and a *Herald-Tribune* reporter was told he'd be shot if he didn't turn over his copy. British reporters weren't allowed to report the incompetence, the atrocities and the concentration camps of the Boer War. About World War I, no newspaper told the truth—a slaughter of millions in the trenches—though H. G. Wells and Arthur Conan Doyle flacked for the military. The American military flatly denied first reports of radiation sickness in Hiroshima. No one wanted to publish Martha Gellhorn's early reports from Vietnam. To be sure, there have been war correspondents who made up stories for their editors, or who decided on their own to protect the public from bad news or had a rooting interest in one side or another and suppressed news. Hemingway, for instance, went easy on the Republicans in the Spanish Civil War. There have been gloryhounds, and danger-junkies, and even some reporters who were also spies. But since 1856 the basic story has been reporters trying to do their job and governments trying to shut them up. There has never, however, been a war that looks like this one.

Live, from the Al Rashid in downtown Baghdad, Luke Skywalker and The Tracers. From palmy Dhahran, the "Wild Weasels" of the 35th Tactical Fighter Wing and Raytheon's own anti-missile Patriot missile. From the columbarium at the Pentagon: Pac-Man and Nintendo briefings. On the screen in your face by remote control, a round-the-clock high-tech, fuzz-grunge telethon, in weird green cyberspace; a seamless web of SCUD alerts bounced off starfish satellites, unlicensed spin-doctors, whey-faced anchorpeople and Hertz rent-a-generals, into microreceivers in the fillings in our teeth. After the pregame show, the interviews with coaches and players, the color analysis, instant replay and halftime stats, the video toasters and the neurojacks, all that's missing is the Game itself, the sudden death in overtime.

I hate using sports metaphors for the real world. I'd prefer to talk about what we're seeing on TV as the raw material of journalism, a gathering of bits and pieces before a story's written, a talking out loud to editors and producers in search of narrative and coherence. But what we're getting between glitzy commercials for "smart" bombs and dumb Arabs is the sort of filler that clogs up ears during an endless baseball rain delay, a stalling technoblab. Inside this glitterdome we are poked, twitched, probed, jolted and hypnotized into believing that we actually see a war, when 90 percent of it's hidden, like Iraq's air force and mobile missile launchers. We miss not only the action but the *meaning*: historical memory and critical intelligence. Nor will the Pentagon help us, with its pools, nannies and pruning shears— and euphemisms like "collateral damage" when what it really means is dead people. On television, except in Israel, nobody ever seems to die, as if the *Washington Post* hadn't already reported what refugees on Jordan's border are saying about Baghdad and Basra and Kuwait; as if the body bags aren't already on their way to Dover Air Force Base in Delaware. What made Vietnam different wasn't the carnage; carnage is what wars have *always* been about. It was the film-at-eleven of that carnage that turned the public's stomach. That's why nobody waging a war wants any more Vietnams in our living rooms. When we know what it looks like, we don't want to do it. This one's just begun. In the primetime to come, beware of magic shows, of Disneyland.

GULF WAR (4): WHATEVER HAPPENED TO CIVILIZATION?

Whether Ramsey Clark is right about thousands of Iraqi civilians dead in Basra, it occurs to me that Basra, according to one school of thought, was the original Garden of Eden. It's also where Sindbad the Sailor took off to find his floating islands and monstrous fish, serpents and diamonds, rocs and rhinoceri, cannibals and talking apes. We're likewise hitting on Abraham's birthplace and Jonah's tomb and Nebuchadnezzar's fiery furnace. So long, Babylon and Ninevah, Samarra and Ur. Not to mention Uruk, where all of us started writing newspaper columns.

I've never been to Basra, Baghdad, Cairo, Damascus or, for that matter, Mecca. I've been only to Jerusalem, where my head hurt from all that history, religion, beauty and death.

And that had been between assaults on the Wailing Wall and Haram al-Sharif: gunfire in the Muslim compound in 1982; the plot to blow up the mosques in 1985. It was possible on a single day to spend the afternoon at the Dome of the Rock, looking down; an evening hour at the Wall, looking up; to still have time for dinner in East Jerusalem, and be back at the swimming pool at the King David before you heard a ram's horn. Two religions are on top of each other, a third next door, archeologists digging underneath, and what they've opened is a vein. Solomon built the first temple; Babylonians destroyed it. Herod built the second; Romans did it dirt. The Wall is all that's left, propping up the plateau with the Mosque of Omar, built by Greek slaves. From the rock where the gold dome sits, the Prophet went to heaven on a white horse. When the Crusaders came in the eleventh century, the Muslims fled to the roof of the Dome, where they were slaughtered anyway. Inside the Dome, as if inside a clock, under the golden mosaics and gaudy Ottoman tile work, there's something scary. Let your eye go into an arcade, stare at a vinescroll. What it sees are the insignia of vanquished empires, the breastplates, crows and double-winged diadems of Byzantium and Sassanid. In stockingfeet, you get the creeps. The Dome is a trophy case: Look what Daddy brought back from his Holy War. They have been throwing rocks at prophets in this desert for 3,000 years. Only the Uzis and the napalm are contemporary.

Like most of us, I'm dangerously ignorant. Where, for example, is Yemen? Just south of Saudi Arabia, in fact, but still a stranger. We cut off aid to this pauperized Arab country when they abstained from backing us at the UN in the good old days last fall when all we said we wanted was Kuwait, before we upped the ante to *off satanic Saddam*, before we decided that a ground war was preferable to talking *ever* about the Palestinians. And all I know about this country is what I read in books like Eric Hansen's *Motoring with Mohammed: Journeys to Yemen and the Red Sea.*

It sounds exotic. Drop in on the fabulous capital city of San'a, with a call to prayer from a white minaret; gingerbread fantasy and geometric squiggle; a sawtooth pattern, a zigzag frieze and the nippled domes of Ottoman mosques; a restaurant lunch like a rugby scrummage and a bathhouse rubadub over slow fires fed by cow skulls, old rubber thongs and worn-out truck tires. Sit in the Cafeteria of Hope and wait for a call that never comes from the Slave of God. See at dawn a white dove, a dervish and a beggar in a wheelbarrel. Motor with a guy named Mohammed who'd rather shop for sheep than stop for sights. Stop at Zabid, a twelfth-century center for Koranic studies; and Yafrus, the original home of the Kabbala, as well as a hangout for Sufi pharmacists; and Barakesh, to get shot at in the 1,500-year-old calcite ruins.

Meet people at weddings or on fishing boats: eccentric Orientalists; French jailbirds; "Fingernail Factory" security cops; Peace Corps volunteers building public toilets, paleontologists who "chortle over globular stomatopoda in the way some men discuss women's breasts"; and little boys playing darts with discarded hypodermic syringes. Kill an afternoon with medical students, a water pipe and some *oud* music, chewing the mildly narcotic *qat*. Go to prison and find out that Islamic justice is subtler than the West supposes: "Yemenis, like other devout Moslems, recognize five types of human behavior. According to the Koran, an act is obligatory, permitted, neutral, reprehensible, or prohibited. There are no other possibilities."

Of course the off-shore islands, the border areas, the archeological sites and the oil fields are off-limits for security reasons. They might be training camps for the PLO. The Saudis sponsor a lot of border trouble. The Russians are said to off-load military supplies somewhere near Salif. The goat smugglers are also smuggling assault rifles, for civil war in Ethiopia.

I didn't know any of this because I don't know much at all about the Middle East that I'm so busy bombing back into the Stone Age, before the first city and the first wheel, both of which, you may remember, happened in Mesopotamia.

GULF WAR (5): HOW TO LOVE AN ARAB

Sunday's text was supposed to have been a Monday night TV movie, called *Long Road Home*, about the westward trek of the Dust Bowl dispossessed in 1937, in jalopies instead of prairie schooners, from bank foreclosures on their farms to stoop-labor and piecework pay and penal servitude in the picking fields of California. I'd use this text to opinionize on John Steinbeck, Edward R. Murrow and Cesar Chavez. I'd remember that my own children had been old enough to read before they finally asked, "Dad, what's a grape?"

Then I'd wonder out loud why unions show up so seldom on primetime television, and only if they're corrupt. I'd tie this to the union-busting Reagan years, the deregulation of greed. I'd mention air traffic controllers, Pittston coal miners, Hormel meat packers, Eastern Airlines mechanics, TWA flight attendants, Greyhound bus drivers and the nine unions on strike against the *Daily News*. Japan gets along without these troublemakers, and so did the nonprofit police states in Eastern Europe, before Solidarity. If the people are hungry, let them eat grapes.

This opinion was written down Thursday, tape-packaged Friday, TelePromptered Saturday and canceled Sunday, because of war. For six hours Sunday I sat in the War Room at CBS News, trying to form another opinion. Looked down on by banks of monitors and Middle East maps and clocks that told me the time in Tel Aviv and Dhahran, I envied General Michael Dugan his magic Madden pencil. In the very cerebellum, the synaptic cleft, of a modern communications giant, I scribbled on my Prompter copy. In this wilderness of smoke and mirrors, it was a mercy they didn't call on me. Bouncing off my own satellites, I would have been part of the problem.

The problem, it seems to me, is how to be a good citizen when they don't give you enough computertime or cyberspace to think. Thursday night, I'd gone to Riverside Church to hear Dan Ellsberg be optimistic about the Soviet peace proposal. Friday afternoon, I'd gone to a meeting of media types, peace movement people and academicians, at *The Nation*, only to be told that Bush had already set a deadline. Saturday morning of "High Noon," who had the leisure to compare the terms of a Soviet three-week plan with an American twenty-four-hour ultimatum, before the digital countdown started on CBS, before ABC watched London's Big Ben strike, ah, er, *five o'clock?*

World War I began after Serbia accepted all but one of Austria's conditions. The "unacceptable" condition was that Austria conduct its own investigation, on Serbian soil, into who killed the archduke. Still, the UN Security Council was in session, wasn't it, even as the oil burned? And Gorby was on the hot line. And Tariq Aziz was rumored to have said... "Saturday Night Live": a ground war. I went to bed and Schwarzkopf didn't. I'd lost my grapes.

Sunday, then, there was nothing left to think about, was there? The way we think is that we gather information, consult experience, feel and reflect, make distinctions and connections, arrive at some moral intelligence, then decide on a course of action. In such a syntax, there are parentheses and subordinate clauses. But deadlines, ultimata, countdowns, "unconditionals" are all exclamation marks. We're slapped, twitched and jazzed into impatience and expectancy: The action-adventure! The adrenaline overload! After which, we're promptly polled. The war had begun without us, and the best we could hope for was death in single digits, and we sought coherence from raw data, and we tried to imagine through the grid of multinational censorships whatever story they were writing in blood on the dunes, and who needs, not now, another opinion?

Especially since, as Charles Kuralt kept reminding us Sunday, and William Safire would confirm in Monday's *Times*, the decision had been made to go two weeks before we went. There had never been the slightest chance Bush would change his mind. Even if we'd had time to think, it wouldn't have mattered what we thought. All that diplomacy just got in the way, requiring what Safire calls "white lies"—to the meddlesome Gorby and to the rest of us, citizen-patsies.

Monday after reading Safire, I had a lot of work to do—books to read, articles to write, bills to pay, apologies to tender, doubts to snuff. Instead I went to the movies, to *The Silence of the Lambs* that afternoon, to a preview screening of *The Doors* that night. I forgave myself for this irresponsibility because it happened to be my birthday. But in fact it was time to form, with the cookie cutter, a whole new batch of opinions from a brand-new batter of subjects. For instance, in *Dances with Wolves*, Kevin Costner wants to be an Indian. We know this because he cross-dresses. This is what happens to Americans. After the land grab and the slave auction, after the Gatling gun and the lynch mob, we always fall in love with the very culture we've dispossessed—with the beads and the blues. It happened to us again in Asia. We'll probably love the *idea* of Arabs once we've killed enough of them.

GULF WAR (6): THE SOFTWARE IN THE SYSTEM

Although I really want to talk about India—where I just spent ten days contending with monkeys, goats, camels, bears, sacred cows, sacred art and secular intellectuals—India will have to wait a week. Why not, for once, be relevant? This is a newspaper, after all. It is, in fact, the newspaper that broke the bulldozers-in-the-desert story. The bulldozers-in-the-desert story excited lots of comment in Bombay and Delhi, most of which missed the point.

I mean, so what if our First Mechanized Infantry Division attached bulldozer blades to their Abrams tanks, rolled parallel to the Iraqi trenches, and buried the enemy alive? This may have violated one or another nitpicking Geneva Convention. And perhaps some journalist would have said so at the time, if journalists had been permitted to accompany the tanks and file any copy. And I'm surprised there's been so little follow-up in the watchdog press, no sidebars—they must have *practiced* stuffing the Saddams, mustn't they have?

But war is hell. What war isn't, not even in the Middle East, is *Lawrence of Arabia*, the best movie ever made about sand. We've always prettied up our wars; otherwise, no one would go. In *The Face of Battle*, John Keegan made fun of our storybook picture of Agincourt:

> *It is pre-Raphaelite, perhaps better a Medici Gallery print battle, a composition of strong verticals and horizontals, and a conflict of rich dark reds and Lincoln greens against fishscale greys and arctic blues. It is a school outing to the Old Vic, Shakespeare is fun,* son-et-lumiere, *Lawrence Olivier in armour battle; it is an episode to quicken the interest of any schoolboy ever bored by a history lesson, a setpiece demonstration of English moral superiority and a cherished ingredient of a fading national myth.*

But Agincourt, really, was an abattoir, with sword and lance. Waterloo, too, was a slaughterhouse, with rifle and musket. The Somme was our first "multiple-missile war," with machine guns and toxic-gas particle projectors. Whether we go to battle on top of an elephant, hoping to behead the enemy, or in the belly of a tank, intending to bury him, our bloody business is the same. It's always incredibly noisy, and we're always terribly afraid. We're also, traditionally, drunk on mead or doped on mushrooms; and we would run away if we weren't afraid of our own officers; and we'd surrender if we weren't afraid the Other would eat our parts for breakfast.

One of the nice things about the Navy is that, in the middle of so much water, you can't run away. The rest is just painters and poets. According to Shakespeare:

> *For I must go where lazy Peace*
> *Will hide her drowsy head;*
> *And, for the sport of kings, increase*
> *The number of the dead.*

How much do you suppose it mattered to the average Iraqi—they were mostly peasant conscripts and reservists in those trenches—whether he was buried alive or found himself on the wrong end of a Standoff Land-Attack Missile, with a "walleyed" video data link to its 500-pound warhead? Or crushed, asphixiated, incinerated by one of our Fuel Air Explosives, a fireball out of a vapor cloud? Or the target of a Multiple Rocket Launch System with its 950 antipersonnel "bomblets" and its 8,000 antipersonnel fragmentation grenades? Whether he had to sit still for a laser-guided, or a "slurry," or a "cluster," or a "penetration" bomb; the Rockeye II or the Tomahawk cruise? How about 15,000 pounds of ammonium-nitrate "Daisy Cutter," dropped from the bowels of a Big Blue 82? In your face, raghead.

Beneath the cyberpunk slanguage of the microsofties, the computer chippies, the sonic boomers and the circuit bores of the American Military Industrial Occult, on the road to Basra, he's still dead: the software in the system.

Maybe what bothers us about the bulldozers is that we bought the Pentagon cover story of a Gulf War against *real estate*. We heard so much about "surgical strikes," we must have thought we were going to a hospital. But 93 percent of the bombs we dropped on the Iraqis were "dumb" instead of "smart"; they were *not* precision-guided. Welcome to "collateral damage." By whatever means, wars are for killing people. That's the whole idea.

In India, it occurred to me that, ever since Hiroshima, everybody we have killed, all those people, by whatever means, have been, happenstantially, yellow and brown. We've gone easy on the melanin-deprived. Now *there's* a story.

TAKING BACK THE NIGHT

The women began to gather in Battery Park in the late afternoon last Thursday, with bedrolls, sleeping bags and backpacks. They said hello to the Portosan, which they called the Jane. They ran ropes through the branches of the trees and hung exhortations. They painted butterflies on sheets and hung those, too, like harps and shields. Like Bedouins, they pitched a tent.

Just in time for the first of the hungry neighborhood children, the women laid tables with bread, cheese, mixed nuts, Evian water, apples and bananas. These children do not belong to these women, but one of the things that women do is feed children, after which the children blow up balloons and kick a soccer ball.

I am variously a stranger: the only male, the single "media" representative, and I won't be spending the night because I have to go home and watch the basketball game and worry about Fiji.

These women (a playwright, a nurse, a stock-market analyst, a college professor, teachers of high school and Sunday school, secretaries, grandmothers) have spent three nights in a city park every year for the past four years. They belong to Anonymous Women for Peace, or Chelsea Against Nuclear Destruction United (CANDU), or both. They "Camp for Peace." Usually, they camp in Madison Square Park, but they were in Battery Park on Thursday night to hook up with last weekend's Peace Flotilla to signify their opposition to nuclear missiles in New York Harbor.

Yes, of course, a peacenik sleepover, a radical pajama party...but you weren't there. Perhaps instead you were playing poker or adultery in the Hamptons. And I wasn't there myself for a while. The women had formed a circle on the lawn, a tribal wheel. I felt irrelevant and impertinent, and so I went away, past the monument raised on the occasion of the seventy-fifth anniversary of the Battle of Manila Bay, down to the waterfront to talk to the gulls. A three-masted sloop named *Petrel* tacked in the lap of the Statue of Liberty. Did you know that they leave poems at the black wall of the Vietnam Memorial in Washington, D.C., as if it were for Wailing?

When I came back, the women invited me to join their wheel. They filled out medical forms for the nurse, in case of emergency. They planned an action for the morning rush hour to remind stalled motorists what it might be like to try to evacuate the city at the threat of nuclear attack. They agreed on no drugs and no alcohol; this was not the Hamptons. They organized litter pickup and security shifts. (Some of the men who care about these women will show up later, to stand watch around the park until dawn. Last year, after a heavy rain, the outside violence came from rats instead of people. But these women seemed capable of taking care of themselves, as they had taken care of everything else.)

At nine-fifteen, the women lit candles. We walked through the park to the water. Ships moved on engines of light, like capsized hotels, huge electrified sugar cubes. At the seawall the women made another circle of their flames. And then they told one another why they were there, where they'd come from and what they hoped for. This wasn't a media event, a photo opportunity, a levitation of the Pentagon. Nor was it, as in China's Cultural Revolution, a struggle meeting, a Speaking Bitterness. It was a gathering of fugitives—reaching out from what they knew in their separate solitudes to make a community of conscience, to ease into their witness and their signifying. Besides me, the only one who was watching was Admiral Dewey, safely dead.

Except: As the women spoke, there was a saxophone softly down the way. It belonged to a black man with a snap-brim hat, a Bolshevik goatee and a leather jacket full of moon-peelings—a perfect dream-dude. He played as the women talked, a counterpoint, and only stopped when they started singing "We Shall Overcome." Then he came over to ask, "Why are you singing *my* song?" The women explained why, and who they knew themselves to be. "Peace," he agreed and returned to his sax.

Well, this was a little too good to be true, which is exactly what we need a whole lot more of, and I was there with my wallet-sized reporter's notebook, and I missed my basketball game because it was wonderful to see this weave of women affirming themselves, and to be around for a while as they took back the night from the predators, and when they went into their Bedouin tent under the harps and shields, one of the feelings I felt was envy.

BUCHANAN KNOWS WHAT
HE DOESN'T LIKE

My favorite theater critic, *Newsday*'s Linda Winer, found herself last week in a place one imagines she'd least like to be of all the world's swampy recesses—in bed with Pat Buchanan. Both of them want to abolish the National Endowment for the Arts: Winer, because it's become so compromised and politicized as to have outlived any usefulness; Buchanan, because he sees it as a sanctuary for people who are subsidized by the taxpayer to do dirty things to one another.

Permit me a passionate dissent. It is the obligation of the men and women in worthy institutions in foul weather to hunker down and ride out the storm. It is the obligation of the rest of us to articulate that worthiness, to fight for every hank of hair and splinter of bone—even the knee that jerks and the bleeding heart.

The revenge of Jesse Helms on art that scares him is nothing new. Helms doesn't think of himself, of course, as a mullah or commissar. He'd just rather the government didn't waste its money encouraging art that offends him, when that money could be better spent subsidizing the tobacco barons. But he's also point man for everybody who believes the Feds shouldn't spend a dime on weird people like artists who, anyway, ought to behave themselves or suffer for it. The explanation for Pat Buchanan may be more complicated: Just what is it he's afraid of, under his bed? Maybe he's afraid he'll go to prison and meet Marlon Riggs.

Except briefly during the Great Depression, our government has supported the arts only, oddly, since Richard Nixon. And ever since Nixon, not so oddly, bureaucrats who determine the pattern of that support—to libraries and museums, symphony orchestras and repertory theaters, companies of dancers and publishers of poetry—have been looking anxiously over their shoulders at Big Brothers like Helms or Buchanan. I know because I was one of those bureaucrats.

They were happy part-time years, first as a member of the literature panel of the National Endowment for the Arts, and later as chairman of that panel, reporting to the National Council on the Arts. We met mostly in Washington or New York, but I remember Berkeley, Calif, where paranoia against Easterners like me ran amok, even though I'd gone to college there. And Savannah, Ga., where we were asked to admire the house where Conrad Aiken's father murdered Conrad

Aiken's mother. And San Antonio, Tex., where Rosalind Russell rode a barge downriver, and six mariachi bands trailed us from room to room in a hacienda where the shower stalls were big enough to stable horses, and Clint Eastwood and Eudora Welty took us to a Dixieland jazz joint.

But mostly I remember long smoky hours in hot little rooms devising programs that would put poets into schools, novelists on radio, paperbacks in bookmobiles. We were trying to keep difficult people from starving because we believed these difficult people at their difficult craft would ultimately transfigure us. Think of it as seeding for a Gross National Product of mystery and magic. It was guesswork, but a nation dreams itself in its literature. Who knew where the next shock of recognition would come from, what farm or barrio, houseboat or mountaintop?

·Once we gave a grant to a poet who used it to write, instead, a best-selling novel. The poet's name was Erica Jong, the novel was *Fear of Flying*. Congress was appalled and our budget was in trouble, but somehow the nation survived this zipless whatever.

Let's be clear about something: Artists are in business to surprise us. If we could imagine what they will do next, we wouldn't need them. And we do need them, not only for pleasure and beauty, or to bind up our psychic wounds, but as stormbirds, as early-warning seismic systems on the fault lines of the culture—before the cognitive dissonance and the underground tremors convulse us. If you want congraulations, buy a greeting card and mail it to yourself.

Buchanan's professed bête noire in the primaries has been the documentary "Tongues Untied" on the public-television series *P.O.V. P.O.V.*, partially funded by the NEA, means "point of view," and the point of view of "Tongues Untied" was that of a black gay man with AIDS, and what Marlon Riggs tried to tell us, in a collage of skits, poems, dance, autobiography, newsreel footage, rap, camp and music video, is how it felt to be black and gay and doubly disdained in straight white America. Some of this was funny: a barbershop quartet singing "Baby, Come Out Tonight." Some of it was angry: at straight black activists with no time for gay men; at a white gay subculture with no time for black men; at homophobic entertainers like Eddie Murphy. Some of it broke the heart: like listening to Billie Holliday. And ten or so minutes were shocking: even on cable TV, we seldom see full frontal male nudity, or black men kissing each other.

Never mind that most of what the NEA does is about as controversial as sponsoring a quilting bee. Nor that "Tongues Untied," like all the *P.O.V.* programs, was safely tucked away on a summer night so as not to perturb any Pledge Weeks. (Even so, seventeen public broadcasting stations in the top fifty markets refused to show it.) The real question is: Why *shouldn't* we be shocked? Shocks of recognition are what public television, and art, too, for that matter, *ought* to be about. PBS was *supposed* to be an alternative, not just for those who are into the Civil War, or British mysteries, or spoonbilled bee-eaters, midwife toads and whatever else a consortium of oil companies has decided is good for its image. After so many hours on the gentle Tasady and the awful Ik, why not gay black Americans, fellow citizens who speak a different anguish?

Why not a reality check, after which perhaps some empathy? We should watch public television as we read difficult novels: to imagine an Other, hear strange music, deepen ourselves, discover scruple. What's happening, instead, with the cutbacks and the timidity, is a squeezing out of local programming, a freezing out of independent producers, and a sycophantic pandering to corporate fatboys and middlebrow taste. And after we've abolished the NEA, PBS will almost certainly become the next target. Whatever demons secretly torment Pat Buchanan when he contemplates naked black men, what he's really saying is that the market ought to determine art. If the market determines art, *of course* it should determine television, too.

But markets have never been any better for art than they have for children (and schools). As a decent culture invests in its children, a vigorous civilization invests in symbolic representations of itself, which means taking a chance on difficult creative people. Mozart depended on court commissions; Voltaire hid out with Frederick II. Think of Machu Picchu and the Pyramids, the Taj Mahal and The Alhambra. The Parthenon in Periclean Athens was built with taxpayers' money. A Medici prince, a Russian czar, kings of France and England, caliphs of Moorish Spain, the City Council of Vienna were all patrons and subsidizers, and all surprised at what they got.

"The world's a king," said Beethoven, "and like a king desires flattery in return for favor." What's really weird in our culture is this idea that artists are lazy lowlife pinko parasites and perverts. The WPA was a terrific program, and so is the NEA's Poets-in-the-Schools. Besides the comparative pennies spent on the experimental, the nickels and dimes that go to museums, libraries, regional theaters and orchestras and dance troupes, we need a broader and healthier definition of *public* art, like the land-grant college and the national park: public space to celebrate ourselves as citizens. Leave it to the market, and what we'll get will look like the South Bronx, sound like Muzak, read like comic books and numb the gums like prime-time television.

PATTERNS AND GHOSTS

Our French friend Sylvie will have to think up another excuse for coming to New York; she just ran out of ten-year-olds. It has been Sylvie's project in recent summer seasons to export herself and one of her children from the City of Light to the Crystal Palace as a sort of geographical puberty rite, or tenth birthday party, for the child. Leah, who will eat anything, is the last of these children. Besides Ninja Turtle lollipops, Leah especially admired the polar bears at the Central Park Zoo. You would agree with her if you'd ever endured a French zoo.

By visitations like Sylvie's, we, too, are roused—from a lethargy that's almost abstract, from surreal smears of sullenness. We rediscover harbors, bridges, museums and street fairs; a sidewalk Turkish cafe, the West Street Trotskyist mural, the Cloisters bus, and the surprise concerts in the little playgrounds between megaliths. Did you realize that Monday nights in Battery Park there are public readings of *The Great Gatsby*—as if to pitch the Romance of Money, by Tibetan prayer wheel, to the whited sepulchres of stock fraud and pension rip-off?

But there I go again. Only Sylvie and Leah could have gotten me out of the house Saturday afternoon, where I should have been thinking about the Year of the Woman and the Crisis of the Cities and the Hole in the Ozone, to the Winter Garden at the World Financial Center, down in the Hong Kong part of town, for a sampling of panels on the AIDS quilt. The last time I looked at the AIDS quilt was on television, in 1989.

You may remember that the NAMES Project started its AIDS Memorial Quilt, a patchwork of grief, in San Francisco in 1987. Designed by friends and loved ones, each panel, three feet by six, commemorates a life lost to plague. On TV in October 1989, in the HBO documentary "Common Threads," we walked on runways among 10,500 of these panels, covering fourteen acres of the Ellipse behind the White

House, in Washington, D.C. We were accompanied by the narration of Dustin Hoffman and the music of Bobby McFerrin. We looked at clips of famous talking heads, from C. Everett Koop to Eddie Murphy. We met five of the victims—a decathlon athlete, a landscape architect, a naval officer, a little boy with hemophilia and an IV drug user too late kicking his habit. And we read a scroll of dread statistics—59,000 Americans dead in the decade of the eighties, more than died in Vietnam; 150 new deaths every day; one new case every minute.

There are now more than sixteen thousand panels in this quilt, and just last week we heard that the incidence of AIDS, worldwide, may be triple the previous estimates, and this wasn't nearly as newsworthy as the Buttafuoco brouhaha or Princess Di's bulimia because AIDS as a story flickers in and out of fashion, as if a healthy majority needn't concern itself with social policy questions like disease control and insurance rip-offs, workplace discrimination and pharmaceutical profiteering; as if we'd decided that the threat to white heterosexuals isn't all that grave and our ghettos deserve whatever they get. Besides, we've got the tricycles of our careers to pedal.

To make a quilt you stitch two layers of fabric together with a soft thickness between them. Quilts have been around for thousands of years, doing duty in Europe, Asia and Africa as cloaks, military doublets, cheap armor, petticoats, bed covers. The best quilts—patchworks of bright medallions on white muslin, with design variations on the Tree of Life—were North American. In the eighteenth and nineteenth centuries our quilting was deemed a minor art...minor, of course, because it was practiced by women. The sewing machine was thought to have abolished this art.

Not so. The AIDS quilt is also a comforter—a binding together, for warmth, of color and love and the fabric of memory.

On HBO, the panels had been laid out like a carpet. In the Winter Garden, they were hung up like tents or sails. You could, if you chose, read out some of the names yourself, at a lectern with a microphone. My wife did so, Saturday. My wife has a theory, still in formulation, of a new political protest art that brings beauty into the world instead of more insults, rites beyond mourning to healing, other colors besides blood.

Like ten-year-olds, Sylvie, Leah and I watched from the book boutique as my wife sounded out the names of the lost, across a ghostly sea of banners—as if, from a Navajo sand painting, they had fashioned mizzenmasts and topgallants and moonsails; as if, from a requiem mass, they had somehow imagined pennants...and kites...and caravelles.

GRAHAM GREENE
FORGIVES KIM PHILBY, BUT I HOLD
A GRUDGE

Graham Greene is dead. I ought to be thinking about novels. But I want to use him to think about something else, the way he used his characters to think about God. A couple of years ago, when Greene came back from a Moscow visit with Kim Philby, he gave a newspaper interview. He told London's *Sunday Telegraph* that he "forgave" Philby his treason because, after all, Philby had been "fighting for a cause he believed in. He wasn't doing it for the money."

This annoyed my children; even the history they get at school (which is mostly the story of what white men do in the daytime) is full of true-believing troublemakers who ought somehow to be held accountable, who ought at least to apologize before my children will forgive them.

Philby's cause, of course, was Stalin's, and he knew more about Stalin's monstrosities than almost anybody else outside the Gulag. Maybe all the agents whose covers Philby blew in his years as a "mole" eventually would have forgiven him, but we don't know because they're dead.

Was Greene really saying that the nature of the cause and the details of the behavior don't count so long as we are sincere in our beliefs?

If so, then nobody's to blame for anything. The enemy is faceless: the social system, the nuclear family, the computer program; recessive genes, angry gods, lousy weather; the Mafia, the Zodiac, the Protocols of Zion; probability theory, prime-time television, demonic possession. What ideologues can't explain away by waving wands of rhetoric, the designer therapists will excuse with their good news of a sanctioning self-love.

And yet: The teeth of the police grinning in the windows of our midnight are sincere, and so is the hooded hangman, and so is the terrorist, that burning bush, and the pink-cheeked bomber of abortion clinics. About their sincerity there is the glisten—the electricity—of the baby eel. They are Shining Path, as in Peru. They run amok, like the long knives of Suharto, after which there were 500,000 dead Indonesians. Torquemada believed in a cause, and so did Robespierre, and so did Goebbels. Say hi to Pol Pot.

It's amazing how much damage can be done by people who aren't doing it for the money.

John Wilkes Booth, meet Sirhan Sirhan. The guy who shot Gandhi was serious about his Hinduism. I've just read the memoirs of Mansur Rafizedah, the former chief of Iran's SAVAK (and covert CIA "asset"), and he feels unappreciated. Think of the Reverend Jim Jones and his Electric Kool-Aid Acid Test. Consider what Lebanese Christians did to Palestinian Muslims with or without Sharon's permission. Contemplate the obdurate South African Botha and the elusive cosmopolite Carlos. Or Pinochet and Quing Jiang. Or Idi Amin and the Ayatollah. The heretics and witches these days, those who must be murdered in order that the rest of us create, are schoolchildren on a kibbutz, Polish shipyard workers, Olympic athletes, tourists in wheelchairs, a young American mechanical engineer who dressed up as a clown and rode a unicycle in the streets of El Cua in the evil empire of expansionist Nicaragua.

Maybe sincerity is overrated. It's obviously antisocial. We sloganeer in the blood of innocents. Let a poet talk back to the novelist Greene. Wallace Stevens was thinking about "the politics of emotion" when he reported in "Esthetique du Mal" on a meeting between Victor Serge and Konstantinov. Serge had helped the Russian Revolution and then had run away from it. Konstantinov was still punching holes in people's heads, filling Serge with "a blank uneasiness":

> *He would be the lunatic of one idea*
> *In a world of ideas, who would have all the people*
> *Live, work, suffer and die in that idea*
> *In a world of ideas. He would not be aware of the clouds,*
> *Lighting the martyrs of logic with white fire.*

In the unlikely event that a Konstantinov or a Philby should ever seek forgiveness, who is entitled to give it to them? God, maybe, with whom Graham Greene had a love/hate relationship. But otherwise? Certainly these lunatics of one idea, and the rest of the true-believers, can't be permitted to forgive themselves, no matter what they're told by their commissar or their therapy group. And I'm not sure Graham

Greene has earned the right to forgive them, either. Try this on for size: Whites and blacks, men and women, fathers and children—if we believe that behavior counts, then only the victim of that behavior is entitled to forgive it.

If we don't believe that behavior counts, we are indecent.

1992: FEAR AND LOATHING ON THE CAMPAIGN TRAIL

IF MARIO DOESN'T RUN, THE REST OF US MAY HAVE TO

If memory serves, instead of just standing around waiting for something to happen, it went this way. John Foster Dulles, Ike's secretary of state, had just come back from Latin America. Whittaker Chambers, in a letter to William F. Buckley, Jr., wondered: "Mr. Dulles was in Peru (what on earth could have taken him there—hints from the Incas on how to lose an empire?)."

Mr. Bush goes to Korea, where nothing happens, and to Japan, where he throws up. (The Philippines didn't want him, any more than they want our naval base.) Because it's an election *and* a recession year, he says he's looking for some sort of trade agreement that will mean more jobs and more votes here at home. But I've been to the Far East several times, and I think what Bush really wants are hints on how to be a god-king, like Tokugawa, the banana fish of shoguns in his Momoyama gaudiness; or Tangun, the great shaman and fertility cultist who, in 2333 B.C., launched Korea in the first place; or Jayavarman VII, the big pinecone of Khmer gangsterism who lolled about Angkor, between bloodlettings.

What you need to be a god-king—a *deva-raja*—is some sort of warrior caste, like the Samurai. Or chivalric code, like Hwarangdo. Plus a messianic faith, in *kami* or Maitreya. It's, you know, a Buddha or a Vishnu or a Shinto thing.

On the other hand Bush could just forget to bring Lee Iacocca back from Nagoya, the Detroit of Japan. By the end of the millennium, eight years hence, their cars would be as lousy as ours. Something's happened to American capitalism. We've lost our Mandate of Heaven. We no longer make anything anybody wants except blue jeans. What we do instead is speculate on fluctuations of the mark or yen. We're into mergers and acquistions and hostile takeovers and liquidations. It's one big Maxwell where nothing gets *made* but paper profits. This isn't capitalism; it's more like superstition, stock-exchange voodoo, invisible credits that move in the night from the memory bank of one computer to another, quoting, in green decimals, a kind of spider-speak.

Let these imaginary banknotes fly away like butterflies or postage stamps. I wish for Bush something else in Asia: an encompassing and a serenity. He's always had the makings of a Taoist. Just looking at him on TV, so fervent in his faith in a capital-gains tax cut, I am reminded of the Tao master who told us that "the mind of a perfect man is like a mirror. It grasps nothing, but repulses nothing. It receives, but does not sustain." But the man is a fork; he needs to play with his food instead of stabbing it. In Kyoto, at Ryoanji, he should have sat for a while to contemplate the Zen rocks and wonder why he'd ever wanted to be a president, much less a god-king, since he isn't interested in doing the job, just getting it. He might have read some Natsume Soseki: *Prior to looking at themselves in shame as immoral, they looked at themselves in wonder as stupid.*

Sigh. I'd really rather write about baseball. Or Nadine Gordimer. Or—because another Nobel Prize winner didn't get the attention she deserved—Daw Aung San Suu Kyi of Myanmar. But there was our only president on TV the other night, blaming Congress for the recession. And nobody laughed in his face. And it's time for Mario to get into this thing and hurt some feelings.

It's not just that Mario has some poetry. He has some anger, too. And he speaks his poetry and his anger in his own accent. So accustomed is the culture to ghostwritten speeches, staged documentaries, retouched photographs, edited tapes and ventriloquists' dummies, that we can't think anymore. All we do is feel bad, which the pollsters report to the ad agencies so they can fabricate a tranquilizer. An angry poet is what we need to cut through the fat in our heads.

We've been lied to. This isn't new, but never before have we been so much inclined to take it for granted. We used to get mad about it. In my own racket, literature, it used to matter that Homer was probably a committee, like the King James Bible. That Aesop may never really have existed, no matter what you read in Plutarch, who made things up. That Solon tacked a few extra verses onto the *Iliad* and Cicero was fiddled with as late as 1582. That Ossian never existed. But these days, postmodernist writers specialize in pastiche and parody. And postmodernist critics would abolish the Author-God entirely, substituting their own "deconstructions" of some "meta" text. And everybody is amused, until it turns out Paul de Man was a part-time fascist.

In art, that "Renaissance" bust of Savonarola, or of Lorenzo de Medici's favorite mistress, was probably knocked off by Giovanni Bastianini in 1855. Before there were Rolex watches and Dali lithographs (for sale cheap!), there were Babylonian monuments, Maori war clubs, Dürer and Hogarth prints, and a whole series of amazing Vermeers, all of them by H. A. van Meegeren, not to mention the 1,700 terra-cotta pots in German museums thought to be "Moabite" until Mommsen denounced them. The Met in New York was had by a fake Greek maiden and a fake Goya. The Getty in Malibu shelled out $7 million for a marble *kouros* that is, perhaps, 2,600 years younger than it ought to be. None of this seems to matter in a modern era of assembly-line art, the mass-production of the totemic, color copies of Van Gogh, inflated stock on the Pop exchange when Andy Warhol signs a Brillo box or Jasper Johns a Ballantine beer can.

And why should it when every movie is a "hommage," which we used to call stealing? When science proceeds from the Piltdown Man, to Cyril Burt's faked data on the IQ differences between blacks and whites, to the guys who invented "cold fusion," right there in the Great Salt Lake, as if finding a solution to our energy problem on a brand-new golden plate from the Angel Moroni? When television commercials, selling us cars, promise adventure; or, selling us beer, promise friendship? Our very emotions are falsified. We have entered a twilight zone of mockery, that "cyberspace" of computer simulations the hackers call "Virtual Reality."

To these falsifications of art, science and the emotions, add history. Once upon a time, Ike was embarrassed about lying to us on the U-2 flights. But nothing embarrassed Nixon, and just look what's become of the political culture: Watergate, Koreagate, Abscam, Wedtech, Iranamok, Chappaquiddick, S&L, BCCI, Elliott Abrams. It's as if our novel had been written by the "dirty tricks" department at the CIA. We've been Disformed. We are Counterintelligent.

Oddly, we seemed to feel almost as bad about Milli Vanilli as once upon a time we felt about the quiz show scandals, when Van Doren and Garroway wept like little mermaids. Where is it written that lip-synching is all right for presidents like Reagan and Bush—anthologies, after all, of the wit and wisdom of the Peggy Noonans of this world—and yet somehow offensive to the faith of the Republic when other dummies do it? Why should we insist on higher standards for MTV than we do for the Oval Office?

I'd like to be at least as nice a person as Barbara Ehrenreich. In *The Worst Years of Our Lives*, Ehrenreich imagines herself on the highway in "a 4-cylinder slug." She's the sort who slows for *strollers*; her kids call her "Road Worrier"; her bumper sticker reads I'D RATHER BE PER-FORMING ACTS OF KINDNESS. But she's always being passed in the fast lane by a turbocharged Porsche 944 or a 375-horsepower Corvette ZR1. At the wheel of this killer-car is the type who gets his kicks by taking out vanloads of nuns at 180 miles per hour. On *his* bumper is another sort of sticker. It reads: HE WHO DIES WITH THE MOST TOYS WINS.

So it's time to draw a line, to start all over again in wrath with a Whitmanesque yawp and a Ginsberg howl, to scourge the thieves of our pride—the ragpickers, paperhangers, junkmen and wiseguys in red suspenders who would lie to their mothers for a slice or an edge or a sound-bite at the Great Trough, on the Magic Box, in the blue ether where the egos whistle.

On the other hand, Jesse Jackson was an angry poet, too.

THE WOMEN ARE RESTLESS

So it turns out Clarence Thomas had an opinion on abortion, after all. Imagine that. And it was exceedingly useful of Harry Blackmun to re-mind us in time for November that he's eighty-three, and won't last forever. *Roe v. Wade*, however nibbled on and gnawed at, seems safe, in its essentials, for at least another season. Never mind that these es-sentials no longer include the reproductive rights of *poor* women, or of teenagers. It would be nice if Congress passed a "Freedom of Choice Act" in time for Bush to veto it before we go to the polls, but that may have to wait till seven new senators who happen to be women are elected this fall, after which, perhaps, the Judiciary Com-mittee will look a little less like Skull & Bones.

From the *Times*, we learn that *Zan-e-Ruz*, the antiliberal Iranian women's magazine, is in a lot of trouble for having published a sewing pattern said to resemble the profile of the late Ayatollah Khomeini. This would be worth more than a chuckle—oh, that

Islam!—if we hadn't also heard, in *The New Yorker*, that nine women
were just elected to Iran's parliament, which is more than four times
as many women as there are, for the moment, in the U.S. Senate. Randall Terry and William Rehnquist must be wondering: What's the
percentage in a theocratic state, if you wimp out by empowering
noisy broads?

Among the slogans, printed up and handed out for chanting at the
pro-choice rally Monday afternoon in Times Square, were SEPARATE
THE CHURCH AND STATE/ YOU CAN'T MAKE US PROCREATE! and
KEEP YOUR ROSARIES/OFF OUR OVARIES! My group left after remarks by Geraldine Ferraro and Ruth Messinger, to the Village, for a
showing at the Film Forum of Gail Singer's *Wisecracks*. Not all the female stand-up comics in *Wisecracks* were angry, but the brilliant bits I
saw of the Clichettes led me to imagine their impersonating justices of
the Supreme Court lip-synching "You Ain't Nothin' But a Hound
Dog." Back home late at night, there were a dozen messages on the
answering machine, none of them for me.

None of these messages was for me, because my house has somehow become in the last several weeks a Baby Bell nerve center for the
women's movement. My wife has been rounding up bodies for Freedom Summer 1992, a cross-country caravan of idealists organized by
the young feminists of the Third Wave, a sort of Anita Hill Brigade
seeking to register some 500,000 new voters. My wife and her
daughter are also organizing volunteers for *The Getting It Gazette*, the
daily newspaper to be published by New York feminists during the
Democratic Convention. And all this is between Wednesday-night
meetings of WAC (Women's Action Coalition).

About Freedom Summer 1992, you should know that it's cospon-
sored by everybody from the Ms. Foundation to the YWCA. Buses
leave New York on August 1.

About WAC, you should know their symbol is the Blue Dot, used
on TV to bleep out the faces of the victims. Inside this Blue Dot,
"WAC Is Watching." Already, they've been to the St. John's rape trial;
and to Grand Central on Mother's Day, to remind us of how often
men default on child support; and to the new, downtown Whitney,
to protest its exclusion of artists who aren't male and pale. WAC
showed up, too, for Sunday's Gay Pride Parade and Monday's pro-
choice rally.

About T*he Getting It Gazette* you should know that Jane O'Reilly,

Judy Daniels, Ellen Sweet, Barbara Ehrenreich, Anne Smith, Susan Cheever and many others are involved. This *GIG* will be a "broadsheet," on "hot pink" paper. (Many jokes about this, of course, and also "Hot Flashes.") Besides inside info, dread statistics, killer quotes, essays and profiles and a "Peter Meter" measuring male politicians by the strength and stamina of their commitment to "women's issues," it will also include restaurant and bathroom advice for the Madison Square Garden area. "Sherpas" enlisted by my wife have already fanned out to collect these data, and will also distribute *GIG* in in the delegates' hotels and outside the convention. Gloria Steinem, Gail Sheehy, Pat Schroeder and Time-Warner (!) have helped with *GIG*'s budget. I have personally pledged to contribute as much as John Kenneth Galbraith. So far, this hasn't cost me as much as it should have.

Some of these women were at the house the other afternoon, telling ghost stories about last April 5, when they all got up early Sunday morning to go by bus and car and train to Washington for the rally in support of *Roe v. Wade.* For these women, so many strangers heading in the same direction, there had been a giddy sense of empowerment, as they floated down the city streets at dawn. Anne Smith remembers a cabbie turning to tell her, "There's a revolution happening. But don't worry. They're all women." Smith was furious—until the driver explained himself: "I mean," he said, "it's a revolution where they won't shoot anybody."

Yes, there are other stories. Tuesday morning, the cops began their preconvention sweep to rid Penn Station of the unsightly homeless. The transplant of a baboon's liver suggests that there's still hope for Congress. Norway's declared war on whales, again; and so has S. I. Newhouse on his magazine editors. But the biggest story of the season is the sewing pattern of the women; it looks, if not quite like Joan of Arc, then at least a lot like the Rhenish mystic Hildegard of Bingen, who laid her nuns end to end upon the earth to stop the diggers from exhuming the body of a revolutionary buried on the convent grounds.

MADISON SQUARE GARDEN:
THE PILLSBURY DOUGHBOYS GO TO A SUN DANCE

For the Democrats in New York last week, harmony was the magic word. As if on Groucho Marx, all the ducks came down with it and bet their lives. Whether this "harmony" is actually a hallucinogen, we won't know till November. Clinton's twenty-four-point lead over Bush in the popularity polls may be meaningless, but there's meaning in this very meaninglessness. All *any* poll amounts to is a transient reading on a rectal thermometer stuck up the body politic. Our fevers subside, as variable as the weather. Remember the polls after Desert Storm?

Anyway, by Thursday night, these Democrats were lolling about like a bunch of Aryan warriors, maybe 4,000 years ago, throwing dice and juiced on soma. Harmony: something perhaps fermented; or cannibis; or the agaric mushroom of the Siberian shamans; or the Iranian desert weed *Peganum harmala*—some sort of plantlike "enteogen," bestowing visions of the "other" and the "sacred realm," 1600 Pennsylvania Avenue. According to a hymn in the *Rig-Veda*:

We have drunk Soma; we have become immortal,
We have gone to the light; we have found the gods.
What can hatred and the malice of a mortal do to us now,
O immortal one?

In this Indian scheme, Clinton would be an Indra with his thousand testicles. Or an Arjuna, who was always reluctant to fight. (In which case, who's Vishnu? Disguised as Krishna, maybe FDR: "Whenever there is a decline of *dharma* and a rise in unrighteousness [*adharma*], I send forth myself. For the protection of the good, for the destruction of the wicked, for the establishment of *dharma*, I am born in *yuga* [time cycle] after *yuga*.") Or Siddhartha on his white horse, Katanka, altogether untroubled by Mara's monstrous armies of Lust and Discontent, Hunger and Thirst, Desire, Sloth and Drowsiness, Cowardice and Doubt, Hypocrisy and Stupor. (Siddhartha, too, was a policy wonk: "These armies of ours, which the world of men and gods cannot conquer, I will crush with understanding as one crushes an unbaked earthern pot with a stone.") Or King Asoka, who founded the Maurya Empire; who built rest houses, planted shade trees, established hospitals, imported medicinal plants and herbs, taught respect for teachers and the elderly, and was, besides, kind to animals.

I'm trying to be mythic. Elvis won't wash in the grander precincts, and there's a Kennedy copyright on Camelot. It might help, for instance, to think of Al Gore as a Taoist—like Joseph Needham's twelve-year-old, who replied to a Confucian braggart: "The ten thousand things and we belong in the same category, that of living things, and in this category there is nothing noble and nothing mean. It is only by reason of size, strength or cunning that one particular species gains the mastery over another....Mosquitoes and gnats suck his skin; tigers and wolves devour his flesh—but we do not therefore assert that Heaven produced man for the benefit of mosquitoes and gnats, nor to provide food for tigers and wolves."

And it's not such a stretch to imagine in the Thursday night boogie of Bill and Hillary, of Al and Tipper, at Madison Square Garden, to Fleetwood Mac, some semblance of Crazy Horse and the famous Sun Dance. Having prayed to Wakan Tanka, the Great Mysterious, by piercing their flesh with eagle claws or buffalo skulls, the Ghost Dancers were positive: *The father will descend,/ The earth will tremble....We shall live again,/ We shall live again.*

I was less a newspaper columnist during this agitated week than a newspaper widower. Not only my wife, but almost every other woman I know is involved in *The Getting It Gazette*. Since I haven't wanted to be on the floor of a party convention since Chicago 1968 (when I couldn't hear anything except on the TV monitors, and all the action anyway turned out to be on the streets and in the parks), what I did during the daytime was wander the naked city from one demonstration to another, and then drag myself home each night to watch the Sun Dance on C-SPAN.

Saturday afternoon, for instance, I made it to the Great Lawn in Central Park in time for a volleyball game at the end of a Walk, from Union Square, for Homeless Children. There I discovered that if white fiftysomething journalists can't jump, at least these homeless are disinclined to spike the ball. From the Great Lawn I wheezed downtown for five minutes at *The Gazette*, an hour in Washington Square, then on to St. Francis of Assisi on Thirty-second Street, half a block from the Garden, where the Coalition for the Homeless had organized a nightly chicken dinner, medical care and legal advice, voter registration and a candlelight vigil, after which those with no place else to go were encouraged to sleep in the sanctuary of the courtyard of the church.

Oddly, the Coalition got started in this courtyard during the last New York Democratic Convention twelve years ago when we thought the problem was temporary. There are now a million homeless nationwide, three million who're homeless off and on, seven million just one paycheck from the streets—a third of them single women with children. The Coalition wants those $25 billion cut by Reaganauts from the affordable housing construction budget; Section 8 housing as an entitlement, like food stamps; and a job-creating public-works program.

It was possible to get from St. Francis of Assisi to Bryant Park in plenty of time for the big Welcome Media party, but if the AIDS protestors on the west side of Sixth Avenue weren't allowed into the park, neither was I. It was also possible before, during and after *The Nation* party Sunday night at the Village Gate, to freeload at half a dozen other fetes, including the Lebenthal do for the Idaho delegation, but when I couldn't find Molly Ivins *or* Kurt Vonnegut *or* Pete Seeger at the Village Gate, I headed for the homeless encampment at the Chelsea Playground on West Twenty-eighth Street, after which it was too late to make the concluding session of the Fannie Lou Hamer "alternative convention," at the Abyssinian Baptist Church on West One Hundred Thirty-eighth.

Not finding Molly at the Village Gate was a big blow. My favorite columnist in the Western world is suddenly famous, with a book, *Molly Ivins Can't Say That, Can She?*, on the best-seller list. But she's also unemployed, since her Dallas newspaper folded. One of the yuppie reporters at this Dallas paper once asked Molly about some professional possibility: "Do you think this is a shrewd career move?" He was talking to a woman who lost her job at a smutty-minded *New York Times* when she tried to slip "chicken-plucker" into its grim gray pages. If Molly ever dies, and we can't let her, what they will say on her tombstone is: SHE FINALLY MADE A SHREWD CAREER MOVE. Besides, she once spent a Thanksgiving weekend in my house when nobody else would.

But I missed her at the Village Gate, where I was politically incorrect. It seems to me that my friends at *The Nation*, in their preposterous enthusiasm for "Flat-Tax Jerry" Brown, have been smoking spotted bananas. Just look at Jerry and you know he's mean, like William Blake's Urizen, "self-clos'd, all repelling": *"Dark, revolving in silent activity,/ Unseen in tormenting passions,/ An activity unknown and horrible,/ A self-contemplating shadow,/ In enormous labors occupied."* Jerry's about-face on California's notorious Proposition 13, once he'd read the polls, contributed to the bankruptcy of an entire state. (They have cut back so on courses that it takes an undergraduate six years now to graduate from a California state college or university.) This June, he couldn't even win his own primary. But for the personality disorder of the Left, a romantic death wish is as crucial as a predisposition to fratricide. Like the White Lotus Buddhists who rose in China against the Mongols, or the Society of the Harmonious and Righteous Fist that rose against the Manchus and the British, our Left enjoys imagining that its ritual boxing, inner powers and magical amulets will protect it from the bullets of the enemy. One also thinks of Amos Oz, who was thinking about his own Israeli Left when he defined a "phalanx":

> *soldiers in a closed-square formation, their backs to one another, their faces to the enemy, lances and spears pointed outward in all four directions, full cover to one another in every direction...The moderate, dovish Israeli left sometimes resembles a reverse phalanx: a square of brave fighters, their backs to the whole world and their faces and their sharpened, unsheathed pens turned on one another.*

At *The Nation* party, there were a lot of these unsheathed pens, and many Brownies, but no Molly to wipe my brain pan with an SOS magic scouring pad—to talk about a man so ugly "that when he was a little boy his momma had to tie a pork chop around his neck before the dog would play with him"; an attorney general so mean "he wouldn't spit in your ear if your brains were on fire"; a congressman so slow "if his IQ slips any lower, we'll have to water him twice a day"; a Reagan so dumb that "if you put his brains in a bee, it would fly backwards"; an Oliver North so sincere that, when he lies to Congress, he's enough "to gag a maggot"; a Dan Quayle who "looks exactly like Princess Di, while Mrs. Quayle looks exactly like Prince Charles." If politics bring out the mythmaker in me, in Molly they rile the peach-orchard wild boar: "It's illegal to be gay in Texas again. They reinstated our sodomy statue, so people can legally screw pigs in public, but not each other in private." She has recommended that the CIA start a chapter of "Nun Killers Anonymous." She had no use at all for the great and glorious Gulf War to MAKE THE WORLD SAFE FOR ISLAMIC FIEFDOMS. In her opinion "there's not a thing wrong with the ideals and mechanisms outlined and the liberties set forth in the Constitution of the United States. The only problem is the founders left a lot of people out of the Constitution. They left out poor people and black people and female people. It is possible to read the history of this country as one long struggle to extend the liberties established in our Constitution to everyone in America."

We need more of this, in the nation and *The Nation*, where Molly is advertised more often than she's published. What this whole country sorely needs is more political reporters like Molly, with her Shakespearean vulgarity, her righteous combination of Lily Tomlin and Mother Courage, and Bill Greider, the last of the shoe-leather I. F. Stones. Did you see Greider on public television, talking about "The Betrayal of Democracy"? He may write these days for *Rolling Stone*, but Greider is almost the exact opposite of their previous political correspondent, Hunter S. "Gonzo" Thompson, picking up radio signals from Klingon starships in his asbestos stuffing. Just by sitting there, in front of all those white men in suits—congressmen, lawyers, lobbyists, media heavies, the canned opinionizers of the think tanks in their bow ties and Beltway blister packs—while they tried to avoid his low-key questions, and then by switching to the faces of black, brown, female and cowboy citizen-dissidents, in Seattle or San Antonio, at Love Canal or in Institute, West Virginia, where Union Carbide poisons people, Bill Greider managed to lower our spirits and raise our temperatures.

Not that he was easy on the facts. He told us about the CIA, and the mining of Nicaragua's harbors, and our contempt for the World Court. He mentioned that there were fewer than 200 registered lobbyists in Washington, D.C., in 1971, and a decade later there are more than 2,000. We heard, whether we wanted to or not, that a U.S. Senator seeking reelection has to raise at least $3,000 a day, seven days a week, for all six years of his term in office. With Greider, we sat there while Robert Dugger, chief economist of the American Bankers Association, tried to dream up a plausible excuse for S&L bailout money being voted through Congress every odd-numbered year, while the subject goes entirely undiscussed in even-numbered years—when, of course, there are elections. We were also told that the auto industry fought off air bags for twenty years. That the EPA, in two decades (!) has managed to regulate only 7 of the 275 industrial chemicals polluting our environment. That twelve years after Superfund, only 63 of 1,200 targeted sites have been cleaned up. And that our kindly government still has a backlog of $87 *billion* in uncollected taxes from corporations and wealthy individuals.

Greider's argument is that all of Washington is one big "Great Bazaar" of fast-buck buyers and sellers. That incumbent politicians in both parties are deformed creatures of PAC money. That corporate lobbyists smother legislation on health care, worker safety, clean air, and toxic-waste disposal in the *regulatory* process, while nobody's looking. That the bankers basically wrote the S&L bailout as they are basically writing next year's commercial banking bailout, so that civilians will have to foot the bill for greedhead bungee jumping. That the media won't tell us what's happening because they're too cozy with the pols they are supposed to monitor—too chemically dependent on favors and leaks.

If you missed his TV program, buy a copy of his book, *Who Will Tell the People?*, a longer and much more disturbing Bill Greider of Indictment. *Who* is an *Almanach de Gotha*, a *Newgate Calendar* and a *Tabula Smaragdina* of footsie and malefaction. Just look at one small portion of these compromising particulars—on the cozy and dependent media—which didn't make it to public television: Did you know that Thomas L. Friedman, the *New York Times* correspondent who covers the State Department, plays tennis with the Secretary of State? That Brit Hume, who covers the White House for ABC, plays tennis with George Bush? That Rita Beamish of the Associated Press jogs with George? That George and Barbara stopped by and were videotaped at a media dinner party in the home of Albert B. Hunt, the *Wall Street Journal* bureau chief, and his wife, Judy Woodruff of the *MacNeil/Lehrer Newshour*? That one reason Andrea Mitchell, who covers Congress for NBC, shows up so often in the presidential box at the Kennedy Center is because she just happens to live with Alan Greenspan, chairman of the Federal Reserve Board?

Maybe it's time the media, like packages of cigarettes, ought to wear Consumer Warnings. We are entitled to wonder, after a reading of Greider and of Eric Alterman's forthcoming *Sound & Fury: The Washington Punditocracy and the Collapse of American Politics*, just what kind of journalism it is we're afflicted with—when a White House Thuggee like John Sununu replaces Buchanan on *Crossfire*. When a George Will, who was still ghostwriting speeches for Jesse Helms during his trial period as a columnist for the *Washington Post*, preps Ronald Reagan for one of his debates with Jimmy Carter and then reviews Reagan's performance the morning after in his column, and later on actually writes a speech that Reagan delivers to the British House of Commons. When Morton Kondracke and Robert Novak collect thousands of dollars from the Republican party for advice to a gathering of governors. When John McLaughlin, who settled one sexual harassment suit out of court and faces the possibility of at least two more, permits himself to savage Anita Hill on his own *McLaughlin Report*. When Hugh Sidey of *Time* magazine, in return for sycophantic past favors, is the *only* journalist invited to a Bush state dinner for Gorby. When Henry Kissinger, on ABC television and in *his* syndicated column, defends Deng Xiaoping's behavior during the Tiananmen Square massacre without telling us that Henry and his consultancy firm had a substantial finanicial stake in a Chinese status quo.

Besides their ethics, there's their judgment. From Alterman's quotes we learn that George Will thinks Bruce Springsteen's "Born in the USA" is "a grand, cheerful affirmation" of American life; that the homeless should be relocated "to some place where they are simply out of sight and no longer visible"; that America ought to have gone to war on Syria after U.S. Marines were killed in Beirut; and actually wrote, on November 9, 1989, the day the Berlin Wall came down, that "liberalization is a ploy...the Wall will remain." That Morton Kondracke on *The McLaughlin Report* blamed the murder of six Jesuit priests and their cook and her daughter on left-wing guerrillas instead of the Salvadoran army; and later asked all Americans to boycott the sponsors of Roseanne Barr's sitcom because her singing of the "Star-Spangled Banner" at a baseball all-star came was "unpatriotic" and "down on the country." That Fred Barnes and Robert Novak assured us there was absolutely no chance we'd send troops to the Middle East because of Kuwait. That Evans and Novak, in syndication, and Suzanne Garment, in the *Wall Street Journal*, were personally responsible for Ollie North's keeping his job (and thus for Irangate), when the National Security Council wanted to send him back to the Marines. That the *Journal*, in lobbying in 1981 for deregulation of the S&L "thrifts," not only promised a boom-boom effect, but also chortled that "the beauty of these solutions is that they're cheap." That David Broder missed the point of Irangate, as he'd missed the point of Vietnam, as Jeane Kirkpatrick missed the point of Marcos, as Kirkpatrick and Will, Evans and Novak, William Safire and A. M. Rosenthal, Charles Krauthammer and Jim Hoagland, entirely missed the point of *glasnost* and *perestroika*. Every one of these deep thinkers would later learn to love the Gulf War, including Anthony Lewis of the *Times*. And not one of them later on would notice any hanky-panky at the Atlanta branch of the Italian Banca Nazionale del Lavaro (BNL) implicating Bush and the Justice Department and the CIA in a cover-up of arms credits for Iraq—except Bill Safire, who, to his credit, keeps screaming about it in his *Times* column; and, at least covertly, Kissinger, who managed to resign from BNL's Advisory Board about a minute before the indictments came down.

No wonder I watch C-SPAN and miss Molly and seem to hear, late at night, a country music song Molly has assured me is authentic: "I Am Going Back to Dallas to See If There Could Be Anything Worse Than Losing You." Besides *The Getting It Gazette*, the best reporting from this convention has been *Spy* magazine's parody of the *New York Times* for July 15—PEROT SET TO PICK TV'S OPRAH WINFREY AS RUNNING MATE—which was also the funniest thing *Spy*'s done in years. While most of my peer-group chuckled over the Abe Rosenthal send-up, I preferred Maureen Dowd's long day with Hillary Clinton, the reluctant cookie-pusher: "For the final stop of the day Mrs. Clinton caught a cab to a downtown clinic to get an abortion. 'This is my fourth or fifth,' she said. 'I wanted to take care of this before the campaign really moves into high gear.'" Equally risible was the news that Sony, "the giant Japanese consumer electronics and entertainment company," had bought "troubled Columbia University" and named Benno Schmidt its new president: "Sony, which acquired Columbia Records in 1988, and Columbia Pictures in 1989, was said to have been seeking to purchase a university for months."

At one of last week's many power breakfasts, Speaker of the House Tom Foley told journalists that if the election went to the House, they would vote on January 5. Well, then, who would be president from January 2 through January 4? Why, of course, Speaker Foley—who would have to resign from Congress but was more than willing to do so, because being an *ex*-president is so leisurely and lucrative. After dodging Charles Kuralt's question about where he'd locate the Foley Presidential Library, the Speaker also admitted possessing a special identification packet in case of catastrophe. It seems that back while there was still an Evil Empire, they played war games in Washington. In this particular scenario, a nuclear strike took out both president and veep, Foley was missing, and somehow the top job ended up with the secretary of agriculture, who refused to relinquish it when at last they found the Speaker. *Boys just want to have fun.*

From such a power breakfast, one needs to hit the streets. My daily route, from Monday through Thursday, took me from the First Amendment quarantine compound in front of the post office behind police barricades, across from the Garden on Eighth Avenue, to whatever demonstration had been scheduled for whatever cause wherever else in the city they stashed the dissidents, like George Will's homeless, "out of sight." There were more than enough television cameras to cover some of this territory, too. But they chose not to. I saw many cameras Monday afternoon at the First Amendment compound where there were also many homeless and more soup-kitchen chicken and a terrific gospel choir of rehabilitated addicts, which didn't make the nightly news because the nightly news on all the local channels went with film of a single disruptive crazy.

I would always make it a point to leave Eighth Avenue, for wherever—Columbus Circle, for the "Take Back Our Lives" march, or Times Square for the gay protest, or Central Park for jobs at home and peace in Central America—before the Brownies descended in self-righteousness. "DEMAND THE HUMILITY AGENDA," indeed. Later in the week, after Clinton had wowed the Women's Caucus, and Ross Perot—either Puff the Magic Dragon or one of T. S. Eliot's Old Possum Mystery Cats: *McCavity's not there!*—took himself off to count the money he will save, when I was off with some AIDS doctors, or the WAC shock troops, or an ad hoc alliance of teachers who don't think Whittle and Benno are the cure for what ails American public schools. Mario Cuomo, in return for his endorsement of the ticket, got some semi-prime time and, maybe, the promise of a Supreme Court appointment, while Flat-Tax Jerry, in return for his nonendorsement, got precisely the shaft he deserved. I don't care if Jerry does sleep with Joan Didion and John Gregory Dunne on his New York pit stops. I find I am no more interested in Jerry's Great Zen Snit than I was in Mario's slice of Hamlet on wry toast. At least Jesse Jackson knew how to put his injured feelings on hold long enough to rouse the rabble with a stem-winder, even though the reporter from the *Times* apparently slept through it, to the front-page embarrassment of our newspaper of record, as if they were not unacquainted on West Forty-third Street with some Siberian soma of their own.

But we are done with the primaries, and they weren't rigged, and if Mario and Bradley and the rest of the Best and the Brightest never got into it, they should consult their image doctors on a new profile, with some more courage. Call me yup-deviationist, incrementalist bourgeois wishy-washy, and maybe even psychobabble-copacetic, but the homeless, who are everywhere except in the Garden and on television, really can't wait for a perfect candidate or the ever-receding, glorious and radiant Revolution. Neither can the Supreme Court and the rest of the judiciary, not with a Justice Department that goes to war for a gag rule on family-planning clinics; nor the thirty-seven million Americans without the safety net of health insurance; nor gays in these plague years of backlash and bashing; nor a broken economy and the wounded earth itself. If we can't have everything, we can't *afford* Bush. This ticket meets at least the minimum daily requirement of decency, with the soft promise of some equitable income redistribution. While I wish the Man from Hope, that country & western jukebox, weren't such a gleeful supporter of the death penalty, not to mention Arkansas's right-to-work law, I am not a purist. I've lost too often and the nation, as well as *The Nation*, is running out of time. If there's a real chance to send George Bush back to his hotel room I will vote, in spite of my modified rapture, for the Southern Baptist Pillsbury Doughboys. At least, which could never have been said for George McGovern, or Jimmy Carter, or Walter Mondale, or Mike Dukakis, they seem to *like* to Sun Dance.

THE REPUBLICANS IN HOUSTON, WITH KALI AND GILGAMESH

For the House of Atreus in ancient Greece, "family values" were incest, infanticide, parricide, matricide, cannibalism and other gaudy dysfunctions. The Brothers Karamazov also come to mind. And the Mafia. Not to mention Charles Manson.

I suppose Jim Baker stayed out of this just long enough to cop a plea.

After the tantrum of the God Squad cadres, it wouldn't much matter what Bush said by way of extenuation Thursday night, and just as well. He went on even longer than Clinton. The Old Smog meets the New Covenant. Bring back Perot, either as a fire hydrant or a maddened fruit bat, in one ear and out the other of Larry King. It appeared to some of us that, just as one kind of counterculture seemed, on television in 1972, to have taken over the Democratic party—in its blood lust postponing George McGovern's acceptance speech till most of Middle America had quit to milk the cows—so had another species of counterculture, twenty years later, seized the Republicans and declared a Holy War that another George will lose.

That dreadful opening night, in fact, Pat Buchanan went on so long that The Ronald himself slipped out of prime time. This muddied what was already a conceptual mess. Reagan should have preceded Buchanan. From Mircea Eliade's books on religion, we know that the basic archaic Neolithic origin myth speaks of the "ritual [that is, violent] death of a primeval giant, from whose body the worlds were made and the plants grew." Ever since, quaint activities like cannibalism, head-hunting and human sacrifice may be seen as ritual reenactments of this "pattern drama...intended to strengthen and increase the harvest." But by the time our primeval giant fell grinning on his sword, Buchanan had already opened up with an Uzi:

> *There is a religious war going on in this country for the soul of America. It is a cultural war, as critical to the kind of nation we shall be as the Cold War itself, for this war is for the soul of America. And in that struggle for the soul of America, Clinton & Clinton are on the other side, and George Bush is on our side.*

He went on to tell a little white lie about the Los Angeles riots, during which, according to Buchanan, the Eighteenth Cavalry had to take back the streets and an old people's home from a mob of black terrorists. In fact, the old people's home took care of itself. Nevertheless, like the Eighteenth Cavalry, "we must take back *our* cities, and take back *our* culture, and take back *our* country." And not only from mobs of color, either. In addition to "the raw sewage of pornography that pollutes our popular culture" there are also all those gays Out There about whom Pat's always been so hot and bothered. He described last month's Democratic convention in Madison Square Garden as "a giant masquerade ball...where 20,000 radicals and liberals came dressed up as moderates and centrists in the greatest single exhibition of cross-dressing in American political history." And just to be sure the delegates got his point, he added that "a militant leader of the homosexual rights movement could rise at that convention and exult 'Bill Clinton and Al Gore represent the most pro-lesbian and pro-gay ticket in history.' And they do."

The next night, Pat the Robertson would take up where Pat the Buchanan had left off. (So many Pats to keep track of in the popular culture: Buchanan, Robertson, Boone, [Mrs.] Nixon, Jerry's father, Edmund G. "Pat" Brown, New York's Senator Daniel P. "Pat" Moynihan, a Sajak, a Riley and a Summerall.) "The people of Eastern Europe

got rid of their left-wingers," Robertson confided; "it is time we in
America got rid of our left-wingers." The Berlin Wall may have fallen
down but the centralized U.S. government is an "equally insidious
plague"; "the carrier of this plague is the Democratic party"; and the
standard-bearer of that party, Guess Who?, has already hatched "a
radical plan to destroy the traditional family." (The day after the convention, Robertson upped this ante in a letter to his Christian Coalition storm troopers, describing "the feminist agenda" as "a socialist,
antifamily political movement that encourages women to leave their
husbands, kill their children, practice witchcraft, destroy capitalism
and become lesbians.")

But the non-Pats were just as pat-ible. For instance, Phil, the key-
note speaker (Senator Gramm of Texas): "Don't you know the Democrats are lonely tonight! In all the world, only in Cuba and North
Korea and in the Democratic party in America do we still have organized political groups who believe that the answer to every problem is
more government." And: "In any hut in any village on the planet, one
world leader is loved, honored and admired above all others. Spoken
in a thousand dialects, his name is still George Bush." Or Rich as in
Bond, the Republican party chairman, who not only told Maria Shriv-
er on NBC that "we Republicans are America, those other people are
not America," but went on to suggest that if Bill Clinton won, Jane
Fonda "will be sleeping in the White House as guest of honor at a
state dinner for Fidel Castro." Plus Newt, as in Gingrich, a member of
Congress: Clinton leads a "Democratic majority that despises American values and denies the basic goodness of the American people."
And Dan, as in Quayle, a vice president, who, his first day in Houston,
told the God Squads, "It's always good to be with people who are *real*
Americans," and would later tell the convention that "Americans try
to raise their children to understand right and wrong, only to be told
that every so-called 'life-style alternative' is morally equivalent. That
is wrong. The gap between us and our opponents is a cultural divide.
It is not just the difference between conservative and liberal, it is a difference between fighting for what is right and refusing to see what is
wrong." And he stamped his foot:

> *I know my critics wish I were not standing here tonight. They don't like our
> values. They look down on our beliefs. They're afraid of our ideas. And they
> know the American people stand on our side. And that's why, when someone*

*confronts them and challenges them, they will stop at nothing to destroy him.
And I say to them: You have failed. I stand before you, and before the American people—unbowed, unbroken, and ready to keep fighting for our beliefs.*

Even George, the president, was not above innuendo early in the
week. On the Democratic Congress: "They gave new meaning to the
words *closet liberal*." And, on Clinton's confidence in victory: "I half
expected, when I went over to the Oval Office, to find him there measuring the drapes." And I haven't even mentioned Marilyn Quayle,
who seems to have ad-libbed her queasiness about such sixties' "life-
style choices" as "draft dodging," "pot smoking" and "adultery." I
will think about Marilyn Quayle in a minute, but to these spoken texts
we ought to add a written word or two—Republican platform planks
opposing not only abortions for victims of rape and incest and "ef-
forts by the Democrat party to include sexual preference as a protect-
ed minority receiving preferential status under civil-rights statutes,"
but opposing as well any and all birth-control information programs
in our public schools except incantations of "abstinence"—plus the
buttons, stickers, posters and signs for sale, with such heartwarming
slogans as "Family Rights Forever! Gay Rights Never!," and "Smile If
You've Had an Affair with Bill Clinton," and "Committee to Save Gay
Whales," and "Hispanic Lesbians Against Racism."

For *New York Newsday*, Jimmy Breslin writes of Houston as if it were a
suburb of modern Serbia, in a frenzy of "ethnic cleansing." Elsewhere,
"lynching bee" has occurred to someone, and "Nuremberg rally" to
others. My female friends, in town to distribute their *Getting It Gazette*,
discovered themselves disdained by and isolated from almost everybody but the whimsical Southern Belles for Safe Sex, who handed out
condoms to offended Young Republicans. It's an isolation easy to come
by in this Gulf port, one of those cities where social disorder, by design, is hard to see. So much of its petrochemical business is in smoky
skycrapers, and maximum-security hotels. So much of its consumption
goes on, as inconspicuously as possible, in theme parks like Neiman-
Marcus. So much of its pedestrian traffic is underground in weather-
proof labyrinths. There is almost no public transportation, so the races
never even have to pretend for a second that they're headed in the same
direction. Wealthy whites hide in River Oaks behind their trees. Poor
blacks roam the sun-stunned streets, where they can be picked off by
snipers. Without street life, it's hard to make waves, even on a Gulf.

And party apparatchiks made it even harder, stashing potentially troublesome delegations like California and New York in out-of-the-way hotels where not a single caucus room had been booked. There was no place for uppity women to agitate about child care, child support, family leave, domestic violence or pay equity. After all, 86 percent of employed women work to support themselves and their families, and even Republican women still earn only 71 cents on the male dollar. Did you know that the number of women appointed to federal courts has steadily *decreased* during eleven years of Republicanism? (Under Carter, women made up 15.5 percent of the appointments to the bench; under Bush, 9.9 percent.) That women account for just 16 percent of all our elected officials? Meanwhile, more than two million American women are physically assaulted by male partners every year, 25 percent of violent crimes in the U.S. are wife assaults, and 33 percent of homeless women and children are fleeing family violence? While we're at it, did you know 40 percent of homeless women get no prenatal care? That more than 70 percent of working single mothers do not have a health plan covering their children? That sexual harassment costs the typical Fortune 500 company $6.7 million a year (and the federal government $133 million a year) in turnover, absenteeism and productivity?

Family values! Most astonishing to me are the facts about breast cancer. Nobody seems to know why, but one in nine American women will get breast cancer in their lifetimes, up from one in twenty in the 1960s. The breast-cancer rate for American women is five times higher than for Asian or African women. In 1990, 175,000 American women were diagnosed as having the disease, and 44,500 died from it. This makes even AIDS look kind and gentle. And yet the National Institutes of Health reauthorization bill—earmarking tens of millions of dollars for breast-cancer research—was vetoed by our only president. Why? He says he was afraid that women would run out and abort themselves in order to flesh-peddle fetal tissue.

But I digress. Every placard and poster and T-shirt had to be preapproved before you got onto the floor of the Astrodome. You were searched at the portals for illegal signs. Some of the uppity women, closet members of NOW, fashioned pro-choice scarves for themselves—white, with blue lettering. These subversive scarves, puffed up in the pockets of their dresses, were seized! This remarkable confiscation went unreported anywhere in the national media, as those media had failed to report the demonstrations of the homeless outside Madison Square Garden in July. Welcome to the theocratic state.

It wasn't just that the Republicans decided to run for reelection against Murphy Brown and Planned Parenthood; against working women and welfare mothers and pinko perverts and Oxford hanky-panky; against condoms and communism, Cuba and Watts. It was as if the Democrats, by actually seeking office, proved themselves to be, at best, heretics, at worst infidels, and, somewhere in between, some sort of Freemason conspiracy, a Trilateral Commission, like Mesmer's Order of Universal Harmony or Cagliostro's Egyptian Rite or the Chevaliers de la Rose-Croix or the Bavarian Illuminati. Kabbalism and Theosophy! The Areopagus and the Zinnendorf System!

I'm semi-serious. It's not so hard to imagine Buchanan, before he opened fire, up there in one of the maximum-security ziggurats, daubed like one of Sumer's warrior-kings with sesame oil, gorged on goat, pulling up his sheepskin kilt, donning his leather-plated armor, hefting his bronze sword and *tingli* drum, imagining himself pic-tographed, bloody and heroic, on the Stela of the Vulture. (According to *The Lamentation over the Destruction of Ur*: "In the wide streets where feasting crowds would gather, scattered they lay. In open fields that used to fill with dancers, they lay in heaps.") Nor to imagine Robertson in boar's teeth and elk's antlers, a Scythian petitioning his Thunder God ·with a bucket of blood from the slit throat of a POW. (Or bringing Bill Clinton, as the Akkadian Semite Sargon the Great brought a defeated King Lugalzaggisi, to the gate of Enlil in the collar of a dog.) And those Christian Coalitionists and Young Republicans— warrior Kurgans, or Indo-European *Männerbund*, or Near Eastern *mari-annu*, in bear pelts and wolves' heads; storm-cloud Maruts, outlaw Finnians, berserkers, *Eihenjahr* and Myrmidons. (Tacitus is quoted, in Rick Fields's *The Code of the Warrior*, on "the terrifying Harrii": "Fierce in nature, they trick out this natural ferocity by the help of art and season: they blacken their shields and dye their bodies; they choose pitchy nights for battles; by sheer panic and darkness they strike terror like an army of ghosts. No enemy can face this novel, and as it were, phantasmal vision: in every battle after all the eye is conquered first.")

And what of Marilyn Q? We will have grievously misunderstood her if we take her at face value. She was not born to blush unseen. There is about her a Boudicca, a Scathach and a Kali. Like Fa Hui, the first of the Chinese Women Warriors back in the time of Shang, Marilyn will be buried with seven thousand cowrie shells, four hundred and ninety bone hairpieces, two hundred ritual vessels, one hundred and thirty bronze weapons, ninety-five jade objects, seventy stone sculptures, twenty arrowheads, sixteen sacrificed Homo sapiens, and six dogs. Like all the others, our Marilyn was hard on Hillary, with her headbands and her legal monographs. You'd have thought poor Hillary was, well, somebody outrageous, like Hypatia of Alexandria.

Hypatia of Alexandria, the last scientist of the Post-periclean golden age, invented the astrolabe, which measures the positions of the sun and stars and calculates the ascendant sign of the zodiac; and the hydroscope, which determines the specific gravity of any given liquid. Because of her sexy neo-Platonism, Hypatia was pulled out of her chariot by zealous Christian monks, in 415 A.D. They stripped her naked, razed her skin, rent her flesh with shells, quartered her dead body and burned those quarters to black ash. Western science wouldn't recover from this martyrdom for another thousand years, when the Arabs taught us all how Hypatia used to do it.

But Marilyn was hard on all women who had made choices different from her own, and the whole convention was a-howling at such succubi, as if the Republican platform were a *Malleus Maleficarum.* What are they so afraid of? Listen to what E. William Monter says, in *Becoming Visible: Women in European History:*

> *The tradition of night-flying female cannibals or* strigae *gradually merged with the originally separate tradition of the malevolent sorceress or* malefica, *who could harm man or beast through magic herbs and spells. Both these stereotypes were, starting in the thirteenth century, assimilated into the Inquisition's stereotypes about heretics, who habitually met after dark to engage in secret orgies and who reputedly worshiped the devil. But some of the key elements in this new history of witchcraft came only very late. For example, the fact that when the devil has sexual intercourse with witches his penis and semen are ice cold…The modern name for the Witches' Sabbath, or* sabbat, *also comes very late; the older term it replaced was* synagogue, *which strongly suggests the confusion between witches and Jews or other heretics.*

Moreover, it seemed to me that Marilyn was talking to somebody else that Wednesday night—not to me, not to us, not to them, not to George, and certainly not to Dan. I think, secretly, she was speaking to

Pat the Buchanan, her kind of warrior-king, over the ruins of Ur. Marilyn sounded to me like the goddess Inanna, beseeching heroic Gilgamesh:

> *Come, Gilgamesh, be thou my lover!*
> *Do but grant me of thy fruit.*
> *Thou shalt be my husband and I will be thy wife.*
> *I will harness for thee a chariot of lapis and gold...*
> *Thou shalt have storm-demons to hitch on for mighty mules.*
> *In the fragrance of cedars thou shalt enter our house.*

Alas, as you're aware if you've read the epic, Gilgamesh was disinclined. He had, anyway, to wait around for the worm to fall out of the nose of his dear dead buddy Endiku.

Imagine that.

Well, so is the party of Abe Lincoln dead, like Endiku. And what we saw in Houston was the worm in its nose.

PART II:
BOOK WORLD

AT WAR AND PEACE ON
THE HOME FRONT

TONI MORRISON: SHE CAN GIVE YOU DREAMS

From a newspaper clipping about a fugitive slave in Ohio who killed her own infant child rather than see her returned to bondage in the South—"Now she would never know what a woman suffers as a slave...I will go to the gallows singing"—Toni Morrison made *Beloved*. From a photograph in James Van der Zee's *Harlem Book of the Dead* of the body of a young girl, shot at a party by a jealous boyfriend, who died refusing to identify her assailant ("I'll tell you tomorrow"), Toni Morrison has made *Jazz*. All you need is genius.

In Harlem, in 1926, a fifty-year-old sample-case beauty products salesman falls in "deep-down spooky love" with a high-school girl for whom "everything was like a picture show...and she was the one on the railroad track, or the one trapped in the sheik's tent when it caught on fire." She goes dancing without him, so he shoots her. And then his crazy wife, who irons hair, will crash the funeral and try with a knife to disfigure the dead girl's face. To find out why any of this happened, all of it on the *first* page of *Jazz*, you'll have to listen to the end of Morrison's song—as if Sidney Bechet had met the Archduke Trio; as if Ellington had gone Baroque.

You will get the City, designed for tall dreams, electric danger and getting away with it; for desire instead of love; for "smelling good and looking raunchy." You will get the music of colored men who float down from the sky blowing saxophones; rooftop clarinets, and drums for the dead, and a flourish of fingered horns in the barrel hooch, juke joint and tonk house; the six-stringed blues guitar and a brass cut so fine "you would have thought that everything had been forgiven." You'll hear about newspapers like *The Messenger* and *The Crisis*, unions like the Pullman Porters, political parties like the Readjustors, race riots like East St. Louis; about polishing shoes, rolling tobacco and selling #2 Nut Brown door to door, along with a vanishing cream. You will have to swim back from this risky city, against the migratory tide, South again to Virginia, the sugarcane and hibiscus; the mules and possoms and walnut trees; a butter press, a broken plow, a rainbow and a fox; a blade of blackbirds and a portent of redwings and a tree on a river called Treason, whose roots grow backwards, climbing toward leaves and wind and light; a cave where one mother is a wild thing, and a well where another mother drowns.

Jazz is a book of dispossession and of haunting. Novel by novel, Toni Morrison reimagines the lost history of her people, their love and work and nightmare passage and redemptive music. It's a brilliant project, a ghostly chorale, a constellation of humming spheres with its own gravity, and now this brand-new star, which is even trickier than usual. If jazz is a music the performer composes himself, then this novel she calls *Jazz* is a book that composes itself: "I have watched your face for a long time now, and missed your eyes when you went away from me." It also *surprises* itself. But I'll get to that modernist wickedness in a minute.

> *If anything I do, in the way of writing novels (or whatever I write) isn't about the village or the community or about you, then it is not about anything. I am not interested in indulging myself in some private, closed exercise of my imagination that fulfills only the obligation of my personal dreams— which is to say yes, the work must be political.…It seems to me that the best art is political and you ought to be able to make it unquestionably political and irrevocably beautiful at the same time.* (Toni Morrison)

Beautiful, certainly. I find that I want to roll around in the books, not a reviewer but an epicure, even a voluptuary. Give me, instead of overviews, her banquet of butter cakes and babies' ghosts, conjuring and "graveyard loves," Chicken Little and cooked flesh, a spittle web of spiders and the breath of snakes, laws of hospitality and "men with the long-distance eyes"—after which, I want to fall into that Shadrack sleep "deeper than hospital drugs; deeper than the pits of plums, steadier than the condor's wing; more tranquil than the curve of eggs." This, of course, isn't criticism; it's gourmandizing. But don't you already know as much as you want to about African oral traditions, Uncle Remus, sermons, slave songs and the blues?

Morrison has said that their music no longer belongs exclusively to her people, so novels are going to have to sing those origin myths and archetypes. I suppose that she is what happened to Zora Neale Hurston once she grew out of Franz Boas: *Mules and Men* for the space age; *Their Eyes Were Watching Some Other God*. She presumes Phyllis Wheatley, Lucy Terry and Harriet E. Wilson; Jesse Fauset, Georgia Douglass Jackson and Alice Childress; Paule Marshall and Gwendolyn Brooks; plus Harriet Tubman, Sojourner Truth, Rosa Parks and Fannie Lou Hamer. She also presumes Richard Wright, James Baldwin, Ralph Ellison and their literature of grievance. She presumes, as well, the Bible and Shakespeare. She ate Faulkner for a snack.

In what way, though, is she political? She never bothers to explain to her readers the epidemiology and the ecosystems of racist oppression; they already know that stuff. But eavesdrop on this art—"You don't listen to people," Circe dissed Milkman; "your ear is on your head, but it's not attached to your brain"—and you hear about an Other America bearing no resemblance to such salacious confabulations as a "culture of poverty" and an affectless "underclass." She's not some Sojourner Dante, touring the limbos of welfare motherhood, circling a crackhead hell. Her people aren't *victims*, at least not pathologies; they have choices and resources, styles and survival skills, and their own business to get on with, inside the white whale that swallowed them. Except in *Tar Baby* and *Beloved*, Morrison's white folks are outside the main action of her characters. "We" are their bad weather and bad luck. Just as her sex and violence are *mystified* (become pity, howling, rainbows, waste), so the dominant culture is oddly, almost mischievously *abstracted*...like probability theory (or maybe Neoplatonism). Such overt political action as occurs (a protest march in *Sula*, assassins in *Song of Solomon*, the mournful drums in *Jazz*) seems always peripheral to some other drama of baffled hopes, family wounds, confused paternity, broken connection or historical amnesia, in a separate republic of dreams. But inside this republic of dreams, what goes on is *identity*-making. And if we don't understand that identity is political, we don't understand anything at all.

How does it *feel* to a white reader to be bad luck, like chemicals in a lake? As if we're not, every minute of the day, so important? As if maybe there were complicated reasons for a Malcolm X, as there are for a Louis Farrakhan; and, for equally complicated reasons, Josephine Baker has more resonance than Madonna? When Sula makes fun of poor black Jude, the rest of us (that's everybody male and pale who's ever appeared in a suit, a tie and a Beltway blisterpack on Ted Koppel's *Nightline*) are merely incidental: "I mean," says Sula,

> *I don't know what the fuss is about. I mean, everything in the world loves you. White men love you. They spend so much time worrying about your penis they forget their own. The only thing they want to do is cut off a nigger's privates. And if that ain't love and respect I don't know what is. And white women? They chase you all to every corner of the earth, feel for you under every bed...Now ain't that love? They think rape as soon's they see you, and if they don't get the rape they looking for, they scream it anyway just so the search won't be in vain. Colored women worry themselves into bad health just trying to hang on to your cuffs. Even little children—white and black, boys and girls—spend all their childhood eating their hearts out 'cause they think you don't love them. And if that ain't enough, you love yourselves. Nothing in this world loves a black man more than another black man. You hear of solitary white men, but niggers? Can't stay away from one another a whole day. So. It looks to me like you the envy of the world.*

Worse, what could be more political than the fact that Morrison—with her wit, poetry and passion, breadth of sympathy, depth of feeling, range of interest, grasp of detail, powers of imaginative transformation, command of time, character, scruple, generosity and radiance, and magical mastery of the Mother Tongue—turns out to be the best writer working in America?

We should have known she was something special from the first two sentences in her first novel, *The Bluest Eye* (1970): "Quiet as it's kept, there were no marigolds in the fall of 1941. We thought, at the time, that it was because Pecola was having her father's baby that the marigolds did not grow." The surprise now, after the celebrity that sears and seals, is that back in 1970 she'd wanted to call herself by her *given* name, Chloe Anthony Wofford, but failed to persuade her publisher in time. Considering how crucial names always are in her fiction—Breedlove, Peace and Soaphead Church; Ajax and Jade; Baby Suggs and Stamp Paid—this looks stranger as the years go by. *Naming*, after all, is one of the great orchestral themes of *Song of Solomon*: If not for a Pilate and a Guitar, Macon (Milkman) Dead would not have learned to fly.

But the becoming was there to begin with, in this End-of-Childhood novel: the community and the scapegoat; caste and class; *rootedness* and the supernatural; prose you can sing as well as read; dreams of flight and transfiguration. Pecola imagines that if only she had blue eyes, she'd be as lovable as Shirley Temple was to Bo Jangles. She ends up crazy, "beating the air, a winged but grounded bird...picking and plucking her way between the tire rims and the sunflowers, between Coke bottles and milkweed, among all the waste and beauty of the world..."

Who will mother poor Pecola, when her own mother cares more about the little white girl in the house she cleans? Not Claudia, a faithless friend. Nor the sugar-brown hollyhocks girls from Meridian and Mobile who straighten their hair with Dixie peach and wash with Lifebuoy to rid themselves of "the dreadful funkiness of passion." Nor even those avatars of Black Motherhood who once upon a time felled trees, cut umbilical cords, loaded bales, rocked babies, plowed all day and came home nights "to nestle like plums under the limbs of their men." These avatars have declared themselves unavailable, past "lust and lactation, beyond tears and terror." Something's missing in this Lorain, Ohio, of kerosene lamps and dandelion soup and whores with names like Poland and China. Everybody seems to want Pecola's baby dead—"in a dark, wet place, its head covered with great O's of wool, the black face holding, like nickels, two clean black eyes, the flared nose, kissing-thick lips, and the living, breathing silk of black skin."

What's missing, as we will discover later on in Morrison's novels, is some figure like the Ancestor, that elder—down South, back in Africa—who connects her questing characters to the wisdom and solace of the textured past; the logic of lions. If Cholly Breedlove, *even* Cholly Breedlove, on his Georgia passage to find his father, had discovered such an Ancestor, he might never have raped his daughter. Cholly, instead, seems to be predicting *Jazz*:

The pieces of Cholly's life could become coherent only in the head of a musician. Only those who talked their talk through the gold of curved metal, or in the touch of black-and-white rectangles and taut skins and strings echoing from wooden corridors, could give true form to his life. Only they would know how to connect the heart of a red watermelon to the asafetida bag to the muscadine to the flashlight…and come up with what all this meant in joy, in pain, in anger, in love, and give it its final and pervading sense of freedom. Only a musician would sense, know, without even knowing that he knew, that Cholly was free. Dangerously free.

Sula flew away to big cities like Nashville and New York and came back, a plague of robins. "In that place, where they tore the night-shade and blackberry patches from their roots to make room for the Medallion City Golf Course, there was once a neighborhood." In *Sula* (1973), this neighborhood, a Bottom in the hills above an Ohio river town, is the narrator, a kind of chorus. It has its ways of dealing with crazies like Shadrack, witches like Sula, and white folks like us:

They did not believe doctors could heal—for them, none had never done so. They did not believe death was accidental—life might be, but death was deliberate. They did not believe Nature was ever askew—only inconvenient. Plague and drought were as "natural" as springtime. If milk could curdle, God knows robins could fall. The purpose of evil was to survive it and they determined (without ever knowing they had made up their minds to) to survive floods, white people, tuberculosis, famine and ignorance. They knew anger well but not despair, and they didn't stone sinners for the same reason they didn't commit suicide—it was beneath them.

Which isn't to say that these stoical communities are invariably wise. There's something self-serving about their forbearance. ("As Reverend Deal moved into his sermon, the hands of the women un-folded like pairs of raven's wings and flew high above their hats in the air…And they saw the Lamb's eye and the truly innocent victim: themselves.") They've a taste for scapegoats and pariahs. Lorain, after all, failed Pecola. Medallion feels better about itself with Sula around to behave so badly. Sula, who caused an innocent child to drown; Sula, who stole her best friend's husband; Sula, who watched her mother burn to death; Sula, with the flowering birthmark that seems to Nel a rose, to Jude a snake, to Shadrack a fish—this Sula, laughing at their God, is "the most magnificent hatred" the Bottom has ever known. They lay broomsticks across their doors at night; sprinkle salt on porch steps. But no more than failed crops, sick children, rednecks, social workers or plague, will this "strange young woman keep them from their God."

Some God. No wonder the rain freezes, silvering Medallion. And Nel cries "a fine cry—loud and long—but it had no bottom and it had no top, just circles and circles of sorrow."

But Sula *isn't* evil: "Had she paints or clay, or knew the discipline of the dance, or strings; had she anything to engage her tremendous curiosity and her gift for metaphor, she might have exchanged the restlessness and preoccupation with whim for an activity that provided her with all she yearned for. And like any artist with no art form, she became dangerous." Whatever she found *elsewhere*, even South, it wasn't sufficient; it wasn't Ancestral. Only the Bottom will take her back in, and even Nel lets her down. Still, Morrison needs this return of the prodigal daughter as much as Nel, "like getting the use of an eye back." Who else can love as Sula loves Ajax:

> *If I take a chamois and rub real hard on the bone, right on the ledge of your cheek bone, some of the black will disappear. It will flake away into the chamois and underneath there will be gold leaf. I can see it shining through the black. I know it is there...*
>
> *And if I take a nail file or even Eva's old paring knife—that will do—and scrape away at the gold, it will fall away and there will be alabaster. The alabaster is what gives your face its planes, its curves. That is why your mouth smiling does not reach your eyes. Alabaster is giving it a gravity that resists a total smile...*
>
> *Then I can take a chisel and small tap hammer and tap away at the alabaster. It will crack then like ice under the pick, and through the breaks I will see the loam, fertile, free of pebbles and twigs. For it is the loam that is giving you that smell...*

Already with this black, gold and alabaster; three Deweys and one-legged Eva in her wagon; a plague of robins and a ghostly ball of fur, hair and muddy strings floating in the light, we have moved out of Faulkner and into García Márquez, where the mindscapes are miraculous.

For instance: blue silk wings and red velvet rose petals and a bag of human bones; a horse named President Lincoln, a cow named Grant and a hog named General Lee; peacocks and bobcats and a spice-sweet ginger smell at night "that made you think of the East and striped tents and the *sha-sha-sha* of leg bracelets...the way freedom smelled, or justice, or luxury, or vengeance." If her other novels circle, and they do, *Song of Solomon* (1977) soars—from Not Doctor Street and No Mercy Hospital on Detroit's Southside, "where even love found its way with an ice pick"; to a ruined plantation, a cave of the dead and a witch named Circe, on the Susquehanna; to Shalimar, on nobody's map of Virginia, where everybody's name is Solomon, and the children sing a riddle-song, which proves on its decoding to be all about how you can ride the very air to Africa.

To be sure, we hear about Macon Dead Jr.'s money-making from his rent-houses, and the lakeshore vacation cabins he builds for the black bourgeoisie. And we go with his son into bars and barbershops, to talk about Kennedy and Elijah and meet those Seven Days assassins who revenge themselves for Emmett Till and Birmingham. ("Hitler's the most natural white man in the world," says Guitar; "He killed Jews and Gypsies because he didn't have us.") We're vouchsafed details on life insurance, raffle tickets, policy slips, bootlegging, Playtex garter belts and pink-veined marble, Dairy Queens and Belgian silk brocade, White Castles and domestic dread.

But *Song of Solomon* is really about naming, especially the ghosts. Macon Dead III is called "Milkman" because his mother nursed him a lot longer than, decently, she should have. But his father is Macon Dead Jr. and his grandfather was Macon Dead period, because of a drunken Union soldier on the journey north in a wagon-load of ex-slaves. His aunt is called Pilate, his sisters Magdalene and First Corinthians, and his cousins Reba and Hagar, because that's where the finger pointed in the family Bible. Circe asks Milkman, "Where'd you get a name like yours? White people name Negroes like race horses." Guitar says, "Niggers get their names the way they get everything else—the best way they can." Milkman thinks of the names black men got "from yearnings, gestures, flaws, events, mistakes, weaknesses. Names that bore witness." His father dreams of an ancestor with onyx skin and "a name that was real. A name given to him at birth with love and seriousness. A name that was not a joke, nor a disguise, nor a brand name."

This is the name Milkman discovers, where Charlemagne turns into Shalimar, and Sugarman to Solomon, and the ghost who cries out "Sing!" is actually naming his Indian wife. Like a sort of bodhisattva-wannabe out of *The Dream of the Red Chamber*, Milkman escapes his northern matriarchy into this lush South of peaches and turkeys and Calvins and Luthers, where he finds in folk memory and child-song not only a black Daedalus, but his own lost grandfather, who came to freedom "out of nowhere, as ignorant as a hammer and broke as a convict," and tamed the wilderness, and so, of course, "they shot the top of his head off."

Never mind that Guitar waits with a gun. Nor whether we can altogether admire a Daedalus who flies, no frills to Africa, leaving behind his wife and kids. What's compelling here is that, while Milkman never meets Solomon/Daedalus nor his ghostly grandfather Jake, he does at last recognize his own aunt Pilate. *Pilate* got him to go South, into American history and racial memory. *Pilate*—born without a navel ("a stomach as bald as a knee"); wearing her own name on a scrap of paper in the brass snuffbox earring; keeper of the eggs and bones; having hoed, fished, plowed and planted, grown vegetables, picked fruit, raised cattle, sold tobacco, made whiskey and talked to the dead—*Pilate* is the Ancestor, the Identity-Maker, an agency of levitation.

I fell off the truck with *Tar Baby* (1981). It still seems overly didactic, somehow brittle, her only novel you can't sing, the least operatic. Maybe if it had been more about Therese and Gideon, and less about Jade, the model who has been to Paris, or Son, the dreadlocked drifter who wants only to go home again, I might have had more patience with her Caribbean island and its fearful fish, puzzled clouds, stingless bees, rain forests full of angel women and ghosts of blind slaves; the various royalties (Catherine the Great, Valerian, Marie Therese) and so many sugar metaphors; all that anthropology and Caliban; Will Shakespeare meets Uncle Remus.

But Jade looks into the eyes of the wife killer with the "Mau Mau, Attica, chain-gang hair" and sees "spaces, mountains, savannas." And Son looks into the eyes of this arty young woman who thinks "Picasso *is* better than an Itumba mask" and sees "gold, cloisonne and honey-colored silk." He won't like imperial New York, she'll *hate* down-home Eloe, and the rest is soldier ants.

Not quite, of course. There are wonderful arias in *Tar Baby* (about stolen labor, insupportable innocence and, warming up for *Jazz*, black women in the big city); and some licorice stick lyricism ("the fruit of the banana trees puffed up stiff like the fingers of gouty kings"); and Valerian may be right when he says that the typical anthropologist is "a purveyor of exotics, a cultural orphan who sought other cultures he could love without risk or pain").

Must, however, a white woman torture her baby while a white man listens to the Goldberg Variations in a greenhouse? When Jade gets stuck in tar, couldn't we have gotten along without those tree women with "their sacred properties," their "pace of glaciers" and their smug faith "that they alone could hold together the stones of the pyramids"? Just the news; hold the Gaia. Would Toni Morrison, after all she's done, want to live in Eloe any more than Jade does? I am sorry that for Son there'll never be lions or a mating dance; that he's stuck with dice instead of tusks, a job instead of a journey. But those are the breaks. I'd like to have been a Druid myself.

About Son and Jade, we're read this lesson: "One had a past, the other had a future and each one bore the culture to save the race in his hands. Mama-spoiled black man, will you mature with me? Culture-bearing black woman, whose culture are you bearing?" While it's a lesson sufficient to float most modern novels, it seems thin for a Toni Morrison. She lets Son off too easily; and she denies, to Jade, all that leftover Sula.

But now we get a masterwork. *Beloved* (1988) imagines what's left out of the slave narratives. Morrison even went to Brazil to look at choke collars and leg irons you won't find in any of *our* museums, and then she wrote a ghost story about history. At its center is an act as awful as anything reported by the Hebrews, the Greeks or the Elizabethans. Inside *Beloved*'s circle of space-time—spell-bound, dream-dazed—the living and dead talk to and lay hands upon each other. Madness and memory cohabit. From this history, like a collective unconscious, the dead, like the repressed, return.

Though the novel begins in 1873, it has more than twenty years of explaining to do before we understand how Sethe, her nineteen-year-old daughter, Denver, and a ghost happen to be hiding from the neighbors and the past at 124 Bluestone Road in Cincinnati. We must go back to Sweet Home, Kentucky, in the early 1850s. Sethe, a teenaged mother then, pregnant with her fourth child, remembers

Sweet Home so : Two white boys "with mossy teeth, one sucking my breast the other holding me down, their bookreading teacher watching and writing it up." And the cowhide that left a scar-tree on her back that flowered red roses. And black boys "hanging from the most beautiful sycamore trees in the world." The flight as if from Egypt; Denver's birth in a boat, "under four summer stars" on the river passage to the free state of Ohio; and "one whole moon" of "unslaved life" before Schoolteacher on horseback arrived and Sethe like a black Medea raised her handsaw and Denver swallowed her sister's blood "right along with my mother's milk."

And this is what Paul D, "last of the Sweet Home men," recalls of Schoolteacher, Georgia prisons, the Civil War and his years on the road till Sethe: Sethe's husband, with his crazed head in the butter churn, "greased and flat-eyed as a fish"; Sixo, who had stopped speaking English "because there was no future in it," set on fire; a three-spoke neck collar, and an iron mouth-bit; the rockpile and the chain gang; sleeping in coffins, hiding in caves and fighting for food with owls and pigs; bad whiskey, hissing grass, "song-murders," "laughing dead men," and "a witless coloredwoman jailed and hanged for stealing ducks she believed were her babies."

Paul D wants to put his story, of "sucking iron," right next to Sethe's story, of stolen milk and river passage, and imagine a future for them. But first he must chase the ghost out of the house. The ghost—a spiteful "pool of red and undulating light" that tips tables and leaves palm prints on the butter—is, of course, Sethe's murdered baby. Once chased, she'll be replaced by a huge young woman, risen from the water with "midnight skin," sugar-devouring, diamond-hungry, exactly the age Sethe's baby, grown up, would be: Beloved. And Beloved chases Paul D.

What chance have Paul and Sethe? From his travels, Paul knows it's best to love everything "just a little bit, so when they broke its back, or shoved it in a croaker sack, well maybe you'll have a little love left over for the next one." Sethe misbelieves that "the future was a matter of keeping the past at bay"; her love is "too thick." Even this land isn't theirs. Sethe can't forgive herself for recalling the sycamores before she recalls the black boys hanging from them: "It made her wonder if hell was a pretty place too."

Morrison does a thousand splendid things in her circling. She introduces us to Baby Suggs, Sethe's mother-in-law, the Ancestor, who

used to preach of grace before she became ashamed of God and retired "to ponder colors" on her quilt, deciding, "There is no bad luck
in the world but whitefolks." And to Amy, a barefoot white girl on
her way to Boston to look for velvet, stopping just long enough to put
spiderwebs on the bloody tree on Sethe's back and deliver Denver.
And also to Stamp Paid: watchman, soldier, spy, busybody, torment-
ed by the song and sadness of "the people of the broken necks, of fire-
cooked blood and black girls who had lost their ribbons."

She acquaints us too with the unendingness of women's work,
even out of slavery: At home, wringing out sheets "so tight the rinse
water ran back up their arms," shoveling snow from the path to the
outhouse, breaking ice from the rain barrel, scouring and boiling last
summer's canning jars, packing mud in the hen house cracks and
warming chicks with their skirts. Away from home, besides the
cradling of white babies, there's laundry at the orphanage or asylum;
corn shucking at the mill; fish to clean, offal to rinse, stores to sweep,
lard to press, sausage to casepack and tavern kitchens to hide in so
white folks "didn't have to see them handle their food."

In fact, instead, these women gather in front of 124 (a way-station,
after all, for fugitive slaves, a place where history stopped), and their
voices search "for the right combination," the code that breaks the
back of words. When they find it there's "a wave of sound wide
enough to sound deep water and knock the pods off chestnut trees. It
broke over Sethe and she trembled like the baptized in its wash."
Beloved, "a naked woman with fish for hair," "thunderblack and glis-
tening," runs from the house to the woods and the river and is gone.
Exorcized. For now.

Amazing how all these little words of one, two or three syllables
strung together beadlike turn into a necklace or a whip. (Shakespeare
did it, too.) Put them together with the Baby Suggs "appetite for
color" and helpful Cherokee Indians. Add Paul's longing "to get to a
place where you could love anything you chose—not to need permission for desire." And find a woman like Sixo's: "a friend of my
mind...She gather me, man. The pieces I am, she gather them and
give them back to me in all the right order. It's good, you know,
when you got a woman who is a friend of your mind." But not in this
history, which is out of happy endings.

Ghost story, history lesson, mother-epic, incantation, folk and fairy
tale—of lost children and men on horseback; a handsaw, an ice pick

and a wishing well; Denver's "emerald light" and Amy's velvet; spiders
and roosters and the madness of hummingbirds with needle beaks as
dead babies are offered up to a shameful God; a devouring past of
everything that is unforgiven and denied; a hunger to eat all the love in
the world—*Beloved* belongs on the highest shelf of our literature even if
half a dozen canonized Wonderbread Boys have to be elbowed off. I
can't now picture our literature without it, between Whitman and
Twain, the Other in Faulkner, an African Flannery O'Connor, and who
knows what other cultures she's looked into, which masks she's put on
like a shaman, her secret antihistamines. Where *was* this book that
we've always needed? Without *Beloved*, our imagination of America had
a heart-sized hole in it big enough to die from. It didn't win every prize
it deserved, and the word was that some of the critics didn't believe in
ghosts. Like Shakespeare's clowns and Freud's dreams, Morrison's
ghosts always tell the truth. If I had voted against *Beloved*, I'd find it convenient, too, not to believe in ghosts.

> *"Watch out for her; she can give you dreams."* (Denver to Beloved,
> about their mother.)

Joe Trace, besides cosmetics, sells trust: "I make things easy." He
has a sad eye "that lets you look inside him, and a clear one that looks
inside you." In his opinion, his wife, Violet, "takes better care of her
parrot than she does of me. Rest of the time, she's cooking pork I can't
eat, or pressing hair I can't stand the smell of." He wishes he could remember their young love, coming north from Virginia, but has a
tough time "trying to catch what it felt like." He tries to dismiss "the
evil in my thoughts" because he isn't sure "the sooty music the blind
twins were playing wasn't the cause. It can do that to you, a certain
kind of guitar playing. Not like clarinets, but close." What Joe wants
at age fifty is to be free, not "to break loaves or feed the world on a
fish. Nor to raise the war dead, but free to do something wild." In
this, the City and *Jazz* conspire.

Names again: Joe's name is "Trace" because when he was abandoned down South as a baby, his parents "left without a trace." He is
that Trace.

. Violet had her spells even before Joe met Dorcas: falling down in the
street through "dark fissures in the globe light of the day"; conversations in her head with a corpse; "tears coming so fast she needs two

hands to catch them." Once, she even stole a baby. But, mostly, till she went to the funeral, she ironed hair and took care of her birds, who got to look at themselves in mirrors she arranged, including a parrot who said "Love you!" When she learns of Joe and Dorcas, she loses the birds and finds a knife. Later, she'll laugh at herself, "trying to do something bluesy, something hep, fumbling the knife, too late anyway." But the abandoned parrot keeps on crying at the window pane, in the snow: "Love you!" And the mirrors have nothing to look at.

"The children of suicides," we are told, "are hard to please and quick to believe no one loves them because they are not really here."

Dorcas, *exactly* like Josephine Baker, is a child of the East St. Louis race riots, which consumed her clothespin dolls and her parents. She's taken in by her aunt Alice, who makes clothes (and do) while hating the city and the "complicated anger" and the "appetite" of its "dirty, get-go-down music." But this music, that "bends, falls to its knees to embrace them all, encourage them all...why don't you since this is the it you've been looking for," is all Dorcas cares about besides movies and looking good, with her pencil-thin eyebrows and green shoes, despite "hoof marks" on her cheeks from acne. Is Dorcas the child Violet miscarried, or the one she tried to steal, or maybe Violet herself, equally motherless, archetypal orphan? Mothers and ghosts!

In *Jazz*, they are all trying to change the way they look, or in business to change the way somebody else looks, even with a knife.

So, too, is the City. Morrison has lived in New York City ever since she stopped teaching English to Stokley Carmichael and Claude Brown, down at Howard in the nation's capital. But the only time she ever wrote of it till now was, briefly, in *Tar Baby*, where Son was bewildered and Jade transcendent: "New York oiled her joints and she moved as though they were oiled. Her legs were longer here, her neck really connected her body to her head." *Jazz*, though, sings the City like a Whitman, "thriftless, warm, scary, full of amiable strangers"; a razor-slant of daylight; nightskies gone so purple with an orange heart that "the clothes of the people on the streets glow like dance-hall costumes"; "bright steel rocking above the shade below" and blocks, lots and side streets where what goes on is "anything the strong can think of and the weak will admire"; where there's a breath each morning that brightens the eye, the talk and the expectations like laughing gas; where "in halls and offices people are sitting around thinking future thoughts about projects and bridges and fastclicking trains underneath" because "history is over, you all, everything's ahead at last." To this city black folks came from "want and violence" and stayed "to look at their number, hear themselves in an audience, feel themselves moving down the street among hundreds of others who moved the way they did and who, when they spoke, regardless of accent, treated language like the same, intricate, malleable toy designed for their play."

Joe and Violet rode north in 1906 in the colored section of the Southern Sky:

When the train trembled approaching the water surrounding the City, they thought it was like them: nervous at having gotten there at last, but terrified of what was on the other side....The quick darkness in the carriage cars when they shot through a tunnel made them wonder if maybe there was a wall ahead to crash into or a cliff hanging over nothing. The train shivered with them at the thought and the trembling became the dancing under their feet. Joe stood up, his fingers clutching the baggage rack above his head. He felt the dancing better that way...

And so the young country couple, "laughing and tapping back at the tracks," danced into the City, which is itself a kind of jazz improvising its days and nights and blues, its dangerous freedom. And here they are—after a railroad flat in the Tenderloin, working domestic service and whitefolks' shoe leather, the cleaning of fish at night and of toilets in the daytime, the riots of 1917—in Harlem in 1926 where there are mailboxes but no high schools, bootleggers but no banks. And, suddenly, a Dorcas. When Joe went looking for the little tramp with a gun, who was he really missing? When Violet went with a knife to the funeral, who was she really cutting up?

If you know Toni Morrison at all by now, you know she'll go South again; if need be, all the way back to antebellum, not only for the servitude, the foreclosures, the lynchings and the mutilations, but for those ghostly waters and that bag of ancestral bones. For that phantom father who came home at last from his politicking with his gold ingots, reed whistles, dollar bills and a tin of Frieda's Egyptian Hair Pomade, too late to save Violet's mother, Rose Dear, from throwing herself down a well "so narrow, so dark it was pure, breathing relief to see her stretched in a wooden box." For the trail of ruined honeycombs, bits and leavings of stolen victuals, the blue-black birds with the bolt of red on their wings, and the gopher-freezing music of running water and high-tree wind, in search of Wild, *Joe's* mother, and her secret cave and her circle of stones and buttons of bone. This is the South of their own minds: why Joe has eyes of different colors, and Violet falls through cracks, and what the music's all about—"I could hear," we are told by the Voice that narrates *Jazz*, "the men playing out their maple-sugar hearts, tapping it from four-hundred-year-old trees, and letting it run down the trunk, wasting it because they didn't have a bucket to hold it and didn't want one either"—and why, when she bleeds to death, even Dorcas, while seeing the bright oranges, also hears something: "Listen. I don't know who is that woman singing but I know the words by heart." It is also, of course, the ultimate South of Sula: past black and gold and alabaster, down to the fertile loam and a song of reconciliation.

I haven't even mentioned Malvonne, who lives alone with "other people's stories printed in small books," or her nephew Sweetness who steals uncanceled letters from the post office. Nor Neola, partly paralyzed since her fiancé abandoned her, "as though she held the broken pieces of her heart together in the crook of her frozen arm." Nor True Belle and Vera Lee and Golden Gray, whose own father comes as such a shock. Nor Hunter, nor Acton, and not even Felice, who is everything that Dorcas wasn't, and whose father is happy working on the Pullman. No matter what our narrator tells us is going to happen after Felice enters the novel, "with an Okeh record under her arm and carrying some stewmeat wrapped in butcher paper, another girl with four marcelled waves on either side of her head," nobody *this* time is going to shoot *anybody*.

You will have to think about who's telling you this story, and I might as well admit I got too clever doing so. Picking up on the epigraph to *Jazz*—from "Thunder, Perfect Mind" in *The Nag Hammadi*—and knowing that Morrison now spends part of every week at Princeton with Elaine Pagels, who wrote the book on *The Gnostic Gospels*, I said, alas, "Aha!" "Thunder, Perfect Mind" is the revelation of a *feminine* power: "I am the whore, and the holy one. I am the wife and the virgin. I am (the mother) and the daughter..." And so on. All this missed the obvious point.

This Voice, with a "sweet tooth" for pain, complains that she hasn't any muscles and so can't defend herself; has lived too long in her own mind, really ought to get out more, but is tired of having been "left standing" while her partner falls asleep; accuses herself of carelessness when things go wrong; wants to "dream a nice dream" for the reader, "be the language that wishes him well, speaks his name, wakes him when his eyes need to be open"; feels predictable, even a bit false—"What would I be without a few brilliant spots of blood to ponder?"—and apostrophizes:

I love the way you hold me, how close you let me be to you. I like your fingers on and on, lifting, turning. I have watched your face for a long time now, and missed your eyes when you went away from me.

It finally occurred to me that I wasn't being talked to by a goddess, or a clarinet: "If I were able I'd say it. Say make me, remake me. You are free to do it and I am free to let you because look, look. Look where your hands are. Now." Where my hands were *then* was holding on to my copy of *Jazz*. The Voice is the book itself, this physical object, our metatext...a whimsy and a wickedness worthy of a Nabokov. And out of this Pandora's box comes not only "something rogue, something else you have to figure in before you can figure it out," but all the love in the world—the love that Beloved was so hungry for and Pecola never got from anybody and Joe Trace thought he couldn't remember and Sula knew would only come to her after "Lindbergh sleeps with Bessie Smith and Norma Shearer makes it with Stepin Fetchit"; even Hagar's "graveyard love" for Milkman, the kind that made "women pull their dresses over their heads and howl like dogs" and sat men down in doorways "with pennies in their mouths"; but most of all, with a wink and all that radiance, Toni Morrison's surpassing love for her people and her readers.

Jazz, yes; but also Mozart.

KURT VONNEGUT: THE LAST INNOCENT WHITE MAN IN AMERICA

Hocus Pocus seems to me to be Vonnegut's best novel in years—funny and prophetic, yes, and fabulous, too, as cunning as Aesop and as gloomy as Grimm; but also rich and referential; a meditation on American history and American literature; an elegy; a keening. "How is this for a definition of high art?" we are asked by the antihero, Eugene Debs Hartke: "'Making the most of the raw materials of futility'?"

But *Hocus Pocus* has been not so much reviewed as consumer-tested like a bar of chocolate, as if all Vonneguts were Hersheys, needing only to be categorized as Semi-Sweet, Special Dark or Bitter Almond. Without even bothering to cut a new stencil, critics perceive him an amusing atavism of the sixties. Or a celebrity-guru who's reached the bottom of his cracker barrel. Or a pet rock. Or an old fart. It makes you wonder why a writer ever tries to do something different. It also makes you wonder what it is the reader really wants from a writer who's been around so nobly, so long.

We take our leave of a Vonnegut novel, even of *Hocus Pocus*, feeling…what? Certainly not comforted, nor galvanized, nor whammied. More…reflective, as if emerging from the vectors of a haiku. I spent a Christmas with him years ago in New Hampshire. We happened in an orchard on black apples stuck to a stricken bough. During the October picking season, helicopters had sprayed Stop-Drop on these apples, and then an early frost had killed them off, and so they hung there, very Japanese. Vonnegut said, "If you don't write about those apples, I will." He never did. Maybe they were too conveniently symbolic. (Stop-Drop, after all, is a kind of Ice-9.) But that's not how a novel of his feels, either.

Another time, in Maine I think, Vonnegut got down and dirty with Ray Mungo, who explained that his communards were leaving for the wilds of Canada because, "We want to be the last people living on the earth." Vonnegut wondered, "Isn't that a sort of stuck-up thing to want to be?" And, of course, stuck-up writers are a dime a dozen: warthog postmodernists, the history-devouring sage, Umberto Eco. We never feel after reading Vonnegut that he thinks he's better than we are, even though he probably is. We feel that a sad man, inside his funny jokes, despairs of our ever getting his plainspoken point, and we're grateful that he goes on anyway trying all over again to make us braver and wiser, but the mind clouds as the teeth grin…and we go about our chastened business with a blank uneasiness. He's such a…*fatalist.*

Let me try again: At the end of the *American Playhouse* public-TV production of Terence McNally's play *Andre's Mother*, the mother (Sada Thompson) and the lover (Richard Thomas) go to Central Park to mourn Andre's death from AIDS. Unable to speak their grief, they send up little white balloons. It is a kind of naming. That's what a Vonnegut feels like, only his balloons are black, like those apples.

We began taking him for granted after his megabucks Dresden novel, _Slaughterhouse-Five_. Part of it was his own fault. His next time out, in _Breakfast of Champions_, he detached himself from his creations, cut the strings, as if they were marionettes or kites. He was fifty years old: "Under similar spiritual conditions, Count Tolstoi freed his serfs. Thomas Jefferson freed his slaves. I am going to set at liberty all the literary characters who have served me so loyally during my writing career." Readers hate this, which is why Arthur Conan Doyle had to bring back Sherlock Holmes, and why Nicolas Freeling is resented for having lost interest in Van der Valk. Besides, with _Breakfast_, weird personal stuff started creeping into Vonnegut's fiction—like his dead father. He dropped the "junior"; he came back to Earth.

But by that time, we felt we'd gotten the message, and it wasn't "Greetings!" _The Sirens of Titan_ asked us how to cause "less rather than more pain," how to "love whoever is around to be loved." _Mother Night_ warned that, "We are what we pretend to be, so we must be careful about what we pretend to be." Bokonon, in _Cat's Cradle_, told us to "Pay no attention to Caesar. Caesar doesn't know what's _really_ going on." _God Bless You, Mr. Rosewater_ wanted to know "how to love people who have no use." Billy Pilgrim in _Slaughterhouse-Five_ overheard Eliot Rosewater telling his psychiatrist, "I think you guys are going to have to come up with a lot of wonderful _new_ lies, or people just aren't going to want to go on living."

Art, of course, is a wonderful lie. After catastrophes and revolutions, Hiroshima and "the Nazi monkey business," God was telling us through Vonnegut that we'd have to invent the meaning of "all this" for ourselves—dream it up. This is why his characters left town so often, left Mother Earth herself, for outer space, for Tralfamadore. On Tralfamadore, the novels have "no beginning, no middle, no end, no moral, no causes, no effects"; they're just clumps of symbols. Vonnegut seems to need Tralfamadorians the way García Márquez needs angels and Toni Morrison needs ghosts and Shakespeare needed clowns. Just maybe, by the transcendent power of the imagination, we could reverse the charges, call back the bombers over Dresden:

American planes, full of holes and wounded men and corpses, took off backwards from an airfield in England. Over France, a few German fighters flew at them backwards, sucked bullets and shell fragments from some of the planes and crewmen...The formation flew backwards over a German city *that was in flames. The bombers opened their bomb bay doors, exerted a miraculous magnetism which shrunk the fires, gathered them into cylindrical steel containers, and lifted the containers into the bellies of the planes.... When the bombers got back to their base, the steel cylinders were taken from the racks and shipped back to the United States of America, where factories were operating day and night, dismantling the cylinders, separating the dangerous contents into minerals. Touchingly, it was mainly women who did this work. The minerals were then shipped to specialists in remote areas. It was their business to put them into the ground, to hide them cleverly, so they would never hurt anybody ever again.*

Then again, maybe not. *Breakfast of Champions* was gloomier. Imagination was not enough. In *Breakfast*, the science-fiction novelist Kilgore Trout imagined "a dialogue between two pieces of yeast. They were discussing the possible purposes of life as they ate sugar and suffocated in their own excrement. Because of their limited intelligence, they never came close to realizing that they were making champagne." Bummer! So much for a chrono-synclastic infundibulum.

But Vonnegut went on dreaming after *Breakfast*—without his critics. ("Yes," he said in *Slapstick*, "and while my big brother meditated about clouds, the mind *I* was given daydreamed the story in this book. It is about desolated cities and spiritual cannibalism and incest and loneliness and lovelessness and death...") It's just that he dreamed his way into different sorts of heads, heads attached to symbolic citizens—writers, soldiers, artists and politicians—whose moral autonomy wasn't what it ought to have been. The weather inside these heads rained confusion; history came down hard and hurt; we were killing the planet. The transforming powers of the romantic self needed some group help, some civic assistance, a home front.

Slapstick is a fairy tale set in the future instead of the past. There are monsters who mean well, a witch, a Tom Thumb (he's Chinese), a noble steed named Budweiser ("golden feathers hid her hooves"), a perilous journey with a gift (a Dresden candlestick stolen from a sleeping chieftain's tent), an Island of Death (where "people lit their homes at night with burning rags stuck in bowls of animal fat") and a ceremony (the hundreth birthday party for the last American president, who's writing his memoirs, which is the book we are reading). There are three ideas many another postmodernist would kill for: a gravity that's as variable as the weather, a Church of Jesus Christ the Kidnapped, and a blueprint for abolishing loneliness like this:

A computer would establish 10,000 brand-new "extended families," giving "proportional representation to all sorts of Americans, according to their numbers," by randomly assigning everybody in the country a new name that consists "of a noun, the name of a flower or a fruit or a fish or a mollusk, or a gem or a mineral or a chemical element—connected by a hyphen to a number between one and twenty." Thus, every individual instantly acquires 190,000 cousins (same middle name) and 10,000 brothers and sisters (same middle name and number). Daffodils, Orioles, Berylliums, Chipmunks, Bauxites, Strawberries and Pachysandras form clubs and even "parliaments" to take care of one another.

One more misbegotten "granfalloon," like the Communist party...

And yet: *Slapstick* also proposes that, even if we aren't "really very good at life," we must nevertheless, like Laurel and Hardy, "bargain in good faith" with our destinies. And there are instruction manuals for this bargaining: *Robert's Rules of Order*, the principles of Alcoholics Anonymous, and the Bill of Rights.

None of these books was written by a Tralfamadorian.

Jailbird is about Harvard and Nixon, Sacco and Vanzetti, Hiss and Chambers, labor unions, corporate greed, the Holocaust and Watergate, not to mention Roy Cohn. There are catacombs under Grand Central and harps on top of the Chrysler Building and even Nixon's "unhappy little smile" looks "like a rosebud that had just been smashed by a hammer." Some fairy tale! "Strong stuff," says Starbuck, whose girlfriend tells him: "You can't help it that you were born without a heart. At least you tried to believe what the people with hearts believed—so you were a good man just the same." And she reads Starbuck's books the way we should read Vonnegut's, "the way a young cannibal might eat the hearts of brave old enemies. Their magic would become hers."

To the three how-to manuals mentioned in *Slapstick*, *Jailbird* adds a couple more: Lincoln's *with malice toward none* Second Inaugural— Vonnegut may look like Mark Twain, but he feels as bad as Honest Abe: "Strange mingling of mirth and tears, of tragic and grotesque, of cap and crown, of Socrates and Rabelais, of Aesop and Marcus Aurelius," said Ralph Ingersoll of Lincoln—and, most radical of all, Jesus Christ's Sermon on the Mount. Kilgore Trout, one of the few Von-

negut characters besides Wanda June to survive the Defenestration of
Breakfast, is in jail for treason because he has preached the Sermon on
the Mount.

Galapagos is about evolution, and *Dead-Eye Dick* is about the neutron
bomb, and *Bluebeard* is about the Abstract Expressionism of Evil.
Strong stuff!

Like Starbuck in *Jailbird*, Rabo Karabekian in *Bluebeard* tries "to believe what the people with hearts believed," so perhaps he's a good
man "just the same"—a child of survivors of the Turkish massacre of
the Armenians, which gives us one more genocide to grieve; a veteran, like all Vonnegut's antiheroes, of World War II, which he spent
commanding a platoon of artists "so good at camouflage that half the
things we hid from the enemy have never been seen again"; postwar
intimate of Pollock and Rothko; once divorced, once widowed, twice
a failed father. Although Rabo paints, he isn't very good at the modernist art that paints "absolutely nothing but itself." Much of his own
work has been destroyed, "thanks to unforeseen chemical reactions
between the sizing of my canvases and the acrylic wall paint and colored tapes I applied to them." He rusticates in misanthropic Hamptons exile, with an empty pool and a locked potato barn, inside which
we meet his last will and testament, his secret witness.

There are the usual dark chords. We are reminded of the industrial
know-how a genocide needs "to kill that many big resourceful animals cheaply and quickly, make sure nobody gets away, and dispose
of mountains of meat and bones afterwards." (On the college lecture
circuit, Vonnegut speaks of "humanity itself [as] an unstoppable glacier made of hot meat, which ate up everything in sight and then made
love, and then doubled in size again.") But there are also the usual
grace notes, those lovely moments that seem to fall in Vonnegut's
pages like autumn leaves. According to Rabo, for example, God Himself "must have been hilarious when human beings so mingled iron
and water and fire to make a railroad train."

But what we've picked up, of importance, along the way in these late
novels are more books of recipes—Shakespeare, *Don Quixote*, Goethe's
Faust, Picasso's *Guernica*, *Gulliver's Travels*, *Alice in Wonderland*. This is a library of how-to (and etiquette) instruction manuals, cookbooks and
sacred civilizing texts; a nest of brains where we sit ourselves down to
read the latest novel by a Johnny Appleseed of decencies, a Space-Age

Buddha—the first Green and the last innocent white man in America, Vonnegut at sixty-eight.

We should know he's up to something special in _Hocus Pocus_ just from the name of his antihero, Eugene Debs Hartke. Debs of course was the American labor leader who said, "While there is a lower class I am in it. While there is a criminal element I am of it. While there is a soul in prison I am not free." Debs tried to keep us out of World War I, but lost out to a more practical-minded Samuel Gompers. He'll lose out again with Hartke, who wanted as a boy to go to the University of Michigan but who ends up instead, after cheating in a high school science fair, at West Point. From the Point, he goes to Vietnam. ("If I were a fighter plane instead of a human being," he says, "there would be little pictures of people painted all over me.") From Vietnam, he goes to teach the dyslexic children of the Anglo-Saxon filthy-rich, at Tarkington College in upstate New York, where there's a Somoza Hall and a Pahlavi Pavilion. From Tarkington he goes to teach black and Hispanic illiterates at the New York State Maximum Security Adult Correctional Facility at Athena—"a brutal fortress of iron and masonry on a naked hilltop"—directly across the valley from the college.

For different reasons, in the year 2001, learning-disabled children of the filthy-rich and illiterate black and Hispanic dopedealers can't read the Writing on the Wall. Even if they could, says Hartke, "Just because some of us can read and write and do a little math, that doesn't mean we deserve to conquer the Universe."

We are reading the story that Hartke has written down on stray scraps of brown wrapping paper and the backs of envelopes, while awaiting trial—like Howard Campbell in _Mother Night_, like Kilgore Trout in _Jailbird_—for treason. There has been a failed revolution. The blacks and Hispanics escaped from Athena, crossed the frozen lake in the valley, ate the horses and the campus dogs, and killed some white people in the "diamond-studded Oz or City of God or Camelot" of Tarkington. Before they all got murdered in their turn, they declared a sort of Paris Commune. Since it is assumed by the triumphant military government that blacks and Hispanics could not possibly have plotted this revolt on their own, Hartke must have done it for them. Besides waiting for his trial, he is also adding up the number of women he's gone to bed with, and the number of men he's killed, and he's afraid he will arrive at the exact same body-count.

I won't tell you about Hartke's crazy wife and his mother-in-law, who make spiderwebs of toilet paper all over the house. Or just how our prisons came to be "color-coded." Or what we're supposed to think of GRIOT, the computer program of the sociobiologists. Or why Hartke thinks "the two principal currencies of the planet are the Yen and fellatio." And never mind what goes on at the Black Cat Cafe. But there are some things you need to know.

In the year 2001, Japanese run our prisons and hospitals, though they were smart enough to pass on our inner-city schools. Koreans own the *New York Times*. Italians own the St. Louis Cardinals. Among the trustees of Tarkington College are a thinly disguised William F. Buckley and a thinly disguised Malcolm Forbes—who shows up with Elizabeth Taylor on a motorcycle. These trustees are told, although they refuse to believe it, that they have treated America as a "plantation." Now that "the soil is exhausted, and the natives are getting sicker and hungrier every day, begging for food and medicine and shelter," and the water mains are broken and the bridges are falling down, "You are taking all your money and getting out of here."

This happens in a valley where once upon a time they used to build the covered wagons that went West, the prairie schooners for the fast-food Donner Party. There are also in the valley Indian ghosts, floating castles, severed heads and twenty-seven perpetual-motion machines "with garnets and amethysts for bearings, with arms and legs of exotic woods, with tumbling balls of ivory, with chutes and counterweights of silver." As if to balance this "magic of precious metals"—as everything in *Hocus Pocus* is exquisitely balanced, from the dyslexics and the illiterates to the number of women loved versus the number of men murdered—there is a carillon of thirty-two bells made "from mingled Union and Confederate rifle barrels and cannon balls gathered up after the Battle of Gettysburg." At Gettysburg, in fact, the man who started Tarkington College was shot by Confederate soldiers because he looked so much like Abraham Lincoln.

Mention is also made of Lee, Custer and Westmoreland.

A critic doesn't have to work very hard to figure out that, for Kurt Vonnegut, the Civil War between whites and blacks is far from over, and the Civil War between rich and poor has only begun, and that's what he's writing his novel about. Nor need you be a semiotician to notice that he does his dreaming about the Civil War inside the fevered head of American literature.

Its not just that these prisoners skating over the frozen lake are right out of _Uncle Tom's Cabin._ Nor that we meet James Fenimore Cooper, Theodore Dreiser and a mortician with the name of "Norman Updike." Nor that, like Mailer and Arthur Miller, Hartke can't stop brooding about Marilyn Monroe. Edgar Allan Poe is quoted. We're actually introduced to Moby Dick (at least his penis). I'm sure there are New England Transcendentalists hiding like angels in these hardwood trees. "Tarkington" probably refers as well to Booth, like Vonnegut an Indiana novelist, although he went to Fitzgerald's Princeton instead of Vonnegut's (and Pynchon's) Cornell. Remember the _Penrod_ and _The Plutocrat?_ Like Cheever's _Falconer, Hocus Pocus_ is a Sing Sing/Attica novel. Hartke's scraps of paper remind me of those "odds and ends of thoughts" that Dr. Reefy in _Winesburg, Ohio_ scribbled down and "stuffed away in his pockets to become round hard balls." I wouldn't even be surprised if one reason Vonnegut left all the dirty words out of _Hocus Pocus_ was because he felt as playful as Mark Twain felt when he left all the weather out of _The American Claimant._

If I seem to be working too hard, it's because nobody else did...except Vonnegut. Like Walt Whitman (and Allen Ginsberg), when Vonnegut goes to Civil War, he's a male nurse. _Leaves of Grass_ is another of his sacred texts. American literature itself, the lens through which he looks at history, bloody history, is a comfort—and a subversion. According to Hawthorne: "'Faith!' shouted Goodman Brown, in a voice of agony and desperation; and the echoes of the forest mocked him, crying, 'Faith! Faith!,' as if bewildered wretches were seeking her all through the wilderness." And Meville, on reading Hawthorne, stopped to shake his head: "For, in certain moods, no man can weigh this world without throwing in something, somehow like Original Sin, to strike the uneven balance...this black conceit pervades him through and through."

Black conceits, black apples, black balloons...Strong stuff!

DON DELILLO:
WHO KILLED JOHN F. KENNEDY? (THE CIA)

Don DeLillo's cold and brilliant novel begins with thirteen-year-old Lee Harvey Oswald and his mother—that American Medea, Marguerite—watching television in the Bronx. For "inward-spinning"

Oswald, his mother *is* a television. Her voice falls "through a hole in the air." She stays up late to compare test patterns.

Libra ends with a hole in the ground, and Marguerite's apostrophizing, "They will search out environmental factors, that we moved from home to home. Judge, I have lived in many places but never filthy dirty, never not neat, never without the personal living touch, the decorator item. We have moved to be a family. This is the theme of my research."

Between these solitudes, someone else is doing the research. DeLillo, who's shy, has found himself a surrogate: Nicholas Branch, CIA (Retired), sits exactly like an author-god at a desktop computer in a glove-leather chair in a book-lined fireproof room full of "theories that gleam like jade idols." He follows "bullet trajectories backwards to the lives that occupy the shadows." He feels "a strangeness...that is almost holy. There is much here that is holy, an aberration in the heartland of the real." Branch is writing, at the Agency's request, a secret history of Dallas—those "six point nine seconds of heat and light" on November 22, 1963. The Agency has given him more than he needs to know. For instance:

> *The Curator sends the results of ballistics tests carried out on human skulls and goat carcasses, on blocks of gelatin mixed with horsemeat...bullet-shattered goat heads in closeup...a gelatin-tissue model "dressed" like the President. It is pure modernist sculpture, a block of gelatin layered in suit and shirt material with a strip of undershirt showing, bullet-smoked.*

Equally modernist, of course, is the Warren Commission Report, "with its twenty-six accompanying volumes of testimony and exhibits, its millions of words":

> *Branch thinks this is the megaton novel James Joyce would have written if he'd moved to Iowa City and lived to be a hundred....Everything belongs, everything adheres, the mutter of obscure witnesses, the photos of illegible documents and odd sad personal debris, things gathered up at a dying—old shoes, pajama tops, letters from Russia. This is the Joycean Book of America.*

And what does the historian decide—after his access to goats' heads and pajama tops; psychiatrists and KGB defectors; confidential Agency files and transcripts of the secret hearings of congressional committees; wiretaps, polygraphs, Dictabelt recordings, postoperative X rays, computer enhancements of the Zapruder film, Jack Ruby's mother's dental chart, microphotographs of strands of Oswald's pubic hair (smooth, not knobby), FBI reports on *dreams*...and the long roster of the conveniently dead?

Branch decides "his subject is not politics or violent crime but men in small rooms." To be sure, his own Agency may be "protecting something very much like its identity," but rogue elements of that Agency have conspired in their small rooms to write an enormous fiction. They will mount an attempt on the president's life that's intended to be a "surgical" near-miss. They will leave a "papertrail" that leads from this attempt to Castro's Cuba, their "moonlit fixation in the emerald sea." They require someone like an Oswald, a fall-guy *figment*, to point the way.

Libra deconstructs the official story and reimagines the dreary principals whom we know already from the pages of the Warren Report and the fevers of Jim Garrison. But it also peoples the parentheses of this shadow world with monsters of its own—agents disgraced at the Bay of Pigs; cowboy mercenaries shopping for a little war; Kennedy-hating Mafiosi, international remittance men, Batista swamp-rats; myths (salamanders out of Paracelsus) and freaks (geeks, androgynes). If his surrogate Branch is a stay-at-home, DeLillo flies by night, and enters, an exorcist, into rooms and dreams. In each room, he finds a secret and a coincidence, a loneliness and a connection, even a kind of theology: "the rapture of the fear of believing."

Win Everett, for instance, is the Agency author-god of the JFK plot, for whom "secrets are an exalted state," "a way of arresting motion, stopping the world so we can see ourselves in it." In his small room with Elmer's Glue-All and an X-Acto knife, he invents the Oswald-figment out of fake passports, false names, phony address books, doctored photographs; "scripts" him "out of ordinary pocket litter." He has, if not misgivings, at least forebodings:

There is a tendency of plots to move toward death. He believed that the idea of death is woven into the nature of every plot. A narrative plot no less than a conspiracy of armed men. The tighter the plot of a story, the more likely it will come to death. A plot in fiction, he believed, is the way we localize the force of death outside the book, play it off, contain it....He worried about the deathward logic of his plot.

But the Agency's bound to forgive him: "What's more, they would admire the complexity of his plan...It had art and memory. It had a sense of responsibility, of moral force. And it was a picture in the world of their own guilty wishes."

He sounds like any old modernist at the keyboard of his master-work, his Terminal Novel, his grand harmonium of randomness. Imagine his surprise on finding that there really *is* an Oswald, sitting there in a Speed Wash laundromat in Dallas at midnight reading H.G. Wells's *Outline of History*. It's creepy. Dyslexic Lee, who grew up dreaming of Lenin and Trotsky, "men who lived in isolation...close to death through long winters in exile or prison, feeling history in the room, waiting for the moment when it would surge through the walls..." Ozzie the Rabbit in Tokyo: "Here the smallness had mean-ing. The paper windows and boxrooms, these were clear-minded states, forms of well-being." A Marine defector who cuts his wrist to stay in Russia; a wife abuser who gets "secret instructions" from "the whole busy air of transmission...through the night into his skin"; a Fair-Play-for-Cuba mail-order assassin whose stated ambition it is "to be a short story writer on contemporary American themes"—he's spent his whole life converging on a plot that is itself just eight months old.

Learning there is a *real* Oswald, Everett feels "displaced": "It pro-duced a sensation of the eeriest panic, gave him a glimpse of the fic-tion he'd been devising, a fiction living prematurely in the world."

His co-conspirator, Parmenter, a member of "the Groton-Yale-OSS network of so-called gentlemen spies," is grateful to the Agency for its understanding and its trust: "The deeper the ambiguity, the more we believe." During the overthrow of Arbenz in 1954, Parmenter's radio station, "supposedly run by rebels from a jungle outpost in Guatemala," was really in Honduras, broadcasting disinformation: "rumors, false battle reports, meaningless codes, inflammatory speeches, orders to nonexisistent rebels. It was like a class project in the structure of reality. Parmenter wrote some of the broadcasts him-self, going for vivid imagery, fields of rotting bodies..." A *real* Oswald makes him laugh: "It was all so funny...Everyone was a spook or dupe or asset, a double, courier, cutout or defector, or was related to one. We were all linked in a vast and rhythmic coincidence..."

But the president dies of coincidence, and so does Oswald. Like Os-wald, *everybody* is writing fiction "on contemporary American themes." One conspirator, Mackey, works with a private army of Cuban exiles: "Alpha was run like a dream clinic. The Agency worked up a vision, then got Alpha to make it come true." Another, Wayne, lives on Fourth Street in Miami: "Judo instructors, tugboat captains, homeless Cubans, ex-paratroopers like Wayne, mercenaries from wars nobody heard of, in West Africa or Malay. They were like guys straight out of Wayne's favorite movie *Seven Samurai*, warriors without masters willing to band together to save a village from marauders, to win back a country, only to see themselves betrayed in the end."

So much bad art. This is Joan Didion's territory, isn't it, paranoia and blank uneasiness? Just so, the Mafia boss Carmine Latta, with his wiseguy contempt for social orders not his own, seems to have wandered in from Saul Bellow, Chicago instead of New Orleans. But with Didion, paranoia is personal, and so, for Bellow, is contempt. DeLillo is loftier, in a room that hangs above the world. He's part camera, of course, with a savage eye on, say, pretty Marina with the "breezes in her head," or Ruby, whose desperate jauntiness breaks the heart:

> *If I don't get there in time, it's decreed I wasn't meant to do it. He drove through Dealey Plaza, slightly out of the way, to look at the wreaths again. He talked to Sheba about was she hungry, did she want her Alpo. He parked in a lot across the street from the Western Union Office. He opened the trunk, got out the dog food and a can opener and fixed the dog her meal, which he left on the front seat. He took two thousand dollars out of the moneybag and stuffed it in his pockets because this is how a club owner walks into a room. He put the gun in his right hip pocket. His name was stamped in gold inside his hat.*

But language is DeLillo's plastique. Out of gnarled speech, funny, vulgar, gnomic, he composes stunning cantatas for the damned to sing. *Libra* is as choral as it's cinematic. Marguerite is the scariest mother since *Faust*, and David Ferrie, with his homemade eyebows, mohair toupee, and the land mines in his kitchen, his expertise on cancer and astrology, seems to speak to us through the cavities in our teeth: "All my fears are primitive. It's the limbic system of the brain. I've got a million years of terror stored up there." For Ferrie, "astrology is the language of the night sky, of starry aspect and position, the truth at the end of human affairs." Oswald is a Libra, which means Scales: "You're a quirk of history," Ferrie says; "you're a coincidence."

But we say coincidence when we don't know what to call it: "It goes deeper...There's a hidden principle. Every process contains its own outcome." On learning Kennedy's motorcade route, Ferrie is beside himself: "We didn't arrange your job in that building or set up the motorcade route. We don't have that kind of reach...There's something else that's generating this event. A pattern outside experience. Something that *jerks* you out of the spin of history. I think you've had it backwards all the time. You wanted to enter history. Wrong approach, Leon. What you really want is out."

But, thinks Ferrie: "*There's more to it. There's always more to it. This is what history consists of. It's the sum total of all the things they aren't telling us.*"

I'm inclined to believe him; I'm not a buff anymore; the assassination hurt my head. Maybe there was a second gunman on the grassy knoll. Maybe Ruby owed money and a favor to the mob. Certainly the shadow world is full of rogues. We read about the novels they have written every day in the funny papers.

DeLillo, though, is an agnostic about reality itself. With its command of the facts and the fantasies, its sliderule convergence, its cantatas and its hyperspace, *Libra* is plausible. But it's also art, the peculiar art he's been perfecting since the antihero of *Americana* abandoned the Vietnam war on television in New York for another war in the American interior. Since, in *End Zone*, football became a metaphor for Armageddon. Since, in *Great Jones Street*, a grotesque rock 'n' roll amalgam of Jagger and Dylan hid out in the East Village from the thought police and from the terror he had himself sown in "the erotic dreams of the republic." Since, in *Ratner's Star*, the superstitions of astrophysics were deployed in a galaxy of time running out and space exploding. In *Players*, terrorists want to blow up the Stock Exchange, with some deracinated Yuppie help. In *Running Dog*, secret agents, pornographers, Buddhists and Hitler all end up in Dallas. In *The Names*, a "risk analyst" for a company insuring multinational corporations against accidents of history goes to Athens, Ankara and Beirut, to find out that he really works for the CIA, in the service of "new kinds of death." In *White Noise*, Nazis make a comeback in middleamerica in the cognitive dissonance at the heart of the consumer culture, where our universities are indistinguishable from our shopping malls, and we lie to ourselves in euphemisms on the TV set and in our dreams, and one of the ex-wives of a professor of Hitler Studies is a part-time spook: "She reviewed fiction for the CIA, mainly long serious novels with coded structures."

At the end of these DeLillo novels, there was nothing left but relative densities of language. He was limbering up for the big dread.

With the White Knight gone, there's no coherence, no community, no faith, no accountability, merely hum. In a faithless culture, death is the ultimate kick. In a random cosmos (those accidental stars, that coincidental static), we need a new *black* magic, "a theology of secrets." Against anarchism, nihilism and terrorism, why not an occult of the intelligence agency, the latest in Gnostic heresies? Against alienation: paranoia. Against meaninglessness: conspiracy. It's all modernist mirrors: disinformation and counterintelligence. Beckett, Borges and Nabokov; Conrad, Kafka and *The Wasteland*...poor Fyodor: crime without punishment.

Oswald, of course, was the Underground Man. The deepest of covers is lunacy.

In Asia and the Middle East, in Latin America and in Dallas, *They* are writing our novel, our meta-fiction, and they are insane.

MAXINE HONG KINGSTON: BUDDHA IN BERKELEY

We won't get anywhere with *Tripmaster Monkey* unless we understand that Maxine Hong Kingston is playing around like a Nabokov with the two cultures in her head. In *Ada*, by deciding that certain wars, which were lost, should have been won, Nabokov rearranged history to suit himself. There were Russians all over North America, making trilingual puns. This odd world was a parody of Russian novels. In *Tripmaster*, America in the sixties is looked at through the lens of a half-dozen Chinese novels, most of them sixteenth century.

First, a disabusing. What everybody seems to have wanted from Kingston, after a decade of silence, is another dreambook, like *The Woman Warrior*. Or another history lesson, like *China Men*. Anyway: more magic, ghosts, dragonboats, flute music from the savage lands. Never mind that she's earned the right to write about whatever she chooses, and if she chooses to write about looking for Buddha in the wild, wild West, to reimagine one culture in the literature of another, we'd better pay attention because she's smarter than we are. Nevertheless, from her first novel the reviewers are demanding more memoir. Where's the female avenger?

Instead of a female avenger, we get Wittman Ah Sing, a twenty-three-year-old fifth-generation Chinese American male, Cal English major, playwright, draft dodger. This Wittman, singing himself in Berkeley and San Francisco in the early sixties, in the parenthesis between the countercultures of Beat and Hippie, will lose his job in the toy section of a department store and apply for unemployment; read Rilke aloud to startled passengers on a bus and look in the woods for his abandoned grandmother; act up and act out. He wants to be an authentic American, but America won't let him. Racist jokes enrage him—but he also worries that a rapprochement of black and white may still exclude his very own yellow, which color determines his wardrobe, his slick performance. Wittman may or may not be legally married to Tana, the folksinger/office worker, but she's too "gringo Anglo" for him; she's not Nanci Lee, who represents Cal "at the intercollegiate (Chinese) beauty-personality-good-grades contest at UCLA." He's done time at a dog pound, and among DNA biologists, and they all look alike: "A liberal-arts education is good for knowing how to look at anything from an inquisitive viewpoint, to shovel shit and have thoughts." He is into movies, drugs, comic books and modern masters. He wants to be, if not Lenny Bruce or Allen Ginsberg, at the very least "the first badass China Man bluesman of America." And what he'll do, like Judy Garland, is put on a show in his garage, a kind of Cantonese *Götterdämmerung*.

In other words: Huck Finn, Holden Caulfield, Augie March, maybe even Stephen Daedalus, and probably Abbie Hoffman. Wittman is a "tripmaster," a friendly guide to the stoned in their travels through acid-time. But he's also, and this is where it gets tricky, an incarnation of the Monkey King in Wu Ch'eng-en's sixteenth-century *Journey to the West*, a kind of Chinese *Pilgrim's Progress*. He's the rebel/mischiefmaker who helped bring back Buddha's Sutras from India; the shape-changer (falcon, koi fish, cormorant) who fussed Lao-tse by eating the peaches of Immortality, even though he wasn't invited to the party of the gods. And the week-long play this Monkey stages to finish off Wittman's "fake book" is nothing less than a reenactment of *The Romance of the Three Kingdoms*, a kind of Chinese "Terry and the Pirates." And the actors he press-gangs into service for that play—everybody he knows in California, including his Flora Dora show-girl mother, his "aunties," and a kung fu gang—are nothing less than symbolic stand-ins for the 108 bandit-heroes of *The Water Margin*, a kind of Chinese "Robin Hood": the enemies of a corrupt social order, hiding out in a wetlands Sherwood Forest, like Chairman Mao in misty Chingkangshan or the caves of Yenan.

This Wittman is stoned on books. Imagine one culture, ours, reimagined in the classic literature of another's, late imperial Ming, so much older and no less bloody. Sixties grandiosity!

A word here about language. What so excited readers of *The Woman Warrior* and *China Men* was that shiver of the exotic, the Other's static cling. It was as if we'd eavesdropped on a red dwarf and picked up these alien signals, this legend stuff from an ancestor-culture that despised its female children, that bound their feet, and threw them down wishing wells, and killed their names. Kingston achieved such a shiver by sneaky art—disappearing into people who couldn't think in English, and translating for them. She had to invent an American language commensurate with their Chinese meanings. In the way that Toni Morrison arrived at all the transcendence in *Beloved* by stringing together little words *just so*, rubbing up their warmth to a combustion, Kingston dazzled us by pictographs, by engrams.

She made it look easy, but imagine the price: denying, abolishing, the self. There wasn't room for a grown-up Maxine in her portraits of the mother who devours her children and the father who buries wine bottles upside-down in the garden so that "their bottoms made a path of sea-color circles." This grown-up Maxine, after all, was a Cal English major, just like Wittman; a reader of Proust and Pound and Joyce and Eliot, the original Whitman and his grandchild Ginsberg, Charles Olson and Gary Snyder and Brother Antoninus. From these books dissolved in brain, from a slang of be-in's and love-in's and trippings-out in the psychedelic sixties, from radical chitchat and the calisthenics of Left Coast Zen, an adult Kingston had fashioned a language of her own, but she'd no place to put it in her first two books. Like Bak Goong in *China Men*, forbidden to talk on the Hawaii sugarcane plantation, she shouted into a hole in the ground. To sing herself, she needed someone like the unbuttoned Wittman.

The result in *Tripmaster* is less charming but more exuberant. Instead of falling into pattern or turning on a wheel—there's something inevitable about everything in *The Woman Warrior* and *China Men*, something fated—this language bounces, caroms and collides; abrades and enflames. Instead of Mozart, Wittman is rock 'n' roll.

Not that Kingston altogether trusts him. He babbles a lot, and he's just as much babbled at: by Mrs. Chew, who skins peaches; and the upwardly mobile civil servant Lance Kamiyama; and the downwardly mobile Yale Younger Poet, hiding out in the bowels of the department store. If Wittman's the sort who asks in a restaurant, "Are you the one I can tell my whole life to?" he's also the sort to whom confiding strangers talk their stories about how the red fox got from China to Oakland, or what noodles with Jell-O tasted like on Angel Island. He has a philosophy, sixties Digger-Buddhist: "Do something, even if it's wrong." He believes, with Kierkegaard: "To think up reasons why something would not work guarantees that it will not work. Never do feasibility studies. Get on with creation. Do the most difficult thing. Keep the means moral." And: "Do the right thing by whoever crosses your path. Those coincidental people are your people."

But his paranoia is also sixties: Through his "metaphor glasses," poor and super-serious psych major Judy turns into a blueblack boar, with "a blue-red tongue showing between silver teeth, and two ivory sword tusks." Seeing inside Tana's head, he is beside himself: "He should never have taken drugs. No miracles ever again. Can't tell the gods' chimeras from freaks of my own." At a Kamiyama party he wonders, "What if Chubby Checker does not mean us well? What if Chubby Checker is up to no good?"

Wittman's too easily wowed. He's a one-man *I Ching*, "a book and also a person dressed in yellow" jumping from "reality to reality like quantum physics." He needs watching. And a female narrator (usually affectionate, always ironic, occasionally annoyed) looks down on him. Don't ask me how I know the narrator's female. I just do. She's as old as China, and remembers what happened in five dynasties and three religions. She also foresees the future: America will lose the war in Vietnam that Wittman's dodging; the sixties will be sadder than he hopes; feminism is on the way. She explains things Wittman has no way of knowing: "Gary Snyder had gone to Japan to meditate for years, and could now spend five minutes in the same room with his mother." And: "Ho Chi Minh's favorite reading was *The Romance of the Three Kingdoms*, and it's a text at West Point, too. Uncle Ho and Uncle Sam were both getting their strategy and philosophy from Grandfather Gwan, god of war." Though not a bully, at one point she tells Wittman to shut up.

It's a nice tension. Wittman wants "to put on a show that would make us braver and scare them not to fuck with us. And also to find the level of paranoia that is just right for living in this country without going insane. The 'them' he especially wanted to get were the innocent. Nobody has a right to be innocent." But he's himself the ultimate innocent, the last romantic, all virtue, passion, energy and funk. He'll go up like a balloon in every weather: "They hung over the balcony and watched the skaters going around. If we run downstairs and rent skates, could we be Orlando and the Russian princess zipping on the frozen Thames above the apple woman in the deep ice? Maybe if he, a fool for books, swears off reading, he would find his own life."

His Watcher and Keeper is amused; knows better. Fond as she is of Wittman, attached, he's less a balloon to her than a kite. (The Chinese, remember, invented the kite; and the wheelbarrow: Yang and Yin.) She pulls his string. Having seen our future, she's aware that Wittman's play won't end the war or save the world. It won't even assimilate him into America, or America into him. (Either assimilation's a two-way street or it's a sellout.) But without his innocence and excess, there would be no way at all of imagining alternative futures: "But, Uncle, we bad. Chinaman freaks. Illegal aliens. Outlaws. Outcasts of America. But we make our place—this one community house for benevolent living. We make theater, we make community."

Now about that play. *The Romance of the Three Kingdoms* is required reading for every literate Chinese child. (If you don't already know this stuff, you probably wonder if you need to. Only if you want to get a tenth as much out of Kingston's novel as she's put into it.) It glorifies a third-century revolt of Liu Pei and his mentor, Chu-ko Liang, against the military dictatorship of Ts'ao Ts'ao. Chinese in America have staged one version or another of it in theaters and opera houses all over in this country since the railroad and Gold Rush days. Like Mao's favorite, *The Water Margin*, it's a treasure trove of stories, "chock full," as Kenneth Rexroth pointed out,

of ghosts, innkeepers who make hamburgers of their guests, giants of superhuman strength, beautiful women in distress, wily intellectuals, crafty merchants, tireless lechers, heroic gluttons, sensitive scholars, arson, rape, murder, hairbreadth escapes, pitiful deaths....To produce something like it would require the collaboration of Rabelais, Petronius, Defoe and Dickens, with, I suppose, details from I. Babel.

Maybe it's not the best Chinese novel. (Which is probably *The Dream of the Red Chamber*, about a Bodhisattva-in-the-making—from which Kingston also borrows in *Tripmaster* for a killer game of mah-jongg; like the Bodhisattva, Wittman must escape domination by his female relatives, the hidden matriarchy at the heart of Chinese society.) But it's the most popular, and a very Grimm fairy tale. In it, all the good guys die.

This of course isn't good enough for Wittman. As well as the god of warriors, Gwan was the god of actors, writers, gamblers and immigrants. Wittman will rewrite *Three Kingdoms*. His play is a "fake war." He will substitute his theater for all the wars in the history of the world. From the Monkey King and Havoc Monster, Pure Green Snake and White Bone Demoness, Dwarf Tiger and Dry Land Water Beast, American movies and Peking opera, vaudeville and puppets and brothel music, fireworks and kung fu, he will ordain a Peaceable Kingdom: "The windows were filled with night mirages reflecting and magnifying—a city at war and carnival. All aflare and so bright that we understand: why we go to war is to make explosions and lights, which are more beatiful than anything."

And this Peaceable Kingdom will include his "coincidental people." Just listen:

The sheriff will surely come soon, and stop the show with a cease-and-desist-disturbing-the-peace order. Jail us for performing without a permit, like our brave theatrical ancestors, who were violators of zoning ordinances; they put on shows, they paraded, and they raised chickens within city limits. They were flimflammers of tourists, wildcat miners, cigar makers without the white label, carriers of baskets on poles, cunic air breathers, miscegenists, landowners without deeds, kangaroo jurists, medical and legal practicioners without degrees, unconvertible pagans and heathens, gamblers with God and one another, aliens unqualifiable for citizenship, unrelated communalists and crowders into single-family dwellings, dwellers and gamblers in the backs of stores, restauranteurs and launderers who didn't pass health inspection, droppers of garbage into other peoples cans, payers and takers of less than minimum wage...look-alikes of Japs and Viet Cong, unlicensed manufacturers and exploders of fireworks. Everybody with aliases. More than one hundred and eight outlaws.

Well, the Hippies wanted to be Indians. Why not, instead, Chinese bandits? And what after all was the Trial of the Chicago 7 but Wittman's sort of theater? And wouldn't it have been something if the Quakers, the Women Strike for Peace, Martin Luther King and the vegetarians had prevailed? Instead, the Garrison State—which had most of the violence—stopped this show, and the Left regressed to little-league Leninism, a tantrum of a cadres, Weatherpeople, Baader-Meinhof. And the rest is Heavy Metal. "It must be," thinks Wittman, "that people who read go on more macrocosmic and microcosmic trips—Biblical god trips, The Tibetan Book of the Dead, Ulysses, *Finnegans Wake* trips. Non-readers, what do they get? (They get the munchies.)"

But you can stop looking for The Novel of the Sixties. It took 3,000 years on its Journey to the West. But here are the peaches and here are the Sutras.

NORMAN MAILER: THE TROUBLE WITH HARRY

In 1976 in *New York* magazine, Mailer sneezed black-magic metaphors all over Watergate and the CIA, Marilyn Monroe and Howard Hughes, Kafka and the Mormons. At once a shaman and an exorcist, he changed shapes and split the lips of his wound: "Is America governed by accident more than we are ready to suppose, or by design? And if by design, is the design secret?

> *Trying to understand whether our real history is public or secret, exposed or—at the highest level—underground, is equal to exploring the opposite theaters of our cynicism and our paranoia.... What a crazy country we inhabit. What a harlot. What a brute. She squashes sausage out of the minds of novelists on their hotfooted way to a real good plot.*

Harlot's Ghost is the elephantiasis of that article: a lot of sausage, spicy and nourishing as far as it goes, but not going far enough. On the book's own calendar, it's still short twenty years. Mailer will try to talk his way around this gap. His editor, Jason Epstein, has already told the *New York Times* that *Harlot's Ghost* is a "test for reviewers—one that I fear will find many of them wanting." But this is preemptive condescension. After 1,300 pages of often brilliant tease—Popol Vuh and Victorian gothic, Vico and Nietzsche, Italian opera and Mahler symphony, Book of Kells and Book of the Dead—Mailer fails to deliver the ultimate intimacy. TO BE CONTINUED, he tells us, but we've waited almost as long for his CIA novel as we waited for his Egyptian novel and it's like waiting for Zapata or the Red Sox.

I was not in the CIA to become a bureaucrat but a hero. (Harry Hubbard)

Suppose Julien Sorel had joined the CIA instead of the Roman Catholic Church, or C.P. Snow had written *Strangers & Brothers* about modern-day Templar spooks instead of social-climbing sliderules. The "Company" may be America's Prep School and Episcopal Church, our Counterreformation and our Fourth Crusade, but it is also Norman Mailer's spirit world—his Scathach and Xibalda, his Jigoku and Jahannam, his karmavacara and his Universal Baseball Association.

Just kidding. Or am I? "Irrationality," Mailer says, "is the only great engine of history." So much for the class struggle. Skip the next several paragraphs if you hate a plot synopsis.

New England blueblood Herrick "Harry" Hubbard joins the CIA in 1955, fresh out of Yale and "as pretty as Montgomery Clift." He is joining his father "Cal" (a Robert Lowell reference I don't pretend to fathom) and his godfather "Harlot" (Hugh Tremont Montague, who brightened Harry's boyhood by teaching him to climb rocks). Harry is posted to Berlin at the time of the Tunnel, where he consorts with pistol-packing William King Harvey; to Montevideo, where he trafficks with the Arbenz-bashing E. Howard Hunt; to Miami, in time for the Bay of Pigs, the Cuban missile crisis and Operation Mongoose, where he beds down with playgirl Modene Murphy (an avatar of Judith Campbell Exner), thus communing with Sam Giancana, Frank Sinatra, Jack Kennedy, Fidel Castro, Howard Hughes and Marilyn Monroe. What happens to Harry after the assassination of JFK is not entirely clear because most of it's been omitted. *A 1,310-page novel about the CIA leaves out Vietnam, Watergate, Nicaragua and Iranamok, not to mention running drugs, laundering money and fingering Mandela.* This much, we are vouchsafed:

Between 1964 and 1984, Harry saves the life of Harlot's wife, Hadley Kittredge Gardiner Montague, who is not only "an absolute beauty," a Jackie Kennedy look-alike, but also a "genius" who develops her own anti-Freudian theory of personality while working of course for the CIA. After Harlot kills his son and cripples himself climbing more metaphorical rocks, Harry steals Kittredge for himself, while continuing to counterspy for Harlot. In 1984, Kittredge, in turn, is stolen by Dix Butler, an Agency "asset" and bisexual megabucks *übermensch*, and Harlot's body, with its face shot off, washes up from Chesapeake Bay. Did Harlot kill himself? Was he murdered? Or has he, in fact, defected to the KGB? Harry leaves Maine for Moscow, to find out. In Moscow, among these many mystifications, he is abandoned by his Creator. And that's all I'm going to tell you because from now on, instead of reviewing this novel, I intend to haunt it, like the pirate ghost Augustus Farr, like the CIA in America's kinky closet. (We are *spooked!*)

What, indeed, did Picasso teach us if not that every form offers up its own scream when it is torn? (Norman Mailer)

We learn about the trouble with Harry from two manuscripts—a shortie called "Omega," set in Orwell's 1984, and a gargantua called "Alpha," maybe the longest flashback in world literature, covering everything else up to 1964. These manuscripts correspond to the two halves of the human psyche as identified by Kittredge for the CIA. They also try out almost every narrative form known to the Mother Russian Novel: picaresque and epistolary; *Bildungsroman* and *roman à clef*; the historical, the gothic, the pornographic; the thriller and the western. There are also journal-jottings, cable traffic, interoffice memoranda and transcripts of wiretaps.

For so many species of story, there are as many tics of prose; seizures and afflatus. When his battery's charged, Mailer windmills from one paragraph to the next—baroque, anal, Talmudic, olfactory, portentous, loopy, coy, Egyptian; down and dirty in the cancer, the aspirin or the plastic; shooting moons on sheer vapor; blitzed by paranoia and retreating for a screen pass, as if bitten in the pineal gland by a deranged Swinburne, with metaphors so meaning-moistened that they stick to our thumbs, with "intellections" (as he once put it) slapped on "like adhesive plasters." When he chooses to, he also speaks in tongues. Harlot sounds like Whittaker Chambers. Modene Murphy sounds like Lauren Bacall. Bill Harvey sounds like L. Ron Hubbard or Lyndon LaRouche. The guilt-ridden Uruguayan double agent Chevi Fuentes sounds like Frantz Fanon and Octavio Paz. Harry sounds like Rousseau's Emile when he isn't sounding like Wilhelm

Reich, and Kittredge sounds like Flaubert's Salammbo when she isn't sounding like Hannah Arendt, and together they sound like Nichols and May. And everybody sounds like Mailer, as if picking up quasar signals from Sirius the Dog Star through a plate in the head; as if bodies, vegetables and objects all had distinctive vibrations, special stinks and personal divinities, angels in the meat loaf, demons in the Tupperware. Even money comes "in all kinds of emotional flavors." Ghosts! Pirates! Indians! Animism! Alchemy!

You either like this stuff or you don't, and I do.

Nor are the usual obsessions neglected, like boxing, bulls and booze. And Marilyn Monroe: Harry's father, Cal, has a theory that Hoffa bumped her off, hoping to pin the rap on Bobby. And Hemingway: Cal says he beat Papa at arm wrestling one dark and stormy Stork Club night. And LSD: Kittredge seems to have invented it in a lab at Langley. And Martin Buber: I'm convinced Mailer has rendered Harry, for all his Waspishness, "one-eighth" Jewish just so Harlot can tell him to read *Tales of the Hasidim*. And of course manhood: Like all Mailermen, who are happiest in motion, in boats and in beds, Harry finds that "happiness is experienced most directly in the intervals between terror," which may be "our simple purpose on earth." If we "surmount that terror...we can, perhaps, share some of God's fear."

This means a lot of rock climbing, some polo and an invasion of Cuba. Thinks Harry:

> *So many of these soldiers had spent their lives getting ready for a great moment—it was as if one lived as a vestal virgin who would be allowed to copulate just once but in a high temple: The act had better be transcendent, or one had chosen the wrong life.*

If this Prep School Ethos is hard on Kittredge, tough darts:

> *I gave up the thought of explaining to her that the natural condition of men's lives was fear of tests, physical even more than mental tests. Highly developed skills of evasion went into keeping ourselves removed from the center of our cowardice...So I could not help it—I admired men who were willing to live day by day with bare-wire fear even if it left them naked as drunks, incompetent wild men, accident-prone. I understood the choice.*

It's even harder on Castro, but he's so Neolithic macho, he will surely understand:

> *I would mourn Fidel if we succeeded, mourn him in just the way a hunter is saddened by the vanished immanence of the slain beast. Yes, one fired a bullet into beautiful animals in order to feel nearer to God: To the extent that we were criminal, we could approach the cosmos only by stealing a piece of the Creation.*

You need no longer wonder: Why Are We in Vietnam? Or Iraq. Or Marilyn Monroe.

> *I could say, to stretch a point, that we were being schooled in minor arts of sorcery. Are not espionage and magic analagous?* (Harlot)

If paranoia is our culture's weather, all that lightning, then Mailer, bless him, puts up a kite instead of an umbrella. But having grown up on him, we already know that we have enemies. It's harder to amaze us. It's a tough break for the old exorcist that Don DeLillo, Joan Didion and Stan Lee in *Dunn's Conundrum* have already covered so much of his territory; that Robin Winks has already written his book about Yale and the CIA; that Tom Mangold has just published a biography of James Jesus Angleton; that Robert Gates twists in the Senate wind; that Pete Brewton's S&L stories, and the magnitiude of the BCCI scandal, are so much more fantastic to contemplate than the CIA conspiracy in *Harlot's Ghost* to finance itself by cashing in on insider tips on when the Federal Reserve Board is about to fiddle with the interest rates. What's *new*, Norman?

Well, he really likes these guys. And why not? If you can identify with Gary Gilmore, not to mention Menenhetet, how hard can it be to identify with Allen Dulles? Besides, the old Social Bandit has been soft on Wasps since the moonshot, when he mindmelded with the astronauts. And he's summered forever in New England with its sermons, charades and whalingship watergames. Of course: Harry will lose his innocence and Harry *is* America—that's the point of these many pages—but what a boys' club it seems to him at the start, what a Skull and Bones, a *safe* house, a happy hunting ground of Hopelites, Berserkirs and Samurai, storm-cloud Maruts and Taoist warrior-sages, Gilgamesh, Achilles, Arjuna, Crazy Horse—with secret books, sacred seals and nifty computer graphics. It's Rosicrucian, Kabbalistic, Druidical! I mean, they have castles on the Rhône, châteaux in the Loire, temples in Kyoto. Why not great Baals with glowing redhot bellies and Tantric miniatures depicting Kundalini; Nuremberg Maidens with heartsful of nails; ramsing, the horn of Tugs, hanging from a banyan; the altar of sacrifice to Yaldaboath; menhirs, tesseracts, an orgone box, a Swedenborg deathmask, a black Celtic virgin (for Sergius O'Shaugnessy) and, in the reliquary, the foreskin of Hermes Trismegistus? (I'm sorry; it's catching.)

But what we get instead is Harlot. Harlot seems to be Mailer's version of James Jesus Angleton, the Fisher King of counterespionage. Like Angleton, he's suspicious of everybody else at Langley, and was taken in by Kim Philby, and doesn't really believe in the Sino-Soviet split. As Angleton was referred to variously at the Agency as Mother, Poet, Fisherman and (aha!) Gray Ghost, so Montague is referred to not only as "Harlot" but also as "Trimsky" (for a Trotsky-like salt-and-pepper mustache), and "Gobby" (for "God's old beast"). Instead of orchids, rocks.

Angleton shows up as a character in dozens of fictions, from Ludlum to Bellow. Even after he was forcibly retired in 1974, he was still obsessed that a Soviet "mole" had penetrated to the nation's very cerebellum. Everywhere he looked, he saw "doubles." If *he* could imagine it, *they* must be doing it. It's with Angleton that we associate the phrase "wilderness of mirrors." He had been, after after, a Futurist poet at Yale, and published a literary magazine, *Furioso*, full of difficult Modernists like Pound, whose enthusiasm for Mussolini was apparently contagious. T.S. Eliot was a buddy of young Angleton's; Thomas Mann came to lunch. No wonder that when he looked in the Labyrinth at Langley for the pattern in the magic carpet, all he saw were "doubles" and "moles," counterfeit identities, masks of the Other. Dostoyevsky, Conrad, Kafka, Nabokov, Wastelands: alienation of the self, by the self, against the self. And no wonder writers love him so much: What else is Modernism but Counterintelligence? Our paranoia is a *text*.

In *Libra*, DeLillo imagines an "occult" of intelligence agencies, a "theology of secrets," the latest in Gnostic heresies, gone to holy war against nihilism, terrorism, inauthenticity and incoherence. Robin Winks tells us in *Cloak & Gown* that John Hollander, then on the Yale faculty, was so struck while reading Sir John Masterman's *The Double-*

Cross System by the code names in the book (Mutt and Jeff, Brutus and Bronx, Zigzag and Tricycle) that he sat down and wrote a book-length poem, *Reflections on Espionage*, "with spies standing for writers and thinkers, living a kind of hidden life in the actual world," with Pound and Auden and Lowell in code.

This is weird stuff, made-to-order for gonzo novelizing. But Mailer shies away from most of it, as he shies away from seeing Latin America or Europe as anything other than geographies of the Agency mind, pale-fire Zemblas. Yes, he has fun with the minor players. If Howard Hunt isn't quite as flamboyant here as his own alteregos in his own David St. John thrillers, Bill Harvery comes on like Henderson the Rain King. The old shaman has even more fun with code names: In Berlin: BOZO, GIBLETS, SWIVET and CATHETER. In Montevideo: AV/OCADO, AV/ANTGARDE, AV/OIRDUPOIS, AV/EMARIA. And in Miami, to sort out the bedfellowship of Mafia and Camelot in Operation HEEDLESS, Jack Kennedy is codenamed IOTA, Sam Giancana is RAPUNZEL, Murphy/Exner is BLUEBEARD and Frank Sinatra is STONEHENGE. I love it.

But the old Druid hasn't given Harlot enough juice to be an Angleton, a paranoid synecdoche. Harlot's supposed to wow us, as he wows Harry, Dix and Arnie Rosen in their early Agency days. But when he talks about a Third World still clinging "to pre-Christian realms—awe, paranoia, slavish obedience to the leader, divine punishment," or explains that the CIA buys up bankers, psychiatrists, narcs, trade unionists, hooligans and journalists because "our duty is to become the mind of America," he seems to belong more to a Bill Buckley/Blackford Oakes pennydreadful than a John le Carré requiem mass. Just once, brooding on relations between Dzerzhinsky, the godfather of the KGB, and the White Russian Yakovlev, does Harlot sound like an Angleton:

When seduction is inspired...by the demands of power, each person will lie to the other. Sometimes, they lie to themselves. These lies often develop structures as aesthetically rich as the finest filigrees of truth. After a time, how could Yakovlev and Dzerzhinsky know when they were dealing with truth or a lie? The relationship had grown too deep. They had had to travel beyond their last clear principles. They could no longer know when they were true to themselves. The self, indeed, was in migration.

But that is the last we hear from Harlot on this subject for another 800 pages. And then there's what I take to be the crucial exchange between Harlot and Bill Harvey, although they are talking to Harry instead of each other, from opposite ends of the novel. First, we get Harlot:

> *The aim is to develop teleological mind. Mind that dwells above the facts; mind that leads us to larger purposes. Harry, the world is going through exceptional convulsions. The twentieth century is fearfully apocalyptic. Historical constitutions that took centuries to develop are melting into lava. Those 1917 Bolsheviks were the first intimation. Then came the Nazis. God, they were a true exhalation from Hell. The top of the mountain blew off. Now the lava is starting to move....Lava is entropy. It reduces all systems. Communism is the entropy of Christ, the degeneration of higher spiritual forms into lower ones. To oppose it, we must, therefore, create a fiction—that the Soviets are a mighty military machine who will overpower us unless we are more powerful. The truth is that they will overpower us if the passion to resist them is not regenerated, by will if necessary, every year, every minute.*

Later, it's Harvey, larger-than-life like DeLillo's David Ferrie, a paranoid's paranoid:

> *There is opposition to entropy. The universe may not necessarily wind down. There is something forming that I would call the new embodiment. Entropy and embodiment may be as related as antimatter and matter....Yes, the forms deteriorate and they all run down to the sea, but other possibilities come together in their wake to seek embodiment. Blobs are always looking to articulate themselves into a higher form of blob. There is a tropism toward form, Hubbard. It counters decomposition.*

What does this mean? Jason Epstein has found me wanting. On Mailer's last page, we are told that Harlot is *Harry's* embodiment, but otherwise this sounds remarkably like one of those rough beasts slouching out of a Yeats poem to be born-again, a mystagogic man-god. And Harry has gone to Moscow to sit at Dzerzhinsky's feet, and this embodiment of Harlot would seem to be whispering that God is the Ultimate Spy, that evolution is just a Cover Story, that the universe is basically Disinformation. Maybe, but the novel itself has no more got us to such a realization than it has bothered to flesh in the migration of Harry from the innocence of Lovett in *Barbary Shore* to the savage savvy of Rojack, that American Dreamer. And I can't help identifying with a character in DeLillo's *White Noise*, the ex-wife of the professor of Hitler Studies, whose job it is to review books *for* the CIA, "mainly long serious novels with coded structures."

Curiously, yet logically, there is one vice...that tempts both narcissist and psychopath. It is treachery. (Kittredge)

I like Modene more than Kittredge, who is Omega to Harry's Alpha. Besides being a tease, Kittredge is snotty. She hates Lenny Bruce, makes fun of A. J. Ayer, and condescends to Freud. Harry has his doubts about her, too, wondering if she began her affair with him "because she wanted to learn whether she could run an operation under [Harlot's] nose and get away with it."

This crossreferencing of sex and espionage is one of the novel's principal conceits. Harlot tells his boys: "Our studies move into penetralia. We search for the innermost sanctum, 'the shuddering penetralia of caves.'" The old Orgone Boxer is asking us to think of spies as voyeurs; of the double-backed beast as another double agent; of adultery as a sort of treason; of sex itself as quest and conspiracy, guerrilla warfare and the coup d'état. Our behavior in history has a lot to do with our behavior in bed. Politics is a sex crime. Imperialism is a gangbang.

Sex can also be divine: Coupling with Kittredge, Harry tells us, is a "sacrament," letting him "see God when the lightning flashed and we jolted our souls into one another." And sex, of course, is death: Harry smells "the whiff or murder beyond every embrace of love"; Sam and Modene even make it in a graveyard, on top of his dead wife's mausoleum.

It seems to me that the trouble with sex as the ground of being is that it puts too much of a burden on sex; we all still have to go to work in the morning, even spies. But I'm not ready yet to discuss Mailer and sex. That comes last. What *about* Alpha and Omega?

Well, according to Kittredge, they aren't metaphors. They are, in each of us, separate unconsciousnesses, with their own egos and superegos. Alpha is our male component, "creature of the forward-swimming energies of sperm, ambitious, blind to all but its own purposes...more oriented toward enterprise, technology, grinding the corn, repairing the mill, building the bridges between money and power, *und so weiter.*" Whereas Omega, our female component, "originated in the ovum and so knows more about the mysteries—conception, birth, death, night, the moon, eternity, karma, ghosts, divinities, myths, magic, our primitive past, and so on."

In other words, double the trouble and goose the guilt, but also someone else to blame it on when things go wrong. What isn't right-brained/left-brained in this, or gussied-up Carl Jung, or old-fashioned schizophrenia, seems, as so often happens when the vapors take Mailer, to be a kind of Trojan zebra, foisting more of his Manichean dualisms on the unwary reader—courage and fear, sex and death, Alpha and Omega, Simon and Garfunkel—the way Aristotle once foisted the unconscious dualisms of Greek grammar on an unsuspecting cosmos.

What the hey. If Yeats can believe in faeries, Pound in funny money, Doris Lessing in flying saucers and Saul Bellow in Rudolf Steiner, the old Rosicrucian has a right to his Alphas and Omegas, however much they remind me of Randall Jarrell on W. H. Auden: "The theological ideas which Auden does not adopt but invents are all too often on the level of those brownpaper parcels brought secretly to the War Department in times of national emergency, which turn out to be full of plans to destroy enemy submarines by tracking them down with seals."

But Mailer as usual is out to get Freud. Freud, says the insufferable Kittredge, "really had no more philosophy than a Stoic. That's not enough. Stoics make good plumbers. The drains go bad and you've got to hold your nose and fix them. End of Freud's philosophy. If people and civilization don't fit—which we all know anyway—why, says Freud, make the best of a bad lot."

This is bumptious. It omits, among many other important matters, Freud's tragic pessimism. Okay, the guy was saying that civilization depends on a certain amount of repression of the instincts, and Mailer would like to think that he operates entirely on instinct, so he's bound to resent this bad news, as well as civilization, at least since the Enlightenment. (Mailer belongs, in fact, to Isaiah Berlin's team of anti-Enlightenment "swimmers against the current" like Vico and Hamann and Herder, like Moses Hess and Georges Sorel.) But you'd think that as much as he identified in *Ancient Evenings* with Menenhetet

on the Boat of Ra, he'd identify even more with a brave pariah who
dropped by bathysphere _into himself_ to see why people hurt the way
they do; the dream-decoder; the first Deconstructionist. Isn't this
Mailer's own detective method, a consulting of the suspect self, plow-
ing through magnetic fields, lighting up the wounds of God?

Besides, Harry in _Harlot's Ghost_ has to kill off two fathers.

I wish the old Kabbalist had spent less time thinking about Hemingway, and no time writing about Marilyn, and some years working
through Freud, after which he could take on Marx, thus killling off,
instead of kissing off, both _his_ fathers. (Anyway, if Jean-Paul Sartre
could churn out 800 pages on Freud when John Huston asked him for
a screenplay, think what Mailer might have managed, especially with
his old buddy Montgomery Clift as Sigmund.) Nor has he really ever
answered the shrewd question put to him by an interviewer in _Pieces
and Pontifications_: "Why can't the unconscious be as error prone as the
conscious?"

Just because Kittredge had ghostsex with the pirate-shade of Augustus Farr, who "submitted me to horrors," doesn't mean Harry has to
heed her every fatuity. He's better off listening to Chevi Fuentes.
Among other good advices, Fuentes warns Harry against the
labyrinth-maker Jorge Luis Borges: "Never read him. In five pages, in
any of his five pages, he will summarize for you the meaninglessness
of the next ten years of your life. Your life, particularly."

> _Capitalism, says Fuentes, is essentially psychopathic. It lives for the mo-
> ment. It can plan far ahead only at the expense of its own vitality, and all
> larger questions of morality are delegated to patriotism, religion, or psycho-
> analysis. "That is why I am a capitalist," he says. "Because I am a psy-
> chopath. Because I am greedy. Because I want instant consumer satisfac-
> tion. If I have spiritual problems, I either go to my priest and obtain abso-
> lution or I pay an analyst to convince me over the years that my greed is my
> identity and I have rejoined the human race. I may feel bad about my self-
> ishness but I will get over it. Capitalism is a profound solution to the prob-
> lem of how to maintain a developed society. It recognizes the will-to-power
> in all of us."_

Chevi used to be a Communist back in Montevideo, before Harry
"turned" him. By the time he tells Harry that he's a capitalist, in
Miami, Chevi has also become a homosexual. Listen up:

You will judge me adversely for being a homosexual, yet it is you who is more of one than any of us, although you will never admit it to yourself because you never practice! You are a homosexual the way Americans are barbarians although they do not practice barbarism openly. They keep their newspaper in front of the light. They go to church so as not to face death, and you work for your people so that you will not have to scrutinize yourself in the mirror.

Our Harry? What's going on? Sure, Kittredge is a drag. Still, isn't there Modene? But something, at the very least androgynous, seems to have happened to Mailer since he came back from Egypt. If you used to worry about his preoccupation with anal sex, as we all of course have worried about Updike's preoccupation with oral sex, you are entitled to worry even more.

In Berlin in 1956, after taking him to a seedy S/M bar where the house speciality is "the golden shower," Dix Butler, Agency *übermensch*, makes a pass at Harry. Harry declines this invitation, not because he isn't excited, but because he fears such an act would oblige him "to live forever on this side of sex." Dix goes both ways, we are told, because he was raped as a child by his brother. But later it's clear that Arnie Rosen, another of Harry's schoolmates in Langley's entering class of 1955, is also gay, and by choice, although forced in the fifties to be furtive.

This isn't to suggest that the CIA goes in for ritual pederasty—as seems to have been the case among Spartans, Celts and the Sambia of New Guinea, if you believe Rick Fields in *The Code of the Warrior*—though it's not hard to imagine, at the Agency, as in prep school, a homoerotic bonding of the blue-eyed boys, reading their spagyrics and their necromantiums, pulling on their Tomar Towers and their Luxor Obelisks, speaking their Vattan cryptosystems. To join the eighteenth-century Bavarian Illuminati, you underwent a trial by a knife. Their candles were black, their hoods were white, and they bound up your testicles with a poppy-colored cordon: standard Skull and Bones hotstuff. However, I digress.

No. Mailer evokes the fugitive sensibility as yet another metaphor for the secret life: undercover, as it were; the double or fictitious identity. But think for a minute about Chevi. In being "turned," wasn't he raped, like Dix? And hasn't he seen Harry in action on another front, too, smitten by the notorious prostitute Libertad, who turns out to be a hermaphrodite? And, suddenly, one begins to wonder what all these men, like STONEHENGE and RAPUNZEL, are really up to. And I must explain the _Tequila Sunrise_ Paradigm.

In the movie _Tequila Sunrise_, Mel Gibson and Kurt Russell are high-school buddies who grew up on opposite sides of the law. They compete for Michelle Pfeiffer. If not to them, what's clear to us is that Gibson and Russell really want to go to bed with each other. Since they can't, they go to bed with Pfeiffer. She's the go-between, the trampoline, a universal joint, a portable gopher-hole, a surrogate and a Chinese finger puzzle. Once you have seen it in the movie, you'll see it everywhere. In Pynchon's _Vineland_, for instance, it's obvious that Vond, the fascistic prosecutor, is murmuring to Zoyd, the rock piano player, through the holes in poor Frenesi's body. The _Tequila Sunrise_ Paradigm might even explain serial killers like Bateman in _American Psycho_, unless you believe that when yuppie Bateman rapes the Aspen waitress with the can of hair spray, nails Bethany's fingers to the hardwood floor, and sodomizes a severed head, he is really criticizing Late Capitalism and the Fetishism of Commodities. (And I'm the king of Bavaria.)

Now take a look at the relationships in _Harlot's Ghost_, not just among Harlot and Harry and Kittredge and Dix, or Dix and Harry and Chevi and Modene, or Modene, Jack, Frank and Marilyn, but, let's say, _historically._ Just suppose that Sam Giancana really wanted to go to bed with Frank Sinatra, and Sinatra wanted to go to bed with Jack Kennedy, and Kennedy wanted to go to bed with everybody, including that "beautiful animal," Fidel Castro. And Marilyn and Modene (or Judith) were the closest they could get, except, of course, for an invasion. There is no question, even in the pages of Arthur Schlesinger, Jr., that the Kennedy Boys had a hard-on for Castro.

Talk about spooky. It shudders the penetralia of caves. Whatever else he's done or failed to do in _Harlot's Ghost_, Mailer—our very own Knight-Errant, Don Quixote, Tripmaster Monkey, Zapata and Scaramouche—has at last made the personal political. Which leads one to wonder whether, all this time, he really wanted to play ball with Arthur Miller and Joe DiMaggio.

E. L. DOCTOROW: BOY GANGSTER

To the radical politics of *The Book of Daniel*, and the revisionist history of *Ragtime*, and the collective, elegiac American dreamworlds of *Loon Lake* and *World's Fair*, E. L. Doctorow has added some amazing grace and made a masterwork. Though *Billy Bathgate* meditates on many matters—mobsters and orphans, the East Bronx and the Great Depression, the politics of sex and the psychology of class, "how ritual death tampers with the universe" and "the amphibian journey" from desire to identity—think of it, like Scott Fitzgerald's *The Great Gatsby* or Horatio Alger's *Ragged Dick*, as a fairy tale about capitalism. And color it wonderful.

Of course, this capitalism is in its first stages of primitive accumulation—by extortion, murder and the numbers racket. The gangster Dutch Schultz dies of his failure to evolve into the higher, monopolistic forms. Dutch lacks the corporate vision of a Lucky Luciano. Still, like the Church, the army, trade unions and professional sports, organized crime has always been a launching pad for the upwardly mobile. And dirty money is the medium through which young Billy in 1935 levitates out of boyhood and the Bronx into "a large, empty resounding adulthood booming with terror" and "even greater circles of gangsterdom than I had dreamed, latitudes and longitudes of gangsterdom": the modern world, where everybody lives alienated ever after.

Billy is a fifteen-year-old high school dropout and amateur juggler. His immigrant Jewish father abandoned him in infancy. His immigrant Irish mother, who works in a laundry, is the neighborhood crazy. ("When I was little I thought all rugs were in the shape of men's suits and trousers. She had nailed his suit to the floor as if it was the fur of some animal, a bearskin..." Their apartment smells of burning wax, "the smoke of wicks" from guttered candles: "Now when I looked behind me into the kitchen it was illuminated with my mother's memory candles, this one room glittering like an opera house in all the falling darkness...and I wondered if my big chance hadn't a longer history than I thought.") Like any Horatio Alger hero, he wants glamour, status, a destiny, "the mythological change of my station." Just listen to him:

> there was something in me that might earn out, that might grow into the lineaments of honor, so that a discerning teacher or some other act of God, might turn up the voltage of this one brain to a power of future life that

everyone in the Bronx could be proud of. I mean that to the more discerning adult, the man I didn't know and didn't know ever noticed me who might live in my building or see me in the schoolyard, I would be one of the possibilities of redemption, that there was some wit in the way I moved, some lovely intelligence in an unconscious gesture of the game, that would give him this objective sense of hope for a moment, quite unattached to any loyalty of his own, that there was always a chance, that as bad as things were, America was a big juggling act and that we could all be kept up in the air somehow, from night to day, in the universe of God after all.

But fairy tales in the West tend also to be oedipal. Billy wants a father, too, and in gangsterdom he has his choice. There's bossman Dutch, born Arthur Flegenheimer, all passion, energy, menace and "rudeness of power," a sort of bad-seed Henderson the Rain King. And there's Abbadabba Berman, the gang's accountant, a natural pedagogue, wise in his numbers, a dandy even if a humpback in his "summer yellow double-breasted suit and a panama hat."

Dutch is capitalism's past—Social Darwinism. He moves in a "realm of high audacity," "contriving a life from its property of danger, putting it together in the constant contemplation of death," in "an independent kingdom of his own law, not society's." The law, he says, "is the vigorish I pay, the law is my overhead." Each hit's "a planned business murder as concise and to the point as a Western Union telegram. The victim after all had been in the business. He was the competition." This laissez-faire attitude toward the morality of economic relations translates into an equally laissez-faire attitude toward the economy of moral conduct: "I like the idea of women...I like that you can pick them up like shells on the beach, they are all over the place, like pink ones and ones with whorls you can hear the ocean." Even his sudden conversion to Catholicism has this greed about it: "I give you my word I couldn't be more sincere, Father. I brought it up, didn't I? I live a difficult life. I make important decisions all the time. I need strength. I see men I know take their strength from their faith, and I have to think I need that strength too. I fear for my life like all men. I wonder what it's all for. I try to be generous, I try to be good. But I like the idea of that extra edge."

On the other hand, Abbadabba is capitalism's future: the managerial revolution. Having seen this future, he knows it belongs to Luciano. It's like railroads: "You look at the railroads, they used to be a hundred railroad companies cutting each other's throats. Now how many are there? One to each section of the country. And on top of that they got a trade association to smooth their way in Washington. Everything nice and quiet, everything streamlined." Besides, according to Abbadabba Berman:

> *At a certain point everyone looks at the books. The numbers don't lie. They read the numbers, they see what only makes sense. It's like numbers are language, like all the letters in the language are turned into numbers, and so it's something that everyone understands the same way. You lose the sounds of the letters and whether they click or pop or touch the palate, or go* ooh *or* aah, *and anything that can be misread or con you with its music or the pictures it puts in your mind, all of that is gone along with the accent, and you have a new understanding entirely, a language of numbers, and everything becomes as clear to everyone as the writing on the wall.*

It is Billy's juggling—of a barter economy of "two rubber balls, a navel orange, an egg and a black stone"—that first commends him as a "capable boy" to the troubled Dutchman and to Abbadabba. He insinuates himself into the Schultz gang as a bagman, go-between, good-luck charm, sorcerer's apprentice and spy. He'll be there for the tugboat murder of Bo Weinberg in tuxedo and cement booties; and the kidnap of Bo's upper-class inamorata, the fair Drew Preston; and their grumpy hiding-out in upstate Onondaga, among farm foreclosures, till Dutch is tried for income tax evasion; and the protracted planning, as if for Kitchener's advance on Khartoum, of a hit on District Attorney Tom Dewey; and in the men's room of the Palace Chop House in Newark on October 23, 1935, for the tabloid massacre: "Murders are exciting, and lift people into a heart-beating awe as religion is supposed to do..."

As in any fairy tale the hero will scale a dark tower, in this case the fire escape at the Max and Dora Diamond Home for Orphans, "the black ladder of my love." He will don various magic cloaks: the reversible satin jacket with the team name Shadows on it; the Little Lord Fauntleroy suit Drew makes him wear for his upstate Bible studies of "the desert gangs"; the polo shirt he puts on to tail Dewey. He will rescue a fair maiden, though not without a qualm: "How could I be sure of anything if I didn't know everything, I wanted a moving shield around her like a fountain of juggled balls, like a thousand

whirling jump ropes, like fireworks of flowers and the lives of innocent rich children." And he will find a buried treasure, "pirate swag,"
by deconstructing the last words, "an insane man's riddle," of the
dying Dutch.

There is also an enchanted wood, a "sinking darkness of forest"
where Drew and Billy walk "hand in hand like fairy-tale children in
deep and terrible trouble." And a sacred cave, the cellar of the orphanage, where Arnold Garbage is in business "to love what was broken,
torn, peeling...to love what didn't work." And an evil wizard: "I was
shown into a heavily draped bedroom that smelled of apples and wine
and shaving lotion, a very atmospheric habitat that did not appear to
include any open windows. And there propped atop the covers on a
grand bank of pillows, in a dark silk robe, with the hairless legs of an
old man protruding, was James J. Hines himself, the Tammany
leader." And a pair of gnomes—humpbacked Abbadabba and midget
madam Mugsy—adding up the bill for an orgy "like a stunty little
couple in a fairy-tale, an old woodcutter and his ancient wife puffing
their magic white weeds of smoke and child mystification and having
a conversation in their language of numbers."

Why do you suppose that gangsters show up so often in novels by
serious writers like Doctorow, William Kennedy and Saul Bellow?
Maybe because, for the immigrant trying to Americanize himself, one
myth is as good as another—baseball, Hollywood, Tin Pan Alley,
Murder, Inc. Or maybe it's otherwise hard to think about our American romance with money—the unmentionable in Henry James, the
obsession in Dreiser, the peculiar poetry of Fitzgerald. Trilling said
somewhere that money is "the great solvent of the solid social fabric
of the old society," the jumping beans of a new culture and status system. And surely its absence is an oppression. And yet for the most part
ours is a literature of loners and losers. And we can't talk about serious
money from the point of view of deerslayers or whaling captains,
river pirates or the Lone Ranger, not even a private eye, not even Huck
Finn. And so, sorting among pop icons, we arrive at the urban outlaw.
We drop, as if by bathysphere, into the primordial greed, and consult
the original Crab. We inquire into metastasis.

Doctorow has as much fun as Kennedy and more than Bellow
among these lowlifes. He seems especially to enjoy their mannered violence, their arabesques. To be sure, he writes beautifully about
everything—from food and water to sex and horses, from corrupt

unions to the country poor, from "the contours of the ocean bed" to "the contours of the white Miss Drew." As Billy levitates by money, Doctorow levitates by language, through circles of light and suspensions of childhood, the deepest chords and finest bloodthreads, on his way from the cityscapes "where we come out sliming...where we make our tracks and do our dances and leave our coprolitic spires" to "the black mountains of high winds and no rain," where moral awareness waits in ambush.

But to the executions of a West Side numbers boss (in a barbershop, after the hot towel has been applied "wrapping it the way they do like a custard swirl, so that only the tip of the nose is visible") and the luckless Weinberg (dainty "as some princess at a ball" on the tugboat, placing one foot at a time in the tub of wet cement which "made a slow-witted diagram of the sea outside, the slab of it shifting to and fro as the boat rose and fell on the waves"; singing "Bye Bye Blackbird"), he brings such fierce relish, such lovely precision, that we either blush or gasp. The absurd is dignified.

And yet he obviously doesn't *like* these gangsters as much as Kennedy and Bellow seem to. It's as if, for all their "supernatural warrior spirit," they had somehow let him down. Unlike the bootleg dreamer Gatsby, they don't know what to do with the money once they've got it: "It was all for survival, there was no relaxed indolence of [their] right to it..." And so Doctorow takes the poetry of their money, their imaginative capital, and gives it to the white Miss Drew. For Doctorow, as much as for the smitten Billy, Drew Preston, half a tourist in the underworld and half Persephone, is what the magic of money is really all about. Which is why Billy must rescue her from a frantic Dutch who "needed more death, he was using up his deaths so quickly now that he needed them faster and faster"—like Third World markets. Of Drew, Billy rhapsodizes:

> *I don't mean just her free access as a great beauty to the most advanced realms of power and depravity, she had chosen this life for herself when, perhaps for her same reasons of starting meditation, she might have chosen life in a convent, say, or to be an actress on the stage. I mean rather how she knew this place would be here. How familiar woods were to her. She knew about horses...about sailing and oceans, too, and beaches to swim from with no crowds on them and skiing in the European mountains of the Alps and in fact all the pleasures of the planet, all the free rides of the planet that*

you could have if you knew where they were and had the training to take them. This was what wealth was, the practiced knowledge of these things so you could appropriate them for yourself.

This tiresomely insouciant Drew, American aristocrat, golden girl, Daisy-chain, "covered her tracks...trailed no history...would never tell her life because she needed no one's admiration or sympathy or wonder, and because all judgments, including love, came of a language of complacency she had never wasted her time to master." So what if "she took off her clothes to gunmen, to water, to the sun"? "Life disrobed her." And so on. This is why we kill our fathers. It's also an awful lot for any twenty-two-year-old female to have to be in any novel's scheme of things, even a blonde. No wonder she disappears. It's a vanishing act, like Shane's. The white Miss Drew seems to me to be not so much a woman, not even a Persephone, as a credit card, by means of which Billy is enabled to multiply his opportunities for social and erotic disappointment. In her, sex and money, Freud and Marx, are more mixed up than Leslie Fiedler, than Herbert Marcuse. And hard as it is to believe in her, the baby-in-a-basket is impossible.

But never mind. Doctorow's whole point is to call into question the authenticity of Billy's identity-making, his juggling act. So much for the "metaphysical afflictions" that inspire "art, invention, great fortunes and the murderous rages of the disordered spirit." The Dutchman dies, going out with a tantrum. So, too, does Abbadabba die, though *his* last words are the combination of a lock. And Billy sees, through a boy's eyes in the animal skin of grown-up language, that

I am resentful, I feel fatherless again, a whole new wave of fatherlessness, that they have gone so suddenly, as if there were no history of our life together in the gang, as if discourse is an illusion, and the sequence of this happened and then that happened and I said and he said was only Death's momentary incredulity, Death staying his hand a moment in incredulity of our arrogance, that we actually believed ourselves to consequentially exist, as if he were something that did not snuff out from one instant to the next, leaving nothing of ourselves as considerable as a thread of smoke, or the resolved silence at the end of a song.

That's Doctorow talking, the Doctorow who improves Dutch's delirium, that mad death-bed pastiche William S. Burroughs arranged into a screenplay in *The Last Words of Dutch Schultz*, with a little Lear-like rage, some Molly Bloom and some Long John Silver. But he warns us:

> *While this monologue of his own murder is a cryptic passion, it is not poetry, the fact is he lived as a gangster and spoke as a gangster and when he died bleeding from the sutured holes in his chest he died of the gangsterdom of his mind as it flowed from him, he died dispensing himself in utterance, as if death is chattered-out being, or as if all we are made of is words and when we die the soul of speech decants itself into the universe.*

For Doctorow language is the agency of moral awareness. Moral awareness is the "content" of any serious discourse. This works for a writer of his quality, and for Toni Morrison, and for almost nobody else. Is it sufficient for Billy? His decoding of the Dutchman's "cryptic passion" will make Billy rich. (Happiness is some other category.) But to do what? An adult Billy isn't saying. "Who I am in my majority and what I do and whether I am in the criminal trades or not, and where and how I live must remain my secret because I have a certain renown." Among the several endings to this subversive fairy tale—a mother rescued from her "distractions," the lovely hymn to the Bronx that was, the surprise package from Persephone—we are encouraged to choose for ourselves the one we need. I found a bitter chocolate sadness in Billy's floating, his tumble in free-fall, his vertigo among the memory candles. He tells us:

> *I will confess that I have many times since my investiture sought to toss all the numbers up in the air and let them fall back into letters, so that a new book would emerge, in a new language of being. It was what Mr. Berman said might someday come to pass, the perverse proposition of a numbers man, to throw them away and all their imagery, the cuneiform, the hieroglyphic, the calculus, and the speed of light, the whole numbers and fractions, the rational and irrational numbers, the numbers for the infinite and the numbers of nothing. But I have done it and done it and always it falls into the same Billy Bathgate I made of myself and must seemingly always be, and I am losing the faith it is a trick that can be done.*

America by the numbers; a countinghouse. It seems to me that Billy—like Bo Weinberg in concrete on the tugboat; like window washers falling from the midtown skyscraper because they didn't pay their dues; like his own lost father in the long history of the big chance; like the orphans—is singing "Bye Bye Blackbird." Once upon a time he had had a huge heart, our Billy, Billy Budd, Huck Finn, call him Ishmael; but they broke it forever.

THOMAS PYNCHON: DOWN AMONG THE THANATOIDS

Vineland—a multimedia semi-thriller, a Star Wars for the Counterculture—is easier to read than anything else by Pynchon except *The Crying of Lot 49*. Like *Crying*, it's a brief for the disinherited and dispossessed, the outlaws and outcasts of an underground America. Also like *Crying*, I suspect it's a breather between biggies. It doesn't feel like something obsessed-about and fine-tuned for the seventeen years since *Gravity's Rainbow*. It feels unbuttoned, as if the Author-God had gone to a ball game. Another darker magisterial mystification is implied, maybe the rumored Mason-Dixon opus. This doesn't make *Vineland* a Sunday in the park with George, but at least it can be summarized without my sounding too much like an idiot.

I. *Where is "Vineland"?*

In the northern California redwoods, "a Harbor of Refuge" since the middle of the nineteenth century "to Vessels that may have suffered on their way North from the strong headwinds that prevail along this coast." It's also a republic of metaphors, a theme park of sixties obsessions—television, mysticism, revolution, rock 'n' roll, Vietnam, drugs, paranoia and repression. And it refers as well to the Vinland of the old Norse sagas, what the Vikings called America. (I wasted time looking up the Vikings. How far did their dragon-ships get? Explain that Icelandic tower in Newport, Rhode Island, and those Minnesota runes. Was Quetzalcoatl actually a Viking? Is Pynchon singing some rock saga about another of his unmapped kingdoms, like Vheissu, the "dream of annihilation" at the heart of *V*?) Anyway, it's symbolic: a Third World.

II. *What happens to whom, and when, in this "Vineland"?*

In Orwellian 1984 midway through the Reagan gerontocracy, refugees from the sixties are having a hard time. Zoyd Wheeler, who used to deal dope and play piano in a rock band, is a "gypsy roofer" trying to take care of his teenaged daughter, Prairie. Prairie's in love with a Heavy Metal neofascist, and misses the mother she hasn't seen since babyhood. This mother, the almost mythical Frenesi, belonged in the sixties to a band of guerrilla moviemakers—the Death to the Pig Nihilist Film Kollective. But she was more or less abducted by the malign federal prosecutor Brock Vond and "turned" into an "independent contractor" for FBI sting operations. When Justice Department budget cuts "disappear" Frenesi from the government computer, Vond's frantic. Expecting her to show up in Vineland, he plots to frame Zoyd, kidnap Prairie and scorch every pot plantation north of "San Narcisco." (Think of Panama.)

In other words, "the State law-enforcement apparatus...calling itself 'America'" declares total war on the leftover flower children. It's a made-for-TV rerun. Back in the sixties Vond's Feds destroyed a college-campus People's Republic of Rock 'n' Roll and trucked the student revolutionaries off to camps for a Political Re-Education Program (PREP). This is where Vond turned Frenesi. When Vond invades Vineland, Zoyd and Prairie are assisted in their resistance by the Woman Warrior DL Chastain; by the Japanese private eye Takeshi; by a DEA renegade and television addict Hector Zuniga; by the Sisterhood of Kunoichi Attentives, a convent of Ninjettes in the karmic adjustment racket; by Vato and Blood, who steal cars and traffic with ghosts; by punk rockers, Jesus bikers, Mafia hoods and three generations of Left Coast Wobblies, including Frenesi's mother, Sasha, who may or may not be a member of the Party...

III. *Is any of this funny?*

Of course it's funny. Not only does Pynchon know more than we do about almost everything—communications theory, stimulus-response psychology, rocket science, Catatonic Expressionism, entropy, gauchos and stamps—but what he doesn't know, he makes up. In *Vineland*, for instance, PingPonging between the sixties and the eighties, he makes up TV movies: John Ritter in *The Bryant Gumbel Story*, Peewee Herman in *The Robert Musil Story* and Woody Allen in *The Young Kissinger*. Not to mention a docudrama about the Boston Celtics, with Paul McCartney as Kevin McHale and Sean Penn as Larry Bird. And not even perhaps to think about *The Chipmunks Sing Marvin Hamlisch*.

There are, besides, the Bodhi Dharma Pizza Temple ("a classic example of the California pizza at its most misguided") and a controlled-environment mall called the Noir Center, with an upscale mineral-water boutique (Bubble Indemnity), a perfume-and-cosmetics shop (The Mall Tease Flacon), and a New York deli (The Lady 'n' the Lox).

Of all the funny names—Weed Atman, Ditzah and Zipi Pisk, Ortho Bob, Mirage—my favorite is Isaiah Two Four, Prairie's Heavy Metal squeeze named by his parents for the swords-into-ploughshares, spears-into-pruning-hooks passage from the Bible. No wonder Isaiah wants to start a chain of Violence Centers, each to include "automatic-weapon firing ranges, paramilitary fantasy adventures...and video game rooms for the kids." These centers would presumably compete with the "fantasy marathons" of the Kunoichi Sisterhood that feature "group rates on Kiddie Ninja weekends..." I also laughed at a Sisterhood self-cricticism session devoted to "scullery duty as a decoding of individual patterns of not-eating." And, of the many songs Pynchon's written for his various musicians, the funniest is "Just a Floozy with-an U-U-zi."

IV. *Can we count on the usual entropy, paranoia and Manichaeanism?*

Yes, as well as some terrific rhapsodies on water, cars and parrots. And the paranoids are right. *They* (narks, RICOs, yuppies, television anchorfaces, earth-rapers, treekillers, random urine-sniffers, sexhating deathloving Wasteland thought police) are out to get *Us* (whomever: civil liberties, due process, readers of Pynchon and *The Nation*). *And* they use *Us* against *Us*. At PREP,

> *Brock Vond's genius was to have seen in the activities of the sixties left not threats to order but unacknowledged desires for it. While the Tube was proclaiming youth revolution against parents of all kinds and most viewers were accepting this story, Brock saw the deep—if he'd allowed himself to feel it, the sometimes touching—need to stay children forever, safe inside some extended national Family....They'd only been listening to the wrong music,*

breathing the wrong smoke, admiring the wrong personalities. They needed some reconditioning....the long-haired bodies, men who had grown feminine, women who had become small children, flurries of long naked limbs, little girls naked under boyfriends' fringe jackets, eyes turned down, away, never meeting those of their questioners, boys with hair over their shoulders, hair that kept getting in their eyes...the sort of mild herd creatures who belonged, who'd feel, let's face it, much more comfortable, behind fences. Children longing for discipline.

Only this time *We* win. You have to understand entropy not just as the heat-death of a culture, but also as *equilibrium*. As Pynchon clued us in his first famous short story with nods to Henry Adams, so he clues us here by quoting another American crazy, William James. According to *Varieties of Religious Experience*: "Secret retributions are always restoring the level, when disturbed, of the divine justice. It is impossible to tilt the beam. All the tyrants and proprietors and monopolists of the world in vain set their shoulders to heave the bar. Settles forever more the ponderous equator to its line, and man and mote, and star and sun, must range to it, or be pulverized by the recoil."

For Pynchon, this is remarkably cheerful. But how are *We*, a bunch of dopers in the California redwoods, to prevail against the Geeks: Virgin vs. Dynamo? See below.

V. *Will we care any more about these characters than we did about, say, Benny Profane and Tyrone Slothrop?*

Probably not, except for DL. Like a Buddhist or a Hume, Pynchon doesn't really believe in the "self." He's more interested in states of being and becoming. Zoyd attitudinizes, Frenesi's a computer dream of patterns, Takehi's inscrutable, Hector's a clown and Sasha's one of Tolstoy's supergoody clean old peasants; even Vond, "like any of the sleek raptors that decorate fascist architecture," adds up to little more than an upwardly mobile social-control freak with a flashy line of psychic yardgoods. But as Vond talks to other men through the holes in women's bodies, so Pynchon talks to his readers through the holes in his cartoon zanies. What he wants to talk about is "official" reality (a media fabrication) versus "unofficial" alternatives (see below).

Frenesi is Pynchon's excuse to make fun of film. According to her

"Kollective": "A camera is a gun. An image taken is a death performed. Images put together are the substructure of an afterlife and a Judgment. We will be the architects to a just Hell for the fascist pig. Death to everything that oinks!" Vond tells her, "Can't you see, the two separate worlds—one always includes a camera somewhere...the other always includes a gun, one is makebelieve, one is real? What if this is some branch point in your life, where you'll have to choose between worlds?" To the People's Republic of Rock 'n' Roll the night of its destruction, Frenesi brought a gun *and* a camera, not to mention fast-film 7242 and a Norwood Binary light meter, for the helicopters and the troops in blackface and "the high-ticket production of their dreams." This is "Reality Time" versus "all that art-of-the-cinema handjob." She'll emerge from hiding and go to Vineland only because Hector promises to star her in *his* movie.

Hector is an excuse to talk about television. Although almost everything happens in *Vineland* in "sullen Tubeflicker," not always "Primetime"; and odd birds sit in palm fronds to sing back at the commercials; and Zoyd, dropping acid, hopes that Prairie will be there "to help him through those times when the Klingons are closing"; and Takeski believes that television "mediates death"; and even Frenesi feels "that the rays coming out of the TV screen would act as a broom to sweep the room clear of all spirits"; and all over Vineland, rival cable TV riggers exchange gunfire, "eager to claim souls for their distant principals, fighting it out house by house"—only Hector is addicted, a Brady Buncher. When his wife kills their TV set with a frozen pot roast, Hector arrests her. He'll escape from a rehab for "Tubabusers." Television is the white noise of the Garrison State, the elevator Muzak of Repression going down.

Zoyd is an excuse to talk about music, from rock ("romantic death fantasies...the terrible about-to-burst latency just ahead, the hard-on") to Heavy Metal ("nuke-happy cyberdeath," "Septic Tank and Fascist Toejam") to New Age ("audio treacle," "mindbarf"), even Bach ("the best tunes ever to come out of Europe"). And everybody's freaked by computers. Prairie worries "how literal computers could be—even the spaces between characters mattered. She wondered if ghosts were only literal in the same way. Could a ghost think for herself or was she responsive totally to the needs of the still-living, needs like keystrokes entered into her world, lines of sorrow, loss, justice denied?" Frenesi, the absentee mother, is also metaphysical:

it would all be done with keys on alphanumetic keyboards that stood for
weightless, invisible chains of electronic presence or absence....We are all
digits in God's computer, she not so much thought as hummed to herself to a
sort of standard gospel tune, and the only thing we're good for, to be dead or to
be living, is the only thing He sees. What we cry, what we contend for, in our
world of toil and blood, it all lies beneath the notice of the hacker we call God.

Whereas Sasha is Pynchon's excuse to talk about one of the alternatives to media reality—a lost history of radical politics in the American West, long before Pacifica or Savio or People's Park; the organizing of loggers and miners and canneries; the strikes against San Joaquin
cotton, Ventura sugar beets, Venice lettuce; Tom Mooney, Culbert
Olson, Hollywood craft unions and fifties blacklists. This repressed
progressive history and its media denial seem at first the subtext to
Vineland. These people did more for the Revolution than sing about it,
or dope themselves stupid. Nor did they surf.

But this is to reckon without the alternative (and competing) unofficial realities of the Indians and the dolphins and DL Chastain, the
kick-ass Woman Warrior.

In every Pynchon novel, there is a woman we love—Rachel Owl-
glass in *V*, Oedipa Maas in *Crying*, Katje or Greta in *Gravity's Rainbow*—
because in the satiric muddle she seems to point true-north to a magnetic pole of decencies. DL is the one we care about here. Though
trained in a variety of martial arts strategies, from the Vibrating Palm
and the *Kasumi* Mist to "the Enraged Sparrow, the Hidden Foot, the
Nosepicking of Death and a truly unspeakable *Gojira no Chimopira*,"
and equally at home among the Kunoichi Sisters and the YakMaf, she
is nevertheless Frenesi's loyal friend, *and* Prairie's resourceful protec-
tor, *and* Takeshi's eventual lover. Like her comrades on a rescue mis-
sion into "the Cold War dream" of PREP, we believe in DL's "propri-
etary whammies" the same way that "in those days it was possible to
believe in acid or the imminence of revolution, or the disciplines,
passive and active, of the East." She is also Pynchon's door to the Orient, into which, it seems to me, he disappears.

VI. *Now I can sound like an idiot.*

I haven't mentioned the Thanatoids, nor their Vineland suburb of
Shade Creek. You reach Shade Creek by water and darkness, with the

help of Vato and Blood, strippers of cars and souls. It's a ghost town, except the ghosts aren't dead yet. They are "an unseen insomniac population," refugees from history, residues of memory, the victims of "karmic imbalances—unanswered blows, unredeemed suffering, escapes by the guilty—anything that frustrated their daily expeditions on into the interior of Death, with Shade Creek as the psychic jumping-off town—behind it, unrolling, regions unmapped, dwelt in by these transient souls in constant turnover…"

Thanatoids, instead of rock 'n' roll, sing songs like "Who's Sorry Now?" "I Got a Right to Sing the Blues" and "Don"t Get Around Much Anymore." They watch television, although they learned long ago "to limit themselves, as they always did in other areas, only to emotions helpful in setting right whatever was keeping them from advancing further into the condition of death. Among these the most common by far was resentment, constrained as Thanatoids were by history and by rules of imbalance and restoration to feel little else beyond their needs for revenge."

Weed Atman, the Leary-like mathematics professor who rose implausibly to guru of the People's Republic of Rock 'n' Roll before Frenesi betrayed him, is a Thanatoid. So are many Vietnam veterans, like Ortho Bob. Ortho Bob explains to Takeshi that "in traditional karmic adjustment…Death was the driving pulse—everything had moved as slowly as the cycles of birth and death, but this proved to be too slow for enough people to begin, eventually, to provide a market niche. There arose a system of deferment, of borrowing against karmic futures. Death, in Modern Karmic Adjustment, got removed from the process." Takeshi, like the Sisterhood of Kunoichi Attentives, sees the money-making possibilities of a "Karmology hustle." So, apparently, do Vato and Blood, Charons on the Shade Creek Styx. When Vond goes looking for Frenesi, he will meet Vato and Blood instead, while the leftover flower children are at a picnic with the leftover Wobblies and a Russian punk rocker who wandered into the redwoods. According to Takeshi, if none of the other stuff works, "we can always go for the reincarnation option." Takeshi's into *The Tibetan Book of the Dead*, with souls in transition, denying death, unable to distinguish between "the weirdness of life and the weirdness of death." So, of course, are Thanatoids. But…

In a way, everybody in *Vineland* is a Thanatoid, full of bad faith; guilty, resentful and nostalgic; under ghostcover, in motion through varying thicknesses of memory and light toward a reckoning. Zoyd's sixties surfer band found "strange affinities" with the subculture of "beer riders of the valley": both rode a "technowave…Surfers rode God's ocean, beer riders rode the momentum through the years of the auto industry's will." DL in her "Ninjamobile" has an L.A. freeway vision of screaming black motorcades, cruisers, huge double and triple trailer rigs,

> *flirters, deserters, wimps and pimps, speeding like bullets, grinning like chimps, above the heads of the TV watchers, lovers under the overpasses, movies at malls letting out, bright gas-station oases in pure fluorescent spill, canopied beneath the palm trees, soon wrapped, down the corridors of the surface streets, in noctural smog, the adobe air, the smell of distant fireworks, the spilled, the broken world.*

Frenesi dreams of a "Gentle Flood," of standing just above the surf,

> *looking toward a horizon she couldn't see, as if into a wind that might really be her own passage, destination unknown, and heard a voice, singing across the Flood, this wonderful song…telling of the divers, who would come, not now but soon, and descend into the Flood and bring back up for us "whatever has been taken," the voice promised, "whatever has been lost"…*

But there were ghosts before the sixties—the Yurok Indians. Early Russian and Spanish visitors to Vineland felt some "invisible barrier" the Indians "might have known about but did not share—black tips of seamounts emerging from gray sea fringed in brute-innocent white breakings, basalt cliffs like castle ruins, the massed and breathing redwoods, alive forever…the call to attend to territories of the spirit." And there were ghosts before there were Indians. Past the lights of Vineland, "the river took back its oldest form, became what for the Yuroks it had always been, a river of ghosts," with spirits called *woge*, "creatures who had been living here when the first humans came," who went away, eastward over the mountains, or "nestled altogether in giant redwood boats, singing unison chants of dispossession and exile." Without warning, trails "would begin to descend into the earth, toward Tsorrek, the worlds of the dead." Ecofreaky Hippies tell Vato and Blood that

> *this watershed was sacred and magical, and that the* woge *were really the porpoises, who had left their world to the humans, whose hands had the*

same five-finger bone structure as their flippers...and gone beneath the ocean, right off Patrick's Point in Humboldt, to wait and see how humans did with the world. And if we started fucking up too bad,...they would come back, teach us how to live the right way, save us...

What's going on? If we put together Shade Creek, flood dreams, technowaves, porpoises and *woge*, with Vheissu in *V*, and the Tristero underground in *Crying* (clairvoyants, paranoids, outcasts and squatters swinging in "a web of telephone wires, living in the very copper rigging and secular miracle of communication untroubled by the dumb voltages flickering their miles") and the "Deathkingdoms" and "death-colonies" Blicero apostrophizes in *Gravity's Rainbow* ("waste regions, Kalaharis, lakes so misty they could not see the other side," Original Sin, Modern Analysis), we end up with something that looks a lot like, if not a comic-book Bardo, then maybe that Buddhist "Global Novel" that Maxine Hong Kingston's been going on about recently in the pages of *Mother Jones* and on, gasp, The Tube. For that matter Zoyd, Prairie, Takeshi, DL and the Wobblies look a lot like the 108 bandit-heroes of *Water Margin*, the Chinese Robin Hood Kingston has so much fun with in *Tripmaster Monkey*.

According to *The Tibetan Book of the Dead*, dying takes time. We experience the supreme void as pure light, and hope it takes us straightaway to Amitabha, which is for Buddhists what One Big Union was for Wobblies. If the pure light won't take us, we must wrestle with our past, our karma. Only after apparitions both beautiful and monstrous are done with our "conscious principle" will we be reborn—the "reincarnation option"—as something else, somewhere other, on the great wheel. Tom Pynchon calls this place, in the last word of *Vineland*, "home." Wouldn't it be pretty to think so?

ROBERT STONE: JONAH IN THE WHALE

Call him Ishmael. Robert Stone returns from Melville and the raptures of the Deep to tell us that God and history are both dead, America is sinking fast, and manhood itself may be terminally diseased. America and manhood have always been his texts, through which he looks, with a burning eye, for watermarks of larger purpose, coded meanings. Stone might leave the country (for Vietnam, for Central America, even Hollywood or Antarctica), but it's America confounded that he finds wherever he goes. And although there are plenty of women in his novels, they are doped to the gills, or tortured to martyrdom, or hang themselves and drown, while a man stands around construing his failure to heroize. It's as if this erstwhile Merry Prankster book by book were working his way backwards, out of Mailer and Hemingway, until, of course, he arrives at Melville's *Isolato*. Like Ahab, Stone hounds God—and discovers His absence. According to Owen Browne, the Pilgrim of *Outerbridge Reach*:

> *we are enslaved to these strange stories. Hidden voices, bought and paid for, endlessly repeating them....Someone was always being played for a fool. The very process of telling the stories was a game of withholding. Every narrative was reversible and had its outer and its inner side. They were all palimpsests....Again and again these demands for blind trust. Jump, leap and he may or may not be there. And you—spread-eagled over the ocean—may or may not fall and sink when the wind is contrary. When the wind is boisterous and the sea so big and the boat so small. Endless games. Deceptions without end, infinity to one, all against all. And on the wind, amplified through the stratosphere, stories to give it form. To keep us absolutely fast in the ice and darkness. Stories like false dawns. But ice, darkness, boisterous winds, and false dawns were all true things that had to be lived out...*

Owen Browne is someone new to Stone's fiction: Northeast Middle-class Normal, Dick Tracy Square, Wonderbread WASPy, as if wandering in from a Cheever or an Updike; monogamous husband, worried father, Navy pilot, sailboat salesman. He seldom drinks, never drugs, and listens to the music of Russ Columbo. "He believes," says his wife, Anne, "in all those things people used to believe in," like the Fourth of July and Vince Lombardi. Why should such a man want to sail around the world alone, in a perilous publicity stunt for the Hylan conglomerate that owns him? Because, he thinks, "the heroic age of the bourgeoisie is over." Contemplating the homeless and the hustlers in Penn Station, the "No Can Do" Polish shipwrights at the boatyard, a stock market in free fall and his rugged face in the promotional videos for the yachts he sells, Owen feels himself to be a stranger in his own country and his own bed, "beside his own woman—a stranger but without a stranger's freedom. On the other side of darkness, he imagined freedom. It was a bright expanse, an effort, a victory." To one of his old Navy buddies, he cries out: "You have no idea how shitty my life has been. How fucking pedestrian and dishonorable."

His wife, Anne, a writer for a yachting magazine, subscribes to these same despondencies. The only time they seem ever really to have been happy was in the Navy, in Vietnam, with "the deliciousness of youth and the feeling of fuck the world, the proud acceptance of honor, duty and risk." And what has become of them now in the big house built by the owner of a clipper ship? She drinks, he mopes and their daughter listens to Megadeath: "The fall [Anne] feared was deep and dark, more frightening than the empty space between her clifftop and the sea. For a moment she was paralyzed with nameless dread." Anne and this Nameless Dread curl up together with a bottle of wine and a copy of *Middlemarch*.

[*Characters in Stone are always reading books, like* The Martian Chorni- cles, Nicholas and Alexandra, *Calderon, B. Traven, Ruben Dario and Kate Chopin, even* Jurgen. *This is very nineteenth century. Besides* Middlemarch, *Anne reads the New Jerusalem Bible, with Tolkien's translation of Genesis, Nien Cheng's* Life and Death in Shanghai *and, for a second time,* Brideshead Re- visited, *while listening to National Public Radio. On Owen's bedside table, with the naval histories and a* National Geographic *atlas, there is a copy of Melville's* White-Jacket. *When he sails, sailing with him, along with Beethoven, Elgar, Sinatra and Samuel Eliot Morison, will be John Donne, Robert Frost, Ernest Hemingway and* Look Homeward, Angel.]

Enter Strickland, a documentary filmmaker who's read everything, including Neruda, and been everywhere, including Vietnam, and knows how "to work the silences, the white noise and dark frames." Strickland is that self-marginalized, bystanding know-it-all who shows up in every Stone novel: Rheinhardt in *A Hall of Mirrors*, the spiteful alcoholic newscaster; Converse in *Dog Soldiers*, the heroin-smuggling tabloid journalist; Holliwell in *A Flag for Sunrise*, the drunk- en anthropologist "forever inquiring of helpful strangers the nature of their bonds with one another"; or Walker in *Children of Light*, the coke-wasted Hollywood screenwriter. Besides quoting Yeats (and Niet-zsche), these know-it-alls can be counted on to do more damage than the freaks with whom they traffick, to whom they condescend. Knowing doesn't save you.

Strickland is between Third World gigs. In Nam, where he went to make an antiwar film, resentful grunts tied him up overnight in a tun-nel man-trap, to a stake smeared with human shit. He has just returned

from revolutionary Nicaragua with footage of political rallies and religious processions, chopper shadows and flamingos, which he will edit
for public television into a film with the obligatory "left-liberal col-
oration" that also contains "a few home truths for the private delecta-
tion of that tiny band of perceptual athletes whom Strickland regarded
as his core audience." In Managua, he made fun of "internationalists"
in their wire glasses, *banda rojas* and overalls: "You probably went to
progressive camps. Cookouts with food-from-many-lands...Folk-
dancing...interracial sing-alongs." Strickland is his own Third World.

[*Characters in Stone carry around a surprising amount of left-wing baggage
they'd just as soon be rid of. In a New Orleans bar, Rheinhardt screams: "You're
a dirty Lovestoneite...you killed Sidney Hillman!" And Rainey rides to his martyrdom with a crazy old stormbird, flying a red flag, singing out loud of "Hay-
market Square, Gene Debs, Henry George—yeah, and Daniel De Leon,
Hilstrom, Big Bill Hayward, Huey!" Marge, in* Dog Soldiers, *grew up in a
family of left-wing Irish vegetarians and "Hudson River Bolsheviks," and went to
National Guardian parties "with all the folksingers and the tame spades." Holliwell in* A Flag for Sunrise *was taught to sing the "Internationale" by a newsstand vendor, and meets with the CIA the day Paul Robeson dies. And Sister
Justin, besides reading* To the Finland Station, *has already done time in a
Mississippi jail, with Folkways Records, for having served in the black voting
rights campaign. In* Children of Light, *besides Lu Anne's Long Friends, those
"Sorrowful Mysteries" with the dragonfly wings, the ghosts of the Hollywood
blacklist also gather in the Mexican night; fun is made of Sequeiros.*]

Anyway, Strickland is hired by Owen's parent company to film for
posterity a circumnavigation of the globe by its resident tycoon,
Matthew Hylan, a Ted Turner/Bill Buckley type who is also, alas, a
"Captain" Bob Maxwell type; he does a bunk. The p.r. people talk
Owen into substituting in the race for glory. Strickland is pleased by
the Brownes; they are precisely right for his savaging. Like all the
other "pilgrims" and "sleepwalkers" he has filmed, they will impale
themselves on his camera. Owen, he says, is "this dorky fucking citizen, for Christ's sake":

*Browne Agonistes, representative of man the measure...The polite yachts-
man out there for the insulted and injured, the losers and the lost. They could
track him in their atlases day by day, the disappointed, the misled, the self-
sacrificers, as he bore their wounds away and washed them in salt. They
should all feel for Browne, Strickland thought, the soft, wet people of the*

world. They should all honor and admire him, the Handsome Sailor, their chartioteer.

As for Anne...well: "Her bright silky hair was braided behind her head. The color of her eyes was nearly Viking blue, but with a Celtic shadow. Her face was strong, willful and austere, wonderfully softened by her smile. It was a brazen faintly androgynous pre-Raphaelite beauty, daunting, almost more than he thought he could handle." But Strickland will try.

And so, as a cure for his despondency, Owen goes to sea alone. And as a cure for hers, Anne goes to bed with the Third World. And as a cure for ours—because Owen and Anne aren't really interesting enough in their privacy to sustain us through the first 200 pages—we tune in on Strickland's malice and cynicism, his Mephisto style. And that's most of what you need to know...except that the Brownes, objects of Stone's conditional sympathy and targets of Strickland's scorn, *aren't* aristocrats. However WASPy, they don't own this nation; they're indentured to it; they bought a package tour, the Vince Lombardi "narrative," like one of Owen's videos. Owen's father may have thought he was a "tragic exile," instead of a lowly immigrant from England, but he worked as a servant on a country estate on Long Island. Anne's "Newfie" father fought his way up from the docks. (Strickland, naturally, never had a father; he was brought up by his mother, among circus performers, in welfare hotels: the Other America.)

Despite appearances, the Brownes are still on probation, the unfinished children of Outerbridge Reach, that Valley of Ashes down Arthur Kill into a backwater of moldering tugs, gutted ferries, "hulks...scarred in a geometry of shadows. The busy sheer and curve of their shapes and the perfect stillness of the water made them appear fast in some phantom disaster...Thousands of immigrants had died there, in shanties, of cholera, in winter far from home. It had been a place of loneliness, violence and terrible labor. It seemed to Browne that there was something about the channel he recognized but could not call to mind. On the dark shore, a junkyard hound kept barking as though it would go on forever."

[*We've been to such boneyards before in Stone's novels: a graveyard shift at a soap factory. With Rainey among machetes and sugar cane, when women screamed for Jesus, and smoking tar ran from an oil drum on the smouldering rocks of the trash pit, and a figure like a voodoo doll emerged with a rope around its neck. With Hicks, in the L.A. canyons, where "shit creeps out of the night under those sundecks, and they know it," or dying in the desert. With Holliwell underwater, when the coral strikes: "As he pedalled up the wall, he was acutely aware of being the only creature on the reef that moved with purpose. The thing out there must be feeling him…its dim primal brain registering disorder in his motion and making the calculation. Fear. Prey." With Lu Anne, counting the Louisana dead: "where the living and the dead are involved in mixed entertainments. And are not tucked away in the ground but dwell among us. Their hair grows and their fingernails and they go on getting smarter in those ovens under their angels."]*

We are ready now for the last couple of hundred pages of *Outerbridge Reach*, as dazzling as anything in American literature. Once Owen's underway, it almost doesn't matter why he went, but here are a few of his reasons: (1) "the good fight or the right war—something that eased the burden of self and made breath possible." (2) "the way to recoup. A good way. A clean way" (a Heming-way!). (3) "I think most of us spend our lives without ever having to find out what we are made of.…In the present day, a man can live his whole life and never test his true resources." (4) "His fear was not of being overcome but of *failing* from the inside out. Discovering the child-weakling as his true nature and having to spend the rest of his life with it." (5) "All good men have physical courage. Without physical courage there is no other kind."

Such Papa Normanizing, Mailerway. Why is it that when men in American novels feel despondent about their manhood, they invariably abandon their wives and children—Pablo, in *A Flag for Sunrise*, even shot his dogs—for some sort of Aboriginal walkabout to kill other men, or fish, to bag a unicorn and waste a hippogriff? Why don't we see any novels with heroes like Walt Whitman or Johnny Appleseed or Charles Kuralt? Instead of Spanish bull, Quaker oats? But in Robert Stone, while Rheinhardt doesn't really, on purpose, deal death to anyone, he more or less co-conspires at a race riot, not to mention the staving-in of Bingamon's skull with an axe handle; Hicks, imagining himself a samurai, piles up quite a body-count from Berkeley to Mexico with an M-70 grenade launcher; Holliwell is the only anthropologist I ever heard of who stabs a man to death in an open boat; if Walker had stayed in Hollywood, Lu Anne might still be alive; and Owen goes to sea to kill his father, and harpoon himself, and remember Vietnam.

I'm about to suggest that the father Owen seeks to kill is really the

Author of Us All—the Great Signifier. I've gone off the deep end before, reviewing Stone. Ten years ago I got so excited tracking down Gnosticism in *A Flag for Sunrise* that I skimped on the rest of the novel: the CIA, the Comintern, the Mafia, liberation theology, Vietnam as paradigm. I'm doing it again because Stone fessed up to this Gnosticism in an interview on WBAI. He has been arguing with God in all his novels ever since he left the Marist brothers at Archbiship Malloy High School in Manhattan and, like Melville, went to sea instead of college. And what Melville discovered, rounding Cape Horn, in the Marquesas, or on Galapagos, among castaways, deserters, "mongrels," "cannibals," tortoises and slaves, is what Stone has discovered in such seething "green places of the world" as Vietnam and Central America: Imperialism. Not God in History but History as God; not "the just rule of the Lord," but "poverty and revenge...cooking oil, excrement, incense, death."

Because Stone's God-hounding has so often been confused in the past with the alcoholic deliriums and drug hallucinations of his characters—e.g., Rheinhardt's "yellow liquid terror," his "White Light" and his "Whirlies"; Marge on Dilaudid and heroin, hoping to "seal some chaste clammy intimacy...while their noses ran and their light bulbs popped out silently in the skull's darkness"; Hicks on speed and Dr. Dope, in his Jungian cave, chemically levitating; Father Egan on rum and reggae seeing Gnosis, and Pablo stoned on Dexedrine seeing "death's heads, swastikas, the ace of spades" and a drunken Holliwell telling his Latin audience, "Mickey Mouse will see you dead"; Walker, on scotch, vodka and cocaine, seeking "fire, motion, risk," while Lu Anne on Quaaludes is chewed on at her fingertips by infant teeth in the shaven skulls of "blue-baby-colored" dragonfly Long Friends—we tend, in reviewing him, to scant his obsessional interest, his itch for the metaphysical. Yet some sort of Christ is nailed to almost every other page.

In *A Hall of Mirrors*, Rheinhardt quotes Dante and finds himself in a graveyard at a latticed gate, from which "a small, iron Christ stared down in a wide-eyed rusty death from the gibbet of a green, oxided cross"; Rainey hears voices of "the dread procession of God's stricken world"; and Geraldine in a dead-baby dream recalls the Bible verse about "the terrible bright blossoms of that almond tree...where the fears were." In *Dog Soldiers*, under Dieter's bell tower, facades are painted with bibical scenes of the serpent with rattles tempting Eve, and Christ in judgment wearing the feathered headdress of a cacique, and martyrs carrying their heads in their hands; a lamb is crucified. Even in *Children of Light* there's a fire-blackened crucifix, a "seared Christus figure"; Lu Anne looks up to see "that the hanged Christ nailed to the beams had become a cat. It was burned black as the figure had been, its fur turned to ash, its face burned away to show the grinning fanged teeth." And of course *A Flag for Sunrise* can't be read without this stuff: St. Ursula and her virgins put in an appearance almost immediately. Jesus Christ, in a glass-box coffin, looking like Che Guevara, reappears throughout. Holliwell himself was Jesuit trained, and seeks in Tecan "people who believed in things, and acted in the world according to what they believed." Sister Justin may have given up her Savior—"the Holy One, the Hanged Man"—for the Revolution, but He appears to her anyway, when she's tortured. Father Egan, "the Christian humanist witness in a vicious world," traffics instead with heresy. Near a jungle pyramid, in front of Toltec stelae depicting human sacrifice, he speaks of "Errant Sophia, the whore of wisdom, who in her foredoomed passion to comprehend the Holy One, underestimated the depths of the Abyss and became lost"; of each man's sundering from his own true self, a "mislaid" God we must reassemble from buried sparks and particles of light, angelic messengers and a Demiurge.

[*Stone has also whistled tunes in the bare ruined choirs of most other world-religions, too. Rainey consults a copy of the* Gita: *"He opened it and turned to the transfiguration of Krishna, God's self-litany in the war chariot: 'I am the Man-Consumer, spewer of skulls/ I am the cunning of Dice Play/ I am Time, waster of the Peoples.'" Converse is familiar with the* Ramayana *and Hicks is a student of Zen, as well as bodhi swasha, T'ai Chi and your basic Kundalini herpetology. Showing up at sunrise in Tecan, besides Toltecs, there are also Olmecs, Incas, Mayans and Aztecs, with jade animals, bone carvings, chacmools, hierogylphs and Rain God Seven.*]

Shia is mentioned in *Outerbridge Reach*, and Calvin and Luther and the Plymouth Brethren, and the name of Owen's personal boat is *Parsifal*. But there's no more weight to these mentions than to similar nods at Trotsky and Ayn Rand, until at last Owen braves the Atlantic. It's almost as if Stone had scourged himself in his first four novels: Evil, maybe; God, no. He seems also to be just saying no to drugs. Strickland's usage is strictly recreational. Maybe Stone sobered up himself after all the self-destructiveness in *Children of Light*. (One good reason for never going to Hollywood is that then you don't have to write a novel about it.) If movies aren't poetry, then neither is dope, a snuff movie of the mind. Heroin, anyway, was never an apt metaphor for the disintegration of American culture. Smack had no more to explain to us about greed and racism than the opium pipe in any way symbolizes Tao or Nirvana; it was another sort of Demiurge. We now see what Hicks saw, at the end of *Dog Soldiers*, in the vibrating mountains:

> *You know what's out there? Every goddamned race of shit jerking each other off. Mom and Dad and Buddy and Sis, two hundred million rat-hearted cocksuckers in enormous cars. Rabbits and fish. They're mean and stupid and greedy, they'll fuck you for laughs, they want you dead.*

Put this together with what Holliwell sees at *Sunrise*: Positive Thinkers dealing death "in the name of God or Humanity or some Larger Notion...How could they convince themselves that in this whirling tidal pool of existence, providence was sending them a message?

> *Seeing visions, hearing voices, their eyes awash in their own juice—living on their own and borrowed hallucinations, banners, songs, kiddie art posters, phantom worship. The lines of bayonets, the marching rhythms, incense or torches, chanting, flights of doves—it was hypnosis. And they were the vampires. The world paid in blood for their articulate delusions, but it was all right because for awhile they felt better. And presently they could put their consciences on automatic. They were beyond good and evil in five easy steps—it had to be O.K. because it was them after all. It was good old us, Those Who Are, Those Who See, the gang. Inevitably they grew bored with being contradicted. Inevitably they discovered the fundamental act of communication, they discovered murder.*

Holliwell had one last thing to tell Sister Justin whom he loved: "God doesn't work through history...That's a delusion of the Western mind." He had several things to tell himself: "When I decide what happened, I'll decide to live with it." And: "The absence of evil was the greatest horror." Finally: "A man has nothing to fear who understands history." (By which he meant: History is meaningless.) This is seeing through everything. And with such ferocious eyes, like Strickland's, we now examine the Pilgrim of *Outerbridge Reach*.

It's not enough that Owen's never done this sort of thing before. He must be wounded in the foot like Achilles before he even leaves harbor. It's not enough that the carpenter dismantled his cabin after a fight about Vietnam. Anne, with her beef jerky, forgot about his solar panels; and his fiberglass cracks into "spiderwebbed craze patterns" in the first storm: "Bad workmanship and sharp practice. Phoniness and cunning....Sold our pottage, overheated the poles, poisoned the rain, burned away the horizon with acid. Despised our birthright. Forgot everything, destroyed and laughed away our holy things. What to do for our children's terrible laughter?" Nor is it enough that he seldom eats, can't sleep and is monitored day and night by transponders signaling from his mast, a ship-to-shore telephone and a short-wave radio. He will also on this radio be propagandized by demented missionaries, with Bible lessons in Cantonese, Korean and Tagalog ("Listeners may remember that when our Lord was pursued by his enemies, Saint Matthew tells us that He went by ship into a desert place apart..."); by equally demented particle physicists, babbling on of "absolute future," "absolute past," "absolute elsewhere" and "imaginary time"; by a punmaking, chess-playing, teenaged ham operator (who is blind); *and* by the ghost of his dead father, quoting the drowned Shelley. None of this is enough because God gangs up on Owen.

Imagine a plague of insects, "pale yellow and black, with delicate spotted wings against the thorax," infesting the wind, covering the cabin windows, crawling up mainsail and mast, smothering the surface of the water "as though the swarm had displaced the ocean." And a great strange cloud that obscures the sun just before the shadow of an enormous shark appears, "its dorsal fin...silently shearing an inch or two of the breathing world." And a blue sky suddenly assailed by curving bands of violet and dark green light, an aurora "beyond the compass of the human will," reminding Owen of tracer rounds and parachute flares in the Song Chong Valley, in Vietnam, in 1969. And a towering "mytsical" iceberg embellished in shapes "unknown to geometry, beautiful but useless in any sort of measurement...a psychological principle." And the pilgrim lashed inside his bubble, through whistling gales and slackening shrouds, surfing into vertigo as if the vessel had been scalded, riding green walls into black waves, freezing rain and "ghostly wands of foam," hearing "the stone annihilation, the locust's shriek magnified from the abyss." And this same Flying Dutchman, "outside randomness" after the engine fails and the masthead light winks out, seeing in a pale blue shimmer "something inexplicable": "In the center of the glow" toward which a petrel leads him "was what appeared to be an inverted mountain range. Peaks hung upside down like stalactites, their points barely touching the surface of the sea." And when at last he finds this island right side up, it proves to be treeless, volcanic, with black gulls. screeching skuas, seething penguins and an albatross; with a lagoon in the crater of the volcano, to which, through winds "like music out of stone," he penetrates by Zodiac; from which, on foot, he passes to a black sand lava beach, where, under a black sky beside a smoky sea, he spies "white shapes…Ice, he thought at first. Coming closer, he saw that the white shapes were not ice. What they might be confounded him. At first they seemed meaningless and without form; closer up, they assumed a geometry with which he was somehow vaguely familiar." Among these shapes, penguins wander "like the citizens of a town." These are the bleached bones—"fin bones like skeletal wings," "head-high pelvic bones and mandibles of peg teeth the size of fists," "cages of five-foot ribs…piled up like the tiers of a stylized prison to a height beyond reach"—of thousands of dead whales.

Instead of God: Darwin.

I'm not even going to tell you about the charred porch, the bright silk dress, the Cape Cod rocking chair, the Mozart and the braided human hair. Nor, in a shattered mirror, a face "dark brown and bearded, wild-eyed, like a saddhu's. Or a dervish's…the face of a man in the grip of something powerful and unsound." No wonder Owen shuts down his radio and telephone, discards his transponder, lies to his journal, "chopping the cup of sea and sky into imaginary angles." As if he'd listened to too much particle physics, what he sees instead of a sun is misshapen discs, a limitless perspective extending forever, to infinity, "in a universe of infinite singularities. In the ocean, they suggested, there would be no measure and no reason. There could be neither direction nor horizon. It was an ocean without a morning, without sanity or light."

Of *course*, this is a passage into Melville. Yes, the shade of Joseph Conrad also hovers, and I suppose, in a sense, that Strickland is Owen's Secret Sharer; but so was Fedellah Ahab's Secret Sharer, six years before Conrad got born. "Annihilation" was one of Melville's favorite words. Owen reads *White-Jacket* prior to setting sail. The original "Handsome Sailor" was Billy Budd, and Owen is also mad Pip, off the *Pequod*. As in *Moby Dick*, Prometheus haunts this novel, too. (The medallion Strickland wears on his neck depicts a man tied to a stake with a vulture eating his eye; Strickland says it's a Mayan god of discomfort, from the Grijalva. Maybe, but then the Mayans must have met Prometheus; besides, like Owen, Strickland is remembering Vietnam.) Not only will we meet so many whales, all of them dead, but we will also encounter, with Owen, Melville's own motto: BE TRUE TO THE DREAMS OF YOUR YOUTH. And when Owen at the bottom of the globe, on bone hooks, swings free "in the ancient deasil motion," whirling clockwise and "congruent" with the sun and stars, "at varying angles to the blue horizon," singing his way into "the interstices" and the "algorithmic Sun Dance," feeling himself attached to "the central pole, the axis of the world," any reader should be reminded of the fate of Ishmael:

> *Round and round, then, and ever contracting towards the button-like black bubble at the axis of that slowly wheeling circle, like another Ixion I did revolve.*

But if *Outerbridge Reach* is a passage into Melville, along the standardized lines of any epic quest—Vedic or Homeric, the Nibelungenlied or the Lay of Igor, an Edda or a Doon—it also has the language and shape of another ancient narrative line. It feels like all great mystic journeys, from St. John of the Cross to William Blake to the flight of the Sufi lapwing. (Note Owen's dervish. Doris Lessing isn't the only novelist to have noticed parallels between Rumi's Persian poetry and modern molecular physics.) As always, Stone's realism picks up speed as it whirls, like a cyclotron, till matter itself explodes into something surtextual. The pilgrim, of course, is the soul. The storms, of course, are symbolic. This is the ultimate migration. In any mystic voyage toward harmony, equilibrium, grace, Union, Marriage, the "geography of the invisible" or the annihilation of the self, there are ravens and hounds, voices and visions, Dark Nights and Rivers of Light. Fasting and insomnia are recommended. A sea talked to St. Catherine of Siena, too. It's amazing how everybody on these journeys—Heraclitus, Siddhartha, Jacob Boehme and William James; Gnostics, Kabbalists and Indian cestatics—agrees, corresponds, with their synonymous detachments and amazements, their ecstasies and trance, their awe and apparitions, their self-abandonment and "saving madness," their eyes and roses and magnets and fish. Logos! Godhead!

It's easiest to understand Owen as symptomatic of a corrupt American ruling class. After all, in this race, he *cheats*. Yachts and Vietnam:

among Boat People, first-class and steerage! But such a comprehension fails to explain why we like him more, even so, than Strickland, the adulterer and voyeur. Having cheated, he then behaves every bit as much like a samurai as Hicks, except this time Stone is talking about despair instead of honor. Owen is empty when he goes to sea, and there he finds emptiness. To the abyss, he brings his built-in precipice. The pilgrim self-destructs; *devolves.* And there's nothing left in this or any other world in which to believe. I'm reminded one last time of Melville:

> *Though nominally included in the census of Christendom, he was still an alien to it. He lived in the world, as the last of the Grisly Bears lived in settled Missouri. And when as Spring and Summer had departed, that wild Logan of the woods, burying himself in the hollow of a tree, lived out the winter there, sucking his own paws, so, in his inclement, howling old age, Ahab's soul, shut up in the caved trunk of his body, there fed upon the sullen paws of its gloom!*

MARY MCCARTHY, R.I.P.

Counting down to the election, I ought to say something about Roger Ailes, who has poisoned the chalice of our franchise. Equally scandalous is that Ronald Reagan on his Japanese boondoggle picked up two million bucks, from the Fuji Corporation, for a couple of speeches and a TV spot. And really outrageous, although only National Public Radio seems to care, is the news that the Republican party, through its busy little conduit, the National Endowment for Democracy, has chipped in *another* two million to bring down Oscar Arias in Costa Rica. The Republican party thus finds itself in bed with Manuel Noriega, who's contributed only $500,000 to torpedo Arias.

But I am instead in mourning for Mary McCarthy, who'd have savaged these lycanthropes with more zest than I can zither up. Even in her mellow years—think of the schoolmarm who civilized the West—she had the biggest teeth at the tea party. *Time* magazine once called her "quite possibly the cleverest woman America has ever produced." It isn't clear whether *Time* meant this as an insult. To call a person clever implies a "merely"; she might have been something grander; she isn't entirely serious. On the other hand, clever is what

Time magazine has always wanted most in the world to be, so maybe they thought they were being nice.

She was clever, ferociously so. And wicked, too. This country loves a Bad Girl, at least one at a time, like Cher. When McCarthy came out of the American West, after a wretched Dickensian childhood, to Vassar and then to New York in the '30s, she must have seemed to the West Side intellectuals, worrying their Marx and Freud, a kind of '20s throwback, a flapper with brains, "a princess among trolls." The reviews she wrote for *The Nation* and *The New Republic* were a kind of SOS magic scouring pad on the brainpan of the culture; we saw the reflection of her grin.

When she moved in with Philip Rahv, he put her to work for *Partisan Review*, reviewing plays. Poor Clifford Odets! When she left Philip Rahv, it was to move in with Edmund Wilson, who encouraged her to write fiction. I doubt he expected himself to turn up in this fiction. Nor could Rahv, Dwight Macdonald, Harold Taylor, etc., have been pleased when they, too, turned up, the living dead. About her novels she once explained, "What I do is take real plums and put them in an imaginary cake."

You must understand that I grew up reading *The Nation*, *The New Republic* and, especially, *Partisan Review*. (In this southern California boyhood, I also subscribed to the *Congressional Record* so I'd have someone to talk to each afternoon when I came home from school.) The intellectuals of the anti-Stalinist Left, the heavyweights of psychoanalysis and modernist literature, were my heroes. In those days, there was a coherent literary culture, and its avatars actually talked to one another. Until I read the satiric novels of Mary McCarthy—swam in the ice blue water of her disdain—it hadn't occurred to me that they also went to bed with one another, just like Gore Vidal and Jack Kerouac...and *embarrassed* themselves.

That some of them had gone to bed with McCarthy was delicious but also frightening. She would know more than they did, like Doris Lessing and Simone de Beauvoir. She was my first crush. Years later, when I did meet her at various Manhattan jolly-ups, she was, of course, kind but firm. Like Lionel Trilling and Hannah Arendt, she took it upon herself to instruct me in my duty, but made it clear there wasn't enough time for me to learn even half of what she'd already forgotten. It is bitter now to contemplate the handful of letters I have

from her. Each blue aerogram from Paris reproves me for some critical or ideological delinquency.

If her novels lack the generosity of great literature, they are full of
everything else that counts, like people, places, plots and ideas;
money, honor, betrayal and sex; a wonderful nineteenth-century en-
ergetic curiosity. *Memories of a Catholic Girlhood* is as good as memoirs
get. *Venice Observed* and *The Stones of Florence* are travel-writing master-
pieces. Her essay on Nabokov's *Pale Fire* is a classic, and her defense of
Arendt, against the critics of *Eichmann in Jerusalem*, was brave and brilliant. In her books on Vietnam, on Watergate and on terrorism, she
followed a blood red moral thread through the labyrinth of a totalitarian century. She read everything, and was indignant about everything, and, yes, clever about everything.

What I'll miss most is her faith that we can know the world, and
choose what we make of ourselves in that world, and maybe even
save it. Literature is publicity now, and politics are public relations.
I'd love to have been in New York back then, when she first arrived
from the West, from the moon, this Diana, this huntress. But I was
born too late. Damn.

HEMINGWAY'S WOMEN

After watching six hours of Stacy Keach as Hemingway on television,
if I were a feminist critic who'd read Carlos Baker, Kenneth Lynn, the
collected letters and Bernice Kert's *The Hemingway Women*, there are
some things I'd have to say about everything I didn't see. Like this:

"She shot very well this good, this rich bitch, this kindly caretaker
and destroyer of his talent." That's Papa, in "The Snows of Kiliman-
jaro," probably talking about Pauline Pfeiffer, his second wife, who
stole him from Hadley Richardson, his first wife, and who would be
robbed of him by Martha Gellhorn, his third, who would relinquish
him to Mary Welsh, the fourth, after which he loved a gun.

Papa said, "No matter how being in love comes out it's sure worth
it all while it's going on." And: "All women worth sleeping with were
difficult." And: "The better you treat a man and the more you show
him you love him, the quicker he gets tired of you. I suppose the
good ones are made to have a lot of wives but it's awfully wearing trying to be a lot of wives yourself."

Of the four—dear sweet little feather kitty (six years), rich bitch (thirteen), Prima-Donna (five) and "camp-follower and scavenger" with the "Torquemada" face (fifteen)—Pauline was most resentful on being dismissed. Having borne him two of his three sons, she actually demanded $500 a month in alimony. She had a right. Her family's cotton-gin and soybean money, like Hadley's trust funds, had supported him in the apprenticeship of his difficult art. Her religion, Roman Catholicism, had at least temporarily improved his sex life, which may be why he converted to it. And at one point he was willing to admit that "she loved me truly and well."

Nevertheless, as Papa prepared to leave her, he wrote a novel, *To Have and Have Not*, in which a woman a lot like Pauline prepares to leave a man a lot like Papa. This woman, "Helen," says: "Slop. Love is just another dirty lie....Love always hangs up behind the bathroom door. It smells of lysol....I'm through with love. Your kind of pick-nose love. You writer."

This is what the pick-nose writers do: they *project*, reversing roles as if they were capes: poor bull. Papa wanted to go, especially to Spain, where he and Martha Gellhorn would be brave together during the Civil War, and so Pauline must be made to decide to leave *him*. It should have been enough for Pauline that Papa understood her *feelings*, that he himself felt *guilty*. Hadley'd never hassled him; Hadley found another man. Pauline went instead into the business of fabrics and bitterness. Brooding about alimony, Papa revised himself: Pauline deserved having done to her what *she'd* done to Hadley. Besides, by this time, her Roman Catholicism had blighted his bed. Whatever else might be said of Spain, coitus interruptus was not its problem.

We're in *Romper Room*. One of Papa's sons, Gregory, has observed, "Papa would suffer for a long time with a woman who was giving him problems sexually, but in the end he would make her suffer more." On the other hand, another of his sons, Jack, suspecting that his father hadn't done all he might to brighten Gellhorn's bed, suggests that he "should have been flattered that Martha's loyalty lasted as long as it did."

Gellhorn took neither prisoners nor crap, at least not much. Of all the females discussed and consulted in Kert's good-humored, evenhanded and engaging book—the four he married, the several with whom he dallied, the dozens of whom he bragged, the two or three about whom he permitted himself merely to fantasize, and even if we include his own mother, the maligned Grace—Gellhorn was the toughest of the cookies; instead of crumbling, _she_ walked out. Ernest, like any other forty-five-year-old American king-baby/boy-man on his way to a Nobel Prize, never forgave her. _He_ was supposed to do the walking, a specialist in Shane-like vanishing acts: to Wyoming, to Constantinople, to bush, to sea, to bag another rhino or kill the big fish.

Much later, Gellhorn would recall their affair with Spain: "I think it was the only time in his life where he was not the most important thing there was." Kert reports a Cuban episode:

> _Another time, when he was roaring drunk after an evening on the town, [Gellhorn] insisted on driving them back to the Finca. All the way out he cursed her and then slapped her, not hard, but enough to send her into a cold rage. Never one to be cowed, she deliberately slowed the car, his beloved green Lincoln Continental, to ten miles an hour, then drove it into a ditch and a tree, leaving him to walk the rest of the way._

Hadley would have ducked; Pauline would have sulked; Mary would have cried. But Martha was writing her own novel. Of course, she was a first-rate journalist, a war correspondent for _Collier's_ magazine, accustomed to paying her own, independent way. But so, too, had Pauline and Mary been journalists. They gave it up for marriage, reporting only to Papa. Gellhorn left him to check out Finland. She dragged him to China to meet Chiang. She wanted him in Europe for the big war; he wanted to stay home playing with his bottles and boats. She tried to explain:

> _But I believe in what I'm doing too and regret fiercely having missed seeing and understanding so much of it these years. I would give anything to be part of the invasion and see Paris right at the beginning and watch the peace....I have to live my way as well as yours or there wouldn't be any me to love you with. You really wouldn't want me if I built a big stone wall around the Finca and sat inside it._

But that's exactly how he _did_ want her. The double standard was his measure. There was just one writer, and his name was Hemingway, and he was either "honest or not, as a woman is either chaste or not." Hadn't he already proved his courage in Italy and Spain? Wasn't he protecting, with his putt-putt _Pilar_ and his rum-soaked cronies, the sands of Havana from German submarines? "I happen to be in a very tough business," he said, "where there are no alibis." He knew this, having looked so hard for them.

Martha must have shamed him, finally, into joining her war. Being famous when he did so, he could choose any magazine or newspaper in the nation for which to correspond. That he chose Martha's own, *Collier's*, left her suddenly on the beach and on the bench, without front-line press credentials: grace under pressure. While Martha, in the boondocks, found the death camps, Papa, in London, was busy drinking champagne with Mary Welsh. Martha seems to have been relieved rather than dismayed; she had already written him, perplexed:

> *I would like to be young and poor and in Milan and with you and not married to you. I think that I always wanted to feel in some way like a woman and if I ever did, it was the first winter in Madrid. There is a sort of blindness and fervor and recklessness about that sort of feeling which one must always want. I hate being so wise and so careful, so reliable, so denatured, so able to get on.*

What if two people, lovers, sought "some common ground which is green and smooth," but each was "a quite odd and burning sort of person"? And yet she, too, was besotted. He mattered more: "You are a much better man than me, but I hope I am not too bad a wife even if I have gone away when I thought you would be away too...I feel ashamed of being happy unless you are." And:

> *You have been married so much, and so long, that I do not believe it [marriage] can touch you where you live and that is your strength. It would be terrible if it did because you are so much more important than the women you happen to be married to.*

Hadley must have felt the same. She forgave him everything, perhaps out of gratitude. He had saved her from spinsterhood, hadn't he? Against her sister's advice, she insisted on saying "obey" at their wedding. At the divorce, she told him, "I took you originally for better, for worse (and meant it!) but in the case of your marrying someone else, I can stand by my vow only as an outside friend." To mystified acquaintances she explained: "If Ernest had not been brought up in that damned stuffy Oak Park environment, he would not have thought that when you fall in love extramaritally you have to get a divorce and marry the girl."

According to Pauline, "You are the punctuation and the grammar as well as the exciting story." She was not unacquainted with scruple, comtemplating Hadley: "Dearest, you and I have something that only about two persons in one or several centuries get....And having it, when we say we can't face life without each other and then deliberately make someone else face life alone, it makes me very afraid about us. Because having all there is, it seems to me, really ought to make us stronger instead of weaker." She endured his fling with Jane Mason— Jane, trying to kill herself, broke her back jumping off a balcony; Ernest was witty to John Dos Passos: "the girl who fell for me literally"—but Martha was too much for her, and, ultimately, for Papa.

Mary sounds like a masochist. She, too, was grateful: he probably saved her life with some quick thinking. But he seems to have stayed in her life because he was too old and too sick to behave anymore like Shane. When, toward the end, he flipped out and was stashed too briefly in the Mayo Clinic, she received a call from Dr. Rome in Rochester: "Ernest was expressing an interest in having sex again, after some months of impotency. Would Mary fly out and spend the night with him? She did as she was told, though she dreaded such an encounter in the locked, barred wing of the hospital. She was right. The experiment was a failure."

They let him out, saying he was cured. Six days later he found his shotgun and must have thought that, like his father, he would die "in a trap that he had helped only a little to set, and they had all betrayed him in their various ways before he died." Mary blamed herself for not having locked up the keys to the storage cellar. No matter that this is silly, even vainglorious: Allow him at least, after his squandering of talent and seed, the dignity and the illusion of free will. Survivor-guilt, too, is a kind of masochism. Just imagine her visit to that clinic...her failure at such therapy. Not even in bed, anymore, could he write a good book.

As for Grace, only one of Papa's many mothers, she is rescued by Kert from his many calumnies. More resourceful than most, and rather proud of him, she deserves better than being remembered merely for destroying the good doctor's Indian collection. Hadley, after all, lost some of the doctor's son's precious manuscripts. And Grace took his infidelities in surprising stride: "She was sorry to hear that his marriage was over, but as far as she was concerned very few marriages deserved to survive. She admitted that she held rather heretical views on marriage but usually kept such opinions to herself."

Such a mother might have invented so many daughters-in-law. Like her, they were all midwesterners. Each new one had to begin by cleaning up the *Finca*: so many broken expensive toys, so much screaming for approval, so many tantrums. It is necessary, after all, for a writer to believe that whatever he is doing or feeling, at *this very moment*, is the right thing to do or feel, because otherwise he can't face his blank page. He needs to believe he is complicated. And then, God help him, all those women know his secrets.

I haven't even mentioned Agnes—"the first one, the one who left him...how he had never been able to kill it," who became the English nurse who had to die so that someone could walk home in the rain. Nor Adriana, the last one, "the Black Horse," to whom he confided, "Probably it would be better if I had never met you that day under the rain...Look, daughter, look. Now you can tell everybody that you have seen Ernest Hemingway cry." Not to mention Lady Duff and Marlene Dietrich and...Did he ever confuse them, in the bagging, with the red snappers and the sharp-tailed grouse, the zebras, wildebeests, waterbucks, guinea fowl, gazelles and trout? Did he confuse himself—falsified, maudlin, self-burlesquing, gone native in Africa?

He shaved his head, carried a spear, dyed his English wool jackets and Abercrombie shirts the Masai orange-pink, and began to flirt with the local women.

Why did all the local women love him? We know he wasn't inclined to spend much money on them: "Martha could not recall that he ever gave her anything except a shotgun and long cashmere underpants from Abercrombie and Fitch suitable for duckshooting on cold days." But he must have spent *something*—this big sad slyboots, this secret reader of the *Partisan Review*. How genuinely empty some of his famous silences must have been. Nothing between the ears but Gary Cooper? Why do we love our children, and why do they run away from us?

About the Hemingway women, who knew his secrets, we can say two things:

First, they were "enablers." By indulging and forgiving, disguising and dissembling, they "enabled" the boy-man to go on being a boy-

man until he surprised himself to death. There is something dangerously sick about "enabling." You victimize yourself.

Second, nevertheless, unlike Papa, and in spite of the fact that
everybody knows women are more emotional than men, not one of
these women ate a gun.

OTHER VOICES, OTHER ROOMS

GABRIEL GARCÍA MÁRQUEZ VERSUS SIMON BOLIVAR

Bolivar, the father of many nations and a child of the Enlightenment,
once complained: "The South Americans have blundered through the
centuries as the blind blunder among colors."

García Márquez begets colors like a Picasso. Among other things, he
has seen

> *The diamonds embedded in the teeth of black grandmothers who sold heads*
> *of Indians and ginger roots sitting on their safe buttocks under the drenching*
> *rain...the solid gold cows on Tanaguarena beach...the blind visionary of*
> *La Guayra who charged two reals to scare off the blandishments of death*
> *with a one-string violin...Trinidad's burning August...the green Hindus*
> *who shat in the middle of the street in front of their shops with genuine silk-*
> *worm shirts and mandarins carved from whole tusk of an elephant...*
> *Haiti's nightmare, its blue dogs, the oxcart that collected the dead off the*
> *streets at dawn...*

Besides these black grandmothers, gold cows, blue dogs and green
Hindus, he's no slouch, either, when it comes to ice, mirrors, magnets and windmills.

Between them, Bolivar and García Márquez invented Latin America.
That one of these continental dreamers should novelize the other isn't
a surprise. What does surprise is that García Márquez has chosen to
novelize the *end* of Bolivar's life—the last wasting days and insomniac
nights on the river Magdalena, when the Liberator was himself almost
blind and had to be read aloud to—omitting the beginning and the
middle, when the colors burned the brightest.

There are some things we ought to know about Bolivar that Gabo
isn't telling us. Permit me to educate myself in public.

I. *"Democracy on his lips; aristocracy in his heart"*

So many Bolivars, so many novels: the wild colonial boy, raised on
Plutarch and Rousseau; Freemason, Jacobin and warrior-prince; Man
of Reason on a White Horse; constitutionalist, emperor and stud; Lear
on the Dover heath; Oedipus at Colonnus.

He was born rich—into the Creole aristocracy of Caracas, in 1783,
with sugar mills and slaves. He was educated as if he were Emile, by a
tutor who had translated Chateaubriand's *Atala* into Spanish. He came
to young manhood in Madrid, where he married a nobleman's daughter; and in Paris, where he read Voltaire, Montesquieu, D'Alambert,
Buffon, Hobbes, even Spinoza. From Madrid, Paris and Rome, he
brought back to South America liberal thought, revolutionary passion,
Romantic afflatus (Goethe! Beethoven! Wordsworth! Camille!) and
some Bonaparte. Decades later the Liberator kept next to him on his
bedside table the very same copy of Rousseau's *Social Contract*, edited by
Diderot, that Napoleon himself had thumbed through on St. Helena.

García Márquez is no more interested in Viennese scrimshaw than
Vladimir Nabokov was, but contemplate this psychogram: Bolivar lost
his father at age three; his mother at age nine; his wife, to yellow
fever, at age nineteen. There would be many women, but only one
great love, the rest of his life, and he died without legitimate heirs—
unless you count Venezuela, Colombia, Ecuador and Bolivia. Revolutionary politics as displaced oedipal rage? He also had a drop, or two,
of "Negro blood," which he didn't like to talk about, though every
time he invented a country he also freed its slaves. It's just that he'd
rather they wouldn't vote. Bad faith?

Anyway, by 1807, back in Venezuela, he was pretending to read
Tacitus and plotting against Spain. (There's the messy business of Francisco de Miranda, a hobnob of Gibbon's, an intimate of Madame de
Stael and maybe a lover of Catherine the Great, who led the first disas-
trous insurrection and seems to have been turned over to the enemy by
the Creole aristocrats, but Bolivar's biographers are mealymouthed on
this subject, Gabo is silent, and I'll take a pass.) In 1811, he freed his
own sugar mill slaves. By 1812, he was on the road—into history and
the primeval—with Homer in his backpack, wading waist deep
through Amazons and crocodiles; over the snowcones of the Andes,
swooping down like a condor. There were the usual atrocities on both
sides, but place names like Puerto Cabello, Cartagena, Orinoco and

Carabobo are as resonant to South Americans as Shiloh, Gettysburg and Appomattox are to us. And Bolivar, like William of Orange, while often defeated, was ever indomitable. Retreating as far away as Haiti, he would regroup and set sail, like Drake or Morgan or Fidel Castro or Don Quixote, in the general direction of Venezuela, with six schooners, a sloop and a printing press. Rousseau would have loved it.

Along the way, he picked up Manuela Saenz, "a perfect mixture of Amazon and courtesan." She could throw a spear, shoot a gun, smoke a cigar and ride a horse, all at the same time. "Her love of animals," one biographer primly notes "caused her to be accused of some amazing depravities." Once, she saved Bolivar from assassination. On another occasion, left behind in Lima, she invaded army headquarters, dressed as a man, brandishing a pistol, to insist that the troops rally to his side. She seems to me the sort of tough cookie, almost prototypical, that Gabo could make much of, but he doesn't. She was arrested after the death of her man, but escaped by boat, with a lock of his hair and a glove, to wind up in the sordid port of Paita, where Garibaldi found her in 1843. Yes, Garibaldi, in a blood red Montevideo slaughterhouse smock, with a ship called the *Mazzini*, flying a black flag with a volcano symbol.

It's all too novelistic. Back in the Old World, Carlyle called Bolivar a Ulysses waiting for his Homer, and Byron borrowed his name for the yacht he used to bring back Shelley's body. It was as if Europe, from whose wishful thinking, from whose mythomania, this American hero derived in the first place, needed him back as a metaphor or a booster shot. To the Ecuadorian poet Olmedo, who wrote overly heroic odes about the Battle of Junin, Bolivar joked: "If I were not so honest and you were not a poet, I could believe you wished to write a parody of the *Iliad* using the heroes of our miserable farce as characters." But poets, of course, will decide who's heroic and who's farcical.

Now look at "Simon the First" in the twilight of his empire building, as constitutions fall like playing cards, and the revolution eats its children: the president of two new countries and the curse of several more, believing always in "one nation, free and unified from Mexico to Cape Horn," but despairing of the anarchy that took over the minute he left the palace; admitting to himself that he was not at all a Talleyrand, with the patience to transform the leaves of the mulberry plant into silk: "I am not capable of playing on such a complicated keyboard, I'd break it."

He was thin-skinned, at the mercy of "the suspicion of any fifth-rate writer in a provincial newspaper." And self-pitying: "Slander strangles me as serpents strangled Laocoon." And also protested too much, especially when he thought he wouldn't get his way: "As far as I am concerned, you may rest assured that I shall not accept the presidency: first, because I am tired of giving orders; second, because I am tired of being accused of ambition..." And he blamed everybody else: "He who dedicates his services to a revolution plows the sea."

He wanted freedom but also order. And while his notion of order wasn't as barmy as Miranda's—who wanted a hereditary emperor called "Inca"—he hadn't the silkworm patience to let these new little nation-states sort out their own borders and squabbles. Simon's idea of a federal union, a kind of "democratic Caesarism" with someone a lot like Simon (or Napoleon) in charge, kept him hopping from Caracas to Lima to Quito to Bogota and back again, putting down minor rebellions by suddenly "disloyal" aides-de-camp. He had two ways of dealing with the ingratitude of men and nations. Men, he got rid of, when he could. Nations, he would encourage to write a constitution that fit him like a glove, which he turned into a fist. The two are related, and this is where the interest of a novelist like Gabo, a Man of the Left, ought to quicken.

A typical Bolivar constitution called for a president, elected for life, and a two-chambered law-making body, with wealthy upper-class Creole families as a substitute for European nobility in one house, and a lower house elected by voters with a minimum of property. For Bolivia, he upped his ante. His best biographer in English, Gerhard Masur, describes his Bolivian scheme as "an elective kingship such as the Catholic Church and the Holy Roman Empire." A President-for-Life was the sun in a planetary system of tribunes and senators and "censors" (guardians of morals, also elected for life), with a hereditary prime minister, usually a buddy of Simon's like Sucre. Left out, you'll have noticed, are "the beggar-proletariat," the recently emancipated but sadly "ignorant" Negroes, and all those "superstitious" Indians who had been around for at least three thousand years. Some social contract.

I'll mention only one of the men he got rid of because he's the one the novelist finds compelling. Without General Manuel Piar, ambitious, theatrical, but also a brilliant tactician, Bolivar would have lost the Orinoco. But Piar made difficulties about "the aristocracy in Caracas" after the fall of Angostura; there were rumors of yet another insurrection; and if it was acceptable to let some intriguers off the hook, well, Piar was a better soldier, and therefore potentially more dangerous. Surprising even his closest confidantes, Bolivar had Piar shot. Eleven years later he was still justifying himself: "The death of General Piar was a political necessity which saved the country. The rebels were disturbed and frightened by him...Never was there a death more useful and more politic and at the same time more deserved." Among Simon's biographers there is a queasiness about Piar, apologetic handstands, because Creole troublemakers like Bermudez and Marino were spared. Piar was a mulatto. He might not even have been qualified to *vote* in, say, Bolivia. It occurs to the novelist that the mulatto general might have been something Bolivar felt guilty about when he went down the Magdalena to his death, in 1830, at age forty-seven.

Of his fellow men-at-revolutionary-arms, San Martin of Argentina went into a very long Old World exile; Jose Gervasio Artigas, creator of the Republic of Uruguay, spent his last thirty years as a farmer in Paraguay; Bernardo O'Higgins, father of Chile, retired to Peru, and died in Lima unnoticed; Sucre of Bolivia was murdered; likewise shot in Mexico were Hidalgo and Morelos, and, in Costa Rica, Moreno. At Bolivar's deathbed at Santa Marta, on a plantation owned by a Spaniard—oh, Magic Realism!—the attending physicians were Dr. Reverend and Dr. Night.

II. *Gabo: The Man with Kaleidoscope Eyes*

Born to colorize: a *mestizo*, whose father was illegitimate. First-hand experience in childhood Aracatca of ice in boxes of frozen fish at a United Fruit Company store; *La Violencia*; Montessori and a scholarship to a high school for the gifted; law student at the University of Bogota, closed down on account of assassination; newspaper columnist from age of twenty; salesman of encyclopedias; Colombia's first-ever film critic; off to Geneva, Rome, Paris; arrested as an "Arab" during the Algerian troubles; *In Evil Hour* and *No One Writes to the Colonel*; Czechoslovakia and the Soviet Union; by Greyhound through Faulkner's American South; in Mexico City, to write ad copy for J. Walter Thompson and movie scripts with Carlos Fuentes; writer's block from 1961 to 1964; thunderstruck in his Opel on the highway, en route to Acapulco, by visitations of the Buendias; back then to "the Cave of the Mafia" to write eight hours a day for eighteen months, and an end to *Solitude*. The rest is Nobel stuff. If you want more look at Gene H. Bell-Villada's *García Márquez* (North Carolina), an agreeable mix of man and metaphor with nifty readings and inside info. Did you know, for instance, that the six chapters of *The Autumn of the Patriarch* not only mimic Bartok's six string quartets, but that they're also closely patterned on Virginia Woolf's *The Waves*? "The great Virginia," Gabo said.

Let's look at this whole business of literary influence. *Solitude* is taught in many courses in Third World Studies programs as a masterwork on colonial rape, and it is. Those who teach it this way, though, tend to resent its being taught any other way—co-opted by Comp Lit Eurocentrics for whom Gabo's a clever child of Faulkner, Kafka, Rabelais and Joyce, the Bible and Sophocles. To talk about a *Patriarch* indebted to Bartok and Virginia Woolf, or a *Cholera* owing something to Proust, Flaubert and Simone de Beauvoir's *Coming of Age*, is to drive these people crazy.

Hard cheese. Gabo grew up on *The Three Musketeers* and *The Magic Mountain*; he read Kafka and Woolf, in translations by Borges(!). *Metamorphosis* blew him away. *Leaf Storm* wouldn't be the book it is, if not for *As I Lay Dying*; nor *Solitude*, if not for *Absalom! Absalom!* (plus Defoe). Nor, to reverse this coin, would *Solitude*—folk myth, fairy tale, medieval/colonial romance, gothic novel, chronicle of exploration, sci-fi—look the same without Afro-Hispanic musical forms like the mambo and bolero, or Caribbean folklore, or Spanish literature since Sor Juana. *Patriarch*'s unimaginable without Suetonius, Plutarch *and* Ruben Dario *and* Domingo Sarmiento.

But no matter how hot the influences or heavy the inspirations, Gabo alone had to master in his eighteen months of *Solitude* dozens of arcane texts on navigation, alchemy, poisons, Sanskrit. And that's the easy part. Then you need magic, or genius: plagues of insomnia and amnesia; ghosts, priests, Indians, Arabs, gypsies; men with machetes hacking their way through "bloody lilacs and golden salamanders" to find, in a swamp, a Spanish galleon; a stream of blood, an umbilical thread, that feels its path across a city from a dying son to his grieving mother; a paterfamilias chained to a tree in the garden, muttering in Latin of memory and desire; a rain of so many tiny yellow flowers that they "covered the roofs and blocked the doors and smothered the animals who slept outside." Thus enthralled, a reader's ready to believe anything: certainly that Macondo was Eden before the Fall, South America before the Conquest, and Colombia during the armed occupation of the United Fruit Company. Gabo may have meant his plague of insomnia to symbolize the Indian loss of bodily peace and spiritual history, but for many of us it also signifies our dreadful century and what we've done to corrupt so many languages. We're allowed: Readers have rights.

The fact is, Gabo is *sui generis*. Nobody else in his own Third World has written a novel as wonderfully encompassing as *Solitude* and neither has anyone else in the First or Second Worlds, not since the Second World War, and maybe not since Proust. Besides, great writers always fatten up on everything that's gone before them, after which we'll feed, in turn, on them. I'd like to see a Comp Lit course on how Gabo himself has influenced literature *since Solitude*. Rushdie, for example, whose *Midnight's Children* tips its turban. Or Toni Morrison, who says she hadn't read *Solitude* before she wrote *Song of Solomon*, but really…Several years ago in Japan, I had dinner with Kobo Abe, who had decided never to write another word because *Solitude* had been translated into Japanese, and Kobo Abe and Gabo were exactly the same age, and the author of *Woman in the Dunes* was positive he'd never write a book as good as *Solitude*, so he'd given up. The next day on a bullet train to Kyoto I heard that Gabo had won the Nobel Prize for literature. *You* know what Japanese writers do when they're depressed. They take gas like Kawabata; or fall on swords, like Mishima. Patched in a panic through Tokyo to Hakone, I got Kobo Abe's wife on the phone. She said he was fine and happily back at work! How could this be? "García Márquez," she said, "has joined the company of the immortals. Abe's no longer in competition with him."

This is un-American, but it suggests the world literature in which we're all complicitous, what Maxine Hong Kingston calls a Global Novel and Rushdie celebrates as "hybridity, impurity, intermingling, the transformation that comes of new and unexpected combinations of human beings, cultures, ideas, politics, movies, songs." It never stops, nor should it. I reviewed *Satanic Verses* here, and it occurs to me that I missed two crucial influences, neither of them Eastern: Blake's *The Marriage of Heaven and Hell* and Bulgakov's *The Master and Margarita*. For that matter, Octavio Paz became more interesting after India. Before *Solitude*, in fact, there was in Gabo's shorter fiction an *excess* of Faulkner and the Frenchies; of DeSica and the gloomy neorealists; of coffins, tumors, incest, doppelgängers, and existential attitudinizing. Except for the sex in "The Sea of Lost Time"—"First they did it like earthworms, then like rabbits, finally like turtles"—you couldn't buy a laugh. And the famous magic had yet to grow up, from the chameleons in *In Evil Hour* that couldn't change colors because they were blind, to those Greek sailors in "Innocent Erendira" who paid women for their favors with "living sponges that later on walked about the house moaning like patients in a hospital and making the children cry so that they could drink the tears."

Seven long years after *Solitude*, with time out for Gabo to be far too soft on Fidel's bashing of dissidents and gays, came *The Autumn of the Patriarch* (1975), to which *The General in His Labyrinth* aspires to be a counterweight. A matched pair, these two novels imagine power. I'll get to *Patriarch* when I get to *Labyrinth*, in a minute. Between *Patriarch* and *Love in the Time of Cholera*, we got the journalistic *Story of a Shipwrecked Sailor* (1972); a backwards murder mystery and send-up of romance novellas, *Chronicle of a Death Foretold* (1982); and the odd little book he wrote for somebody else, *Clandestine in Chile* (1987), the story of Miguel Littin.

Littin was one of Chile's best-known moviemakers until forced into exile when his friend Salvador Allende was murdered in 1973. Gabo met him in Madrid in 1986. Littin had just come back from an undercover visit to Chile (fake beard, fake glasses, fake passport and fake Uruguayan accent), with home movies of Pinochet's dictatorship. It's easy to see why Gabo was intrigued. The man spied on his own country, like writers everywhere. He forged a new identity, counterfeited another self, then had problems feeling authentic—two great modernist themes. And he'd turned politics into a movie; very Latin American. Inside Littin's skin, an itchy Gabo looks for and finds his usual quota of portents: a dream-palace, at the foot of a French garden; babies in their prams dressed up like rabbits; a restaurant where tired seagulls go to sleep. Gabo also bullies Littin into thinking about two of the writer's personal heroes: the martyred Allende, a doctor who learned his politics and chess at the cobble of an anarchist shoemaker; and the poet of love and revolution, Pablo Neruda, who spent *his* Nobel Prize money removing the stable of a castle from Normandy to his own backyard, for the churchlike vaults, the stained-glass windows and the pond full of lotus flowers.

It makes you wonder: Is Latin America just full of this stuff, waiting around for a Gabo to see it, to turn blood into butterflies? Or has

Gabo, the man with kaleidoscope eyes, invented his own Latin America? Or has Latin America invented Gabo out of all its technicolored ambiguities?

Love in the Time of Cholera is a happier story, though not quite the three-hanky job—a kind of Hispanic *Cocoon*—so many reviewers gushed about. Gabo abandons his magic act to tell a tale almost straight, covering several generations in two different centuries in three separate minds. In the last half of the nineteenth century, in an old port city on the Caribbean coast, under the golden domes of the Viceroys, a young Florentino and an even younger Fermina fall in love. They are both from the wrong side of the social tracks; he's illegitimate; her father is a crook. Fermina dreams over Florentino's letters. He composes a waltz for her on the violin. She says she'll marry him if he promises he won't make her eat eggplant. She marries instead the most eligible bachelor in Rionegro, the haute bourgeois Dr. Urbino, famous for ridding the country of cholera. The doctor won't die till he's eighty-one, from a broken spine after falling out of a mango tree in pursuit of a parrot. And then Florentino, with his "mineral patience" and his "Trappist severity" and his "chronic romanticism," the worldly boss of all the riverboats and a secret poet, too, reaffirms his love of the widow Fermina, fifty years, nine months and four days after she kissed him off.

Well, yes, it's a sumptuous portrait of turn-of-the-century self-deception; and a knowing account of marriage as a social compromise; and a book of wonders about neediness in old age as consuming as the last poems of Yeats; and a laudation of the love that would abolish time. And I'm not saying that the cholera isn't real; nor that the gerontoerotics are a mask for some other, ulterior, Marxist meaning; nor that Gabo didn't want to make us feel good. But I will suggest there are "choleras" Dr. Urbino didn't get rid of. There are those fevers and obsessions, like love and poetry and music, immune to the science and subversive of the death-spirit of an indecent social order. There's the cholera of political violence: Up in a hot-air balloon, looking down at corpses strewn on the landscape, what Fermina sees, besides white drool foaming at the lips of the dead, are bullet holes at the backs of their necks: *La Violencia.* And Dr. Urbino, a specialist in "the ethical management of forgetfulness," is of course, a Good Liberal, inadequate to history's rages, the mad passions of illicit love, the daunting silence of the river idol "with her serpent's eyes." Even the port city, consecrated to a Holy Spirit cult, has its own unconscious, a nightmare past: it was the principal slave market of the New World. In its marble ruins, the Viceroys rot with plague inside their armor. *That* plague's symbolic, too.

But Gabo's got us this far on the river, under many colors, including a black flag.

III. *Pick a Patriarch*

Not exactly at Bell-Villada's suggestion, I reread *Autumn of the Patriarch* while listening to Bartok. It's a still masterpiece, and no less difficult. From the beginning, in decrepit light and ancient silence, with cows in the bedroom, lepers under the rosebushes and a body "floating face down on the lunar waters of his dreams," to the end, when this "comic tyrant," a "figment of the imagination," flies through "the dark sound of the last frozen leaves of his autumn toward the homeland of shadows," it is a novel that stares us down, like a Toltec stele or a Quetzalcoatl, as if the Patriarch himself looked back at us "from the slime of his lugubrious Asiatic silences."

Patriarch is a slow, dense, downward book. To be sure, we meet some interesting people: Leiticia Nazreno (an Imelda *and* an Evita), who'll be eaten by dogs. Saturno Santos, "who knew how to change his form at will, turn into an armadillo or a pond." The papal nuncio, who refuses to beatify the Patriarch's mother—that wandering bird-woman who "conceived him standing up and with her hat on because of the storm of bluebottle flies around the wineskins of fermented molasses." The deposed dictators playing dominoes in the rest home on a cliff, "poor presidents of nowhere, grazing on oblivion in the house on the reefs and begging a hello from ships." We're also asked to contemplate the miraculous and the horrific: "disappeared" children, hurricanes and cannibalism, a fixed lottery, the stolen sea. And there are Gabo's usual magic tricks—a prestidigitation of pelicans, iguana eggs, telepathy, mules in the mountains with grand pianos on their backs, sewing machines and severed heads...

But the magic is black; the colors rot. *Patriarch* is heavy, like the man's very feet. Those always dragging feet are a terrific conceit: "dragging his graveyard feet along the corridors of ashes and scraps of carpets and singed tapestries"; "his great feet of a badly wounded elephant begging with wrath"; "thick feet of a captive monarch past the darkened mirrors with the single spur wrapped in velvet so that nobody could follow his trail of gold shavings"; "great feet of a senile elephant looking for something that hadn't been lost to him in his house of solitude"; "great feet of a dying saurian in the steaming bog of the last fens of salvation in the shadowy house"; "great feet of a hopeless insomniac through the last fleeting dawns of green sunrises..." Etc.

In an "ancient city of viceroys and buccaneers," the Patriarch is a cunning thug—nothing more. Having enjoyed "the solitary vice of power" for so many years, all he knows is that "a lie is more comfortable than doubt, more useful than love, more lasting than truth." From other Latin tinpots we have known and loathed, Bolivar's bastard whelps like Gomez, Somoza and Guzman Blanco, Gabo has borrowed this or that character defect: Trujillo, for instance, had a thing for cows; and Peron, a taste for schoolgirls. And from the biographies of their prototypes, the Roman emperors, he steals what he needs for a glaze of the mythic: how Claudius and Domitian dealt with dissidents; the uniform worn by the child Caligula; Nero's kinky passion for his mother, Agrippina; the number of wounds suffered by Caesar. (For more of this, see Bell-Villada, who's also instructive on the linguistic wonders of Gabo's original Spanish.) But why this drag, a gathering mass? I think it's because of the stolen sea.

He let them steal it when there was nothing else left to sell. The quinine and tobacco monopolies had gone to the English, rubber and cocoa to the Dutch, concessions for the railroads and river navigation to the Germans: "The last train on the upland barrens had fallen down an orchid-covered precipice, leopards slept on the velvet seats, the carcasses of the paddlewheelers were sunk in the swamps of the rice paddies, the news was rotting in the mailbags." And so one April, North American nautical engineers took away the Caribbean, "carried it off in numbered pieces to plant it far from the hurricanes in the blood-red dawns of Arizona":

> *They took it away with everything it had inside, general sir, with the reflection of our cities, our timid drowned people, our demented dragons...*

What's been stolen is memory; what remains is a weight of horror: long silence; drowned bodies. Like some pre-Columbian artifact, a volcanic storm god or altar toad, the Patriarch is somehow *forever*, a barbaric abiding. Worship of him is indistinguishable from fear of him, a numb surrender. As superstitious as he is, in thrall to sybils who see death in basin water, to angels with machetes, so are his subjects, spellbound by the madness of the arbitrary and the all-powerful. We know this because what began in Gabo's head as an interior monologue became, triumphantly, a kind of choral mass. Dozens of voices—retainers, victims, ambassadors, peasants, nuns, ghosts—tell us the Patriarch's story in a people's polyphony, a cleansing flood.

(It's wonderful stuff, and we got nothing like it in *El Senor Presidente*, by Miguel Angel Asturias, that Guatemalan windbag; nor in Alejo Carpentier's overpraised *Reasons of State*, though I'm willing to forgive Carpentier almost anything—even his endless precious lists of objects, shapes and smells—for one hilarious paragraph, maybe satirizing Octavio Paz. When the Head is overthrown, with the Communists waiting in the wings, a Professor of Christian Social Democracy takes charge, with "a vertiginous flood of words launched to the four winds:

> *(...moving from Morgan's bank to Plato's Republic, from the Logos to foot-and-mouth disease, from General Motors to Ramakrishna, coming at last to the conclusion—or at least some understood it thus—that from the Mystic Marriage between the Eagle and the Condor, and as a result of the fertilization of our inexhaustible soil by foreign investment, our America would be transformed by the vigorous Technology that would come to us from the North, [and] by the light of our own innate spirituality, a synthesis would be born between the Vedanta, the Popol-Vuh and the parables of Christ-the-first-socialist...)*

This Patriarch, too, is a child of Bolivar's, from a long line that began five years after the Liberator's death, with Rosas, and has since afflicted us with the likes of Jimenez, Batista, Duvalier. Jacobo Timerman is inclined to believe that Castro's not much better, and I'm inclined to agree with him, in spite of the fact that Castro's got Gabo to give him books to read at night as he rambles the streets of Havana in his chauffeur-driven limousine. Castro maintains a house for Gabo in Havana; in return, Gabo will supply him with nocturnal reading matter—for instance, Bram Stoker's *Dracula*. "!Que cabron!" said Fidel to Gabo after *Dracula*: "The bastard! I couldn't sleep!" Nor should any of them sleep, our pols, our caudillos. They should be looking into books as if they were mirrors, and seeing Dracula, Hamlet, Ahab, Frankenstein, Robin Hood, Raskolnikov, Pinocchio, Oedipus and Peter Pan.

"America is ungovernable," declares Bolivar in *The General in His Labyrinth.* "This nation will fall inevitably into the hands of the unruly mob and then will pass into the hands of almost indistinguishable petty tyrants of every color and race":

> *He drew breath and continued: "I know I'm ridiculed because in the same letter I say first one thing and then the opposite, because I approved the plan for monarchy, or I didn't approve it or somewhere I agreed with both positions at the same time." He was accused of being capricious in the way he judged men and manipulated history, he was accused for fighting Fernando VII and embracing Morillo, of waging war to the death against Spain and promoting her spirit, of depending on Haiti in order to win the war and then considering Haiti a foreign country in order to exclude her from the Congress of Panama, of having been a Mason and reading Voltaire at Mass but of being the paladin of the Church, of courting the English while wooing a French princess, of being frivolous, hypocritical, even disloyal because he flattered his friends in their presence and denigrated them behind their backs. "Well, all of that is true, but circumstantial," he said, "because everything I've done has been for the sole purpose of making this continent into a single, independent country, and as far as that's concerned I've never contradicted myself or had a single doubt." And he concluded in pure Caribbean: "All the rest is bullshit!"*

Like the Patriarch, I have dragged my feet. It's not that I expected more Macondo magic, or another installment of the riverboat lovebirds in their frisky dotage. Death and politics are fine by me. But from *Labyrinth*—along with clues as to what went wrong, along with a demystifying of the hero-cult—I did expect some reimagining of Bolivar's "almost maniacal dream of continental unity"; instead of the Patriarch's barbaric mysticism, the true colors of a Latin American Enlightenment. Why can't Bolivar remember Miranda, or his summit meeting with San Martin at Guayaquil, or the Congress of Panama? I don't understand these choices; it's as if Gabo had cut himself down to the size of the old man on the river, as if an unbecoming modesty or piety inhibited him after so much homework and second thoughts. Just because the Liberator didn't believe in magic doesn't mean the novelist has to go cold-turkey.

Not that there aren't earthquakes, volcanos, rockets, bagpipes; cockatoos and clavichords; alligators catching butterflies, bears threading needles, mules eating bedrooms and "nine cages of parrots and macaws that railed against Santander in three languages." But they're almost perfunctory. For the most part, at the end of his tether chewing on his string, Bolivar is picked at with a finicky minimalism, lacking Lear's stricken grandeur, or the insight of blind Oedipus.

It's the Bolivar familiar from the biographies—rational, generous, insomniac; a lover of women, horses and dogs; a hater of firearms, tobacco smoke, bullfights; at his best putting down European know-it-all's with a recital of the "hideous slaughters" in their own history: "Don't try to have us do well in twenty years what you have done so badly in two thousand...Damn it, please let us have our Middle Ages in peace!" And he is, decisively, mestizo: "He had a strain of African blood through a paternal great-grandfather, who had fathered a son by a slave-woman, and it was so evident in his features that the aristocrats in Lima called him Sambo. But as his glory increased, the painters began to idealize him, washing his blood, mythologizing him, until they established him in official memory with the Roman profile of his statues."

Yet he's also diminished. The guilds are against him, and the students, and mobs drunk on corn liquor. There are insults painted on the convent walls. Black widows of his many wars line the riverbank. His hussars sow the "fiery seed" of gonorrhea. His hosts at fancy meals, fearful of his tuberculosis, can hardly wait for him to leave before burying their Bohemian crystal and English China. His favorite, Sucre, has been murdered in ambush, "as he walked alone, his hands in his pockets, through the atrium of the cathedral...On the night he learned of Sucre's death, the General vomited blood." For his consumption, his constipation and his "crisis of coughing," the doctors administer enemas. And so does the novelist. We are meant to believe that, on Bolivar's "return trip to the void," history is what consumes him, and memory purges.

But this isn't, at the harmonium or the synthesizer, memory as forgotten music, the dark chords, muffled cries, children's night-shrieks. It is memory as a laundry list: "twenty years of fruitless wars and the disillusionments of power"; lost in the Orinoco jungle, ordering his

soldiers to eat the horses so they wouldn't eat each other; stoning dogs
to death in a slave quarter; a circling of the turkey buzzards over a
slaughterhouse; "the ill-fated Constitution of Bolivia, the imperial in-
vestiture accepted in Peru, the lifelong presidency and Senate member-
ship dreamed of in Colombia, the absolute powers assumed after the
Ocana Convention." What had it all come to? "I have no friends." And:
"Nobody understood anything." And: "Now we are the widows. We
are the orphans, the wounded, the pariahs of independence."

Even Piar, the mulatto general who had "called on blacks, mulat-
toes, zambos and all the destitute of the country to resist the white
aristocracy of Caracas, personified by the general," is remembered
more as a position paper than a human being, much less a crisis of
conscience, just when the novel ought to be picking up steam:

> *Piar's official advocate did not have to lie when he praised him as one of the
> outstanding heroes in the struggle against the power of Spain. He was de-
> clared guilty of desertion, insurrection, and treason, and was condemned to
> death and the loss of his military titles. Knowing his merits, no one believed
> that the sentence would be confirmed by the General...He revoked the sen-
> tence of demotion and confirmed the sentence of death by firing squad, which
> he made even worse by ordering a public execution...the sentence was car-
> ried out under the brutal sun in the main square of Angostura, the city Piar
> himself had wrested from the Spanish six months before. The commander of
> the firing squad had ordered the removal of the remains of a dead dog that
> turkey buzzards were devouring, and he had the gates closed to keep stray
> animals from disrupting the dignity of the execution. He denied Piar the
> final honor of giving the order to fire and blindfolded him against his will,
> but he could not prevent him from bidding farewell to the world with a kiss
> to the crucifix and a salute to the flag.*

I quote at such length because this passage typifies what's so disap-
pointing about the novel. Thirteen years after the execution of Piar, Bolivar says to his servant: "I would do it again." His servant is pleased.
I'm not. Of course, by this time Bolivar has decided for himself that his
real enemies are the oligarchies in each new nation, who oppose his
dream of unity "because it was unfavorable to the local privileges of the
great families." If he ought then to be a bit more sympathetic to what
Piar was trying to tell him, it isn't Gabo's fault that Simon was a poor
listener and a slow learner. Didn't it *ever* occur to Bolivar that maybe

these brand-new principalities, having thrown off one king, were chary of sticking their necks in the noose of another?

But I'm not pleased for another reason. What we get here is information instead of art, so matter-of-fact flat as to be affectless. The Creole with a mestizo in his closet meets the mulatto with an attitude problem. One of them isn't listening, and there isn't room for both in the same New World. Isn't Piar's death the Passion Play of aborted revolution, a betrayal of the Enlightenment, a paradigm of dissent silenced, of privilege legitimized by firing squad? Bolivar tears out the tongue of a spokesman for those mute and color-blind masses—a historical unconscious—for whom Gabo himself has always testified, thereby dooming them to centuries of patriarchs. Shouldn't we be riled? If Gabo thinks so, he hasn't exerted himself to make us feel it. He's coy and careful, a graduate student so dutiful that the grand idea dies somewhere in the footnotes, as if the French Revolution weren't still being fought all over Latin America, as if Bolivar hadn't embodied its contradictions, a one-man Diderot's *Encyclopedia*.

You'd think the mistress Manuela would excite every color on Gabo's palette, besides giving him something Octavio Paz-like to say about Latin politicians and the way they use their women as virgins, whores, witches, mothers and muses. But he devotes more passion to a one-night stand in Lima with "a young girl who was covered with a fine, straight down over every millimeter of her Bedouin skin." What the Liberator does to this girl as she sleeps is to lather and shave every square inch of her, "leaving her doubly naked inside her magnificent newborn's body."

It's a heartbreaking scene—suggesting demonic possession—but it's lonely in this novel, leading nowhere. Gabo's remarkably incurious as to what Bolivar imagined he might need or find in bed, except for a sponge and a sword. What about that sad first marriage, or the psychology of orphans? Gabo hasn't before had to therapize any of his characters because he's always been able to pull a miracle, an angel or a ghost out of his hat, to symbolize and subvert the usual difficult emotions. But Bolivar, the enemy of superstition and thus an enemy of angels and ghosts, is naked to history, a target for every determinism going, and Gabo seems unwilling to help him.

Why should Bolivar be *less* complicated than a lightweight Littin, *less* substantial than the Patriarch? The Patriarch, however thick with memory and grudge, was also resonant, whereas Bolivar is a shadow of his deeds, a string of scrappy quotes, an unpersuasive dream or two, his vagaries and guilts piled on like pickup sticks and poked at with too much diffidence. The novelist in the archives has been too timid with his razor to go deep, as if fearful of nicking himself, or maybe of cutting the symbolic throat of his symbolic father. If Gabo can't exorcize the Liberator, safely dead, how is he ever going to do the job that's needed on his personal and living albatross, the *barbudo* Fidel? The corruptions of power need all the magic they can get. As the angel comes and the mirror clouds and the clock stops and the radiant voices of the slaves from his childhood sugar mill sing at the morning star, it seems that Simon and Gabo might finally connect, but this is the last delirium and the last page, too late for me, or fiction, or history.

SALMAN RUSHDIE:
TWO BROWN MEN, FALLING HARD

Headlines kept getting in the way. In Pakistan, reactionary nuts are using Salman Rushdie, and the dead bodies of some true believers, to destabilize Benazir Bhutto's government. In Iran, the Ayatollah Khomeini, with Rocks in his Dome, has put out a $5.2-million contract hit on the novelist. In South Africa, Saudi Arabia and at Waldenbooks, *The Satanic Verses* is banned. For a couple of minutes, let's try to see the book through the bonfires of its burning.

As much as Islam, Salman Rushdie blasphemes Thatcherism. He's unkind, too, to V.S. Naipaul. "Pitting levity against gravity," altogether impious, *The Satanic Verses* is one of those go-for-broke "metafictions," a grand narrative and Monty Python send-up of history, religion and popular culture; Hindu cyclic and Muslim dualistic; postcolonial identity crisis and modernist pastiche; Bombay bombast and stiff-upper-liposuction; babu babytalk and ad agency neologism; cinema gossip, elephant masks, pop jingles, lousy puns, kinky sex and Schadenfreude; a sort of *Sammy and Rosie Get Laid* in Doris Lessing's *The Four-Gated City*—from which this slyboots Author-God tip-&-twinkletoes away, with a cannibal grin. "Who am I?" he asks us. "Let's put it this way: Who has the best tunes?"

As we shall see, he's disingenuous. And already I've made the novel sound as daunting as the kipper poor displaced Chamcha has to face so many miles from home, at his first appalling public-schoolboy break-fast: "England was a peculiar-tasting smoked fish full of spikes and bones, and nobody would ever tell him how to eat it." How, indeed?

Saladin Chamcha and Gibreel Farishta were both of them born in Bombay; they are equally inauthentic. Chamcha leaves Bombay's "vulgarity" for England's "poise and moderation," where he eats kippers, marries a blond and well-bred Pamela, co-hosts a popular children's TV show (*The Aliens*), and turns himself into the Man of a Thousand Voice-Overs: "If you wanted to know how your ketchup bottle should talk in its television commercial, if you were unsure as to the ideal voice for your packet of garlic-flavoured crisps, he was your very man. He made carpets speak in warehouse advertisements, he did celebrity impersonations, baked beans, frozen peas. On the radio he could convince an audience that he was Russian, Chinese, Sicilian, the President of the United States." He wants, from Pamela, a child, and can't have one. He is a mimic man.

Gibreel stays home to star on the big Indian screen and in various Bombay bedrooms. When he isn't pretending to be Hanuman the monkey king in a series of adventure movies owing more "'to a certain cheap television series emanating from Hong Kong than it did to the Ramayana," he incarnates "the countless deities of the subcontinent in the popular genre of movies known as 'theologicals.'...Blue-skinned as Krishna he danced, flute in hand, amongst the beauteous gopis and their udder-heavy cows; with upturned palms, serene, he meditated (as Gautama) upon humanity's suffering beneath a studio-rickety bodhi-tree." Recovering from a Christ-like hemorrhage, he'll fall in love with the Everest-climbing ice queen Alleluia Cone and lose his faith.

Instead of kippers, Gibreel eats "the gammon steaks of his unbelief and the pig's trotters of secularism." He is an imposter.

Now, then: Chamcha and Gibreel, the mimic man and the imposter, are on their way from Bombay to "Mahagonny, Babylon, Alphaville," better known as "Proper London, capital of Vilayet," when their jumbo jet the *Bostan* is skyjacked by Sikh terrorists and blown up in mid air, at 29,002 feet. This unlikely pair of pretenders, in a parable of the migration of peoples and of souls, drops from "a Himalayan height" down "the hole that went to

Wonderland...a succession of cloudforms, ceaselessly metamorphosing, gods into bulls, women into spiders, men into wolves. Hybrid cloud-crea-

tures pressed in upon them, gigantic flowers with human breasts dangling from fleshy stalks, winged cats, centaurs, and Chamcha in his semiconsciousness was seized by the notion that he, too, had acquired the quality of cloudiness, becoming metamorphic, hybrid...

Are they fallen angels, "halfway between Allahgod and homo sap...daring to ask forbidden things: antiquestions"? Or are they "just two brown men, falling hard, nothing so new about that you may think; climbed too high, got above themselves"?

(As it happens _Bostan_ is Farsi for garden as well as a poem by the Persian Sa'di on Muslim virtues and the proper behavior of dervishes. "Vilayet," according to the _O.E.D._, was a province of the Turkish Empire in which well-behaved Ottomans got to go to school for three years if they passed a competitive exam. Twenty-nine thousand and two is almost as many feet as Mt. Everest. Was mountain climber Cone named for a much smaller sacred hill in Mecca, or is Rushdie just setting up a later pun on "the ice queen Cone"? For that matter, when the mimic man Chamcha marries "Pamela," isn't he, sort of like Naipaul, marrying the English novel? And so on.)

Anyway, they land in a swamp in Sussex presided over by a crazy woman. And Chamcha has turned into a goat. (Or maybe the devil, Shaitan.) But what he looks like to white England, with his horns, hooves and tail, is Everywog. As a manticore explains to him, the night of his escape from the detention center for illegal immigrants to which Gibreel has betrayed him, "They have the power of description, and we succumb to the pictures they construct." Underground in Vilayet, Chamcha will see his new image become an icon of the underclass. Asians and West Indians, with a lot of help from the police, will riot about race. Though Chamcha, after some funny business with waxworks in a nightclub, will metamorphose once more, by rage, into Shakespeare's Iago, he won't really learn anything interesting about himself till he returns to Bombay for the death of his father and the bed of an old girlfriend, the opinionated Zeeny Vakil.

This is an overmuch of symbolic baggage for any character to have to carry around, but it's nothing compared to the burdens of Gibreel. Gibreel acquires a halo. He may be the Archangel Gabriel, through whom God posted messages to the Prophet. But he behaves more like Azraeel, the exterminating "agent of God's wrath," come to burn down Proper London. On the third hand, having played so many gods in the low-budget "theologicals," maybe he's just crazy. He has terrible dreams: "The universe of his nightmares had begun to leak into his waking life, and if he was not careful he would never manage to begin again, to be reborn with her, through her, Alleluia, who had seen the roof of the world." These bad dreams are what got Rushdie into trouble:

(1) In the ancient sand-city of Jahilia, a Mohammed-like businessman/prophet named Mahound seems to be making up his messages from God—or Gabriel, or Shaitan—to suit his political convenience in a hairshirt-pulling fight with the local matriarchal deities Uzza, Manat and Al-Lat. Even these "satanic verses" are fiddled with by his scribe. Meanwhile, the girls in the local brothel take the names of Mahound's many wives, to spice up their profane business.

(2) In semi-modern Titlipur in the shade of a banyan so immense that "the growth of tree into village and village into tree had become so intricate that it was impossible to differentiate between the two," orphaned epileptic Ayesha hears voices and, wearing nothing but a cloud of butterflies, leads credulous villagers on a pilgrimage to Mecca that ends in death by drowning.

(3) In a modern imperial city, an Imam plots the overthrow of a Middle Eastern state run by a Westernized empress whom he accuses of "sexual relations with lizards," and whom he confuses with Al-Lat (Mother-Goddess). According to this Imam: "History is the blood wine that must no longer be drunk. History the intoxicant, the creation and possession of the Devil, of the great Shaitan, the greatest of the lies—progress, science, rights—against which the Imam has set his face. History is a deviation from the Path, knowledge is a delusion, because the sum of knowledge was complete on the day Allah finished his revelation to Mahound." After *his* revolution: "Burn the books and trust the Book; shred the papers and hear the Word." And: "Now every clock in the capital city of Desh begins to chime, and goes on unceasingly, beyond twelve, beyond twenty-four, beyond one thousand and one, announcing the end of Time, the hour that is beyond measuring, the hour of the exile's return, of the victory of water over wine, the commencement of the Untime of the Imam."

Well. "Mahound" was a term of contempt, used by the Crusaders and in medieval Christian mystery plays, to animadvert Mohammed; he is always a satanic figure. The Jahilia brothel, a "tent of Black Stone called The Curtain," sounds a lot like Ka'aba, regarded by the faithful as the only consecrated spot on earth. The desert scribe who fiddles with the Koran's text is "a bum from Persia" named (surprise!) Salman. While the story of Ayesha, her butterflies and her lemming-like Exodus to a sort of Jonestown may derive from the Sufis and their moths, Ayesha was also the real Mohammed's favorite wife; and she turns up again in the Imam-dream, as the name of the despised empress. Imam is, of course, Khomeini, never notorious for his sense of humor.

Rushdie may say now whatever he wants about "the fictional dream of a fictional character, an Indian movie star, and one who is losing his mind at that." He can say his book "isn't actually about Islam"; it's about, instead, "migration, metamorphosis, divided selves, love, death." But that's not what he was saying last fall. To Madhu Jain in *India Today* (Sept. 15): "Actually, one of my major themes is religion and fanaticism. I've talked about [Islam, which] I know the most about." To Shrabani Basu in *Sunday* (Sept. 18): "It is a serious attempt to write about religion and revelation from the point of view of a secular person....Besides, Mohammad is a very interesting figure. He's the only prophet who exists even remotely inside history."

I'm not saying that for this impudence Rushdie deserves Khomeini's eleventh-century sort of criticism by Assassination. I *am* saying he has played fast and loose. ("Writers and whores," observes his own Mahound: "I see no difference here.") Having said that, I'm sorry so much attention's been paid to less than a third of the novel and so little to the rest of it, which has brilliant things to say about the hatred of women in history; the triumph of the machinery of images—in movies, television and advertising—over ancient myth, classical literature and political science; the displacement and deracination of the modern intelligence in a world of permanent migration and mindless hybridizing; the loss of self and the death of love in a time without decency or roots; wog-bashing in the racist theocracy of the Mad Thatcher.

Talk about your Imams. Listen to this, from one of the New Men, an advertising executive:

Maggie the Bitch...She's radical all right. What she wants—what she actually thinks she can fucking achieve—is literally to invent a whole goddamn new middle class in this country. Get rid of the old woolly incompetent buggers from fucking Surrey and Hampshire, and bring in the new. People without background, without history. Hungry people. People who re-

ally want, *and who know that with her, they can bloody well* get. *No-body's ever tried to replace a whole fucking* class *before, and the amazing thing is that she might just do it if they don't get her first. The old class. The dead men…And it's not just the businessmen. The intellectuals, too. Out with the whole faggoty crew. In with the hungry guys with the wrong educa-tion. New professors, new painters, the lot. It's a bloody revolution. New-ness coming into this country that's stuffed full of fucking old* corpses. *It's going to be something to see.*

Who's left out of this revolution? Well, certainly Chamcha. He may have married Pamela because of her voice, "composed of tweeds, headscarves, summer pudding, hockey sticks, thatched houses, sad-dlesoap, house parties, nuns, family pews, large dogs and philistin-ism"; because, as she says, "I was bloody Britannia. Warm beer, mince pies, commonsense and me." But having fallen from the sky and discovered his brown face, Chamcha's welcome only in Asian ghettos like Brickhall High Street, in cafes like the Shaandaar, among the pista barfi and jalebis, the chaloo chai and vegetable samosas. Al-leluia Cone, herself the daughter of death-camp survivors, asks, "What's a Paki?" A news vendor tells her: "A brown Jew."

Also left out will be Mimi Mamoulian, Chamcha's partner in mim-ickry and impersonation: "I have read *Finnegans Wake* and am conver-sant with post-modernist critiques of the West, e.g., that we have here a society capable only of pastiche: a 'flattened' world. When I become the voice of a bottle of bubble bath, I am entering Flatland knowing-ly, understanding what I am doing and why." Owing to "upheavals of Armenian-Jewish history," Mimi has "an excessive need for rooting." She owns a Norfolk vicarage, a farmhouse in Normandy, a Tuscan bell tower, a seacoast in Bohemia, "all haunted…Chanks, howls, blood on the rugs, women in nighties, the works. Nobody gives up land with-out a fight." There will be, nevertheless, no place for Mimi to hide.

Nor for Alleluia. Her father kills himself, like Primo Levi:

Why does a survivor of the camps live forty years and then complete the job the monsters didn't get done? Does great evil eventually triumph, no matter how strenuously it is resisted? Does it leave a sliver of ice in the blood, work-ing its way through until it hits the heart? Or, worse: can a man's death be incompatible with his life?

She has read "that as a part of their natural processes of combustion, the stars in the skies crushed carbon into diamonds. The idea of the stars raining diamonds into the void: that sounded like a miracle..." It's toward this miracle that she climbs, as high up as her lover Gibreel falls, and she can't hide there, either.

What's going on? History is out of control, and metamorphosis, too. We've left home once too often. No more avatars of Vishnu. Instead of rising out of ashes like a phoenix or resurrecting like a Christ, we are reborn, devolved, into parody, bloody farce, false consciousness, bad faith. Like Mimi, we are haunted. Like Gibreel, our nightmares leak. Like Chamcha, we are on the run. What we see on the streets of Jahilia the night Mahound prevails are "men and women in the guise of eagles, jackals, horses, gryphons, salamanders, warthogs, rocs; welling up from the murk of the alleys have come two-heeled amphisbaenae and the winged bulls known as Assyrian sphinxes. Djinns, houris, demons...slayers of manticores, water-terrorists..." Or, in London the night the goat-Chamcha escapes from Immigration, "men and women who were also partially plants, or giant insects...men with rhinoceros horns instead of noses and women with necks as long as any giraffe. The monsters ran quickly, silently, to the edge of the compound, where the manticore and other sharp-toothed mutants were waiting by the large holes they had bitten into the fabric of the containing fence..."

Talk about alienation! After all Rushdie's cultural anthropology and depth psychology; his comparative religion, apocalyptic politics, World Lit looting, showbiz pratfall, and razzle-dazzle with the likes of Lucretius, Shakespeare, Joyce, Beckett, Eliot, Nabokov; Bentham and Gramsci, Dickens and Naipaul, William Blake and Omar Khayyam, Henry James and Frantz Fanon, *Ubu Roi*, *The Wizard of Oz*, *Dr. Strangelove* and Jerry Della Femina—we end up, all of us, hungry for meaning, demanding to be made new, condemned instead like Chamcha to *The Aliens Show*:

It was a situation comedy about a group of extraterrestrials ranging from cute to psycho, from animal to vegetable, and also mineral, because it featured an artistic space-rock that could quarry itself for its raw material and then regenerate itself in time for the next week's episode; this rock was named Pygmalien, and owing to the stunted sense of humor of the show's producers there was also a coarse, belching creature like a puking cactus that came from a desert planet at the end of time: this was Matilda the Australien, and there were the three grotesquely pneumatic singing space sirens known as the Alien Korns, maybe because you could lie down among them, and there was a team of Venusian hip-hoppers and subway spray-painters and soul-brothers who called themselves the Alien Nation, and under a bed in the spaceship that was the program's main location there lived Bugsy the giant dung-beetle from the Crab Nebula who had run away from his father, and in a fishtank you could find Brains the super-intelligent giant abalone who liked eating Chinese, and then there was Ridley, the most terrifying of the regular cast, who looked like a Francis Bacon painting of a mouthful of teeth waving at the end of a sightless pod, and who had an obsession with the actress Sigourney Weaver...

We've come all this way in as much of a mess as *The Satanic Verses* itself, and I haven't told you anything about the sex and violence, or what you'll probably want to know about Pamela, Alleluia, Chamcha's father and Gibreel's producer, not to mention Uhuru Simba, Jumpy Joshi, the Granny Killer, the race riot, the *Othello* subplot, the female Sikh terrorist or the satirical poet Baal. Nor will I. Somewhere along the line, maybe in "the secret chamber of the clavichords," Rushdie lost control of his novel the way I've lost control of its review. *The Satanic Verses* lacks the ravening power, the great gulp, of *Midnight's Children* and *Shame*. It bites off the heads of its characters instead of digesting their essences. It's got too much on its troubled mind to make a symphonic noise out of so many discords. Of course, in its huge dishevelment, its *Leaves of Grass* lurchings and scourges, whistles and vapors, belly laughs and belly flops, it's infinitely more interesting than those hundreds of neat little novels we have to read between Rushdies.

What Modernism, the new alchemy, is all about is the inventing of a new self. But what if the machinery short-circuits? Is there a way out of these devolving cycles into lesser selves, meaner societies, death-ward-spinning meta-systems? One suggestion, though I'm not sure how seriously Rushdie intends it, shows up in a book by Zeeny Vakil, Chamcha's Bombay art critic/girlfriend (the most interesting, least developed character in the novel): *The Only Good Indian* lambastes "the confining myth of authenticity, that folkloristic straitjacket which she sought to replace by an ethic of historically validated eclecticism, for was not the entire national culture based on the principle of borrowing whatever clothes seemed to fit, Aryan, Mughal, British, take-the-best-and-leave-the-rest?" It's Zeeny who tells Chamcha to get real: "We're right in front of you. You should try and make an adult acquaintance with this place, this time. Try and embrace this city, as it is, not some childhood memory that makes you both nostalgic and sick."

But this seems far too straightforward for a metafiction. I think Rushdie's also proposing something more botanical. When, in Gibreel's dream of Mecca and drowning, the Titlipur villagers leave their mothering banyan tree, they perish. Then there is, for Chamcha, "the tree of his own life," the walnut tree his father planted "with his own hands on the day of the coming of the son." Chamcha explains this tree to Zeeny: "Your birth-tree is a financial investment of a sort. When a child comes of age, the grown walnut is comparable to a matured insurance policy; it's a valuable tree, it can be sold, to pay for weddings, or a start in life. The adult chops down his childhood to help his grown-up self. The unsentimentality is appealing, don't you think?" As usual, Chamcha has missed the point. For his father, that tree was where his son's soul lived while the boy himself was far away, pursuing his unrequited love affair with England. Many pages later, Chamcha will watch a television program on gardening, and witness what's called a "chimeran graft," in which two trees—mulberry? laburnum? broom?—are bred into one:

> *a chimera without roots, firmly planted in and growing vigorously out of a piece of English earth: a tree...capable of taking the metaphoric place of the one his father had chopped down in a distant garden in another, incompatible world. If such a tree were possible, then so was he; he, too, could cohere, send down roots, survive. Amid all the televisual images of hybrid tragedies—the uselessness of mer-men, the failures of plastic surgery, the Esperanto-like vacuity of much modern art, the Coca-Colonization of the planet—he was given this one gift.*

For this, they want to kill him.

THE HIT MEN

I hope hundreds turned out yesterday at the PEN rally to support Salman Rushdie. We need something to wash the taste of gall and aspirin out of our mouths. It's been a disgraceful week. A maniac puts out a $5.2-million contract on one of the best writers in the English language, and how does the civilized West respond? France and Germany won't pubish *The Satanic Verses;* Canada won't sell it; Waldenbooks and B. Dalton abandon ship and the First Amendment; and a brave new philistinism struts its stuff all over Mediapolis, USA, telling us that that Rushdie's unreadable anyway, besides being some sort of left-wing Indian troublemaker you never heard of till the Ayatollah gave him a bad review. And nobody seems in fact to have read *any* Rushdie—certainly not Cardinal O'Connor, nor Jimmy Breslin, nor Pat Buchanan.

In his first novel, *Midnight's Children*, Rushdie suggested that independence for the Indian subcontinent was ruined by the lunatic behavior of Muslims and Hindus. He also made fun of Indira Gandhi. And Indira Gandhi threatened to sue. His second novel, *Shame*, was a savage attack on the bloody coming to power in Pakistan of the Islamic fundamentalist Zia. Pakistan banned it. *The Satanic Verses* is likewise *contemporary*. Among other things, it's a Monty Python send-up of modern England, its money-grubbing and its racism. Maggie Thatcher's more of a target than Mohammed. And so is the Ayatollah Khomeini himself, in thin disguise. Just maybe, the blood-grudge of His Bearded Malevolence is personal. He'd surely have seen himself in Rushdie's portrait of the Imam. This Imam, in angry exile in the modern era in one of Europe's imperial cities, plots the overthrow of a Mideast state run by a Western-educated, secular-minded empress whom the Imam accuses of "sexual relations with lizards," and whom he confuses with the hated Mother-Goddess Al-Lat. He sounds like Tehran radio. Just listen to him: "History is the blood wine that must no longer be drunk. History, the intoxicant, the creation and possession of the Devil...the greatest of the lies—progress, science, rights—against which the Imam has set his face. History is a deviation from the Path, knowledge is a delusion, because the sum of knowledge was complete on the day Allah finished his revelation to Mahound." And: "Burn the books and trust the Book; shred the papers and hear the Word." And, after a revolution exactly like K.'s in Iran: "Now every clock in the capital city of Desh begins to chime, and goes on unceasingly, beyond twelve, beyond twenty-four, beyond one thousand and one, announcing the end of Time, the hour that is beyond measuring, the hour of the exile's return, of the victory of water over wine, of the commencement of the Untime of the Imam."

But all this has been ignored, like the fact that fundamentalist Pakistanis would be rioting to get rid of Benazir Bhutto, a Western-educated woman, whether or not Rushdie had ever written a word. And religious fanatics are killing one another's children in Belfast and Beirut without the excuse of a novel to hate.

You may recall that "assassin" derives from the Arabic *hashishi* ("hashish eaters"). The original assassins were an eleventh-century all-male Persian sect, fanning out from the Alamout mountain in northern Iran. They killed on command of Hassan Ibn Sabbah. What we've looked into for the past shameful week is an eleventh-century mind, an assassin's grin. We've averted our jumpy eyes, ducked our fuzzy heads, scuttled on all fours. Welcome to the Untime of the Imam.

On Thursday in England Roald Dahl, an author of wicked children's books, told TV cameras that Rushdie's novel should be pulped "to save lives"—as if the *novel* had killed anybody. On Friday, pulling *The Satanic Verses* from his shelves, B. Dalton CEO Leonard Riggio explained: "It is regrettable that a foreign government has been able to hold hostage our most sacred First Amendment"—as if Riggio weren't the hostage holder. (You'd think maybe the FBI might be interested in terrorist threats to bookstores and publishing houses, but not according to a Justice Department spokeswoman.) On Saturday in the *New York Post*, Pat Buchanan enjoyed himself at the expense of "the trendy leftist" Rushdie, suggested that he seek sanctuary among Nicaragua's Sandinistas to whom he's been so sympathetic, and allowed as how "the First Amendment has succeeded phony patriotism as the last refuge of the scoundrel"—as if that amendment, the glory of our republic, weren't precisely what protects the right of a Buchanan to his swamp fevers, the privilege of such pips to squeak.

And on Sunday in *Newsday*, Breslin, whom the vapors must have taken as they sometimes seize a Mailer, described Rushdie as "a horrid writer" whose "cheap apology" to Khomeini was "a wretched performance," a "groveling...perfectly consistent with Rushdie's dreadful sentence structure"—as if all the newspaper columnists in America could write for a thousand years, even unto the end of Untime, and ever produce a novel half as wonderful as *Midnight's Children*.

Monday we were told that Cardinal O'Connor would really rather we didn't buy the Rushdie book. We were also told that the cardinal himself won't read it. And where were the other world religious leaders? Not a single one seems to have spoken up on Rushdie's behalf.

They may have deplored the Ayatollah's *fatwa*, but they spent more time sympathizing with the injured feelings of the Islamic multitude; and most thought the book should never have been published; and many in England agitated to expand the blasphemy laws. If the Vatican's performance was disgraceful, so was that of the Archbishop of Canterbury, the Chief Rabbi of the United Hebrew Congregations of the Commonwealth, the Cardinal of Paris, the Archbishop of Lyon and Israel's chief Ashkenazi rabbi, Avraham Shapira. It's as if all of them overnight forgot about Erasmus and Spinoza, Jan Hus and Thomas More, Galileo and Martin Luther, not to mention Socrates and not even to think about Jesus Christ: free speech on the cross.

As Rushdie himself explains, right at the start of *Verses*, when Chamcha and Gibreel are blown out of the sky by terrorists: "Just two brown men, falling hard, nothing so new about that you may think; climbed too high, got above themselves..."

GÜNTER GRASS: BAD BOYS AND FAIRY TALES

They went ahead and did it anyway, the two Germanys—as if the Berlin Wall had been a chastity belt. They are in bed together again, a single two-backed beast, under the sign of the Deutschmark, in spite of Günter Grass, who told them not to. He has been telling them not to for thirty years. He agrees with the Frenchman who said he loved Germany so much, he was glad there were two of them. Which is why Grass has been called—to his face—"a traitor to the fatherland." He hates the very idea of a German fatherland. Look what the fatherland does when the lights are out all over Europe.

This is more than oedipal rage. These fugitive pieces dating back to 1961 all say the same thing. You may feel the war's over; let bygones be bygones; aren't some of our best friends Germans? But Grass began to write because of Auschwitz. Time passes, and Auschwitz hasn't gone away. Writing after Auschwitz, "against passing time," means using "damaged language in all the shades of gray": no more "black and white of ideology," "blues of introspection," "polished literary chamber music," "detergents of all-purpose poetry," but "shame on every page." Maybe another nation could have committed Auschwitz, but only one did. Unless we stuffed our ears with lottery tickets, we must have heard the screaming. "One of the preconditions for the terrible thing that happened was a strong, unified Germany...We have every reason to fear ourselves as a unit." If to say this is to be a traitor to the fatherland, maybe even a "rootless cosmopolitan," well, tell it to the Scarecrow.

According to Grass, nationalism itself is a "bacillus." He'd rather see a confederation, "a linkage of provinces" sort of like Switzerland: "Germany in the singular is a calculation that will never balance; as a sum, it is a communicating plural." Such a plural could communicate in a mother-tongue instead of a fatherland, as German-language writers—citizens of a state of mind—have communicated as far back as Grimmelshausen, who made fun of the Thirty Years' War, and as recently as Group 47.

In his fiction and nonfiction, he's often obsessed about Group 47, the German writers East and West who met sadly and briefly after the war. Some would try again, with beer and potato salad, between 1973 and 1977. They show up in *Headbirths* and he's even projected them backwards, into the seventeenth century, in *The Meeting at Telgte*. At Telgte, we also met the first German novelist, Grimmelshausen, who gave Brecht the idea for Mother Courage and Grass the idea for a *Tin Drum*, a modern *Simplicissimus*. So has the notion of a commonwealth of writers, "a cultural nation" in the no-man's-land of Potsdamer Platz, been kicking about for years in his pages.

But oedipal rage there certainly is—in splendid excess. The Bad Boy of German Letters has been father-bashing, grandfather-bashing and godfather-bashing since he left Danzig. At the gates of Buchenwald, listening to Bach, Nazis wept like wounded bulls. So much for the civilizing surplus value of High Culture. So much for Werther, Brahms and *Buddenbrooks*, for geopolitical fairy tales and Black Forest *Unsterblichkeitsbedürfnis* . There's no forgiving the Mandarins, the ideologues, the lyric poets. He quotes in *Two States* from one of his *Dog Years* fairy tales. Nothing is pure: not snow, virgins, salt, nor Christ, nor Marx. If anything were pure, then the bones,

> *white mounds that were recently heaped up, would grow immaculately without crows: pyramids of glory. But the crows, which are not pure, were creaking unoiled, even yesterday: nothing is pure, no circle, no bone. And piles of bones, heaped up for the sake of purity, will melt cook boil in order that soap, pure and cheap; but even soap cannot wash pure.*

Against this shameful fatherland of the white mounds and the cheap soap, Günter Grass—pariah, traitor, Dennis the Menace—sticks out his Tin Drum. He will wash the taste of shame out of the mouth of the German language. This seems to me exemplary. We need more such brilliant Bad Boys, even if we lose a few great novels.

Grass grew up in a hurry: at fourteen, a Hitler Youth; at sixteen, a soldier in the Panzers; at seventeen, an American POW; at nineteen, an apprentice stonecutter, conscience stricken by "photographs showing piles of eyeglasses, shoes, bones"; at twenty-five, a poet and sculptor; at twenty-eight, off to Paris where—under the lash of Paul Celan—he wrote most of his amazing Danzig Trilogy.

If you know *The Tin Drum* (1959) just from Volker Schlöndorff's pious movie you'll have missed the gusto and maybe the point of this Danzig according to Breughel and Bosch, this rhapsodizing and guffaw, the punning and screaming. Nor am I about to belabor it here. But a brief visit in book two to the western front, where Oskar and Bebra look at the turtle-shaped pillbox Dora Seven, a compound of concrete and puppy-dog bones, gives you the flavor. A proud Corporal Lankes explains:

> *The centuries start coming and going, one after another like nothing at all. But the pillboxes stay put just like the Pyramids stayed put. And one fine day one of those archeologist fellows comes along. And he says to himself: what an artistic void between the First and the Seventh World Wars!...Then he discovers Dora Five, Six, Seven; he sees my Structural Oblique Formations, and he says to himself, Say, take a look at that. Very, very interesting, magic, menacing, and yet shot through with spirituality. In these works a genius, perhaps the only genius of the twentieth century, has expressed himself clearly, resolutely, and for all time. I wonder, says our archeologist to himself, I wonder if it's got a name? A signature to tell us who the master was? Well, if you look closely, sir, and hold your head on a slant, you'll see, between those Oblique Formations...All right, here's what it says: Herbert Lankes, anno nineteen hundred and forty-four. Title: BARBARIC, MYSTICAL, BORED.*

And Bebra says: "You have given our century its name."

There's a disdain here for a lot of poetry, philosophy, psychology, and the nineteenth century's notorious Wagnerian bond with night and death. Oskar, a self-made dwarf whose voice shatters plate glass, isn't symbolic of Nazi culture; nor is he symbolic of what became of the Germans, poor puppy dogs, inside Hitler's 1,000-year pillbox. Oskar instead symbolizes the German artist, who should have been the German conscience but who chose instead to stay three years old forever. Not by accident, as Oskar scrambles with his books up the railroad embankment to look at Dora Seven, does he admit to "losing a little Goethe" in the process. Goethe! *The Tin Drum* is the first of Grass's very Grimm fairy tales. As it ends, the Black Witch is gaining on the three-year-old times ten, in a loony bin: "Black words, black coat, black money."

Likewise I know what to make of Mahlke's grotesque Adam's apple in *Cat and Mouse* (1961). Mahlke's been asked to swallow too much, including the philosopher Fichte. He has swallowed so much, he needs an Iron Cross to cover it up. Nor, for all the time he spent in church and his fixating on the Black Madonna of Czestochowa, is Mahlke any sort of Christ-figure, a Teutonic Billy Budd. As old and as useful to myth as a Son of God, is the Scapegoat, someone who is blamed and punished and expelled from the social order. Scapegoats are usually Jewish.

After the Scapegoat in this fairy tale of history comes the Scarecrow. Amsel the half-Jew constructs these scarerows in *Dog Years* (1963). They are mechanical marching men: the SA. Amsel will be betrayed by his "bloodbrother" Matern, "the bounceback man." Tulla, the satanic pubescent from *Cat and Mouse*, shows up again; and Dr. Brunies, the first in a long line of luckless Grass pedagogues; and many black German shepherds, leading to Hitler's favorite Prinz, and to the equally black Pluto, hiding underground after the war in Brauxel's mine, with an army of scarecrows, all of them waiting for emancipation and a reckoning.

Unfriendly references abound in *Dog Years* to Kant and Hegel, old Celtic Druids, Prussian oak-tree gods, "the goateed Husserl," and the Hoard of the Nibelungs. Besides, "Schopenhauer glowered between bookshelves." But listen to this:

Has a thousand words for Being, for time, for essence, for world and ground, for the with and the now, for the Nothing, and for the scarecrow as existential frame. Accordingly: Scareness, being-scared, scare-structure, scare-vulnerable, scare-principle, scare-situation, unscared, final scare, scare-born time, scare-totality, foundation-scare, the law of scare. "For the essence of the scarecrow is the transcendental three-fold dispersal of scare-

crow suchness in the world project. Projecting itself into the Nothing, the scarecrow physis, *or burgeoning, is at all times beyond the scarecrow such and the scarecrow at-hand…" Transcendence drips from stockingcaps in the eighteenth stall. A hundred caustic-degraded philosophers are of one and the same opinion: "Scarecrow Being means: to be held-out-into Nothing."*

And so the Danzig Trilogy ends with a wicked parody of…Martin Heidegger! Is this any way to talk to your Higher Culture? With a slingshot?

It's generally felt that Grass won't write another novel as completely satisfying as *The Tin Drum.* This is because, after the Trilogy, instead of staying put inside his characters, he was loose on the streets, agitating for social justice and Willy Brandt, animadverting Kiesingers and Globkes, off to Tel Aviv or Managua. John Updike tells us: "Those who urge upon American writers more social commitment and a more public role should ponder the cautionary case of Günter Grass. Here is a novelist who has gone so public he can't be bothered to write a novel; he just sends dispatches to his readers from the front lines of his engagement."

I'd be more comfortable agreeing for once with Updike if he hadn't missed the point of three of Grass's books. But yes, Grass has been on the barricades, and barricades get in the way of the lapidary. Personally, I'd blame movies almost as much as politics for the, ah, dishevelment of his subsequent fiction: the impatient cuts, irresolute fades; camera angles wider than subcontinents; a sacrifice of introspection.

But I also see a career in which novels and politics are twinned. He would democratize the language *and* the social order. He not only answers all the fire alarms in the culture; he often sounds them himself. And the vernacular in which he sounds them—vulgar, sarcastic, satiric, cajoling, blasphemous, absurd, iridescent; seaport street-talk and Magic Realism on the Vistula—has about it the acid vehemence of another great German scourge. Think of him as Martin Luther with a sense of humor. Yes, of course, salvation for Grass is all works, and he'd probably rather sit down for beer and potato salad with Erasmus, but I can't help recalling the Ninety-five Theses nailed to the door of the Wittenberg church, the tract on Babylonian Captivity, and the famous farting contest between Luther and Lucifer. At least in part, the Reformation was all about metaphors. And I do believe we're talking about a second Reformation in a West where every possible indulgence is for sale, plastic accepted.

In his own words, he is one of those writers who "bolt from their desks to busy themselves with the trivia of democracy. Which implies a readiness to compromise. Something we must get through our heads is this: a poem knows no compromise but men live by compromise. The individual who can stand up under this contradiction and act is a fool and will change the world." This almost mandates in his prose something messy, voracious, indulgent, hybrid, partisan, ad hoc, avuncular, treasonable and...well, heroic. How many Calvinos do we need, anyway? Or Robbe-Grillets and Tourniers? Enough, already, of this cult of the petty-bourgeois genius.

He wouldn't publish another novel for seven years. The political speeches were collected as *Speak Out!* (1968), and there's an important play to mention, *The Plebians Rehearse the Uprising* (1966), his account of the workers' insurrection in East Berlin, Leipzig and Magdeburg. *Plebians* was disapproved of in the West because it hadn't followed our line of a popular revolt against communism. It was despised in the East because it was anti-Stalinist, and asked the embarrassing question, Where was Brecht? Grass had to go all the way to India to see it performed again, twenty years later, in Bengali.

In *Local Anaesthetic* (1969), Eberhard Starusch, a fortysomething professor of "German and history," goes to a dentist. There's a TV set to distract the patients. On its screen, Starusch projects his life, his violent fantasies and not a little German history and literature—Goethe again; Kleist and Buchner; "Hegel and Marxengels"; "the late Rilke—the early Schiller"; even Herbert Marcuse—between commercials. Sometimes, this private videotape is the only scheduled program. Sometimes the commercial products (deep freezers, hair rinse) represent abstract problems (memory, disguise). Sometimes the screen writhes in "live" coverage of antiwar demonstrators, including Starusch's brainy, disillusioned student, Scherbaum, who wants to burn his long-haired dachshund, in public, to protest against American napalm in Vietnam.

Surrgoate fathers and prodigal sons: Starusch and Scherbaum educate each other into the basis for action and the requirements of decency. Being rational "doesn't prevent you from being stupid," but neither does being passionate and sincere. If, as we are led to believe,

"humanity is terrorized by overproduction and forced consumption,"
the answer may not be the professor's "pedagogical prophylaxis" (because the modern eats history for breakfast), or the dentist's utopi-
an/anesthetic "Sickcare" (because there will always be pain), but neither is the answer burning dachshunds, nor the mindless violence of
the Maoist teenybopper Vero.

A passionate youth, a kindly elder, an accommodation: Imagine that,
in the sixties. Not exactly, to pick at random, Irving Howe and the New
Left; not even, to go all the back to the fifties, Lionel Trilling and Allen
Ginsberg. Pay attention in *Local Anaesthetic* to the counterpoint of quotations from Seneca and Nietzsche. Grass has his problems with Seneca,
who was to blame, after all, for Nero. But he *hates* Nietzsche.

So much for Goethe, Heidegger, Nietzsche. Now for the Brothers
Grimm. In *The Flounder* (1977), a swamp-monster history of nationalism, religion, nutrition, art, sex and the author, Grass unbuttons himself; and it's quite a sight, like Rabelais and Levi-Strauss doing the
dirty. His nine chapters are the months of pregnancy and the Ages of
Man. They give birth, out of the sea and the amniotic soup, to the
New Woman, who may be almost as revolutionary as the potato.

Our flounder's borrowed from an old Grimm typically punitive
and typically misogynistic folk tale. He pops out of the Baltic, near (of
course) Danzig, the first male chauvinist fish; immortal. In Grimm,
the fisherman who caught this talking turbot was so impressed with
its gift of speech he set it free. In gratitude, the fish promised to fulfill
the fisherman's wishes. This good fortune was subverted by the greed
of the fisherman's wife, Ilsebill, who asked for control of the moon
and the sun.

According to Grass, the flounder, back in Neolithic times, hated
matriarchy, and signed on as a kind of Kissinger to the fisherman,
teaching him power politics, leaking the secrets of metallurgy and the
Minoans, stirring up a stew of war and wanderlust—of restless Goths
and final solutions. Like the fish, the fisherman is immortal, a masculine principle mindlessly replicating itself, and sexually allied down
through the eons with successive Ilsebills: invariably cooks, invariably
pregnant, invariably symbolic of the status of women from the Stone
Age to 1970 in society, fantasy and other metaphysisms. Thus a three-
breasted Awa, who suckles man to happy stupor; Iron Age Wigga,
who invents fish soup; Mestwina, reconciling paganism and Chris-

tianity; ascetic Dorothea, who bakes a Sacred Heart into High Gothic bread dough; Fat Gret, a goose-plucking nun, for whom "young sons of patrician families were an appetizer: tender asparagus tips"; Agnes the kindhearted, Amanda the potato faced, Sophie the Virgin, Lena the Socialist, Billy the Lesbian and Maria of the buttermilk.

We meet Opitz and Gryphius, the seventeenth-century poets who will reappear in *The Meeting at Telgte*. There are broad burlesques of the Teutonic epic: more godfather-bashing. And, before the talking turbot is tried by feminists for crimes against the distaff, there will be many odd recipes, including one for toads' eggs fried in the fat of stillborn baby boys. But we know now that what's really cooking is an entire culture, masculine and capitalist, ballsy and greedy. We eat our role models, those mushrooms and that excrement. It makes a writer want to puke.

The Meeting at Telgte (1979), written as a seventieth birthday present for his old friend Hans Werner Richter, is more oedipal mayhem, anticipating much of what Grass says later on about mother tongues and fatherlands. In fact these poets never made it to Telgte in 1647 to talk about language and peace as the Thirty Years War was winding down. Still, a novelist dreams: What if, like German writers in 1947, they'd met and drafted a statement? After all, poets alone "knew what deserved the name of German. With many 'ardent sighs and tears,' they had knitted the German language as the last bond; they were the other, the true Germany."

Meet Birken ("one wondered why so much beauty should have a need of theory"); Buchner ("so ponderously silent that his mute periods have been cited as figures of speech"); Gryphius ("thunder, even when he lacked lightning"); Rist ("Logau's wit was corrosive because it lacked wholesome humor...because it lacked wholesome humor it was no better than irony...because it was ironical it was not German...because it was not German, it was intrinsically 'un-German and anti-German'"). According to Grass, even the composer Schutz *could* have been there where he wouldn't have heard much music: "To set such a drama to music, one would have to unleash a war of flies." Eavesdropping—naturally—is Grimmelshausen. Grass identifies with Grimmelshausen as Mann identified with Goethe. This is because Grass and Grimmelshausen are both funny. (Goethe told us: "How dare a man have a sense of humor, when he considers his immense burden of responsibilities toward himself and others? However, I have no wish to pass censure on the humorists. After all, does one have to have a conscience? Who says so?")

Thirty years is a long war. These poets would actually *prolong* this war, in order to refine the German language and its "rhymed yearning for death." Instead of soup they "sank their teeth into phrases and sentences; easily satisfied word-ruminants, finding, if need be, satiety in self-quotation." Besides: "No one was willing to give up merely because reality had once again put in an objection and cast mud at art." Finally, of course: "This verdict of universal guilt amounted to a universal acquittal."

They perfect a petition, but as the inn burns down the petition burns up: "And so what would in any case not have been heard, remained unsaid." No great loss: less "soul-mush." But something in Grass is tickled by these poets' clubs: Fruit-bearers, Sweet-smellers and the German-minded; the Upright Cucumber Lodge, an Order of the Elbe Swans. Something in him looks among the beer kegs and milking stools and wanton wenches for a saving "thistle." Honor? Comrades?

Zeus had the first "headbirth," springing Athene. It's "a paradox that has impregnated male minds to this day." It's also a parable of art. Grass Zeusifies. His *Headbirths* (1980) is a lively mess, placenta and all. In no special order, though often in circles, *Headbirths* contemplates the 1980 elections in the German Federal Republic; a dead friend; movies; children; Asia; balls of thread; liver sausage; and a fictitious pair of civil servants, Harm and Dorte, who can't decide if they want a child and can't imagine what history will do to them and their Volkswagen.

Grass approves of children, having sired lots, but he isn't sure the world needs any more Germans, no matter how much authorities deplore a declining birth rate that makes necessary so many Turks to do the coolie work of the republic. After being a nuisance on the *Tin Drum* set, Grass went off with Schlöndorff to the Orient, thinking cinematic. Maybe they'd make a movie on overpopulation. Like nuclear reactors, overpopulation's bad for the ecology. Grass took these notes; we don't know what Schlöndorff did. The dead friend is Nicolas Born, from Group 47.

Meanwhile Zeus looks over his shoulder at critics who ask him to butt out of contemporary politics, as if this morning's news weren't a headbirth of history. At one point he makes himself ten years older than he really is in order to imagine the compromises writers of that age—Eich, Koeppeman, Kästner—must have made with Hitler. To the dead Born, he speaks out loud: "Now that you are dead I am aging more perceptibly. My courage, which was doing fine only yesterday, has furled several sails." (Don't believe him.) And: "I'm ashamed." (He's the only one.)

Mobius on a bender gets looped. In Shanghai, among eleven million bicycles, he wonders, What if the populations of China and the two Germanys were reversed? If there were only eighty million Chinese...and a *billion* Germans in "the alarming process of self-discovery"? But the Germans, unlike the Chinese, are dying out. Will they end up stuffed in their own museums? On your left, Hittites, Sumerians, Aztecs; to the right, Germans who were "not mere warlike barbarians concerned only with sordid gain, mere function without spirit," but victims of an industrial society that depended parasitically for its extravagant standard of living on a South (oil; Turks) which it exhausted. Ought those Germans to have *denied* themselves *anything*?

Grass imagines Harm and Dorte as teachers who met at a sixties rally against the war: liberal puppylove. Harm will quote Marx on the capitalist law of accumulation through redundancy, and deplore "the lack of long-range views." Dorte frisks among computer projections, and deplores "the lack of meaning in general." Both feel bad about their civil-servant privileges, and vote against Franz Josef Strauss. Since Grass needs them to go to overpopulated Asia to "tabulate and classify" the squalor, he will also invent a Sisyphus Travel Agency, to arrange "destitution as a course of study." Harm and Dorte will be booked into slums from Bangkok to Bombay.

Grass directs: "Long shot of the Indian subcontinent. She, cut off at the waist, covering half the Bay of Bengal, all Calcutta and Bangladesh, casually takes the pill: 'It's safe to say that birth control...has been a failure in India.'" It's also safe to say that Grass has more fun with his impossible screenplay than he does with Harm and Dorte, who will weary any reader. When Dorte, inside a Cave of Bats, undergoes a mystical conversion to the cult of the Mother Goddess and withholds her sexual favors from Harm till he agrees to procreate, even Grass is exasperated. With her ball of thread, can't she knit herself a child? Only a movie could make us care about these two. And movies, Grass suggests, are a substitute for the imagination. Take that, Schlöndorff.

But so, Grass implies, are card files and data sheets a substitute for the imagination. They furnish a "vacuum." And the worst possible substitute for the imagination is a politics-as-usual of neglect, a headbirth metastasized. Grass fumes: What nonsense to seek disarmament through rearmament, to combat an energy shortage by stepping up production, to breed reactors instead of Germans, to pile up pork and butter mountains in a world where fifteen million children starve to death each year. If he were in charge he would abolish compulsory education and "emancipate" all civil servants by firing them. To raise the birth rate he would cut off the electric current at night and reintroduce as bedware the traditional German nightcap, to save the heat that escapes through the holes in our heads. He would mandate a switch of political systems every ten years between Germanys East and West, giving the German Democratic Republic "an opportunity to relax under capitalism," while, under communism, the FRG would drain off its cholesterol. More radically, he'd deal with property "as my spiritual property and that of others have been dealt with: 70 years after the author's (that's me) death, his (my) rights enter the public domain; I (as dictator) would extend this benefit by law to all earned or acquired possessions—house, factory, field—so that only the children and some of the grandchildren will be obliged to inherit it or hold it in usufruct. Ones born later will be exempt from this hereditary burden...they will be free to make a fresh start."

Ridiculous of course. Without surplus there can be no value. This is the sort of irresponsible antinovelistic "dispatch" digressiveness that so dismays an Updike he neglected to mention any of it in his review of *Headbirths*.

Finally, Grass would ordain a National Endowment, a Museum without Walls in the psychic space between the two Berlins, promoting the history and, much more important, the literature—the mother tongue—of all the Germanys. Writers, he says, are the best patriots; even a "wounded" language might somehow heal the body politic. "What's wrong with us is neither material nor social, but an emergency of the spirit." Dorte in her sarong confesses: "I'm afraid, Harm. Of us, of everything." Grimmelshausen would advise her: Read Hölderlin. Or Trakl.

Having kissed off the Brothers Grimm in *The Flounder*, in *The Rat* (1987) Grass kisses off fairy tales period. No more ruined towers, magic mirrors, hungry ravens, dead trees, a comb, a belt, a cherry torte and those little bones left over after Adolf ate the sleeping princess. "All hope is gone," he says in one of the little poems that pepper the text, "for fairy tales/ it shall be written here,/ are dying with the forests." The forests are dying from industrial overdevelopment and acid rain. Without forests, of course, "children can no longer get lost."

In one of *Rat*'s subplots, fairy-tale characters seize power and demand a re-greening of Middle Europe. They are exterminated. In another subplot, five feminists, on a barge in the Baltic, search for a vanished matriarchal city; they'll be vaporized. In a third subplot, Oskar the dwarf returns as a middle-aged producer of video cassettes on his way to Danzig-Gdansk, where he will show films he has already made about the apocalyptic future; he, too, will be vaporized. In yet a fourth subplot, an artist who counterfeits Authentic Gothic for needy cathedrals is tried and convicted...of treason!

Where's the Social-Democratic novelist while all of this goes on? Either dreaming or marooned in a space capsule orbiting an Earth on which everything has been obliterated except rats, wood lice, a stinging bluebottle and a flying snail. In either case, a scholarly She-Rat explains the future and disdains the past. We are also told of new punk religions, hybrid rat-men with blue eyes and blond hair, and the posthistorical significance of Solidarity, the then-outlawed Polish labor movement. (Who knew?) An alarmist Grass is having his black fun with movies as fairy tales, with literature as lies, with art and politics as forgeries and with rats as symbolic of all the herrenvolk wants to get rid of, from scruples to children to, of course, the Jews. This is his own sort of poisoned apple: Wake up, before all of us turn into big, bad Germans!

Fed up with "frozen cheerfulness," "stylized warmth behind burglarproof glass," "Social Democratic neither/nor," not to mention people who obsess about the "half-life of their vegetables" and take courses in How to Cope with Grief, Grass sent himself for six months in 1987 to Calcutta, where he found more shame. In *Show Your Tongue* (1988), he measures everything, including himself, by Calcutta: "a city damned to offer lodgings to every human misery"; a city he loves, in spite of itself, for the Bengali lyrics, sitar melancholy, moonlit courtyards; a city that plummets "as if an Expressionist had invented this rush of streets for a woodcut of epileptic collapse. Only the sleepers remain real." In a diary, in anguished little poems and violent smudgy drawings, he limns an "acrid smoke of open fires fed with cakes of dried cow dung"; vultures, crows and "child-bundles" living in a garbage dump; old women on funeral pyres at the crematorium, "sticking out from under the shrouds."

Even at the crematorium: "Only the rich can afford sufficient wood. The free-market economy, death as an overhead expense, like everything else." Temple-hopping with his sick wife; reading Lichtenburg, Schopenhauer and Elias Canetti; among Bengali poets who can't understand a word of Tamil or Urdu, Grass is beside himself:

> *If you lent (for a fee) one of these slum hovels, created from bare necessity, to the city of Frankfurt am Main and had it set down next to the Deutsche Bank highrise where the hewn granite sculpture by the artist Bill says yes, always yes to the towering bank, because as an endless loop it loves only itself, is incontrovertibly beautiful and immaculately endorses the circulation of money stamped valid for eternity—if, I say, you replaced that granite celebrating its flawless self, and set down instead one single slum hovel as authentic as want had made it right next to the glassy arrogance of the Deutsche Bank, beauty would at once be on the side of the hovel and truth, too, even the future. The mirrored art of all those palaces consecrated to money would fall to its knees, because the slum hovel belongs to tomorrow.*

Who'll make the revolution that saves Calcutta? Not Marx, says Grass; nor Mao. He looks to Kali, goddess of destruction, "the terrible black mother" with ten arms and a sword, a spear, a shield and a strangling noose; a necklace of skulls and a girdle of severed hands. This is the Kali we see in the temples under layers of black enamel, palms red, eyes ringed, surrounded by women "equipped with Dracula teeth, holding child-sized men in their talons, biting off heads, hands and cocks." In blood-drunk ecstasy, Kali cast down her consort, Siva, and danced on his stomach. And then, because she was ashamed of herself, she stuck out her tongue. So does Grass.

This is the good liberal, having met despair. V.S. Naipaul went to Calcutta once upon a time, and stayed a minute, holding his nose. Allen Ginsberg went there, too, for a year, and became a nurse. Supposing a Norman Mailer went to Israel? Isn't this the sort of thing a serious writer ought to do—book himself into the nightmares of the century, the unconscious of history, after too many tours of the self?

When Grass left town for Calcutta in August 1987, he was flying away

*from Germany and Germany, the way two deadly foes, armed to the teeth,
grow ever more alike; from insights achieved from too close up; from my own
perplexity, admitted only sotto voce, flying with me. And from the gobbledy-
gook, the where-I'm-coming-froms, the balanced reporting, the current situations, the razor-elbowed games of self-realization. I am flying thousands
of miles away from the superficial subtleties of former leftists now merely
chic feuilletonists, and far, far away from myself as part or object of this
public exposure.*

And now look what they've done: Left and Right, do-si-do, buck
and wing, danse macabre. He should be embarrassed. Instead he al-
lows to be published these unrepentant fugitives—as if a lost cause
mattered. As Martin Luther may or may not have told the Diet at
Worms: "Here I stand. I can do no other."...*A rhymed yearning for death.*

Now that writers can talk, what shall they say to one another: Show
me the way to the next BMW? We are advised by publicists for corporate capitalism that if the nonprofit police state is now bankrupt, so
too, somehow, is social democracy. To be a good liberal, a practical
radical, a ferocious democrat, a self-made orphan, a citizen without
portfolio and a prophet without honor; a Bad Boy and skeptic; a holy
fool instead of a court jester; incapable of simplifying yourself in the
gridwork of profit-taking and self-congratulation; ashamed of your
very own white-male perks—well, it's very thick sausage. And certainly not advisable if you want a Nobel Prize.

In some ways it would be easier to write in opposition, from a
prison or a psycho ward, in one of the Koreas or Latin Americas or the
new black fascisms of emergent and depressing Africa—to have been,
before everything changed utterly in 1989, a Konrad or Kundera or
Sinyavsky. They'd forgive you then your urgency—review your
courage instead of your cleverness. You'd not be asked for more than
one masterwork. Fly the black flag, and everyone salutes. But in our
postindustrialized, postmodernized, post-semioticized, post-toastied
fairy-tale West, a Grass is needed more than ever, and more than mas-
terworks. From men of color in white societies, and from women
everywhere, we expect dissent, abrasions of race and sex and class on
a dominant culture, the music and sinew of the Other. But how many
white male writers of the first rank are Citizens before they are Au-

thor-Gods? How many put down the pen, pick up a sword, cut through the fat, gather unto them the children and say: There are wounds that will not heal?

Grass would hate this comparison, but look at France since the death of Sartre. Primo Levi fell down a stairwell. Amoz Oz also comes to mind, in *Slopes of Lebanon*: "What began with the biblical words 'Zion shall be redeemed by law' has come to 'Nobody's better than we are, so they should all shut up.'" Quoting Isaiah ("Your hands are covered with blood") and Jeremiah ("For they had eyes but they did not see"), Oz grins: "Veteran defeatists, both of them. Troublers of Israel. Self-hating Jews."

Grass ought to have left immediately last Christmas, not for Gdansk, never again to be Danzig, but for lovely, fragile, introspective Prague, to declare himself an honorary Czech. With Havel to Kafka's Castle! Imagine Günter Grass in Prague for the Velvet Revolution, that Sergeant Pepper's Lonely Hearts Club Band. Havel and friends—writers, actors, jailbird intellectuals—met at the Magic Lantern Theater, on a stage set for Dürrenmatt's *Minotaurus*, under a TV tuned to an operetta with the sound off. There they wrote a Social Contract. Timothy Garton Ash tells us that once when they were tired and depressed, students appeared onstage dressed comically as Young Pioneers (red kerchiefs, white blouses, pigtails): "It is the Committee for a More Joyful Present. We have come, they say, to cheer you up—and to make sure you don't turn into another politboro. Then they hand out little circular mirrors to each member of the plenum." So that the members of the plenum might look at themselves.

Citizen Grass is stuck in both his Germanys, but he can look at himself. Now that the Wall isn't there, I see him jumping over it with Christa Wolf, to hold hands and to ban nuclear reactors. The talking turbot and Cassandra: This picture makes me smile.

MILAN KUNDERA WANTS TO BE IMMORTAL

We are at the end of Europe, the end of history, the end of culture and the end of this novel, in deck chairs at a health club with a swimming pool. We can look at ourselves in twenty-seven mirrors on three sides of the rooftop club, or we can look through the fourth wall at a panoramic view of Paris. Milan Kundera is talking to one of his characters in *Immortality*, the accused rapist and guerrilla tire-slasher Professor Avenarius. He seeks a metaphor. To Avenarius, he says, "You play with the world like a melancholy child who has no little brother." Avenarius smiles, very much like a melancholy child, and then remarks: "I don't have a little brother, but I have you."

And we have Kundera, a sixty-two-year-old melancholy child, a little brother of the bloody borders and the lost faith. He has written this novel in front of our eyes, out of chance encounters with enigmatic strangers, and radio news reports of anomalous events, and imaginary conversations among the lofty likes of Goethe and Hemingway, and snippets of books, and shards of memory. He has interpolated little essays—on journalism, sentimentality, coincidence, astrology, and the phases of the erotic moon—that turn out, of course, not to have been digressions at all. Everything fits inside with a satisfying snap, like the hasp on a jewel box or the folding of a fan. Left in the air, like smoke, are ghosts and grace-notes.

I'm sure there's a musical analogue; there usually is in Kundera's fiction: Mozart's *Don Giovanni* or Beethoven's last quartet or any one of sixteen fugues by Bach. "Our lives are composed like music," Kundera told us in *The Unbearable Lightness of Being*, "and if we listen well, they will speak to us in the heightened language of secret motifs, which are really the accidents of our becoming, transformed into significance by a roused imagination."

Certainly, in *Immortality*, there's a lot of Mahler.

But along with linear time, Romantic poetry, modern art, the idea of progress, the ardor of revolution and the consolations of nostalgia, he has also given up on music. "Music," we're told, "can be heard every time some statesman is murdered or war is declared, every time it's necessary to stuff people's heads with glory to make them die more willingly. Nations that tried to annihilate each other were filled with the identical fraternal emotion when they heard the thunder of Chopin's Funeral March or Beethoven's *Eroica*." Kundera himself explains that "music taught the European not only a richness of feeling but also the worship of his feelings and his feeling self....Music: a pump for inflating the soul. Hypertrophic souls turned into huge balloons rise to the ceiling of the concert hall and jostle each other in unbelievable congestion."

Whether this constitutes a symbolic parricide—Kundera's father, mourned so lovingly in *The Book of Laughter and Forgetting*, was a musicologist—I can't say. But it leaves us lonelier in Paris than we were before we ever met Agnes (a computer expert and "the clear-minded observer of ambiguity") or her sister, Laura (an *haute couture* shopkeeper and "the addict of ambiguity") or Agnes's husband, Paul (a clever lawyer and "the simpleton of ambiguity").

Laura, because she thinks she loves Paul, plays Mahler on a white piano and collects money for African lepers in the Paris Metro system. Agnes, because she decides she doesn't love Paul anymore or not enough, leaves Paris for Switzerland, where her father and her money are both stashed. Paul, who's come to deplore Mahler as much as rock 'n' roll, and to despair of Western civilization, drinks too much. Professor Avenarius meets Laura in the Metro when she's humiliated by *clochards*, seems never to have heard of Agnes, and hires Paul to defend him against the charge of rape. (Though there's always a lot of rape in Kundera novels, this one didn't happen.)

I neglect Rubens, who renounced art in favor of erotomania, because he is one of Kundera's several wicked surprises. So I won't tell you about his affair with the Lute Player, also known as the Gothic Maiden, and their stroll among "the severed heads of the famous dead." Besides, you've met him before. Like Zemanek in *The Joke*, Jaromil in *Life Is Elsewhere*, Klima in *The Farewell Party* and Tomas in *The Unbearable Lightness of Being*, he's a compulsive womanizer. There are signs here that Kundera is at last as weary of Don Juan and his roundelay of one-night stands as he wearied earlier of Don Quixote. But there are signs here that Kundera has wearied of everything else, too, even laughter: "Humor," says Avenarius, "can only exist when people are still capable of recognizing some borders between the important and the unimportant."

These people are unhappy because God is dead, and neither sex nor politics will guarantee them a life everafter. They're short on meaning and being. In all of European culture there are only fifty or so geniuses (fifty-one, counting Kundera) who deserve remembering after they have gone. Laura, Agnes, Paul, Rubens and Avenarius are not among these happy few. ("Class inequality is but an insigificant shortcoming compared to this insulting metaphysical inequality.") Kundera plays them on his fiddle. Or, to stick to his own quite wonderful conceit of the clock in Old Town Square in Prague, with the twelve apostles and the bell-ringing skeleton, he pops them in and out of his narrative like marionettes. In a world of "many people, few ideas," not even their unhappiness is original. They've borrowed it like their gestures, from Goethe, Beethoven and Napoleon; from Tycho Brahe and Robert Musil; from Marx and Rimbaud. In one thirty-page section midway through *Immortality* Kundera mentions Lacan, Apollinaire, Rilke, Romain Rolland, Paul Eluard, Knut Hamsun, Cervantes, Shakespeare and Dostoyevsky. In spite of all this culture, Europe got Auschwitz and the Gulag. Somebody must be doing something wrong, so everybody's punished.

According to Paul, who is about to be fired from a radio station where he has a commentary program,

> *High culture is nothing but a child of that European perversion called history, the obsession we have with going forward, with considering the sequence of generations as a relay race in which everyone surpasses his predecessor only to be surpassed by his successor. Without this relay race called history there would be no European art and what characterizes it: a longing for originality, a longing for change. Robespierre, Napoleon, Beethoven, Stalin, Picasso, they're all runners in the relay race, they all belong in the same stadium.*

To which the man who will fire him replies:

> *If high culture is coming to an end, it is also the end of you and your paradoxical ideas, because paradox as such belongs to high culture and not to childish prattle. You remind me of the young men who supported the Nazis or Communists not out of cowardice or out of opportunism but out of an excess of intelligence. For nothing requires a greater effort of thought than arguments to justify the rule of nonthought. I experienced it with my own eyes and ears after the war, when intellectuals and artists ran like a herd of cattle into the Communist Party, which soon proceeded to liquidate them systematically and with great pleasure. You are doing the same. You are the brilliant ally of your own gravediggers.*

This, of course, is Kundera's right brain talking to his left. Indeed the novelist, eavesdropping on this exchange as if he hadn't made the whole thing up himself, is reminded of another of his characters in another of his novels, Jaromil in *Life Is Elsewhere*. Like Paul (and Rimbaud), Jaromil felt it necessary "to be absolutely modern." He, too, was "the ally of his gravediggers." Kundera counts on us to remember on our own that Jaromil—an amalgam of Rimbaud, Lermontov and the Czech "proletarian" poet Jiri Wolker—was everything the novelist despises about Modernism: its confusion of Youth, Poetry and Revolution; its muddling of the vanguard and the avant-garde. Since Jaromil, in the storied Czech tradition of the Bohemian Catholic governors in 1618 and of Masaryk in 1948, was defenestrated, I'm somewhat surprised Paul doesn't take a header out the panoramic window of the Paris penthouse. But the surprise death in *Immortality* is reserved for someone else. Paul, instead, declares it is time "at last to end the terror of the immortals. To overthrow the arrogant power of the Ninth Symphonies and the *Fausts*!"

Clever, yes? Yes. And so are Kundera's "existential mathematics," his listing of the varieties of coincidence—mute, poetic, contrapuntal, story-producing, and maybe even morbid—he has employed to keep us turning his pages. Equally clever is Goethe's reminding Hemingway, in the middle of a chat in the afterlife, that they are both "but the frivolous fantasy of a novelist who lets us say things we would probably never say on our own."

The trouble with this cleverness is that it also reminds us we've been here before, with the send-up of Pavel Kohout in *The Joke*; with the send-up of Dostoyevsky and Gide in *Farewell Party*; with the send-up of Nietzsche, Tolstoy and Sophocles in *Unbearable;* with the send-up of Milan himself as the misogynist Boccaccio in *Forgetting*. The essay in *Immortality* on Imagology (ad agencies, public opinion polls) is inferior to the essay in *Unbearable* on "Kitsch" ("kitsch excludes everything from its purview which is essentially unacceptable in human nature"; "a folding screen set up to curtain off death," to "deny shit"), just as the meditation on *Grund* (a German word for reason in the sense of a cause, "a code determining the essence of our fate") is inferior to the meditations in *Forgetting* on *litost* (a Czech word meaning "upsurge of feeling") and in *Unbearable* on *soucit* (a Czech word meaning "human co-feeling").

It's not as though he hadn't already told us in *Laughable Loves* that sex is powerless against socialism; or in *Elsewhere* that poets will always sacrifice shop girls for the good opinion of the Revolution; or in *Farewell* that "Western culture as it was conceived at the dawn of the modern age, based on the individual and his reason, on pluralism of thought, and on tolerance," has come to a violent end; or in *Forgetting* that cultural progress is no longer possible; or in *Unbearable* that "*Einmal ist keinmal*": the horror of history signifies nothing.

We've even been with him into swimming pools before, maybe for lightness of being.

Nor, really, do we need Laura's skirt flying over her head in the Paris Metro, among rioting *clochards*, to remind us of the humiliation of other women in other Kundera novels: Helena and laxatives; sex-starved Alzhbeta and sleeping pills; pregnant Ruzena and the poison capsules; the spinster, in "Edward and God," on her knees, and Tereza, in shame, on the toilet. Avenarius may be innocent of rape, but Lucie in *The Joke* was a victim of its viciousness, and we were encouraged to believe that Sabina, with her bowler hat, dreamt about it, and we can be pretty sure that Kundera does. About all his eros there is a sado- and a masochistic edge: the whistle of the whip. Even mothers tend to be monsters. Jakub in *Farewell* pictures his own birth: "He imagined his tiny body sliding through a narrow, damp tunnel, his nose and mouth full of slime."

Even women with whom we are expected to identify, like Tamina in *Forgetting*, like Agnes in *Immortality*, belong to men in the molecules of their memory: Tamina to her dead husband, Agnes to her dead father—although there's an indication here that Kundera may have briefly entertained another role for his women to play besides the pathetic, one that's not so metaphysically insulting. I'll make fun of that in a minute.

If there is much that's familiar in *Immortality* from the other novels, there is also a great absence. That absence, except for the clock in Old Town Square, is Czechoslovakia, particularly Prague, the capital of Kafka and forgetting. We're in Paris, to which Kundera fled in 1970, but we might as well be anywhere. Place is irrelevant to *Immortality*, a deracinated novel, a sacred monster-ego, one of those severed heads of the famous dead by which Rubens and his Gothic Maiden stroll. This head makes witty remarks ("Napoleon was a true Frenchman in that he was not satisfied with sending hundreds of thousands to their death, but wanted in addition to be admired by writers"), but it floats, on the water, in the air, trailing its nerve-strings like cut cables.

There's no hint here of the intersection of the personal and political that made *Forgetting* a masterwork: the magic circle of Young Communists, levitating angels in "a giant wreath," from which Kundera fell;

the slit throats of six ostriches and six poets; the passage of the totalitarian state from a Bach fugue to a twelve-tone "single empire" to the abolition of notes and keys; the statues of Lenin growing "like weeds on the ruins, the melancholy flowers of forgetting." This same intersection was also the key to *Unbearable*. Not all the violence belonged to the Russians; there was a lot of it in Tomas before the tanks came to Prague in 1968.

(Oddly, it was this personal violence that was omitted from the overpraised movie version of the novel. Yes, Lena Olin, as Sabina, did for bowler hats what Pythagoras did for triangles and Melville did for whales; she gave them a whole new meaning. But the old meanings got lost. In the novel, the bowler is a sex-games prop, a memento of her father, "a sign of her originality" and something else. When Tomas and Sabina look at each other in the mirror, at first it's comic. But, suddenly, "the bowler hat no longer signified a joke; it signified violence; violence against Sabina, against her dignity as a woman....The fact that Tomas stood beside her fully dressed meant that the essence of what they both saw was far from good clean fun...it was humiliation. But instead of spurning it, she proudly, provocatively played it for all it was worth, as if submitting of her own will to public rape." Likewise, the movie lets Tereza swim in one of Milan's pools with other naked women, but leaves out her dreams about it, in which "Tomas stood over them in a basket hanging from the pool's arched roof, shouting at them, making them sing and do kneebends. The moment one of them did a faulty kneebend, he would shoot her.")

Last summer in Prague, Czech writers complained to us that not only had Kundera deserted them, but he was so busy designing himself a Nobel Prize, he hadn't managed to say a word on the Velvet Revolution, when history resumed, not having come to the end he had predicted; and so did European culture, but strangely without him. I don't know when he finished *Immortality*—the copyright is 1990—and therefore can't tell you whether he chose deliberately to ignore this astonishing and essentially nonviolent sea change, or it arrived too late to be thought about this time around, or he no longer cares at all anymore. Besides, Czech writers gripe a lot.

But history doesn't end; it *can't*; it's internalized, in nations and cultures and families and lovers. There's no reason to believe that we don't evolve, for better or worse, in the history of our cultures like the species in its Darwinian messiness, as much a consequence of chance, contingency, compromise and quirk, as of necessity or design; with some adaptations that are nifty, and some inefficient, and some full of surprising surplus value. Surely cultures are their own feedback loop, susceptible to Chaos and Catastrophe Theory, capable of rearranging themselves in a hot flash after an idea or a bomb, like Islam, the Mafia or the party line. And surely individual citizens tend to recapitulate the culture, as ontogeny recapitulates phylogeny. Or fractals…but let's not get into fractals. A Khmer Rouge was implicit in the brutal kings and the tenth-century Cambodian command economy of slaves that created in the jungle a sandstone cosmology and a vision of thirty-two hells, those golden lions, golden Buddhas, dancing girls, corncob towers and serpent cults, which is probably why Pol Pot let stand so undisturbed those temples and tombs, the bare ruined choirs of Angkor Wat. Maybe despair, like so much else, is cyclic, millennial.

I can be lofty, too. For that matter, it doesn't seem to me that kitsch is anything new. What else are folk songs and fairy tales, lullabies and festivals, the shinbones of saints for sale on the roads to the cathedrals, or the comfort stations of the miraculous, in the Middle Ages? Wasn't "imagology" invented by great religions? Didn't the media, by sympathetic magic, help make possible what happened, another _Eroica_, in Eastern Europe in 1989? And yet in his very own bare ruined choirs, Milan Kundera feels himself beached; and this vastation he patrols in a canary yellow Spenglerian doom-buggy.

What we get in _Immortality_, instead of any Czechoslovakia, is a lot of Goethe. Why, you may wonder, so much Goethe? For two reasons. First, he was

> _the great center…a firm center that holds both extremes in a remarkable balance that Europe will never know again. As a young man, Goethe studied alchemy, and later became one of the first modern scientists. Goethe was the greatest German of all, and at the same time an antipatriotic and a European. Goethe was a cosmopolitan, and yet throughout his life he hardly ever stirred out of his province, his little Weimar. Goethe was a man of nature, yet also a man of history. In love, he was a libertine as well as a romantic. And something else…Goethe knew how and with what materials his house had been constructed, he knew why his oil lamp gave off light, he knew the principle of the telescope with which he and Bettina looked at Jupiter…The world of technical objects was open and intelligible to him._

Not since Mann has another writer wanted so much as Milan to
reincarnate Weimar's wise guy, trashed by Modernism. (Never mind
that Kundera belongs more to Vienna at the turn of the twentieth century than to Weimar on the straddle of the eigthteenth/nineteenth; to
Ludwig Wittgenstein and the Secessionists. His novels are peopled
with Schieles and the wild-haired women of Klimt.)

The second reason for so much Goethe is that Kundera has borrowed, with credit, his brand-new role for women right out of Part II
of *Faust.* According to Paul at the swimming pool on top of Paris,
"Woman is the future of man." (Without knowing it, though Kundera does, Paul quotes Aragon.) Paul has been drinking and thinking
about his daughter and his granddaughter:

> *Either woman will become man's future or mankind will perish, because
> only woman is capable of nourishing within her an unsubstantiated hope
> and inviting us to a doubtful future, which we would have long ceased to be-
> lieve in were it not for women. All my life I've been willing to follow their
> voice, even though that voice is mad, and whatever else I may be I am not a
> madman. But nothing is more beautiful than when someone who isn't mad
> goes into the unknown, led by a mad voice…*Das Ewigweibliche zieht
> uns hinan! *The eternal feminine draws us on!*

How seriously are we supposed to take this? Not very. Paul, after
all, the "simpleton of ambiguity," is the one who says it. Kundera
can't help adding that "Goethe's verse, like a proud white goose,
flapped its wings beneath the vault of the swimming pool." I can no
more imagine this novelist buying into the Eternal Feminine than I
can see him abandoning the (dead) cultures of the great cities for
some woodsy totem worship under the sign of Gaia, the Mother of
Titans. And the last thing women need done to them, anyway, is another abstraction, another metaphor.

But where does that leave the severed head? Being melancholy,
being brilliant, dreaming of gestures. As much as Thomas Mann at the
end, he reminds me of Vladimir Nabokov—another exile, another
Bolshie-basher, another father-phile, another disdainer of the determinisms of Marx and Freud, another sacred monster of immortal art,
opposed to the very idea of a "future," inventor of Zemblas.
Nabokov's magic kits were also full of masks and mirrors, artist-mad-
men and artist-criminals, insanity and suicide, strangled wives and

slaughtered sons and debauched nymphets. But I am also reminded, more surprisingly, of Ingmar Bergman.

What tales Bergman tells on himself in his autobiography. He grew up on masks and ghosts and guilt and Strindberg. Death instead of a cuckoo popped out of the clock in the dining room. His first memory is of vomit. His prayers to get rid of pimples and stop his masturbating "stank of anguish, entreaty, trust, loathing and despair." He hated a brother, tried to kill a sister, almost never sees his many children by his several wives. When he sleeps, he's afflicted by loathsome dreams: "murder, torture, suffocation, incest, destruction, insane anger." Insomnia is worse: "Flocks of black birds come and keep me company: anxiety, rage, shame, regret..." Autoanalysis, Lear-like rage, a madness to see through prison walls to an absent God: The greatest movie director in the history of the world has found the only cure for his dread of the dark in "film as dream, film and music...The mute or speaking shadows turn without evasion towards my most secret room. The smell of hot metal, the wavering picture, the rattle of the Maltese cross, the handle against my hand." All this compensatory genius, from a little boy afraid to die in the dark.

I think *Immortality* is Kundera's *The Seventh Seal*, a game against death. I think he'd feel bad anywhere, like Bergman. (I am also charmed by the title of Bergman's autobiography, *The Magic Lantern*, which was, of course, the name of the theater where Havel, and the rest of the Czechs who hadn't left Prague, sat down to revise their social contract, to write a civil society instead of a novel.) Kundera jumped ship before it suddenly set sail into new meanings and new beings. All his borders are scheduled to disappear next year. Somewhere Marx says that when the train of history turns a corner, all the thinkers fall off. This included Marx. And Kundera. And many other lonely severed heads.

JEAN-PAUL SARTRE: PROBLEMATIC PILLHEAD

Giacometti, who tortured metals, told Jean-Paul Sartre, who tortured ideas: "You're beautiful. You're like Hamlet. Yes. You always think Hamlet was a tall, thin guy, and so on, eh? No, me, I'm sure he was a little fellow who drank beer, eh? A fat little man with hair like yours and eyes like yours. Very beautiful."

On the other hand, Giacometti went to brothels looking for deformed women, and they were beautiful, too.

Sartre as Hamlet? He certainly hated his stepfather. And couldn't make up his mind about the Communist party. But to *be* wasn't his problem. Being had to be turned into meaning by action. We are alone with our thoughts, and history keeps on happening to us, and we must strike back to be free. Heroically, Sartre struck back. He would "think against myself"—against his class, his country and his century, against Marx and Freud and the rest of the big boys. He would even "think against" his own vocation as a writer.

He could have been another Proust or Spinoza. At the start he wanted to be both; in the end, he was neither, but something else, problematic: philosophizing novelist, pamphleteering playwright, celebrity intellectual, "pope of existentialism," tireless ambassador of the French Left to the Third World, one-eyed, chain-smoking, piano-playing boozehound, pillhead, womanizer.

This doesn't seem to bother Annie Cohen-Solal, who's along for the ride with a wicked grin in *Sartre: A Life*. It vexes Ronald Hayman, who likes neat bureau drawers in *Sartre: A Biography*. Cohen-Solal, an Algerian-born and Sorbonne-educated critic of French literature and culture who has also written a book on Sartre's friend Paul Nizan, will love her man even when he behaves badly. Hayman, a British-born and Cambridge-educated biographer of Kafka, Nietzsche and Brecht, lunges at Sartre with a butterfly net and would staple his wings to the wall.

They're stuck with the same ugly duckling superstar who will write the same twenty pages a day Sartre averaged every day of his hectic life, in hotels and cafes or on the barricades or in jail, never alone, losing more manuscript than most writers publish. (For his fiction—and *The Words*, his splendid invention of his childhood—he was crafty and sober. For philosophies and polemics, he was stoned, usually on corydrane, a compound of aspirin and amphetamines. He doped himself up to kill God.)

Poulou—Sartre's childhood nickname—loses his father when he is only one, leaving him conveniently without a "superego." Still, it's harder than he thinks to invent yourself from scratch. The Sartres climbed in three generations from peasant to tenant farmer to men of property to Poulou's grandfather, a country doctor and "radical atheist." The Schweitzers were a long line of left-wing teachers; one of them lost his job for refusing to pledge allegiance to Napoleon III.

(Even his missing father got to the Third World, before Poulou was born, and felt bad for having helped subdue the restless natives, in Indochina's Gulf of Tonkin, from the gun deck of a French naval cruiser called, of course, *Descartes*.)

He loses exclusive rights to his mother at age twelve, when she remarries. He consoles himself with friends like Nizan, and by writing his dirty hands off. (Cohen-Solal summarizes an early novel: a tyrant's head is "stuck through the steeple clock at the Roman numeral XII" so that "he will be excruciatingly aware of each passing second that brings him closer to decapitation at the stroke of noon.") Hayman reports that the Nizan-Sartre group at the Ecole Normale Supérieure would hide in wait on the stairs for the regular boys to come back in fancy jackets from a night out, and then drop water bombs on them, shouting, "Thus pissed Zarathustra!"

In 1929 he meets Simone de Beauvoir, "the Beaver." They sign a two-year lease, with options for "contingency" love affairs. There will be many more contingencies for him—Olga, Wanda, Dolores, Helene, Michelle, Evelyne, Arlette—than for her, but the relationship lasts half a century anyway. (She was his best editor. And, if not exactly lots of laughs dragging him up and down mountains all over the world, she had to have been great to look at with her turban and her clogs and her bicycle.)

Another classmate, Raymond Aron, steers him to the metereological corps for his military service in 1930; he sends up weather balloons and puts down notes on the psychology of the imagination. In 1933, Aron directs him to Husserl and phenomenology, and to Berlin for night school. He wrestles with Heidegger; Heidegger loses. (He will quarrel and break with Aron, then with Camus, then with Merleau-Ponty. He couldn't get along with men his own age. Lucky Nizan, dying young.)

Teaching in Le Havre, he is depressed enough to write *Nausea*, although his students love him; he plays Ping-Pong and poker with them, and proselytizes for Dos Passos and Faulkner. Partying in Paris, he cries at the end of Al Jolson in *The Singing Fool* and imitates Donald Duck on the Left Bank, and, after a bad trip on mescaline, is followed by lobsters. (Odd, this sleepwalk through the thirties, not much affected by the book burnings in Berlin, the Spanish Civil War, the Soviet purges. At the same time that Nizan saw "a reciprocity of suffering," Sartre was worrying "the ethics of marginality" and "the mutual estrangement of subject-object relationships." He dreamed of a wind in the Void.)

Before he goes to war, he has vacationed in a dozen countries with de Beauvoir, published two books on the imagination, one book each on ego and the emotions, a novel and a collection of stories, and he's just warming up. During nine months as a soldier and eight as a prisoner of war, he begins *Being and Nothingness*, ends *The Age of Reason*, fills dozens of notebooks, writes daily letters to three different women, and lectures in the prison camp on Rilke and Malraux. (This wasn't *Stalag 17*, or *Hogan's Heroes*.)

Escaping to Paris, he's a changed man, a collective-minded activist. His Resistance isn't as endangering as Malraux's or Beckett's, but he contributes to Camus's *Combat* and Aragon's *Lettres Françaises*. Novels: *The Reprieve* and *Iron in the Soul*. Plays: *The Flies* and *No Exit*. Philosophy: *Being and Nothingness*, *Existentialism and Humanism* and *Anti-Semite and Jew*. Criticism: *Baudelaire*. Women: of course. (They will weave a web around him. He will write a play for Simone Signoret, who had been his student; and a song for Juliette Greco; and Françoise Sagan will cut his meat for him when he is old and blind.)

There are thirty-seven daily papers in the news-starved, post-censorship Paris of 1945. They all discover Sartre. He speaks: "We are alone without excuses. This is what I mean when I say that man is condemned to be free." And he editorializes, in the first issue of *Les temps modernes*:

> *The writer has a place in his age. Each word has an echo, as does each silence. I hold Flaubert and Goncourt responsible for the repression that followed the Commune because they did not write a single line to prevent it. It was none of their business, you may say. But then was the Calas trial Voltaire's business? Was Dreyfus's sentence Zola's business? Was the administration of the Congo Gide's business?*

Freedom and choice, responsibility and action: "Man commits himself to his life and thereby draws his image, beyond which there is nothing."

Meanwhile, his stepfather dies and a forty-year-old Sartre moves in again with his mother. (In the morning, he plays Schubert on the piano for her; in the afternoon, for the Beaver, he plays Beethoven sonatas and Bach fugues.) There's his peculiar harem to support. (As always, he gives away his money to causes and strangers.) He tries to organize a Left alternative to the French Communist party. (Thorez, the CP chief, was a Stalinist thug.) He visits the United States, and Dolores, for the first time. (Cohen-Solal gives us his excitement at our movies, "the art of the future," and our jazz, "the music of the future," and our skyscrapers.) Not to mention books and plays and magazine-editing and Algeria. (In Cuba, "Che" Guevara tells him, "It's not my fault if reality is Marxist.")

Well: Marx and Freud. He has resisted these twin determinisms, the dialectic and the unconscious. But he will think against himself: Men and women obviously exist in history, at once subjects and objects, knowing and acting. Just as obviously, an individual's upbringing might condemn him to repeat the history of his family *or the history of society.*

Some of what happens now is silly. Imagine him, explaining to workers "the true intersubjectivity of the proletariat." Imagine his trying to talk Thorez into believing that a dialogue with Nothingness is more fun than dialectical materialism. See—instead of Donald Duck imitations—his party-line waddle and goosestep in the early 1950s, and that contemptible *Temps modernes* editorial finding excuses for the Gulag. Hungary in 1956 will put a temporary stop to this bootlicking of the commissars; Czechoslovakia in 1968 will finish it off forever.

But something serious is going on. How can an individual imagination articulate itself in the context of a social imagination? Has history itself an unconscious? Sartre seeks the moment and the anthropology of choice—in his long essays on Kafka, Mallarmé, Baudelaire, Tintoretto and Genêt; in his plays on Kean and Nekrassov; in his screenplay on Freud for an incredulous John Huston; in *The Words.* He is still looking in his three volumes on the bourgeois archenemy Flaubert, and he never even gets to *Madame Bovary.*

There will be more philosophy and plays, and ten collections of essays, but *The Words* is his farewell to literature. No *mot* is any longer *juste*; language itself must take to the streets, rude like a knife. Sartre will refuse the Nobel Prize, as he refused the Legion of Honor, but his celebrity is always available as a blunt instrument in a good cause, as his money is available for newsprint and legal fees, as his time is available for bearing witness in a factory or courtroom.

Other, more effective voices and energies than his opposed the war in Vietnam, although one wishes he had used some of his time with the War Crimes Tribunal to consult Bertrand Russell on Wittgenstein, a philosopher he never came to terms with. And Cohen-Solal makes it clear that he was also peripheral to the liberation theology of May 1968, though those students were his children. But for a free Algeria he risked prison, and bombings of his hotel and office. He was a bulletproof shield behind which the nameless advanced on the machinery of state terror: "You don't arrest Voltaire," said de Gaulle. He understood Frantz Fanon. (And Fanon died before they could quarrel, as they would have, about Israel.)

In the end, he was down among the young—the anarchists and Maoists—as if for their warmth, to rub against their contradictions. They weren't very good at thinking, but the state had banned their newspapers, and so he agreed to be their editor, and sold those papers on the street until the other eye went out.

Don't go to Cohen-Solal for routine chronology, or a gloss on the phenomenological *pour-soi* and *en-soi*, or synopses and decodings. She won't even mention Arthur Koestler. She wants instead to dizzy us with possibilities. Like a shaman, she assumes the skins of French culture and spins, speaking in tongues. Ideas show up in her pages like rainbows. Her style, borrowing a bit from the Dos Passos newsreel, also owes a lot to Sartre's own enthusiasm for jazz and movies. It cuts, jumps, bops and dreams, from close-up to fade-out, gobbling colors, trafficking in ambiguities and hallucinations. What we get is less philosophy than rapture. *This* is what it felt like to be a child of Sartre's century. You will want to stay here awhile.

Whereas Hayman goes about his glum business of spelling everything out, nailing everything down, keeping score. On the quarrels with Camus and Merleau-Ponty, he is persuasive. About the influence of Husserl and Heidegger on style in *Nausea*, he can't be faulted. He is justifiably fierce about the fifties fellow-traveling. But he bullies and nags. He thinks Sartre's sex life must have been unhappy (which may be merely envy), and that his "doctrines about choice have neurotic roots" (which is probably true of all of us), and that his resistance to Freud must mean that he had a lot to hide (which is simply vulgar).

In fact, Hayman's potted psychologizing is a trial throughout. For instance: "In Sartre, as in Freud, a secret wish to be someone else, or at least to be more like other people, had developed into a violent opposition to make the others more like him by imposing his ideas on them." And: "Sartre would have wanted neither to understand why he found it so easy to identify with a man who had a self-effacing father nor to recognize anything Oedipal in his refusal to forgive his stepfather for taking possession of the mother who had once been like a cuddly sister."

Please. The result is that when Hayman finally gets around to questioning Sartre's attitude on violence, I don't want to listen anymore. That's sad, because Cohen-Solal avoids the subject, going on instead about incest, triangular relationships, bad faith and the Other. Sartre, seen through the bloody spyglass of terrorism, of child-killing as a petition for redress of grievance, looks troubled and troublesome out in the void. But since Hayman's been so dismissive of everything else Sartre thought, why should he care what he said about violence?

Let him go. The century used him up. But at least he was consistent in his self-revisions. He talked himself into commitment and stayed there, even at the price of relinquishing his claim on us as a great imaginative writer. He hated the bourgeoisie and late capitalism, and gave away his millions without stint or grudge, and died propertyless and almost penniless, still ferocious about freedom and choice, without excuses, looking in his old fake-leather jacket once again to the young, "a small old tramp" (I quote Cohen-Solal) "carelessly wandering from the Closerie des Lilas to La Coupole, with 'nothing in his hands, nothing in his pockets,'" a Charlie Chaplin with graduate degrees, a hero of the culture who hated that culture, his very own Other.

WOLE SOYINKA: A GARDEN OF TOO MANY CULTURES

Just because the Swedish Academy finally got one right doesn't mean that I forgive them. For years, because I edited a literary magazine, I was invited to submit my nominations for the Nobel Prize. For years, I nominated Vladimir Nabokov, Jorge Luis Borges, Günter Grass and Doris Lessing, in that order. And for years, the gnomes of Stockholm paid as much heed to my nominations as God paid to my various memos on modern architecture and Original Sin.

Nabokov and Borges died un-Prized; Grass is too busy these days greening German politics to write much fiction; Lessing's spaced out on Warp Factor Five, with her *Canopus in Argos* series. And we are supposed to read instead the likes of Karl Gjellerup, Wfadysfaw Reymont, Erik Axel Karlfeldt, Frans Eemil Sillanpaa and Pearl Buck, all of whom have been en-Nobeled.

Actually, the Academicians started to get their act together the minute I stopped nominating. What does this mean? It means as much as the fact that the Mets score after two outs in playoff games during which I swing speechless in the macrame plant-hanger with an ashtray on my head. Still, no reasonable reader can complain about Saul Bellow or Gabriel García Márquez as Nobel Laureates. I'll even go along with the humorless and woman-bashing Bulgar Elias Canetti, whose monomaniacs in *Earwitness* include such lovables as the Corpse-Skulker, the Narrow Smeller and the Woe Administrator. I think of the Swedish Academicians as Narrow Smellers.

Or I did until they gave the Prize last week to Wole Soyinka. This made me look good in front of my students at Columbia. These students are asked to write a dozen short essays each semester, reviewing anything from a movie to a circus to a therapy group. One of these reviews must be of a book. I give them a list: fiction by García Márquez, Grass, Lessing, Milan Kundera, Kobo Abe, Toni Morrison, Salman Rushdie, Maxine Hong Kingston, Paul Scott or André Malraux; memoirs by Nabokov, Jean-Paul Sartre, Arthur Koestler, Norman Mailer, Alexander Herzen or...Wole Soyinka, whose *Ake: The Years of Childhood* would dazzle anybody into sentience.

It's amazing how even the most talented writing students seem to fear or resent unknown books, especially by foreigners they haven't heard of. Kids willing to "deconstruct" a rock lyric as though it would save their sex lives go blank and grim when you mention a Kundera. It's as if they're scared that, by opening the box of somebody else's trapped words, they will be compromised in their splendid singularity; they will be "influenced." In vain I explain that they need all the influence they can get. Something oedipal may be going on: Let's kill all the fathers of our literature by not reading them.

And then a Nobel Prize comes along, and *Ake*, after all, *is* a short book, and maybe reading a Nigerian will improve one's moral posture. I don't care why they are suddenly ready to read Soyinka, so long as they do it. I don't even care if the Narrow Smellers prized Soyinka for the wrong (political) reasons—isn't it Africa's turn, and why not a Yoruba; at least they won the civil war?—because they picked the right man. Begin with the seductive *Ake*, his memoir of growing up from 1935 to 1945, before moving on to the poems, the novels and the bitter plays.

What if Naipaul were a happy man? What if V.S. Pritchett had loved

his parents? What if Nabokov had grown up in a small town in western Nigeria and decided that politics were not unworthy of him? I do
not take, or drop, these names in vain. Soyinka belongs in their company. It's a company of children who grow up without ever forgetting anything, children who sing in a garden of too many cultures.
Ake locates the lost child in all of us, underneath language, inside
sound and smell, wide-eyed, brave, flummoxed. Behind each shrub,
there's an angel or a demon. What Waugh made fun of and Proust felt
bad about, Soyinka celebrates, by touching.

From the beginning, before he was three years old, when he wanted to go to school because school was the place of books, he had a
reputation: "He will kill you with questions," they said. And why
not? Every intelligent child is an amateur anthropologist. The first
thing such a child notices is that adults don't make sense.

He was as bookish as, say, Sartre, but when Sartre came to write his
Words, he'd forgotten how to be a child; he invented himself backwards to come up with an appropriate prototype. Soyinka remembers
absurdity, friendship, ridicule, bed-wetting, pomegranates, goats, bicycle bells, a cutlass cut from a barrel hoop, weddings at which everyone arrived in clothes that didn't fit, snoring in the bedroom, wasps
on the ceiling, shoes and clichés, medicine and prayer: "I noticed that
God had a habit of either not answering one's prayers at all, or answering them in a way that was not straightforward."

He noticed everything. His father, Essay, was with "wicked patience" the headmaster of a Christian grammar school. His mother,
Wild Christian, ran a shop, professed nonviolence, and beat him with
a stick. His uncle initiated him into Yoruba mysteries by using a knife
on his ankles and his wrists. On his worrying out in the bush that a
huge snake might "jump down" from a tree on him, his uncle advised: "Speak English to it."

He was also a troublemaker, following the loud music of the Police
Band well beyond the boundaries of his parsonage, failing to weed
the school lawn, eating the powdered sugar intended for his younger
siblings and refusing to fling himself at the feet of the local king: "If I
don't prostrate myself to God, why should I prostrate myself to you?"

Isn't this enough ambivalence to launch a career in contemporary
literature? We are reading about English colonialism and Yoruba folk
myth, the Bible and the hex, irrational parents, pregnant madwomen,
nightmares of demonic possession, fear of "CHANGE," radio pro-

gramming schedules that begin and end by asking God to save the
wrong king, language as alien as black and white. A "rare event" is "a
grown man who was unabashedly happy." And yet Soyinka, with his
palm oil, kola nuts, cowrie shells, dead dogs, old coins and new
blood; hearing the cries from the marketplace and the chime of the
tower clock; spying on the "songmaster" who leads a procession of
humiliated women house to house down mean African streets past
cemetery, sewing academy, barbershop, repair shack, "mounted div-
ination birds" and "elephant-topped" archways to a fake palace; eating, for joy, black-eyed beans crushed and skinned and mixed with
melon-seed oil, and ingesting, as a cure for the wet bed, roasted
eggnest of praying mantis; dreaming of a dead father and a shoeless
child—this Soyinka somehow, marvelously, makes ambivalence almost cheerful.

If most of *Ake* charms, however, the last fifty pages inspire and con-
found; they are transcendent. The women of Ake perceive an unfairness
in the fact of a new tax law and in the person of a white District Officer.
As they agitate, young Soyinka is their courier, as if from culture to culture, from mother to son. These black women, insulted by a white
man, make a revolution. "You may have been born," they tell the
white man, "you were not bred. Could you speak to your mother like
that?" It then occurs to them to cut off his genitals and mail them with
a message to his mother. They will refrain. You will wish they hadn't.

Strange stuff, maybe, for our privileged young to read, but I can
only teach what I think I know, and I feel strange myself in one of
those franchise fry-shops where we sometimes go for coffee after deconstruction—as if in the wrong country, my wrists stuck out and my
shoulders wrong, having to be tailored, a bob of nose, a change of
name, to the specifications of a culture that wanted someone else. The
beginning of style is a sense of the strange. Score one, then, for the
Narrow Smellers. But they still owe me for Vladimir and Jorge, not to
mention Tolstoy.

DORIS LESSING RETURNS FROM OUTER SPACE

I'm pleased to be here, but intimidated. The writer you're about to meet
has read everything and forgets nothing and hasn't forgiven very much.

Almost the first book I ever reviewed, for Pacifica radio in 1962, was

Doris Lessing's *The Golden Notebook*. I learned more from that novel than I'd really wanted to know, so early in my life, about racism, colonialism, communism, feminism and psychoanalysis. She'd seen *through* these tests, before I got my chance to flunk them. She burned out the fat between my ears. But *The Golden Notebook* was more important in another respect. Another reviewer at that time, one of our preeminent New York intellectuals, said with just a whiff of condescension: "Here, I felt, was the way intellectual women really talk to one another when they feel free and unobserved." Well, maybe. What I felt was much scarier. I'd been *found out*. I saw myself in her pages as an unattractive *Other*. I sought promptly to modify my behavior. I've tried ever since in my male role to behave as if Anna Wulf were watching, and would report to Molly. This of course is ridiculous, as both my wives will tell you. But I say it out loud to suggest that I've been taking Doris Lessing personally for almost thirty years.

If *African Stories* opened my eyes, if *The Golden Notebook* modified my behavior, *The Four-Gated City* changed all the maps in my head. This concluding volume of her *Children of Violence* series depicted a world in which technology and fascism had triumphed, sex and imagination and intelligence had been brutalized; a world of figurative and literal plague for which the only hope was drastic biological mutation. Not a single illusion was left to us, except maybe R. D. Laing.

Instead of getting easier, it's gotten harder to live with Doris Lessing. I had to spend time in hell, and learn to care about cats, and flap with the Sufi lapwing across the Seven Valleys of Mystical Experience toward an Annihilation of the Self. And then she went into Outer Space. I mean, she wrote her way out of Africa and England and the West and this world, to disappear for the five volumes of the *Canopus in Argos* series. Sure, the Queen of Zone Three was neat. So was the glacier on Planet 8. But who wanted to be looked down on by alien carpetbaggers from three different galactic empires, in five different evolutionary time zones, whether they were benign Canopeans or anxiety-ridden Sirians or brutish Shammats? Here and now we were hurting, in our history and our intimacy. It seemed to me in my dismay that we were in no way healed by metaphors of dervishes, from Rumi's Persian poetry or from modern molecular physics.

It's not any fun to be dismayed by a writer you are compelled to read because so much of what you know, you got from her in the first place. I kept sending off my annual postcard to the gnomes of the

Swedish Academy in Stockholm. Any prize for literature that Doris Lessing hasn't won, including the Nobel, embarrasses itself. But I also felt out of "alignment," like one of her Shikastans, as if the Canopeans had turned off that faucet of the "substance-of-the-we-feeling," meaning that famine, pestilence, nukes and unkindness to animals were in store for all of us.

She came back from Outer Space of course, from blue air, archetypes and the whistle of the ether. She had written her prophetic book on Afghanistan, and a couple of novels under the nom de guerre Jane Somers, and *The Good Terrorist*—a kind of bookend to *The Summer Before the Dark*, the satanic flipside of Woman as Organizer, Mother as Minister of Caring. Then she published her short and stunning *The Fifth Child*, and I was obliged to eat, if not crow, then maybe one of those doomed beasts on Planet 8 whose "horns at their base were thicker than our thighs."

Like all the other reviewers, I exhausted myself construing Ben, "the fifth child" born to Harriet and David to punish them "for thinking we could be happy." Alien? Throwback? Dark child of traumatic memory or the British Empire? Murderous ghost? Symbol of the repressed proletariat? "Neanderthal baby," says Ben's mother. He strangles cats, and his siblings lock their doors at night against him. He will join the bikers and rapists, "the hostile tribes" at the gates of the burning city. To me, in his brown shirt, Ben seemed like one of the grotesques in Günter Grass's *The Tin Drum*, the little Nazi the good liberals can't handle, a ferocious beast of the unconscious, a seething neediness. Baby Evil, the Ultimate *Other*.

Never mind. Reviewers sniff and hound *after* God, and bite ourselves in our own meanings. Reading about Ben, I flinched from looking into the eyes of my own children. And he fits into all of Lessing, as if a Shammat, or fresh from Shikasta, while also belonging to the Coldridge dream in *The Four-Gated City* of the clairvoyant priesthood and the emancipating mutants. And to the nightmares of Charles Watkins, in *Briefing for a Descent into Hell*, who knew himself to be a fragment of the consciousness of those superior beings sent down from Venus to save our garden (our Rohanda). Ben's part and parcel and symbolic baggage of a cosmology Lessing's been elaborating her entire career. I should know by now you don't tell a great writer what to write about; you take whatever you can get from her. Fiction writing itself is so peculiar, almost unique in its disregard for the claims of sociability and good behavior. Like a monk, a hermit or a shaman, the writer disappears for years at a time to talk to the ghosts in her machine. We're lucky she comes back at all from this brave solitude in the desert or the Void. And if her weather report from the Void dismays, so be it. "Writers don't give prescriptions" says the poet Ikem in Chinua Achebe's _Anthills of the Savannah_: "They give headaches." And in Toni Morrison's novel, Denver warns Beloved about their difficult mother: "Watch out for her. She can give you dreams."

I've thought a lot about it…and it seems to me this evening that the Nobel Prize no longer deserves Doris Lessing. The rest of us, maybe. But watch out for her; she can give you dreams.

SAD SAM BECKETT

General outcry. (Stage direction in Samuel Beckett's _Waiting for Godot_)

First word from Paris on the Mike Nichols/Steve Martin/Robin Williams Lincoln Center production of _Waiting for Godot_ was that Beckett was not amused. In a letter to Jack Garfein, he was reported to have said, "I deplore the liberties taken in N.Y. Godot, with text and on stage."

Well, you may think, especially if you're among the hundreds of close personal friends of _Newsday_ drama critic Linda Winer for whom she failed to deliver tickets to this must-see show, "So what?" Harold Pinter no longer speaks to Robert Altman because Altman, in an ABC television production of _The Dumb Waiter_, fiddled with Pinter's _pauses_. Get real, Harold.

Then we heard last week from Barney Rossett, longtime Beckett publisher and agent, who had a different take after a Paris chat with Sam. "We were talking about the play," Rossett told _Newsday_, "and he said, well, they were funny, meaning the New York cast. And I said yes. And he said, what's wrong with that?"

Nothing is funnier than unhappiness. (Endgame)

Barney thinks Beckett's problem is that he's too nice: "Sometimes I think he says things to fit the person he's talking to." Garfein, after all, had wanted to mount his own production of the play with Dustin Hoffman.

I think Beckett's just weird. This happens to a writer who has to invent first himself, and then his readers. The masters of modernism are almost always weirder than anybody they write about or for. I remember when *Godot* opened in Boston in 1958. Their business done, the actors stayed onstage, inviting our questions. Dumbstruck, we hadn't any. What a disappointment we must have been to the playwright.

But Beckett has been an acrobat of disappointment since he was born ("under the table," he said). He grew up morose, in a fancy Dublin suburb. According to his biographer, Deidre Bair, he smokes and drinks too much, finds it hard to sleep, suffered a nervous breakdown, and is susceptible, especially in situations of emotional stress, to boils, cloacal cysts, and "idiosyncratic pleurisy." He has also had trouble with his eyes, his teeth, his feet and his mother.

> *I'm looking for my mother to kill her, I should have thought of that a bit earlier, before being born.* (The Unnamable)

I'm as suspicious as you are of writers and their mothers. There's a lot of it going around these days, in biographies of John Cheever and Truman Capote, and in Philip Roth's recent meditation on being a bad boy. But Beckett's mother, mean minded and possessive, seems to have been why he left Dublin for Paris. Bair thinks his trilogy of novels—*Molloy*, *Malone Dies* and *The Unnamable* (which A. Alvarez called "The Unreadable")—was a way of getting rid of her. It didn't work: "Beckett's mother, his wife and other women who have been important to him are all tall, gaunt and androgynous." And only a "womb fixation" could possibly explain his stuffing of so many people into mounds (*Happy Days*), urns (*Play*) and trashcans (*Endgame*).

> *If I had the use of my body I would throw it out of the window.* (Malone Dies)

On the other hand, he is also said to swim, golf, cricket and crack up motorcycles. If, as a lad he liked Schopenhauer (gloom), Sam Johnson (scrofula), Dante and Celine, he was also partial to Gilbert and Sullivan, Charlie Chaplin, Laurel and Hardy. If, in London he was a failure at literary journalism (Connolly told him to get an honest job); if, in Paris he was an errand boy for Joyce (that messy affair with the daughter); if *Murphy* was turned down by forty-two publishers (he has a list of them); and if, after chewing his way to the end of language, all the way down to squeak, he still calls all his stories "miseries"...nevertheless: Nancy Cunard believed in his genius (and paid for it). Peggy Guggenheim went to bed with him (and called him "Oblomov"). Marcel Duchamp was a buddy (his book on chess inspired *Endgame*). Sam was more heroic in the French Resistance than Camus or Sartre. And he did last long enough to win a Nobel Prize, unlike three of his flambouyant peers—Nabokov, Borges and Calvino.

Do you believe in the life to come? Mine was always that. (Endgame)

I like to think of him so drunk with Giacometti one night in the Dome that he trapped himself in the revolving door and whirled round and round, just like modernism. We're more likely to remember that he lived for forty years in the same Paris apartment with a wife to whom he communicated only on the telephone.

Lighten up, Sam. It's only the end of the world.